Learning With the Movies

by Beth Holland

Other Books by Beth Holland

Bread For Life Cookbook
Bread For Life Cookbook Volume 2
Tea Time With Bread For Life
Some Common Nutritional Fallacies
The Coming Famine

Videos by Beth Holland

Bread For Life Class Video
Basic Breadmaking
Advanced Breadmaking

Audio Tapes by Beth Holland

Bread For Life

My special thanks to Bridgett Rowedder. God sent her to me at just the right time in order to take me and my books in hand and make them into the professional looking products they've become. She is the creative genius behind all the Bread For Life publication art work, layout, page set ups, labeling, etc. Without her, I'd still be floundering and wondering how to do all this! It is obvious to me through God bringing Bridgett into my life that creating books, videos, etc., was the direction God intended me to go. I praise God for her and want everyone to know that she is a great blessing in my life and a treasured friend.

ISBN 0-9753922-3-9

Printed in the United States of America

Cover and interior design by Bridgett Rowedder.

I dedicate this book to my wonderful family
who endured my hours at the computer and
who also encouraged my writing and finishing
this book, (and all the others) as well as helping to review movies with
me and for me. Without their help, this could not have been done.

Rachel and Kathryn,
thanks for all the times you shooed me to the computer
while you stepped in and did my job; for the times you cleaned
the house, fixed the meals and stepped up to the plate to do
what had to be done. You are amazing young women.
I love you and am very proud of you.

To Tom,
who has understood his sometimes distracted wife, who doesn't
always hear or respond when intensely focused on the task at hand,
especially when in the midst of trying to find the exact words
while writing. You have endured more than most husbands
would and with a great attitude. Thanks for your love,
support, and belief in me. And thanks for not complaining
about late meals, and for supporting and encouraging
us all. I love you more each day.

To my parents,
who have always been in my corner, no matter what I
decided to try. Without their support and telling me
that I could accomplish whatever I put my mind to,
I'd probably never have tried all that I have. I love
you both, so much.

And to my precious and awesome Lord and Savior, Yeshua
without whom I would not be here, or be the person I am.
Who has loved me, healed me, and brought me closer to Him,
Who has always been there and understood me, even when
I didn't really understand myself. I love you and am constantly
amazed at who you are, how much you love us, and all that you do!
Praise Your Holy Name!

How To Use This Book

This book is an effort to serve the homeschooling community and any families who wish to "learn with the movies;" to make learning come alive through the use of drama and film. As a former actress and singer, holding degrees in Voice Performance, Acting and later, a faculty member in the Department of Drama and Theatre at my alma mater, the University of Georgia, I am asked regularly by my home school support group for recommendations on movies to co-ordinate with a particular chosen study.

There is no doubt that Hollywood has certain biases which are portrayed in film. However, there are films that are worthwhile for viewing and can offer us a way to look into the life and times of historical figures and events. Though not always successful, Hollywood takes great pains to make a film accurate in every possible detail. In a historic film, the clothing, customs, manners, weapons, table implements, jewelry, travel, etc. will be as historically perfect as they can make it. Therefore, I have used film as a culmination to many a study. This allows my children to SEE the time period/person/scientific discovery about which we have studied as accurately as possible in the present time in which we live.

A story has incredible power. It can move us to tears, to joy, it can even change our lives. I have found that my children more highly retain the facts of what we are studying when embedded into a really good story. This same principle holds true for film. If children SEE the time period, person's discovery and/or life in the context of a well done film, then they are much more apt to retain the facts since they have a context or framework into which the facts fit. This is much more enjoyable than the dry, rote memorization of facts.

It is my hope that this will be a great service to the home schooling community [to any families out there who want to "learn with the movies"] and that you and your family will enjoy seeing history, science, music, art, biographies, etc., come alive. This is not a license to just view movies for school, but a (hopefully) beneficial tool to pull it all together in a fun, family way. I have included some good, clean family fun movies as well as those for "academic" reasons. It is my desire to make our family the place my children want to be and wish to bring their friends. Therefore, on occasion, we have a "family night" of movie, popcorn, spend the night guests, and fun. Hopefully, these will aid you to have some family nights of your own.

Since not every family has the same criteria, if I think that there is anything contained in the film to which someone might object, I have tried to note it. However, that does not mean that I have caught every item to which someone might take offense. For your family's value system, parents might wish to view every film before showing them to their family. This will be the only way in which you can be absolutely assured that nothing offensive to you and your values is contained in the film to be seen. After 1939 and the release of *Gone With the Wind*, the barrier of no four letter words was broken. Parents need to decide whether to allow these films, edit them, or skip them entirely. Unless the film is just full of bad language, I have not noted this in the write up as I have put the notice here.

There is a company which makes a filtering box called a Guardian which you can attach to your home theatre. This device removes all bad language from any film you view which has closed caption. For more information, visit their website at: http://www.tvforfamilies.com/questions.htm. I have recently found that some VCRs come with a built in Guardian feature. My family purchased one of these for about $65.00 from Wal-mart.

In the past, Hollywood did a wonderful job in telling the stories of great men and women who have aided our lives and played an important part in our history. I tend to lean to the films of the past as I feel that they hold values closer to most home schoolers and families of today and have less objectionable content. However, there are a few more recent films of note. They are also included with notes if there is concern about any of their content. Also, check out the History Channel, a cable television network. They do some very nice programs on various incidences in history, including the development of weapons, firearms, planes, as well as biographies, battles and wars. However, as with all secular television, there are certain items in some of these programs which I feel are unsuitable for children. If you are going to use one of their programs, it is a good idea to video tape it and preview it before showing it to your children. That way, you can edit anything objectionable.

By NO means have I listed every movie available for a particular time period or for family fun nights. I have tried to list those with which I am most familiar, which I feel best show the period/person/subject and meet the criteria I have for family values. You may have favorites I didn't list; that's fine, by all means use them. These are the ones I felt would best meet the needs of the majority.

Just because a film is listed does not mean that I am endorsing the film or even recommending it! Some films are listed for excerpted scenes only and some with the recommendation that they be avoided.

The space between the actors and the beginning of the write up is **not** a mistake. Many people don't want to wade through a cast list to read the review, so I have made it easy to find the beginning of the write up. Also you will find spaces for notes throughout the book for you to add your favorite movies that I may have missed. Add in, mark out, do whatever you need to do to make this YOUR family's movie guide.

The ratings listed are mine. They are there to give you an idea of how one film, which you may like, should stack up against another with which you may not be familiar. ***** is Exceptional, **** is Excellent, *** is Very Good, ** is Good and * is Fair. NR stands for not rated and TVM for TV movie. If they have been made since ratings of G to R, then that will also be listed. D: stands for the director, followed by the cast list. **V** means that it is available on video tape. **DVD** means that it is available on DVD. I have not listed laser disks as most people have either VCRs or DVD players for home use. If it is not available in one of these two modes there will be no V or DVD, which means that you will have to look for it when it comes on television and tape it, or if you don't get television, ask a family member or friend to do so for you. You might want to give them a list of the films you are looking for so that when one comes on, they will know to tape it for you.

For years, the Christian community scorned the use of visual media. Then, they discovered the power of it and began producing Christian television and films like the *Jesus* film which has been used by Campus Crusade for Christ to bring thousands to salvation, including entire villages and tribes. In the same vein, I hope this will be a new way to make education real, enjoyable and memorable to your children. We all know the old saying, "A picture is worth a thousand words." I hope these pictures will make the subject matter you are studying real and alive to your children, even if it's as far back as the beginning of time!

May God's Richest Blessings be yours!

In the service of the King of Kings,

Beth Holland

Table of Contents

Category	Page

Bible Times/Character

America's Godly Heritage **** (See 1700s America)

Bible Codes, The (1999) NR Documentary by PAX TV.   This explores the encoded information in the Bible, specifically in the Torah. It has both pro and con positions but, in my opinion, proves the Divine authorship of the Bible beyond any doubt. Very interesting and thought provoking. You might want to follow up with Grant Jeffrey's book, *The Mysterious Bible Codes*.

Cross and the Switchblade (1972) **1/2 (See Family Films)

David (1997) **1/2 D: Robert Markowitz. Nathaniel Parker, Leonard Nimoy, Jonathan Price.   Covers the story of King David fairly accurately. Nimoy, who is Jewish, accurately anoints David by *pouring* the oil over his head. Part of the Trimark Home Video series. **V**

Education and the Founding Fathers **** (See 1700s America)

Esther (2000) **1/2 D: Raffaele Mertes. Louise Lombard, F. Murray Abraham.   The story of Esther is well acted and fairly accurately portrayed. A Trimark Home Video series of Biblical stories. **V, DVD**

Greatest Story Ever Told (1965) **1/2 D: George Stevens. Max von Sydow, Charlton Heston, Carroll Baker, Angela Lansbury, Sidney Poiter, Shelly Winters, John Wayne, Ed Wynn, Jose Ferrer, Van Heflin, Claude Rains, Telly Savalas, and more.   Beautiful film with many familiar faces. Some may find it too hard to concentrate on the story due to this, but it still shows the gospel story and is well made. **V**

Hiding Place, The (1975) **1/2 (See World War II)

Inn of the Sixth Happiness (1958) *** D: Mark Robson. Ingrid Bergman, Curt Jurgens, Robert Donat, Ronald Squire.   The true story of Gladys Aleward, who felt that God had called her to China, yet no missionary agency would sponsor her. So, she worked to get there, studying about China the entire time until God opened a door for her. A truly wonderful family film. **V**

In Search of Noah's Ark (1976) ** Narrated by Brad Crandall.   Documentary telling of the many expeditions to find the Ark and eye witnesses of its existence. Not an "A" grade documentary, but definitely contains information worth seeing. Our family learned a lot from it. **[G] V**

Jeremiah (2000) *** D: Harry Winer. Patrick Dempsey, Klaus Maria Brandauer, Oliver Reed.   Based upon the book of Jeremiah, this well done movie chronicles the life of the famous prophet, his calling from God, his obedience to that call, and how he was abused for telling the king and the people *the truth*. It is interesting to see the motivations given to those in authority who stand against the message God gave Jeremiah and helps you to see these people in a much more human realm. There is a bit of Hollywood thrown in, but this film is still well worth seeing. Part of the Trimark Home Video series. **V, DVD**

Jesus *** (NR) D: Peter Sykes and John Kirsh. Brian Deacon.   Produced by Campus Crusade for Christ and based upon the gospel of Luke, this is a very well done production and more Biblically accurate than most. **V**

Joseph (1995) **1/2 D: Roger Young. Paul Mercurio, Ben Kingsley, Leslie Ann Warren, Vincenzo Nicoli. Mercurio plays Joseph with Kingsley as Potiphar.   This film has some really good moments as it shows Joseph working hard and rising to the top by doing his best for those in authority over him. Even though the story is Biblical, I recommend taping this and skipping the part with Potiphar's wife as it is a bit too explicit about her advances to Joseph. Other than that, this is a fairly well done film of the Biblical story and another Trimark Home Video production. **V**

King of Kings (1961) **1/2 D: Nicholas Ray. Jeffrey Hunter, Siobhan McKenna, Robert Ryan.   Narrated by Orson Wells, this not 100% accurate view of the life of Messiah is still worth mention. Beautifully filmed, and containing some dramatic highlights of His life.

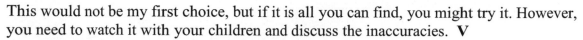

This would not be my first choice, but if it is all you can find, you might try it. However, you need to watch it with your children and discuss the inaccuracies. **V**

Man Called Peter, **A** (1955) *** D: Henry Koster. Richard Todd, Jean Peters, Marjorie Rambeau, Doris Lloyd, Emmett Lynn.   Based upon the book of the same title by wife Catherine Marshall, this is the story of Peter Marshall, a Scotsman and Presbyterian minister who became chaplain to the United States Senate. Worth discussion are some of the choices he makes as pastor of a historic D.C. church when faced with upholding the church's traditions, or changing them as he feels God is leading. A wonderful family film. **V**

Miracle Maker, The (2000) **** D: Derek Hayes. Voices of: Ralph Fiennes as Jesus, Michael Bryant as God, Ken Stott as Simon Peter, Julie Christie as Rachel, Miranda Richardson as Mary Magdalene and William Hurt as Jarius.   This begins when Yeshua is 30. It uses clay figures to tell the story and animation for flashbacks of his life. The actors have cockney accents, but other than that, it all seems accurate and works wonderfully well. To ensure accuracy, rabbis, priests, and ministers were all used as advisors on the movie. Though this is new, it is one of my top picks for the gospel message, especially for children, though adults will like it, too. **DVD**

Prince of Egypt, The (1998) **1/2 D: Brenda Chapman, Steve Hickner, Simon Wells. Voices of Val Kilmer, Ralph Fiennes, Michelle Pfeiffer, Sandra Bullock, Jeff Goldblum, Danny Glover, Patrick Stewart, Helen Mirren, Steve Martin, Martin Short.   Animated musical story of Moses and the Exodus of the children of Israel from Egypt. Includes some different twists like Moses stepping into the Nile when it turned to blood. We thought this would make him "unclean" according to Scripture, but this shows the water immediately surrounding him remaining water. These twists could be from Jewish tradition, since the producer was Steven Spielberg, who is Jewish. Compare with the Biblical account and see what you think. **V, DVD**

Samson and Delilah (1949) **1/2 D: Cecil B. DeMille. Victor Mature, Hedy Lamarr, George Sanders, Angela Lansbury, Henry Wilcoxon, Olive Deering, Fay Holden, Russell (Russ) Tamblyn. George Reeves, Tom Tyler, Fritz Leiber, Mike Mazurki.   An Oscar winner, this *Bible* story has DeMille touches along with fictionalized parts. View first and see if you think it's for you. **V**

Story of Ruth, The (1960) **1/2 D: Henry Koster. Elana Eden, Stuart Whitman, Tom Tryon, Peggy Wood.   Exactly what it says with a bit of license taken. Still, worth seeing and a good family movie. **V**

Ten Commandments, The (1956) ***** (See Ancient Egypt)

NOTES

Ancient Egypt

Caesar and Cleopatra (1946-British) ** D: Gabriel Pascal. Claude Rains, Vivien Leigh, Stewart Granger, Flora Robson, Francis L. Sullivan, Cecil Parker.   Film version of George Bernard Shaw's play. It's been a while since I've seen this, so view it first, but I remember this as having an almost paternal relationship between the leads. **V, DVD**

Cleopatra (1934) *** D: Cecil B. DeMille. Claudette Colbert, Warren William, Henry Wilcoxon. In my opinion, the better of the two. In black and white. Watch first for objectionable parts. **V**
(1963) ** D: Joseph L. Mankiewicz. Elizabeth Taylor, Richard Burton, Rex Harrison, Pamela Brown, Hume Cronyn, Martin Landau, Roddy McDowell, Carroll O'Connor.   Four hours long, in color. Most well know for its production costs! Parents should definitely view this one first. **V, DVD**

Egypt: Quest For Eternity - National Geographic. [NR]   This gives much information about the culture of Ancient Egypt, present day archeology on the temples at Luxor and Thebes and so much more. However, as in investigating any civilization of false gods, there is mention of them. Highly recommend stopping the tape and discussing the inaccuracies with your children, therefore holding up truth to falseness. Discerning truth is a necessary skill for their future. Begin at home and use the time to help them develop this skill. **V**

Prince of Egypt (1998) **1/2 (See Bible)

Ten Commandments, The (1956) ***** D: Cecil B. DeMille. Charlton Heston, Yul Brenner, Anne Baxter, Edward G. Robinson, Yvonne De Carlo, Debra Paget, John Derek and more.   Not 100 % Biblically accurate, but certainly Hollywood at it's best. A wonderful portrayal of the Biblical story of Moses delivering God's people from the oppression of slavery under the rule of Pharaoh. Inspirational especially in the parting of the Red Sea and the giving of the Ten Commandments. Human frailty is shown in the doubting of the people, their unfaithfulness to God in the making of the golden calf. A great culminating, family event for the study of Ancient Egypt. Read the Biblical account first and compare. **V, DVD**

Tut, the Boy King, narrated by Orson Wells. NR   A taped television special showing the treasure of Tutankhamen's tomb when they were on exhibit at the National Gallery of Art. Beautiful close-ups of the treasures, and well worth seeing. However, be aware that Orson Wells definitely plays up the mystical part of Egypt's culture in the narration. Once again, an opportunity for discussion. If it concerns you, watch it first and hear the narration, make notes, turn off the sound and you narrate it to your children. However, I wouldn't miss seeing it since the close-ups of the treasures are really something. **V**

Valley of the Kings (1954) **1/2 D: Robert Pirosh. Robert Taylor, Eleanor Parker, Kurt Kaszner, Carlos Thompson.   The focus of this film is on early 20th century excavation of the Valley of the Kings. Eleanor Parker is looking for information to continue her father's life work in looking for a tomb to prove Joseph's existence and impact upon Egyptian society. I would recommend parents watch this one first as Parker is married to Thompson, who turns out to be the villain, but is drawn to Robert Taylor, who heads the expedition to prove the existence of a tomb showing Joseph's life. There is nothing overt, but you need to see it to decide if it's okay for your family. **V**

Ancient Greece

Boys from Syracuse, The (1940) **1/2 (See Music/Arts)

Chariots of Fire (1981) ***1/2 D: Hugh Hudson. Ben Cross, Ian Charleston, Nigel Havers, Nick Farrell, Alice Krige, Cheryl Campbell, Ian Holm, Sir John Gielgud.   Based on the true story of two men: one a Jewish Cambridge student, Harold Abrahams, the other, a wonderful example for your children, Eric Liddell, both of whom participated in the 1924 Olympic Games in Paris. The influence of Eric Liddell upon his peers, children, competitors and even his King are portrayed. Shown is a man of unmovable conviction, who has to come to grips with his own struggle and the desires of his heart and that to which he feels God is calling him. As the Olympics originated out of Ancient Greece, this can easily be tied in with this study and also be used for a character discussion as well. Highly recommended. [PG] **V, DVD**

Three Hundred Spartans (1962) ** D: Rudolph Mate. Richard Egan, Ralph Richardson, Diane Baker, Barry Coe.   Not the best acting in the world, but worth seeing as this film recounts the historic Battle of Thermopylae. Three hundred Spartan soldiers held off the much larger Persian army and fought alone, without help from any of the other city-states and to the death to defend Greece. According to historical accounts, at the end of the battle, the Persians unleashed so many arrows that they "blotted out the sun." This scene was a challenge to the technical crew, who figured that it would take about 200 arrows released simultaneously to create this effect. Since so many archers were difficult to find, they build 10 machines to release 20 arrows, each, which they coordinated to shoot all at once.

NOTE: **Jason and the Argonauts** (1963- British) * D: Don Chaffey. Todd Armstrong, Gary Raymond, Nancy Kovack, Honor Blackman, Nigel Green.   Though this film is mostly well rated by other reviewers for it's special effects, this is a film I wouldn't show to my children, but will let you make you own choice. Definitely watch this one first, parents, as the occult is prevalent throughout this film and parts of this would be very scary for most children. The acting is really poor. **V**

NOTES

Ancient Rome

Ben-Hur (1959) *****D: William Wyler. Charlton Heston, Jack Hawkins, Stephen Boyd, Haya Harareet, Hugh Griffith, Martha Scott.   Based upon the book by General Lew Wallace, this is a great film showing life in Ancient Rome as well as the Jews, their customs, the customs of the Romans, a fabulous chariot race and most inspiring, the life of Messiah, especially as it integrates with that of Judah Ben-Hur. When we were studying Rome, we read about the legions and their standards. We had an idea about them, but we actually saw what we'd read about in the opening of this movie! General Wallace converted to Christianity as a result of researching and writing the book upon which this is based. The book is wonderful, too! Highly recommended. **V, DVD**

Demetrius and the Gladiator (1954) **1/2 D: Delmer Daves. Victor Mature, Susan Hayward, Michael Rennie, Debra Paget, Ann Bancroft, Richard Egan, Ernest Borgnine.   Sequel to *The Robe*. Demetrius becomes a centurion and turns from Messiah. Later, the Apostle Peter brings him back to the fold. Again, Caesar is after the robe and orders Demetrius to bring it to him so that he can kill a man and use the robe to prove that it can restore life. It doesn't. Demetrius points out that the power is not in the robe, but in the Messiah. One note, Susan Hayward's character is married, but doesn't act like it. You should probably view this one first to see where to edit. **V**

Fall of the Roman Empire (1964) **1/2 D: Anthony Mann. Sophia Loren, Stephen Boyd, Alec Guinness, James Mason, Christopher Plummer, Anthony Quayle, John Ireland, Omar Sharif, Mel Ferrer, Eric Porter.   Again, this is not a documentary, but has some redeeming features. This shows the corruption within the "ruling class" of Rome, and how Caesar was viewed as god and what effect that had upon the Roman society. I recommend parents view this one first. **V, DVD**

Julius Caesar (1953) ***1/2 (See Literature)

Jupiter's Darling (1955) **1/2 (See Music/Arts)

Quo Vadis? (1951) *** D: Mervyn LeRoy. Robert Taylor, Deborah Kerr, Peter Ustinov.   From Henryk Sienkiewicz's novel. Taylor plays a Roman soldier who falls in love with Kerr, a believer. He walks a fine line to keep her out of harm and alive under the reign of an unstable Nero. This is worth-while in that it shows the believers facing the lions, crucifixion and how they faced it as part of the cost, and duty, of following Y'shua. Parents should watch this first and see if they feel all parts are appropriate. **V**

Robe,The (1953) **1/2 D: Henry Koster. Richard Burton, Jean Simmons, Victor Mature, Michael Rennie, Richard Boone, Jay Robinson, Dawn Addams, Dean Jagger, Jeff Morrow.   Based upon the Lloyd C. Douglas novel, this is the story of a Roman centurion who, at the crucifixion, gambles for and wins the robe of Y'shua the Messiah. His servant, Demetrius, takes the robe when freed. The centurion is order by Caesar to find or destroy the robe. This leads to Demetrius leading the centurian to salvation which leads in turn to his martyrdom. There is a lot of emphasis on the power of the robe as the instrument of the power of God, which may be viewed as idolatrous. View it and judge for yourself. **V**

Sign of the Pagan (1954) **1/2 D: Douglas Sirk. Jeff Chandler, Jack Palance, Ludmilla Tcherina, Rita Gam, Jeff Morrow, Alexander Scourby.   The story of Attila the Hun descending upon the Roman empire. This is the only film of which I know that deals with the Mongol's from the east who ultimately brought the end to the mighty Roman Empire. Not a great film, but deals with the subject. Parents may wish to view this first and decide if they feel it is worth showing.

Spartacus (1960) **1/2 D: Stanley Kubrick. Kirk Douglas, Laurence Oliver, Jean Simmons, Tony Curtis, Charles Laughton, Peter Ustinove, John Gavin, Nina Foch, Herbert Lom. VIEW FIRST!!! This film has subject matter which is definitely inappropriate for children. However, it has some scenes which might be worth extracting. Mainly, those of the gladiators in the ring, the battle of Spartacus with the Romans and those which portray the willingness to die rather than return to slavery. This is entirely up to the parent to decide if it is something you wish to use, but please, do you homework first with this one before you begin running the tape or letting them view it on television. V

NOTES

Mayans

Kings of the Sun (1963) **1/2 D: J. Lee Thompson. Yul Brynner, George Chakiris, Shirley Anne Field, Richard Basehart, Brad Dexter.   Tale of Mayan leader (Chakiris) fleeing massacre by a tribesman who wishes to rule in his stead. He brings those who will follow to the shores of American to establish a new settlement. Though this is not the best acted film is does tell the Mayan belief of human sacrifice (not gory at all, but might wish to edit) to please the gods for good crops and the desire of the king to abandon this practice. Yul Brynner plays the chief of a tribe of American Indians whom the Mayans encounter. Not great acting, but interesting.

NOTES

Vikings

The Vikings (1958) **1/2 D: Richard Fleischer. Kirk Douglas, Tony Curtis, Ernest Borgnine, Janet Leigh, narrated by Orson Wells.   Filmed on location in Normandy and Brittany. This is one I recommend parents watch first. The Vikings were a barbaric society and this certainly portrays them as such. It is not as graphic as today's version would be, but does show topics of which certain parents may not approve. On the plus side, it shows the way the Vikings lived, sailed, their beliefs, and fierceness. It also shows the court of England as well. Accurately portrays the Vikings way of life. After watching, if you object to certain parts, you may be able to fast forward them and still salvage part to give your children a living picture of the time. **V**

NOTE: **The Long Ships** (1964 – British-Yugoslavian) * D: Jack Cardiff. Richard Widmark, Sidney Poitier, Rosanna Shiaffino, Russ Tamblyn.   Some reviewers like this movie and recommend it more highly than the one above. I choose to differ with them. This is the story of a group of Vikings battling Moors over possession of a golden bell. I found this movie to be very violent and gory, with no real redeeming values for the watching. **V**

NOTES

Middle Ages

Adventures of Marco Polo, The (1938) **1/2 D: Archie Mayo. Gary Cooper, Sigrid Gurie, Basil Rathbone. Not factual, but a way to introduce this famous explorer. Read and compare. Parents view first. **V**

Adventures of Robin Hood, The (1938) **** D: Michael Curtiz, William Keighley. Errol Flynn, Olivia de Haviland, Basil Rathbone, Claude Rains, Patric Knowles, Eugene Pallette, Alan Hale, Sr. The familiar tale of Robin Hood who robs the rich to give to the poor, well portrayed by Errol Flynn. A sweeping, majestic presentation of chivalry at it's best as Robin Hood, rightfully a nobleman, takes care of the people of England in the absence of Richard the Lion-heart, defending the wrongfully accused Maid Marian, and fighting the usurper, Prince John. It also raises the issue of Prince John "raising" Richard's ransom with the intention of keeping it for himself. This shows the battle of uniting England which contained both Normans and Saxons. Erich Wolfgang Korngold's score won an Oscar. He also wrote the score to another Errol Flynn film, *The Prince and the Pauper* (see Reformation), studied with Gustav Mahler and composed opera. This is one for the whole family to enjoy and cheer for the hero! **V**

Bandit of Sherwood Forest, The (1946) **1/2 D: George Sherman. Henry Levin, Cornel Wilde, Anita Louise, Jill Esmond, Edgar Buchanan. Robin Hood's grown son helps him battle the Regent of England who has plans to kill the boy king and revoke the Magna Carta. The films strongest point is in making known the importance and value of the Magna Carta. Good for family viewing.

Becket (1964) **** D: Peter Glenville. Richard Burton, Peter O'Toole, John Gielgud, Donald Wolfit. Powerful film adaptation of Jean Anouilh's play, adapted for the screen by Edward Anhalt who won an Oscar for it. England's King Henry II is at war with the church. He decides to place a friend in the position of Archbishop of Canterbury, thinking this will bring an end to the contention. What he cannot foresee is how this appointment will affect his friend, Thomas à Becket, whose character demands that he fulfill his duty and honor THE KING to whom he must ultimately answer. I recommend that parents see this first as there is some immorality discussed and there might be other areas of concern. However, I recommend that you edit it however you must and show as much as you can. A powerful film.

Black Rose, The (1950) **1/2 D: Henry Hathaway. Tyrone Power, Cecil Aubry, Orson Wells, Jack Hawkins, Michael Rennie, Herbert Lom, James Robertson Justice, Finlay Currie, Robert Blake, Laurence Harvey. Norman vs. Saxon as Tyrone Power portrays the illegitimate (though not played up as so) Saxon son of a Norman knight. He steals the inheritance left to him by his father, but denied him by his Norman half-brother. Doing so makes him a hunted man and so he flees to the Middle East. This leads him to the armies of the great Kahn and involvement with the brilliant general played by Orson Wells. He ends up in Cathay (China) and it shows the wonders of its civilization of the time. If parents are concerned, they could view it first for content, but I believe most will approve and show it to their family.

Black Shield of Falworth, The (1954) **1/2 D: Rudolph Mate. Tony Curtis, Janet Leigh, David Farrar, Barbara Rush, Herbert Marshall. Based upon Howard Pyle's *Men of Iron* this costumer shows the process of becoming a knight and the political intrigues of the time. A lovely picture for family viewing. **V**

Castle (1983) [NR] David Macaulay. Animated look at the building of a castle, the importance of its location, the fortifications chosen, life in the castle, and the village. Once again, a great presentation of this information with narration by David Macaulay. There is one scene of animated nudity showing the use of a garderobe at night. You might choose to omit this. Other than that, highly recommended. Get the book by the same title and compare. **V**

Cathedral (1973) [NR] David Macaulay. Animated look at the building of a cathedral based upon Macaulay's book of the same title. Wonderful presentation of information in a clear, understandable way. A good video to use toward the end of a study of this period. Combined with the section on architecture in *A Child's History of Art* by V. M.

Hillyer, this shows the importance of the keystone in building arches. Highly recommended. **V**

Connecticut Yankee in King Arthur's Court, **A** (1949) ****1/2** D: Tay Garnett. Bing Crosby, Rhonda Fleming, William Bendix, Cedric Hardwicke.   Based on Mark Twain's classic story, this musical version shows Bing transported to King Arthur's court, deemed a monster and then a wizard as he introduces new ideas and has a wonderful time. It does show the gross difference between the nobility's way of life and the poor/peasant's. It also has Merlin the magician, though he is more of a joke than an introduction to witchcraft. I think most will consider it a family film. **V**

Court Jester, The (1956) ******** D: Norman Panama Melvin Frank. Danny Kaye, Glynis Johns, Basil Rathbone, Angela Lansbury, Cecil Parker, Mildred Natwick, Robert Middleton, John Carradine.   This one will need to be seen by the parents first to see if you approve, need to edit it or skip it. However, it is SO funny (if you like Danny Kaye's humor), that I included it as worthy of mention. Kaye is in the service of the Black Fox (a Robin Hood type) and must protect the rightful infant King from the usurper who seeks his death. Kaye infiltrates the court as the Court Jester which leads to multiple wild situations. In order to fight in a joust of honor, he must be made a knight. A truly funny scene is the one in which they, literally, rush him through the process. The only concern for some parents will be Mildred Natwick's portrayal of a "witch." Watch it and see what you think. Just remember, the pellet with the poison's in the vessel with the pestle and the flagon with the dragon has the brew that is true! Or is it the flagon with the dragon has the pellet with the poison and the chalice from the palace has the brew that is true? **V**

Crusades, The (1935) ******* D: Cecil B. DeMille. Loretta Young, Henry Wilcoxon, Ian Keith.   Young plays a young woman who becomes Richard the Lionheart's (Wilcoxon) queen, and is kidnapped by infidels. This tells a tale of the Crusades and shows a battle with siege towers, catapults and boiling oil. I have not found all of these in another film. A wonderful old black and white film for the whole family. **V**

Hunchback of Notre Dame, The (1939) *****1/2** (See Literature)

If I Were A King (1938) ******* D: Frank Lloyd. Ronald Coleman, Frances Dee, Basil Rathbone.   The tale of the French poet François Villon who vexes King Louis XI (Rathbone) with his verse and must be clever enough to save his head! Not necessarily historically true and accurate, but family fun. Later remade as *The Vagabond King*, Rudolph Friml's operetta based upon this story and written in 1925. **V**

Ivanhoe (1952) ******1/2** D: Richard Thorpe. Robert Taylor, Joan Fontaine, Elizabeth Taylor, Emlyn Williams, George Sanders, Robert Douglas.   Based upon the epic by Sir Walter Scott, this is once again a wonderful portrayal of chivalry at its best, and worst. Filmed in Great Britain, it tells the story of Normans and Saxons; a Saxon knight who left England to fight in the Crusades with King Richard and of his battle to raise the ransom for Richard. It shows the Jewish people in England and well portrays them as a people with no country and the sentiments of the people towards the Jews. The jousting scenes are well done and once again, this is a great film for family viewing. **V**

Joan of Arc (1948) ****1/2** D: Victor Fleming. Ingrid Bergman, Jose Ferrer, Francis L. Sullivan, J. Carrol Naish, Ward Bond, Gene Lockhart, Cecil Kellaway.   Based upon the Maxwell Anderson play, this is the story of Joan of Arc's life, her call from God to deliver her county, her stand for the truth and willingness to pay the price to be true to God. **V**

Lady Godiva (1955) ****** D: Arthur Lubin. Maureen O'Hara, George Nader, Victor MacLaughlin, Torin Thatcher, Robert Warwick.   Not the greatest movie ever made, but an acceptable black and white retelling of this famous story, tastefully done. The children will also learn where the term "peeping Tom" came from and why no good ever comes to one! **V**

Robin Hood (1973) ****1/2** D: Wolfgang Reitherman. Voices of Brian Bedford, Phil Harris, Monica Evans, Peter Ustinov, Terry-Thomas, Andy Devine.   A good introduction for

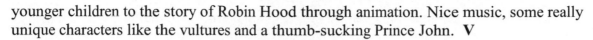

younger children to the story of Robin Hood through animation. Nice music, some really unique characters like the vultures and a thumb-sucking Prince John. **V**

NOTE: *See comments below on the following movies.*

Braveheart (1995) ** D: Mel Gibson. Mel Gibson, Sophie Marceau, Patrick McGoohan, Catherine McCormack.   Because this film has caused a lot of talk, I'd like to comment upon it. I have been somewhat appalled hearing of youth ministers referring to this film and quoting from it to inspire their teens to follow Yeshua! "What fellowship hath light with darkness?" Yes, the tale of William Wallace is that of a very brave man who inspired hundreds of men to follow him in fighting for Scottish freedom. However, this film is very explicit in violence, gore, infidelity, homosexuality, and just plain sin. Personally, I do not find the factual part of the film to overcome or even outweigh the instruction in sin. Therefore, I cannot endorse or recommend this film. It is rated "R" for movie and video release and doesn't fare much better even when edited and "cleaned" up for T.V., which is where I saw it. (I do not see "R" rated films.) So, my best advise is to skip this one.

Camelot (1967) *1/2 D: Joshua Logan. Richard Harris, Vanessa Redgrave, Franco Nero.   I know that this film has been recommended by other home schoolers as well as Disney's *The Sword in the Stone*. In my opinion, neither of these is appropriate for children as the first deals with adultery and the second with witchcraft as primary themes. However, *The Once and Future King* is a well known piece of literature. My suggestion is that you tell the story so that they will know about King Arthur and the legendary kingdom of Camelot (which will play into American history under JFK), and perhaps listen to some of the music from the Broadway album. This musical play was written by Alan Jay Lerner and Fredrick Lowe. The original Broadway cast included Richard Burton as King Arthur, Julie Andrews as Guinevere and Robert Goulet as Lancelot.

Lion in Winter, The Whether seen on stage or screen, in my opinion, this work is not for children. Covering a time in the life of Henry II, (1133-1189) this play is filled with immorality and perversion. The film gets high ratings for the skill of the playwright, and the actors. However, I don't think there is any way to salvage this work for educational purposes for children. A better film on his reign will be found in *Becket*. From there you can study about this king, famous for innovations including trial by jury and circuit courts. He was the father of Richard the Lion-hearted and his crafty brother, Prince John.

NOTES

The Renaissance

Agony and the Ecstasy, The (1965) *** D: Carol Reed. Charlton Heston, Rex Harrison.   Michelangelo's ongoing conflict with Pope Julius II shows the work on the Sistine Chapel, the hardships, the scaffolding and the determination of Michelangelo. **V**

Note: I would recommend getting a library book to see the Sistine Chapel and compare the painting before and after the recent cleaning of the paintings. For years, people thought Michelangelo had painted with rather drab colors. After cleaning, they saw that he had painted his masterpiece with brilliant colors. This would be an interesting way to either kick off a unit on him, or to end a study of him and/or Renaissance painters. (See Music/Arts, too.)

Captain From Castille (1947) *** D: Henry King. Tyrone Power, Jean Peters, Cesar Romero, Lee J. Cobb, John Sutton.   Driven by revenge Tyrone Power strives to avenge his family of the cruel and unjust treatment of the Spanish Inquisition and the false accusations of an Inquisitor (Sutton). He joins the army of Cortez (Romero) on his conquest of Mexico. **V**

Note: The Aztecs believed that a regular diet of the grain amaranth would produce a race of "supermen." Because of their belief in the supernatural qualities of amaranth, it was widely cultivated by the Aztecs and was used in their holy days celebrations. It was mixed with human blood and shaped into birds, snakes, other gods and then baked. These loaves were then consumed in a ritual to maintain their strength and fitness. Cortez was so outraged at this mockery of "Communion" that he killed Montezuma and ordered the destruction of all amaranth seeds and plants. Anyone found with a single seed in his possession would have their hands cut off. This battle is recognized as the end of the Aztec empire. With their source of "strength" gone, they became lost and dispirited. Amaranth has made a recent comeback in the diets of today and has been found to be a highly nutritious grain. You might want to look into its history, nutrition and cook with some for part of your study.

Hamlet (1948-British) **** (See Literature)

Prince of Foxes (1949) **1/2 D: Henry King. Tyronne Power, Wanda Hendrix, Orson Welles, Marina Berti, Everett Sloane, Katina Paxinou.   Costume Renaissance epic of Power as a wandering adventurer who meets and matches wits with the legendary Cesare Borgia. An interesting film of intrigue.

Romeo and Juliet (1968-British-Italian) ***1/2 (See Literature)

Taming of the Shrew, The (1967-US- Italian) ***1/2 D: Franco Zeffirelli. Elizabeth Taylor, Richard Burton, Vernon Dobtcheff, Michael York.   A good, understandable portrayal of the classic play by Shakespeare. It does have some bawdy lines, as Shakespeare was known to do. Accurately showing the period in dress, manner, custom, food, dining, etc. Check it out first to edit any objectionable parts, but it may just be the most watchable film production of a Shakespearian play. **V**

Adventures of Don Juan, The (1948) ** D: Vincent Sherman. Errol Flynn, Viveca Lindfors, Robert Douglas, Alan Hale, Ann Rutherford, Raymond Burr.   Oscar winner for costumes, this is another Flynn swashbuckler. Probably the best version for this tale as most of the "realities" of the situation are tastefully masked. If you feel the need to cover this subject, this is your best bet, but I'd still view it first for content. In history, Don Juan was Philip II of Spain's illegitimate son. Philip pursued the Spanish Inquisition, and sent the Armada to England for the purpose of ridding the land of the Protestant "heretics." **V**

Anne of the Thousand Days (1969) **1/2 D: Charles Jarrott. Richard Burton, Genevieve Bujold, Irene Papas, Anthony Quayle, Peter Jeffrey.   Based on the play, this is the story of Henry VIII and his wife, Anne Boleyn, whom he had beheaded. Not perfectly accurate, but still an engrossing film with fine acting jobs by all. Because of the subject matter as well as some scenes, *parents **need** to view this first* to determine if it is right for their family and if they can edit it for use. **[M/PG] V**

Fire Over England (1937 British) *** D: William K. Howard. Laurence Olivier, Flora Robson, Leslie Banks, Raymond Massey, Vivien Leigh, Tamara Desni, Morton Selten, Robert Newton.   Historical drama about the British-Spanish conflict of the 1500s and the dreaded Armada. Robson is wonderful as Queen Elizabeth I, with Massey in fine form as the villain from Spain. Young Vivien Leigh plays a maiden in Elizabeth's court. **V, DVD**

Luther (1955-Lutheran Church Production) D: Irving Pichel. Niall MacGinnis, John Ruddock, Pierre Lefevre, Guy Verney, Allastair Hunter, David Horne, Fred Johnshon, Philip Leaver; narrator: John Wiggin.   Dramatization of the life of Luther (1483-1546) and the nailing of his 95 theses to the door of the All Saints Church in Wittenberg, Germany in 1517. The film opens with this statement, "This dramatization of a decisive moment in human history is the result of careful research of facts and conditions in the 16th century as reported by historians of many faiths." Not great acting but definitely worth seeing. **[NR] V**

Man For All Seasons, A (1966-British) ***** D: Fred Zimmerman. Paul Scofield, Wendy Hiller, Leo McKern, Robert Shaw, Orson Wells, Susannah York, John Hurt, Nigel Davenport, Vanessa Redgrave. Star-studded cast does outstanding job portraying the film version of Robert Bolt's play of Sir Thomas More's (Scofield) conflict of conscience with King Henry VIII (Shaw) who wishes More's support in breaking with the Pope and forming the Church of England (in 1534) in order to divorce his wife and marry another. Fabulous acting job, all. Shows the power of a man who refuses to compromise what is right, (according to his heavenly King), even for his earthly king. Powerful. Video version should be edited for language. **V**

Prince and the Pauper, The (1937) ***1/2 (See Literature)

Private Life of Henry VIII, The (1933-British) ***1/2 D: Alexander Korda. Charles Laughton, Binnie Barnes, Robert Donat, Elsa Lanchester, Merle Oberon, Miles Mander, Wendy Barrie, John Loder. Historical story of 16th century English king who beheads his wives. Parents preview this one first. **V**

Private Lives of Elizabeth and Essex, The (1939) ***1/2 D: Michael Curtiz. Bette Davis, Errol Flynn, Olivia de Havilland, Donald Crisp, Alan Hale, Vincent Price, Henry Stephenson, Henry Daniell, James Stephenson, Ralph Forbes, Robert Warwick, Leo G. Carroll.   Elaborate, colorful costume drama with Davis at her best as Queen Elizabeth I and Flynn as the dashing Essex whom she loves, but cannot have. Not historically accurate, but still a good film adaptation of the Maxwell Anderson play, *Elizabeth the Queen*. The film is also known by this title. **V**

Sea Hawk, The (1940) **** D: Michael Curtiz. Errol Flynn, Brenda Marshall, Claude Rains, Donald Crisp, Flora Robson, Alan Hale, Henry Daniell, Una O'Connor, Gilbert

Roland.   Rousing tale of swashbuckler Flynn (at his best) on the high seas. A departure from Rafael Sabatini novel of the same name but still good family fun. Another great score by Erich Wolfgang Korngold. The video version has extra footage for the British showing Queen Elizabeth I (of the film) giving a morale building message for the wartime audiences. **V**

Spanish Main, The (1945) **1/2 D: Frank Borzage. Paul Henreid, Maureen O'Hara, Walter Slezak, Binnie Barnes, John Emery, Barton MacLane.   Colorful swashbuckler of Dutch captain Henreid, who is imprisoned by villain Slezak for daring to shipwreck upon his shore. Henreid escapes and takes Slezak's intended bride (O'Hara) hostage, which turns out to be a blessing for her. Fun action film.

Virgin Queen, The (1955) *** D: Henry Koster. Bette Davis, Richard Todd, Joan Collins, Herbert Marshall, Jay Robinson, Dan O'Herlihy, Rod Taylor.   Davis reprises her role from *The Private Lives of Elizabeth and Essex* as Elizabeth I. This film shows her conflicts with Sir Walter Raleigh, as well as her irascible disposition and wily character. **V**

Young Bess (1953) **1/2 D: George Sidney. Jean Simmons, Stewart Granger, Charles Laughton, Deborah Kerr, Cecil Kellaway, Leo G. Carroll, Kay Walsh.   Costumer of the life of Queen Elizabeth I before ascending to the throne. Shown is her estranged and strange relationship with her father, Henry VIII (Laughton) and the effect he had on all around him, especially the terror of being his wife. Her relationship with her brother, who does ascend to the throne for a short period of time is also shown, as well as those who wielded the power behind the young king. Also shown is Elizabeth's (fictitious) love for a fine man (Granger) who is unobtainable for her. Good acting jobs, all. **V**

Note: Forever Amber (1947) 1/2 D: Otto Preminger. Linda Darnell, Cornel Wilde, George Sanders, Jessica Tandy, Anne Revere, Leo G. Carroll.   Even other reviewers calls this one "musical beds." Some recommend this as an example of the moral decay into which England sank after Oliver Cromwell, but I feel that it is simply one example of immorality after another and not worth showing to children. If you wish to consider this one, I feel the parents **must** view it first.

NOTES

1600s

Against All Flags (1952) **1/2 D: George Sherman. Errol Flynn, Maureen O'Hara, Anthony Quinn, Mildred Natwick.   Flynn plays a British soldier who must infiltrate a pirate stronghold, find the map to the cannons and disable them before the British fleet arrives. O'Hara is the key to the armaments. Parents may wish to view this first as Flynn is portrayed as a "ladies man." **V**

At Sword's Point (1952) **1/2 D: Lewis Allen. Cornel Wilde, Maureen O'Hara, Robert Douglas, Dan O'Herlihy, Alan Hale, Jr., Blanche Yurka.   The children of the Three Musketeers (one of whom is a girl!) come to the aid of the Queen, who is fighting for her life and that of her children against the evil Regent who wishes to take control of the kingdom. Beautiful costume film with plenty of swashbuckling. Fun trivia: Wilde's father was an Olympic fencing coach and Wilde was a very proficient swordsman. **V**

Black Swan, The (1942) **1/2 D: Henry King. Tyrone Power, Maureen O'Hara, Laird Cregar, Thomas Mitchell, George Sanders, Anthony Quinn.   Oscar winning cinematography beautifully shows this costumer of swashbuckling Power snatching O'Hara from the grasping clutches of Sanders and Quinn. Just swashbuckling fun. **V**

Captain Blood (1935) **** D: Michael Curtiz. Errol Flynn, Olivia de Haviland, Lionel Atwill, Basil Rathbone.   Errol Flynn's first swashbuckler based upon the Rafael Sabatini novel. Flynn plays Peter Blood, an Irish physician who treats men, not political sides. Because he treated the "wrong" person, he is imprisoned and sold as a slave. Escaping, he becomes a pirate captain who seeks to right the wrongs done to him and his fellow slave/pirates. Justice is done in the end with much action in sea battles and sword fights in between. Real family fun. Score is another by Eric Wolfgang Korngold, a student of the classical composer, Gustav Mahler. Excellent film. **V**

Crimson Pirate, The (1952) *** D: Robert Siodmak. Burt Lancaster, Nick Cravat, Eva Bartok. A Mediterranean swashbuckler full of gags and fun. Burt Lancaster was a circus performer before becoming an actor. The mute in the film is his former partner who joined him for the physical comedy tricks, all of which Lancaster did, himself. No stuntmen! **V**

King's Thief, The (1955) **1/2 D: Robert Z. Leonard. David Niven, Ann Blyth, George Sanders, Edmund Purdom, Roger Moore, Alan Mowbray.   Great costumer of intrigue in the court of King Charles II of England. **V**

Plymouth Adventure (1952) *1/2 D: Clarence Brown. Spencer Tracy, Gene Tierney, Van Johnson, Leo Genn, Dawn Addams, Lloyd Bridges, Barry Jones.   Though based on fact, too much license was taken with this story. The framework is there, but unfortunately, Hollywood decided to turn the story of the Pilgrims into a soap opera, with the captain of the Mayflower (Tracey) lusting after William Bradford's wife! (Tierney) If parents watch this first, most can be omitted and you can still salvage some good parts, including the changing of terms by the Virginia company right before sailing, the use of the printing press to save the ship, the terrible storm they all survived, the birth of Oceanis, and even the mysterious death of Bradford's wife, though there is no evidence for the story line in the film. Parents will definitely need to preview this one and decide if they want to salvage parts of it.

Queen Christina (1933) **** D: Rouben Mamoulian. Greta Garbo, John Gilbert, Ian Keith, Lewis Stone, C. Aubrey Smith, Gustav von Seyffertiz, Reginald Owen.   Considered Garbo's best film, this reteams the famous duo of Garbo and Gilbert in the story of Sweden's 17th century Queen who was renowned for her intelligence as well as for being a good ruler. She renounced her throne for the love of her life, a Spanish ambassador to her court. Parents *definitely* need to preview this one before showing it to their children. **V**

Three Musketeers (1948) **1/2 (see Literature)

America

Allegheny Uprising (1939) *** D: William Seiter. John Wayne, Claire Trevor, George Sanders, Brian Donlevy, Robert Barrat, Moroni Olsen, Chill Willis.   Based on a true story of settlers vs. Redcoats with Wayne a man of principle who believes in the law and fights to uphold it even with his own life at stake when framed for murder. Clean and well done, we had a good laugh when Claire Treavor kisses John Wayne and one of the men says, "If he's a bit warm, it's that kissing business and not the bullet." **V**

America's Godly Heritage **** Documentary.   Produced by Wallbuilders, this is a wonderful look at American history including the perspective which is so often omitted from texts: the faith of our Founding Fathers. Obtain from church libraries or from www.wallbuilders.com. Check their website for more excellent videos and DVDs as well as other resources. Highly Recommended **V, DVD**

Ben and Me NR   Animated version of the book (which is very different) telling of the mouse, Amos, who is responsible for all of Benjamin Franklin's inventions, almanac, sayings, and witticisms! Done by Walt Disney when he was still alive, this is fun for the entire family. Recommend that you read the book first, then compare and discuss it and the movie. The author, Robert Lawson, also did another book, *Mr. Revere and I* about Paul Revere and his horse, from the horse's point of view.

Drums Along the Mohawk (1939) ***1/2 D: John Ford. Claudette Colbert, Henry Fonda, Edna May Oliver, John Carradine.   Story of courageous settlers in upstate New York during Revolutionary War, marrying, settling, building a home, farming, and fighting the Indians for their lives. Well done. **V**

Education and the Founding Fathers **** Documentary.   An excellent Wallbuilders video covering what our Founding Fathers said about education. www.wallbuilders.com has more resources. **V**

Follow the River (1995) TVM D: Martin Davidson. Sheryl Lee, Ellen Burstyn, Tim Guinea, Eric Schweig, Reneé O'Connor.   Based on fact and a book by James Alexander Thorn, this is the story of a group of people captured by the Shawnee in a raid upon their homes. Set in the 1750s, we see the hardship of the captives as well as the indomitable spirit of the leading lady of the story. Very well done. **V**

Johnny Tremaine (1957) *** D: Robert Stevenson. Hal Stalmaster, Luana Patten, Jeff York, Sebastian Cabot.   From the novel by Esther Forbes, this well done Disney film tells of a young apprentice silversmith who gets involved with the Sons of Liberty, the Boston Tea Party, and the Revolutionary War. Read the book first and then see the movie and compare. **V**

Last of the Mohicans, The (1936) **1/2 D: George B. Seitz. Randolph Scott, Binnie Barnes, Heather Angel, Hugh Buckler, Henry Wilcoxon, Bruce Cabot, Phillip Reed.   Probably the only film version not horribly gory to show of the James Fenimore Cooper story of conflict between the British Army and Colonial settlers of the French and Indian War. This book is about a very bloody time in history. Parents should definitely view this first. **V**

Northwest Passage (Book I—Roger's Rangers) (1940) **1/2 D: King Vidor. Spencer Tracy, Robert Young, Walter Brennan, Ruth Hussey, Nat Pendelton, Robert Barrat.   Based on Kenneth Robert's book about the true story of Roger's Rangers (with Tracy in the title role) who faced incredible hardship and insurmountable odds to explore new territory in Colonial America. There are a few scenes parents will wish to edit, so preview first. **V**

Rachel and the Stranger (1948) *** D: Norman Foster. Loretta Young, William Holden, Robert Mitchum, Tom Tully.   Bondservant Young, for propriety's sake, marries [in name only] the widower holder of her papers (Holden) to take care of him and his young son. Mitchum is Holden's friend who decides that Rachel (Young) could do better by marrying him! Frontier life and skills are shown. If the subject matter concerns you, view it first, though I will tell you that this is portrayed very above board by all. **V**

Captain Horatio Hornblower (1951) *** (See 1800s)

Count of Monte Cristo, The (1934) *** D: Rowland V. Lee. Robert Donat, Elissa Landi, Louis Calhern. **V**

(1977) TVM D: David Greene; Richard Chamberlain, Tony Curtis, Trevor Howard, Louis Jordan, Donald Pleasance. Average **V**

(2002) D: Kevin Reynolds. Jim Caviezel, Guy Pierce, Richard Harris, James Frain, Dagmara Dominczyk, Michael Wincott, Luis Guzman. **V, DVD**

Of the three versions, my favorite is the newest. All are based upon the classic story by Alexandre Dumas. It is the story of Edmond Dantes (Donat/Chamberlain, Caviezel) who is wrongfully imprisoned and whose imprisonment was masterminded by Mondego - the man he thought was his friend - who coveted Dante's betrothed for his own. Dantes survives his imprisonment and escapes, returning to exact vengeance upon Mondego. Whichever version you choose, please view it first. I think you'll find the newest version can be easily edited as well as being enjoyable to watch.

Great Garrick, The (1937) *** D: James Whale. Brian Aherne, Olivia de Havilland, Edward Everett Horton, Melville Cooper, Lionel Atwill, Lana Turner.   A tale about a real life English actor, David Garrick, and the Comedieaise (French acting troupe) who believe his ego needs deflating and set their talents to do so! A very fun film with excellent cast and acting.

Horatio Hornblower (1998) **** D: Andrew Grieve. Ioan Gruffudd, Robert Lindsay, Pual McGann, Lorcan Cranitch, Tony Haygarth.   Based upon the books of C. S. Forester, this is an admirably done set, now consisting of three parts. The original set had four episodes: "The Duel," "The Fire Ships," "The Duchess and the Devil," "The Wrong War." The second installment consists of, "Mutiny" and "Retribution" and the third, "Loyalty" and "Duty." They include a wonderful look at the costumes, ships, and warfare of the time. These were produced by A&E and are available for rental or purchase from either A&E's website or through some of the website rental/purchase places mentioned in the appendix, and perhaps may even be found locally. Though they are excellently done, there is still subject matter which parents most probably will want to edit. Therefore parents watch them first and then edit as you wish. The time period covered in this series also includes the 1800s. **V, DVD**

Man in the Iron Mask (1934) *** D: James Whale. Louis Hayward, Joan Bennett, Warren William, Joseph Schildkraut, Alan Hale, Sr. **V**

(1977) TVM D: Mike Newell. Richard Chamberlain, Patrick McGoohan, Louis Jourdan, Jenny Agutter, Vivien Merchant, Ian Holm. Above average **V**

Based upon the Alexandre Dumas tale of twin brothers separated at birth. One is King of France, the other knows nothing of his parentage. The one who has been hidden since birth is now needed to take the throne from his corrupt brother. It is the only way to save France and the monarchy. Due to some of the subject matter, parents would be wise to view this first and decide if this is right for your family.

Note: I do *not* recommend the newest version with Leonardo di Caprio. It is repugnant to the extreme for those who hold family values.

Scaramouche (1952) ***1/2 D: George Sidney. Stewart Granger, Eleanor Parker, Janet Leigh, Mel Ferrer, Henry Wilcoxon, Lewis Stone, Nina Foch, Richard Anderson, Robert Coote.   Set in France, this is an excellent adaptation of the Sabatini novel of a young man who seeks to avenge the death of his friend (Anderson) against the man who killed him (Ferrer) while also seeking for the truth of his parentage. To hide his identity, he joins a Comedia del Arte troupe (about which you can study) and becomes the clown, Scaramouche. He falls in love with Janet Leigh who, with Eleanor Parker's help, tries to keep him apart from Ferrer, an expert swordsman. He secretly studies swordsmanship to be ready to duel with Ferrer. He is elevated to a representative of the people, which brings him into the realm of Ferrer. Tension, action, drama and the longest duel ever filmed. **V**

Scarlet Pimpernel, The (1982) TVM D: Clive Donner. Anthony Andrews, Jane Seymour, Ian McKellan, James Villiers.   Based upon the combined novels of the title and *Eldorado* by Baroness Orcy, this excellently done version has it all. Intrigue, swashbuckling, disguise, costumes, lavish sets as well as the horror of the French Revolution. Due to some of the more graphic scenes, especially with the guillotine, [and a few showing two people in bed together] I recommend parental viewing first. However, remember that the French Revolution was terribly bloody and therefore, these scenes are still cleaner than the reality. Special Mention, Above Average. **V** (There is also a version with Leslie Howard in black and white, (1935) but I feel this one is better.)

Tale of Two Cities, A (1935) **** D: Jack Conway. Ronald Colman, Elizabeth Allan, Edna May Oliver, Reginald Owen, Basil Rathbone, Blanche Yurka, Isabel Jewell, Water Catlett, Henry B. Walthall, H. B. Warner, Donald Woods.   Dickens classic story of the 1780s French Revolution and of a man who lays down his life for his friends. Don't miss this one. **V**

NOTE: **Marie Antoinette** (1938) 1/2 D: W. S. Van Dyke II. Norma Shearer, Tyrone Power, John Barrymore, Robert Morley.   You would think that this would be a fine film since it was made in '38, but it is filled with immorality. This predates the old "Hayes Code" by one year. Suggest you pass on this one.

NOTES

1800s

Due to the number of movies set in this time period, I have subdivided them into categories for easier reference, though they are in no particular chronological order within the subdivisions.

The West

Adventures of Bullwhip Griffin, The (See Family) **V**

Alamo, The (1960) *** D: John Wayne. John Wayne, Richard Widmark, Laurence Harvey, Richard Boone, Carlos Arruza, Frankie Avalon, Patrick Wayne, Linda Cristal, Chill Wills, Ken Curtis, Hank Worden, Denver Pyle.   Filmed on location in Bracketville, TX, this rendition of the Battle for the Alamo has all of the pertinent facts in place. A few men, greatly outnumbered, took the stand to defend Texas at the Alamo, knowing there was no hope of their survival, but also knowing the importance of its position. From here came the famous cry, "Remember the Alamo!" a rallying call to all Texans. In this battle Davy Crockett and Jim Bowie died as well as other, now famous, brave men. As with several other films, this story presents the opportunity to discuss those who gave their life for their country and those who did not; the character of those on both sides of the issue and what our responsibility is to our country. **V**

Angel and the Badman (1947) *** D: James Edward Grant. John Wayne, Gail Russell, Harry Carey, Irene Rich, Bruce Cabot.   The daughter of a Quaker family influences gunman Quirt Evans (Wayne) to hang up his guns and live a life of peace. In the meantime, there are a lot of good, moral lessons portrayed, like loving your enemy. A fine family film. **V**

Annie Oakley (1935) *** D: George Stevens. Barbara Stanwyck, Preston Foster, Melvyn Douglas. Based upon the life of the famous sharpshooter, this gives a good picture of American life in the late 1800s. Later made into a musical by Irving Berlin called, *Annie Get Your Gun* (See Music/Arts) **V**

Bend of the River (1952) *** D: Anthony Mann. James Stewart, Arthur Kennedy, Julia Adams, Rock Hudson, Jay C. Flippen, Lori Nelson, Stepin Fetchit, Harry Morgan.   An 1840 Oregon western of wagon train boss Stewart and his fight to get the train through as he battles with one time crony, Kennedy. **V**

Big Country, The (1958) **** D: William Wyler. Gregory Peck, Burl Ives, Jean Simmons, Carroll Baker, Charlton Heston, Chuck Connors, Charles Bickford.   Eastern sea captain Peck comes west for the girl with whom he fell in love while she was in the east. In the west, things begin to appear differently. A wonderful character study with many opportunities for discussion about how things may appear, and how they really are, as well as the character of a man. Highly recommended. **V**

Big Sky, The (1952) **1/2 D: Howard Hawks. Kirk Douglas, Dewey Martin, Elizabeth Threatt, Arthur Hunnicutt, Buddy Baer, Steven Geray, Hank Worden, Jim Davis.   Two backwoodsmen meet and become friends as they hunt for Martin's uncle (Hunnicutt). All get involved in a plan to go where no white man has ever gone before: up the Missouri river to Blackfoot territory to trade for furs. Only problem: a fur company is trying to hold a monopoly on the territory and the fur trade. The group's secret weapon is a Blackfoot princess the captain rescued. Well done western based on a book by A. B. Guthrie, Jr. **V**

Broken Arrow (1950) **** D: Delmer Daves. James Stewart, Jeff Chandler, Debra Paget, Will Geer, Jay Silverheels.   True 1870s story of Apache Chief Cochise (Chandler) and ex-Army man (Stewart) who represents the whites in making a treaty with Cochise. Shows Cochise's struggle in making a decision for his people, his keeping his word and the whites, who do not. Paget is lovely as the Indian wife of Stewart. Very well done. **V**

Buffalo Bill (1944) **1/2 D: William Wellman. Joel McCrea, Maureen O'Hara, Linda Darnell, Thomas Mitchell, Anthony Quinn, Edgar Buchanan, Chief Thundercloud, Sidney Blackmer.   Star-studded cast in colorful biography of legendary western character. **V**

Calamity Jane (1953) *** (See Music/Arts)

Call of the Wild (1935) **1/2 D: William Wellman. Clark Gable, Loretta Young, Jackie Oakie, Reginald Owen, Frank Conroy.   Loosely based upon Jack London's book of the Yukon. Read the book first and then watch and compare, critique. Parents may wish to preview first.

Cheyenne Autumn (1964) *** D: John Ford. Richard Widmark, Carroll Baker, Karl Malden, Dolores Del Rio, Sal Mineo, Edward G. Robinson, James Stewart, Ricardo Montalban, Gilbert Roland, Arthur Kennedy, Patrick Wayne.   Last Western by Ford, about Cheyenne tribe being relocated by the army and then deciding to return to their home; the varying views on this decision within the tribe, the division of the tribe and the hardships each part encountered. This film shows the army's injustice to the Indians as well as a missionary's (Baker) effort to help them. Worth viewing. **V**

Chisum (1970) **1/2 D: Andrew V. McLaglen. John Wayne, Forrest Tucker, Christopher George, Ben Johnson, Glenn Corbett, Bruce Cabot, Patrick Knowles, Lynda Day, Richard Jaeckel, Geoffrey Duel. A highly fictionalized account of Billy the Kid who wishes to start a new life. The catalyst for this new life is a godly, Bible believing Englishman who has a great impact upon his life. Though this movie is obviously not a documentary of Billy the Kid's life, I think that it presents some great opportunities to discuss choices in the face of hard decisions and allows the family the opportunity to cover ground that, eventually, we all will face: how to handle injustice. Will we follow the principles of the Messiah, or take matters into out own hands? Note: the end scene is a fairly violent gun battle. **V**

Dark Command (1940) **1/2 D: Raoul Walsh. Claire Trevor, John Wayne, Walter Pidgeon, Roy Rogers, George "Gabby" Hayes, Porter Hall, Marjorie Main.   This film covers a largely fictitious look at the Quantrill of Quantrill's Raiders. It also raises some interesting character issues ripe for discussion. **V**

Davy Crockett, King of the Wild Frontier (1955) *** D: Norman Foster. Fess Parker, Buddy Ebsen, Basil Ruysdael, Hans Conried, William Bakeswell, Kenneth Tobey.   Wonderful fun for the family, this Walt Disney production (first shown as three Sunday night episodes), tells the story of Davy Crockett. Though not strictly factual, it does show the down-home-spun humor and tall tales for which Crockett was known. Also shown is the fact that he served in Congress, his honor, and truthfulness. For the ending of his life, see *The Alamo*. **V**

Dodge City (1939) *** D: Michael Curtiz. Errol Flynn, Olivia de Haviland, Ann Sheridan, Bruce Cabot, Frank McHugh, Alan Hale, John Litel, Victor Jory, Ward Bond.   Errol tames the town and gets de Haviland. Fun for all. **V**

Eagle and the Hawk, The (1950) ** D: Lewis R. Foster. John Payne, Rhonda Fleming, Dennis O'Keefe, Thomas Gomez, Fred Clark.   Set in 1860s Texas-Mexican territory about two U.S. law officers (O'Keefe, Payne) trying to stop a coup to make Maximillian ruler of Mexico.

El Dorado (1967) *** D: Howard Hawks. John Wayne, Robert Mitchum, James Caan, Arthur Hunnicutt, Edward Asner, Michele Carey, Christopher George, Charlene Holt.   Story of friends, one a gun fighter, the other a sheriff who has become a drunk, and the range war surrounding the sheriff's town. Wayne comes to his friend's (Mitchum) aid, with a young man who can't shoot! (Caan) Range wars were a reality of the West. This film shows the ugliness of them and the old adage, "Power corrupts and absolute power corrupts absolutely." **V**

Escape from Ft. Bravo (1953) *** D: John Sturges. William Holden, Eleanor Parker, John Forsythe, Polly Bergen, William Demarest, William Campbell, Richard Anderson.   Civil War era western. Holden plays a tough cavalry captain at an Arizona fort where Confederate prisoners are held and where Indian attacks are happening. **V**

Far and Away (1992) **1/2 D: Ron Howard. Tom Cruise, Nicole Kidman, Thomas Gibson, Robert Prosky.   This is a film which DEFINITELY has to be edited by the parent, but has a few scenes worth extracting. Included is the story of the difference of classes in Ireland, the Irish immigration, how they were viewed and treated, their contribution to the eastern part of the transcontinental railroad, and the 1893 Oklahoma land rush. Excerpt what you feel would benefit your children to see. If nothing else, shown the land rush scene. It actually happened that way. **V**

Far Country, The (1955) *** D: Anthony Mann. Jimmy Stewart, Ruth Roman, Corinne Calvet, Walter Brennan, Jay C. Flippen, John McIntire, Harry Morgan.   Stewart, a confirmed loner and cattleman, takes his herd to Alaska and finds nothing but trouble in a town run by McIntire who is corrupt and out to steal gold claims and anything else with which he can get away. **V**

Far Horizons (1955) **1/2 D: Rudolph Maté. Fred MacMurray, Charlton Heston, Donna Reed, Barbara Hale, William Demarest.   This opens in 1803 with Jefferson's Louisiana Purchase and the need to explore the new territory acquired by the United States. The explorers chosen were Lewis and Clark. The hardships of the exploration are minimized in favor of a fictitious love story between Clark and Sacegewea, but children can get the flavor of the expedition from this film. A pretty costumer.

Fastest Gun Alive, The (1956) **1/2 D: Russell Rouse. Glenn Ford, Jeanne Crain, Broderick Crawford, Russ Tamblyn.   Moral tale of a peace-loving storekeeper who was a former fast gun and must now live down his reputation, but someone always comes looking for him to make a name for themselves. Tamblyn has impressive dance bit. Parents view first. **V**

First Traveling Saleslady, The (1956) **1/2 D: Arthur Lubin. Ginger Rogers, Barry Nelson, Carol Channing, David Brian, James Arness, Clint Eastwood.   Rogers and Channing are traveling salesladies for girdles, who can't make a go of it in the west, so switch to highly controversial barbed wire! Off beat comedy has its moments. The inimitable Carol Channing is always a joy to watch, but pairing her with a very young Eastwood is a bit bizarre. Nevertheless, the children should enjoy it.

Fort Apache (1948) *** D: John Ford. John Wayne, Henry Fonda, Shirley Temple, Pedro Armendariz, John Agar, Ward Bond, George O'Brien, Victor McLaglen, Anna Lee, Irene Rich, Dick Foran, Guy Kibbee, Mae Marsh, Hank Worden.   The first of Ford's famous cavalry trilogy with Fonda as a by-the-book leader who doesn't get along with anyone. Methodical and well done character development like all of Ford's films. Followed by *She Wore a Yellow Ribbon.* **V, DVD**

Gentleman Jim (1942) **1/2 (See 1900s)

Geronimo (1962) **1/2 D: Arnold Laven. Chuck Connors, Kamala Devi, Ross Martin, Adam West, Pat Conway. Title says it all. **V**   Redone recently by Ted Turner, and reflects its time. Whichever one you see, parents definitely need to preview it.

Great Sioux Uprising (1953) **1/2 D: Lloyd Bacon. Jeff Chandler, Faith Domergue.   Chandler plays an ex-Yankee officer doctor who helps the Sioux and tries to help quell an uprising of the Indians. Good movie about fighting evil.

High Noon (1952) **** D: Fred Zinnemann. Gary Cooper, Thomas Mitchell, Lloyd Bridges, Katy Jurado, Grace Kelly, Orro Kruger, Lon Chaney Jr., Henry Morgan, Lee Van Cleef.   An interesting character study of a marshal who, on the day he is to both wed and retire, learns of a gunman who is coming to find him. The marshal can run, and considers it, as no one will aid him. However, his conscience ultimately won't allow him to do so. **V, DVD**

How the West Was Won (1962) **** D: John Ford, ("The Civil War"); Henry Hathaway, ("The Rivers, The Plains, The Outlaws"); George Marshall ("The Railroad"). Carroll Baker, Henry Fonda, Gregory Peck, George Peppard, Carolyn Jones, Eli Wallach, Robert Preston, Debbie Reynolds, James Stewart, John Wayne, narrated by Spencer Tracy.   All star cast epic of three generations of Western pioneers. I first saw this at the Fabulous Fox Theatre in Atlanta, Georgia as a four year old (my first movie) and still remember it today! It hasn't

aged and will be good, historical fun for the family. **V**

Iron Mistress (1952) **1/2 D: Gordon Douglas. Alan Ladd, Virginia Mayo, Joseph Calleia, Phyllis Kirk.   Story of Jim Bowie and the Bowie knife.

Jayhawkers, The (1959) **1/2 D: Melvin Frank. Jeff Chandler, Fess Parker, Nicole Maurey, Henry Silva, Herbert Rudley.   Chandler and Parker battle for power in the 1850s west. **V**

Jesse James (1939) **1/2 D: Henry King. Tyrone Power, Henry Fonda, Nancy Kelly, Randolph Scott, Henry Hull, Brian Donlevy, John Carradine, Jane Darwell.   Power and Fonda play Jesse and Frank James. Not totally factual, but a good film to introduce children to the famous outlaws. **V**

Little House on the Prairie just about any episode.   This popular television show, based upon the books by Laura Ingalls Wilder, are available in libraries, some video stores, and K-Mart/Wal-Mart. They are wonderful stories filled with family and character building values. A few may contain subject matter of which all families might not approve. **V**

Lone Star (1952) **1/2 D: Vincent Sherman. Clark Gable, Ava Gardner, Lionel Barrymore, Beulah Bondi, Broderick Crawford.   Set at the time of the battle for Texas independence, this is a fun, clean family film to tie in Texas history. **V**

Man Who Shot Liberty Valence, The (1962) **** D: John Ford. James Stewart, John Wayne, Vera Miles, Lee Marvin, Edmond O'Brien, Andy Devine, Woody Strode, Jeanette Nolan, Ken Murray, John Qualen, Strother Martin, Lee Van Cleef, John Carradine, Carleton Young.   Young lawyer (Stewart) comes to town only to find that no one is much interested in the law; all are terrified of a man named Liberty Valence, who picks on Stewart to draw him out. Stewart takes it until he must face him or lose all self-respect. He doesn't know that he's had some secret help. Interesting film and character study. **V,DVD**

Mark of Zorro, The (1940) ***1/2 D: Rouben Mamoulian. Tyrone Power, Linda Darnell, Basil Rathbone, Gale Sondergaaard, Eugene Pallette.   Black and white swashbuckler with Power playing the son of a Californian aristocrat who studied to be a soldier in Spain. When called home, he finds his father ousted and a corrupt governor in his place. Power plays a foppish young man to everyone while secretly fighting against the injustice as Zorro. Rathbone was a swordsman in real life and commented on Power's dexterity with the sword. The scene of their swordfight is one of the best on film. **V**

Mask of Zorro, The (1998) *** D: Martin Campbell. Antonio Banderas, Anthony Hopkins, Catherine Zeta-Jones, Stuart Wilson, Matt Letscher, Maury Chaykin.   This is one of the newer films of note, but would still need to be edited. This is the first film to come close to the fine films of the past since *Indiana Jones and the Last Crusade.* It is the story of Zorro, (played by velvet-toned Hopkins) whose identity was discovered and who was imprisoned for 20 years. His wife was killed, his child stolen and raised by his arch-enemy who has now returned to California and unwittingly given Zorro the opportunity to escape. He stumbles across a young man (Banderas) who, as a child helped Zorro, and trains this young man to become the new Zorro. The training and transformation of the new Zorro is interesting, the sword fights wonderful. Parents should view first to omit several scenes which are not appropriate. The film can be easily salvaged without these scenes, which just goes to show that Hollywood COULD make family films again, if they so chose. **V, DVD**

McLintock! (1963) ***1/2 D: Andrew V. McLaglen. John Wayne, Maureen O'Hara, Patrick Wayne, Stefanie Powers, Yvonne De Carlo, Chill Wills, Bruce Cabot, Jack Kruschen, Jerry Van Dyke. Probably my favorite John Wayne film, this is one for the entire family. Wayne plays George Washington McLintock, who owns a good piece of the West. His wife (O'Hara) has removed herself from their backwater town to go to the capital, but has returned home for the homecoming of their daughter from college. This begins a giant free-for-all of a movie with highlights of a fight at a giant mudslide which will split your sides in laughter, and a public spanking with a fire shovel for O'Hara! Just rent a copy and watch it for a fun family night. **V**

My Darling Clementine (1946) ***1/2 D: John Ford. Henry Fonda, Linda Darnell, Victor Mature, Walter Brennan, Cathy Downs, Tim Holt, Ward Bond.   Ford's famous version of the gunfight at the O.K. Corral in 1881 and what leads up to it including a cantankerous Doc Holliday, and how Wyatt came to Tombstone and to being the Marshal there. One of Ford's best. **V**

Night Passage (1957) **1/2 D: James Neilson. James Stewart, Audie Murphy, Dan Duryea, Brandon de Wilde, Dianne Foster.   Stewart works for the railroad. His brother (Murphy) belongs to a gang planning to hold up the payroll train.

North to Alaska (1960) *** D: Henry Hathaway. John Wayne, Stewart Granger, Ernie Kovacs, Fabian, Capucine.   Action tale of partners in an Alaskan goldmine, claim jumpers and greedy businessmen. Granger's betrothed is to be brought north by partner Wayne. When he arrives in San Francisco, he finds she has married another. Not wishing to return empty-handed, he offers marriage to his friend and a better life to a "soiled dove." Granger's kid brother (Fabian) develops a crush on her and it's sort of a sprawling free-for-all from there. Definitely entertainment as opposed to straight history. Recommend parents watch first to see if they approve. **V**

Old Yeller (1957) ***1/2 D: Robert Stevenson. Dorothy McGuire, Fess Parker, Tommy Kirk, Kevin Corcoran, Jeff York, Beverly Washburn, Chuck Connors.   Based upon the Fred Gipson novel, this is the story of a boy coming of age and the stray dog he takes in. Farm life in 1869 Texas is shown as well as the concern with "hydrophobia" (rabies) and the courage of the boy to do as he must to care for his family in the father's absence. **V**

NOTE: If interested, the children might like to look into the life of Louis Pasteur and his work to find a cure for rabies. Listed in Medicine, you will also find a review of the movie of Pasteur's life.

One and Only Genuine Original Family Band, The (1968) **1/2 D: Michael O'Herlihy. Walter Brennen, Buddy Ebsen, Lesley Ann Warren, John Davidson, Janet Blair, Kurt Russell.   A musical family gets involved in the presidential election of 1888 and the issue of statehood for the Dakotas, which eventually ended up being divided into North and South Dakota. **[G] V**

Painted Hills, The (1951) **1/2 (See Family Films)

Pony Express (1953) **1/2 D: Jerry Hopper. Charlton Heston, Rhonda Fleming, Jan Sterling, Forrest Tucker.   Set in the 1860s, this western tells an exciting, fictitious story of the founding of the Pony Express including the colorful characters of Buffalo Bill and Wild Bill Hickock. **V**

Rare Breed, The (1966) *** D: Andrew V McLaglen. James Stewart, Maureen O'Hara, Brian Keith, Juliet Mills, Jack Elam, Ben Johnson.   I remember seeing this in the theatre when I was little. The story of Vindicator, the Hereford bull who followed his owner, a girl, when she whistled "God Save The Queen" fascinated me as a child. Today, it is the fun story of an English woman and her daughter who bring the bull, Vindicator, to the American west to fulfill her late husband's dream of cross-breeding Hereford and Longhorn cattle. Jimmy Stewart catches the idea and doggedly sees it through. A good one for perseverance, and seeing the hardships of the west as everyone else laughs at the idea and says that Herefords cannot survive the western weather. **V**

Red River (1948) **** D: Howard Hawks. John Wayne, Montgomery Clift, Walter Brennan, Joanne Dru, John Ireland, Noah Beery, Jr., Harry Carey, Sr., Chief Yowlatchie, Hank Worden.   Fascinating movie character study of the clash between a tough guardian (Wayne) and his charge who is now a young man (Clift in film debut) while on a cross country cattle drive. Powerful. **V, DVD**

Rio Grande (1950) *** D: John Ford. John Wayne, Maureen O'Hara, Ben Johnson, Harry Carey, Jr., Victor McLaglen, Claude Jarman, Jr., Chill Wills, J. Carrol Naish, Grant Withers, Pat Wayne.   Last of Ford's famous trilogy (*Fort Apache* and *She Wore a Yellow Ribbon*) takes a look at the code of conduct of the Post Civil War Calvary, as well as the strained relationship between a father and son. **V, DVD**

San Antonio (1945) **1/2 D: David Butler. Errol Flynn, Alexis Smith, S. Z. Sakall, Victor Francen, Florence Bates, John Litel, Paul Kelly.   Well done film of hero Flynn thwarts villains Francen and Kelly while romancing Smith and fighting for justice. **V**

Santa Fe Trail (1940) ** D: Michael Curtiz. Errol Flynn, Olivia de Haviland, Raymond Massey, Ronald Reagan, Alan Hale, Guinn Williams, William Lundigan, Ward Bond, Van Heflin, Gene Reynolds, John Litel, Charles Middleton.   Somewhat confused picture is worth seeing for John Brown's raid. Reagan plays George Armstrong Custer. (whom Flynn portrayed the next year in *They Died With Their Boots On*) **V, DVD**

Searchers, The (1956) **** D: John Ford. John Wayne, Jeffrey Hunter, Vera Miles, Ward Bond, Natalie Wood, John Qualen, Harry Carey, Jr., Olive Carey, Antonio Moreno, Henry Brandon, Hawk Worden, Ken Curtis, Lana Wood, Dorothy Jordan, Pat Wayne.   Wayne searches for years for niece (Wood) who was taken captive as a child by the Indians in a raid on her family's homestead. Excellent film that also covers some difficult subject matter. **V, DVD**

Second Time Around, The (1961) **1/2 D: Vincent Sherman. Debbie Reynolds, Andy Griffeth, Steve Forrest, Juliet Prowse, Thelma Ritter, Isobel Elsom.   Cute comedy of widow (Reynolds) moving to Arizona, being befriended by Ritter and becoming sheriff while being courted by Griffeth and Forrest.

Seven Alone (1975) **1/2 (See Family)

Seven Brides for Seven Brothers (1954) **** (See Music/Arts)

She Wore a Yellow Ribbon (1949) ***1/2 D: John Ford. John Wayne, Joanne Dru, John Agar, Ben Johnson, Harry Carey Jr., Victor McLaglen, Mildred Natwick, George O'Brien, Arthur Shields, Francis Ford, Noble Johnson, Tom Tyler.   Wayne plays a cavalry officer who's about to retire, but realizes that a war is imminent and therefore, is reluctant to leave. This is the second film in Ford's cavalry trilogy and is followed by *Rio Grande.* **V, DVD**

Spoilers, The (1955) **1/2 D: Jesse Hibbs. Anne Baxter, Jeff Chandler, Rory Calhoun, John McIntire, Barbara Britton.   Fifth version of this tale of the Klondike in which Chandler and McIntire own a gold mine. A clever group comes in with a "legal" plot to usurp it from the rightful owners. McIntire sees the plot, Chandler doesn't, which leads to the longest fight scene ever put on film. The gold rush and claim jumpers were a reality of that time. Baxter plays Chandler's girlfriend who owns a casino/saloon. If this is a concern, view it first.

Stagecoach (1939) **** D: John Ford. John Wayne, Claire Trevor, Andy Devine, John Carradine, Thomas Mitchell, Louise Platt.   Interesting character study of people in a stagecoach which comes under Indian attack. A chance to discuss character, people's lives, choices, and where they lead. Parents may wish to view it first to form some questions for the kids to think about. Also note, there is a "saloon girl" in this as well as a gun fighter. In 1939, you can tell there is scorn for them, but no details of their way of life are given in any explicit way. Skip the remakes. (1966) (1986) **V, DVD**

They Died With Their Boots On (1941) *** D: Raoul Walsh. Errol Flynn, Olivia de Haviland, Arthur Kennedy, Charley Grapewin, Gene Lockhart, Anthony Quinn, Stanley Ridges, Sydney Greenstreet, Regis Toomey, Hattie McDaniel, Walter Hampden.   Hollywood version of George Armstrong Custer, played with typical Flynn panache. Covers Custer's life from his entrance to West Point to his death at the Little Bighorn. Watch and then compare to history and see how you think the movie compares with this controversial historical figure. Clean for the entire family's viewing. **V**

3 Godfathers (1949) ****1/2 D: John Ford. John Wayne, Pedro Armendariz, Harry Carey, Jr., Ward Bond, Mae Marsh, Jane Darwell, Ben Johnson, Mildred Natwick.   Three bandits come upon a wagon in the desert. Inside is a woman who is about to give birth. She is dying and knows it. She asks the bandits to get her baby to civilization. This is a character study of "bad" men, who lay down their lives for a child. **V**

Tin Star, The (1957) *** D: Anthony Mann. Henry Fonda, Anthony Perkins, Betsy Palmer, Neville Brand, Lee Van Cleef, John McIntire, Michel Ray.   Former sheriff turned bounty hunter Fonda comes to town where young sheriff Perkins faces a tough job. Fonda gives Perkins pointers in dealing with the problems of his town, mainly fostered by one man. Covered are prejudice, vigilante justice vs. the law, and bravery/honor vs. cowardice. In the end, Perkins ends up teaching Fonda a lesson in return. Excellent drama. **V**

Undefeated, The (1969) **1/2 D: Andrew V. McLaglen. John Wayne, Rock Hudson, Tony Aguilar, Roman Gabriel, Bruce Cabot, Lee Meriwether, Ben Johnson, Merlin Olsen, Michael (Jan-Michael) Vincent, Harry Carey, Jr., Royal Dano, Richard Mulligan, James McEachin, Gregg Palmer, Kiel Martin.   After the Civil War, southerners head west to Mexico for promised freedom. They meet with Wayne and his gang (who were formerly "Yankees") who are delivering horses to the Spanish government. Unfortunately, they are all caught in a military coop that threatens their lives. Though not high drama, this film does show the proximity of the Civil War and the one with Mexico. **[G] V, DVD**

Union Pacific (1939) *** D: Cecil B. DeMille. Barbara Stanwyck, Joel McCrea, Robert Preston, Akim Tamiroff, Brian Donlevy, Anthony Quinn.   The building of the Transcontinental Railroad including a train wreck, the Calvary, and the Indians. **V**

Western Union (1941) *** D: Fritz Lang. Robert Young, Randolph Scott, Dean Jagger, Virginia Gilmore, John Carradine, Slim Summerville, Chill Wills, Barton MacLane.   Bad guys try to stop the Western Union on the last part of it's expansion West in the 1860s. **V**

Westward the Women (1951) ****1/2 D: William Wellman. Robert Taylor, Denise Darcel, Beverly Dennis, John McIntire, Hope Emerson, Lenore Lonergan.   Wonderful story of Taylor going back east to bring women west to be brides. Shows the hardships of wagon travel west and the incredible fortitude of those who tried it. Highly recommended. **V**

World in His Arms (1952) *** D: Raoul Walsh. Gregory Peck, Ann Blyth, John McIntire, Anthony Quinn, Andrea King, Eugenie Leontovich, Sig Ruman.   Peck is a skipper who meets Russian countess (Blyth) thinking that she's a servant of the countess' in San Francisco circa 1850. They fall in love and want to be married, but Blyth is running away from a man she is supposed to marry but to whom she doesn't want to be wed. Peck is taken captive by this man, who is in charge of the Russian settlement in Alaska. She tells him she'll marry him to save Peck. It all works out in the end, with some good adventure along the way. This also covers the purchase of Alaska from Russia and hunting seals. **V**

NOTE: Dances With Wolves (1990) ** D: Kevin Costner. Kevin Costner, Mary McDonnell, Graham Greene, Rodney A. Grant, Floyd Red Crow Westerman, Tantoo Cardinal.   Though an amazing tour de force for first time director Costner, this film troubles me somewhat. Yes, it has some great scenes, especially the buffalo hunt. (which you may want to excerpt) And there is no doubt that the white man took shameful advantage of the American Indians. However, not ALL of the white men of that time were evil. This film goes to extremes to present all whites as evil, savage men, and the truly civilized people to be the Sioux. History does not agree with this interpretation. I am also disturbed that those characters who are portrayed as believers in Messiah are shown to be crazed. Many of Kevin Costner's films have become very real platforms for the philosophy of the New Age movement. Any parent seeing his films needs to be aware of this and look for the underlying messages in them. If you have no problem with this, that is your choice. Families of other faiths need to be aware of what is happening in this film.

Adventures of Mark Twain, The (1944) *** D: Irving Rapper. Fredric March, Alexis Smith, Donald Crisp, Alan Hale, C. Aubrey Smith, John Carradine, Percy Kilbride.   Not 100% factual, but a fine story none-the-less, and well worth seeing. You might compare this with the facts of Samuel Clement's life and see where they differ. **V**

Buccaneer, The (1958) ***1/2 D: Anthony Quinn. Yul Brynner, Charlton Heston, Claire Bloom, Charles Boyer, Inger Stevens, Henry Hull, E. G. Marshall, Lorne Greene, Fran Jeffries.   The story of the Battle of New Orleans in the war of 1812. Heston plays General Andrew Jackson (later President) who comes with his Tennessee volunteers to protect the city. He is aided by pirate Jean Lafitte (Brynner) to win the battle. The story of Lafitte and Jackson is real and the acting is very well done by all. Watch for "Ben Cartwright" (Lorne Green) as a hysterical civilian. Also worth note is the "honor" of Lafitte in not attacking an American ship, and the taking of responsibility for those under him as well as his choice at the end of the film. Good food for discussion and a good film for this time period. **V**

Davy Crocket and the River Pirates (1956) **1/2 D: Norman Foster. Fess Parker, Buddy Ebsen, Jeff York, Kenneth Tobey.   Second Crockett tale originally shown on two Disney programs. Full of the same fun and tall tales of the first. **V**

Davy Crockett, King of the Wild Frontier (1955) *** D: Norman Foster. Fess Parker, Buddy Ebsen, Basil Ruysdael, Hans Conried, William Bakewell, Kenneth Tobey.   Wonderful fun for the family, this Walt Disney production (first shown as three Sunday night episodes), tells the story of Davy Crockett. Though not strictly factual, it does show the down-home-spun humor and tall tales for which Crockett was known. Also shown is the fact that he served in Congress, his honor and honesty. **V**

Diamond Jim (1935) **1/2 D: A. Edward Sutherland. Edward Arnold, Jean Arthur, Binnie Barnes, Cesar Romero.   Biography of the eccentric 19th century millionaire who was noted for loving money, food and Lillian Russell. A recreation of the Gay '90s. Parents should preview this first.

Fighting Kentuckian, The (1949) *** D: George Waggner. John Wayne, Vera Ralston, Philip Dorn, Oliver Hardy, Marie Windsor.   On the 1810 frontier a troop of Kentuckians appear. John Wayne and his sidekick, Oliver Hardy (of Laurel and Hardy) work to stop land-grabbers. Wayne also courts Vera Ralston, a French aristocrats daughter, and runs into traditions of which he's never heard and for which he has little patience. This could spark some interesting conversations of other countries and customs and how we view and deal with them. **V**

Great Moment, The (1944) **1/2 (See Medicine)

I Dream of Jeanie (1952) ** D: Allan Dwan. Ray Middleton, Bill Shirley, Muriel Lawrence, Eileen Christy, Lynn Bari, Richard Simmons, Rex Allen, Lousie Beavers, James Kirkwood, Carl "Alfalfa" Switzer.   Loosely based upon the life of Stephen Foster, the 19th century American composer of "Camptown Races," "I Dream of Jeannie With the Light Brown Hair," "Swanee River," plus many more. Foster's story is also told in *Swanee River.* **V**

Inheritance, The (1997) NR (See Literature. Also known as *Alcott's Inheritance.*)

In Old Chicago (1938) *** D: Henry King. Tyrone Power, Alice Faye, Don Ameche, Alice Brady, Andy Devine, Brian Donlevy.   This Oscar winning period piece leads up to the great Chicago fire of 1871. It tells the legend of Mrs. O'Leary's cow. Parents, preview first. **V**

Little Women (1933) **** D: George Cukor. Katherine Hepburn, Joan Bennett, Paul Lukas, Frances Dee, Jean Parker, Edna May Oliver, Douglass Montgomery, Spring Byington. Louisa May Alcott's book comes to life in this wonderful film version. You may wish to read the book and then view the film to compare how well the book was adapted to film. **V**

Long Gray Line, The (1955) *** D: John Ford. Tyrone Power, Maureen O'Hara, Robert Francis, Ward Bond, Donald Crisp, Betsy Palmer, Phil Carey, Harry Carey Jr., Patrick Wayne. A story of West Point's athletic trainer, his interaction with the cadets, and his many years there. Excellent footage of West Point. **V**

Man Without a Country, The (1973) TVM D: Delbert Mann. Cliff Robertson, Beau Bridges, Peter Strauss, Robert Ryan, Walter Abel, John Cullum, Geoffrey Holder. Edward Everett Hale's classic tale superbly acted, especially by Robertson. The story of Philip Nolan who never wanted to hear of the United States of American again. He was sentenced to living on American naval ships for the rest of his life and no one could mention anything about the U. S. in his presence. A fabulous character study. Highly recommended. Above average. **V**

Many Rivers to Cross (1955) **1/2 D: Roy Rowland. Robert Taylor, Eleanor Parker, Victor McLaglen, James Arness, Josephine Hutchinson, Rosemary DeCamp. Taylor is a loner and backwoodsman for whom Parker has set her sights. They are "hand-fasted" due to the lack of available clergy to marry them (this was a real custom of the time). The danger and war with the whites and Indians is shown. Mostly, a fun film.

Mississippi Gambler (1953) **1/2 D: Rudophe Maté. Tyrone Power, Piper Laurie, Julia (Julie) Adams, John McIntire, Dennis Weaver. Power is a professional, but honest gambler who falls in love with Laurie, who takes her brother's side in a disagreement with Power and holds it against him. He becomes friends with her father as they have a common contact in their past and a true understanding of honor; Laurie's brother does not. Her pride and pig-headedness cause great unhappiness to all, but she eventually wakes up before it's too late. Mostly a romance, but included for the information on honor, chivalry of the 1800s, and the customs of the time. Parents, view first and see what you think.

President's Lady, The (1953) *** D: Henry Levin. Charleton Heston, Susan Hayward, John McIntire, Fay Bainter. Fictional story of President Andrew Jackson's wife, Rachel. Parents, preview first. **V**

Rainbow in the Thunder (1988) TVM D: David Hemmings. Tim Dunigan, Gary Grubbs, Cheryl L. Arutt, Richard Tyson, Samantha Eggar, Matt Salinger, Johnny Cash, David Hemmings. Dunigan is a young Davy Crockett who fights with Andrew Jackson (Salinger) to defeat the Creek Indians. Told in a flashback by the older Davy (Cash) as he visits with President Jackson (Hemmings). Good Disney production, but different from the Crockett stories starring Fess Parker.

Reap the Wild Wind (1942) *** D: Cecil B. DeMille. Ray Milland, John Wayne, Paulette Goddard, Raymond Massey, Robert Preston, Susan Hayward, Charles Bickford, Hedda Hopper, Louise Beavers, Martha O'Driscoll, Lynne Overman. Milland is an attorney who comes to Florida in the 19th century and falls for Goddard who has her eye set on Wayne. A dispute involving a sunken ship and investigating the wreck puts Wayne on the stand and ultimately requires deep sea diving in an exciting scene also involving a giant octopus. Don't watch if you don't want to see Wayne as anything but the hero. **V, DVD**

Seminole (1953) **1/2 D: Budd Boetticher. Rock Hudson, Barbara Hale, Anthony Quinn, Richard Carlson, Hugh O'Brien, Russell Johnson, Lee Marvin, James Best. Only film with which I'm familiar covering the Seminole wars in Florida. Hudson is an Indian who is trying to help save the Indian tribe's effort to stay free being under the rule of the white man.

Shocking Miss. Pilgrim, The (1947) ** (See Music/Arts)

Showboat (1939) *** D: James Whale. Irene Dunn, Allan Jones, Helen Morgan, Paul Robeson, Hattie McDaniel. **V**

(1951) *** D: George Sidney. Kathryn Grayson, Ava Gardner, Howard Keel, Joe E. Brown, Marge and Gower Champion, Robert Sterling, Agnes Morehead, Lief Erickson, William Warfield. **V, DVD**

Both versions are well done and have their own recommendations. The torch-singer, Helen

Morgan plays Julie in the black and white version, but the wonderful William Warfield sings "Ol' Man River" in the later version. Perhaps you should see both and compare! The story is of a young woman, Magnolia, whose family owns a "Showboat" which travels the Mississippi. She is friends with the star of the show, Julie, who is married to Steve. In the opening of the film, we learn that Julie is of mixed blood, [black and white, though she looks white]. When the showboat docks, she is arrested by the authorities, as mixed marriages are a crime in the south. Magnolia must then fill Julie's shoes in the show, opposite Gaylord Ravenal, a gambler whom she later marries. A look at life in the south and a very famous American musical theatre score by Jerome Kern and Oscar Hammerstein II. Songs include, "Make Believe," "Bill," "Can't Help Lovin' That Man," "Ol' Man River," "Why Do I Love You." Musical theatre is a uniquely American art form. This is an example of that art form from the early part of the 20th century. (also see Music/Arts)

Sound and the Silence, The (1992) TVM D: John Kent Harrison. John Bach, Ian Bannen, Vanessa Vaughn, Francis Bell, Elizabeth Quinn. Fascinating and well done account of Alexander Graham Bell's life, teaching of the deaf, meeting his wife, and invention of the telephone and the struggle for the patent against a rival. Covers most of his life. Parents might wish to preview first, but I think most will find it a fine film. Also known as *Alexander Graham Bell: The Sound and the Silence.* **V, DVD**

Story of Alexander Graham Bell, The (1939) *** D: Irving Cummings. Don Ameche, Loretta Young, Henry Fonda, Charles Coburn, Spring Byington, Gene Lockhart, Polly Ann Young. Ameche is a bit over the top in his portrayal of Bell, but the film is entertaining as it covers the famous inventor's life. **V**

Tennessee Johnson (1942) *** D: William Dieterle. Van Heflin, Lionel Barrymore, Ruth Hussey, Marjorie Main, Charles Dingle, Regis Toomey, Grant Withers, Lynne Carver, Noah Beery, Sr., Morris Ankrum. Well made historical drama of President Andrew Johnson's rise to the presidency and his troubles with Congress ending with his impeachment, the first ever in U. S. history.

NOTES

Europe

Beau Brummell (1954) **1/2 D: Curtis Bernhardt. Stewart Granger, Elizabeth Taylor, Peter Ustinov, Robert Morley.   A beautiful costume picture showing Brummell's power in dictating fashion of the time as well as his influence with the king. However, this does show the Prince of Wales' immoral involvement with a widow (this was true) but were I you, I would definitely edit this part. It also shows the king's madness and the effect this had upon the Prince of Wales and his desire to rule. Lastly, it shows how a life spent frivolously can be wasted and end in ruin, a powerful lesson for us all. **V**

Captain Horatio Hornblower (1951) *** D: Raoul Walsh. Gregory Peck, Virginia Mayo, Robert Beatty, Denis O'Shea, Christopher Lee.   Based on C. S. Forester's British sea epic of naval hero of the Napoleonic wars. This film also covers the late 1700s. Parents view first to see what you think. **V**

Captain Lightfoot (1955) *** D: Douglas Sirk. Rock Hudson, Barbara Rush, Jeff Morrow, Finlay Currie, Kathleen Ryan.   Beautifully filmed on location in Ireland, this is a costumer about 19th century Irish rebellion. Hudson stumbles upon one of the heads of the rebellion by stealing English gold. He is then taken in and becomes "Captain Lightfoot." A good conversation starter on the English/Irish enmity.

Dr. Erhlich's Magic Bullet (1940) ***1/2 (See Medicine)

Emma (1996) *** (See Literature)

Florence Nightingale (1985) TVM D: Daryl Duke. Jaclyn Smith, Claire Bloom, Timothy Dalton, Jeremy Colorful story is pretty to see but contains many inaccuracies. White Angel below is better. **V**

Great Waltz, The (1938) ** D: Julien Duvivier. Luise Rainer, Fernand Gravet, Miliza Korjus, Hugh Herbert, Lionel Atwill, Curt Bois.   Music is better than the story of Johannes Strauss the younger. Watch only if you can't find *The Waltz King*. (See Music/Arts) If you do watch this one, parents will need to view it first. **V**

Greyfriars Bobby (1961) **1/2 (See Family Films)

Horatio Hornblower (1998) **** (See 1700s Europe)

Magnificent Rebel (1962) **1/2 D: George Tressler, Karl Boehm, Ernst Nadhering, Ivan Desny, Gabriele Porks.   Disney tale of Beethoven's life shot on location in Germany. May also be used for a study of music. (See Music/Arts for a more detailed write-up.)

Persuasion (1995-British-U.S.-French) *** (See Literature)

Pride and the Prejudice, The (1940) **** (See Literature)

Sense and Sensibility (1995) **** (See Literature)

Song of Love (1947) **1/2 D: Clarence Brown. Katharine Hepburn, Paul Henreid, Robert Walker, Henry Daniell, Leo G. Carroll, Gigi Perreau, Tala Birell, Henry Stephenson.   Biography of composer Robert Schumann and wife Clara, including friendship with composer Johannes Brahms. Overall, an excellent movie, though not 100% factual, is still worth seeing and comparing to good biographies of these three important musicians. The mental illness of Schumann is factual. **V**

Story of Louis Pasteur, The (1936) ***1/2 (See Medicine)

Waltz King, The (1963) **1/2 (See Music/Arts)

White Angel, The (1936) *** D: William Dieterle. Kay Francis, Ian Hunter, Donald Woods, Nigel Bruce, Donald Crisp, Henry O'Neill.   Story of Florence Nightingale is well done. It accurately portrays her total devotion to the call (of God) on her life, the condition of the hospitals and nurses in England, her training in Germany, the stonewall of the medical institution toward trained female nurses, that only 38 nurses accompanied her to the Crimean, the condition of the hospital upon her arrival in Scutari, the soldiers rallying for her when she became ill, the Henry Wadsworth Longfellow poem written in her honor. Worth seeing.

The World

Anna and the King of Siam (1946) ******** D: John Cromwell. Irene Dunn, Rex Harrison, Linda Darnell, Lee J. Cobb, Gale Sondergaard.   So far, my favorite film of the true story of an English governess who becomes teacher to the royal children of the King of Siam. The performances of Dunn and Harrison are superb. If you study the far east, or simply wish to show this story, this one's the best. **V** (See Music/Arts for the musical version entitled *The King and I.*)

Juarez (1939) ****1/2** D: William Dieterle. Paul Muni, Bette Davis, Brian Aherne, Claude Rains, John Garfield, Gale Sondergaard, Donald Crisp, Gilbert Roland, Louis Calhern, Grant Mitchell.   Set in 1863, this is an interesting picture of war between Emperor Maximillian and Benito Juarez. Shown are two men of similar yet differing ideals. Includes touching romance of Maximillian and his wife, Carlotta. Compare with historical accounts. **V**

Kim (1950) *****1/2** (See Literature)

Life of Emile Zola, The (1937) ******* D: William Dieterle. Paul Muni, Gale Sondergaard, Joseph Schildkraut, Gloria Holden, Donald Crisp, Erin O'Brien-Moore, Morris Carnovsky, Louis Calhern, Harry Davenport.   A contortion of the chronology and not 100% accurate, yet the spirit and major facts are shown. Zola's works are shown, but most importantly the film portrays his influence upon France at that time in regard to the conviction for treason of Alfred Dreyfus and *why* he was convicted with no evidence: he was a Jew. Watch and compare to fact or use to kick-off a study on the Dreyfus affair.

Stanley and Livingstone (1939) *****1/2** D: Henry King. Spencer Tracy, Nancy Kelly, Richard Greene, Walter Brennen, Charles Coburn, Cedric Hardwicke.   Tracy's excellent portrayal of the determined and persistent reporter who searches Africa for Dr. Livingstone. A wonderful story of the power of Messiah through Dr. Livingstone having an impact upon the people who know him and upon Tracy in particular. Knowing Dr. Livingstone changes Tracy's life and outlook, which figures into the ending of the film. To go with this, I recommend the *Your Story Hour* tapes on Dr. Livingstone, a remarkable man who was a very talented musician, a minister of the gospel and later, a medical missionary to Africa. **V**

NOTES

Civil War
(The War Between the States)

Gone With The Wind (1939) ***1/2 D: Victor Fleming. Clark Gable, Vivien Leigh, Leslie Howard, Olivia de Haviland, Thomas Mitchell, Barbara O'Neil, Victor Jory, Laura Hope Crews, Hattie McDaniel, Ona Munson, Harry Davenport, Ann Rutherford, Evelyn Keyes, Carroll Nye, Paul Hurst, Isabel Jewell, Cliff Edwards, Ward Bond, Butterfly McQueen.   Margaret Mitchell's Civil War story has become, arguably, the greatest film of all time. Since it is given such a place, I will mention it first. However, I do not recommend showing this to any child, unedited. So far, all my children have seen are excerpts. You will have to make your own call on this one and decide whether to show any or all of it to your family. Without a doubt, it portrays more of the southern experience of the Civil War than probably any other one film. Seeing the opulence and luxury of the pre-Civil War aristocracy and the fall of that civilization might be worthwhile for their understanding. The burning of Atlanta and the road out with the down-trodden, retreating confederate soldiers is also worthy of note as are the soldiers on the tracks when Scarlett goes searching for Dr. Meade, her work in the hospital and its conditions, the deprivation of life at Tara after the war, the reconstruction, shanty town, slave labor, the K.K.K., (their original purpose and what they are now), carpetbaggers, and whatever else you think is of note. In the event that your memory is foggy, or you've never read the book, Scarlett had three husbands, (though two of her children are left out of the movie), the last of whom was Rhett Butler. This is NOT a story of a woman's marriage to one man, but of a woman who survives by her wits as her world comes apart, and who believes herself to be in love with a married man. If you have older children with whom you wish to view this, I think it should be discussed if shown. Were her choices Godly? What of her character, etc. What other choices could she have made? In our present society that has no clue about character and is bombarded with messages from the media that there are no absolutes, the issues in this movie definitely need to be seen with some wisdom from the parents. If you have not read the book, don't assign it to your teen. Read it first and then make that choice as there is more explicit information in it concerning Scarlett's thoughts, choices, marriages and relationship with Ashley. **V**

Abe Lincoln in Illinois (1940) **** D: John Cromwell. Raymond Massey, Gene Lockhart, Ruth Gordon, Mary Howard.   Lincoln's life and career are well acted by Massey with Gordon playing his wife, Mary Todd Lincoln. **V**

Autobiography of Miss. Jane Pittman, The (1974) Above average D: John Korty. Cicely Tyson, Barbara Chaney, Richard Dysart, Katherine Helmond, Michael Murphy.   Tour de-force performance by Tyson as a 110 year old slave recounting her experiences from the Civil War to the civil rights movement. Based upon Ernest J. Gaines novel. Won nine Emmy awards. Once again, parents might want to view this first. **V**

Belle Starr (1941) **1/2 D: Irving Cummings. Randolph Scott, Gene Tierney, Dana Andrews.   This is the only film about which I know that covers this real-life, female, Confederate spy.

Birth of a Nation, The (1915) **** D: D. W. Griffith. Lillian Gish, Mae Marsh, Henry B. Walthall, Miraim Cooper, Robert Harron, Wallace Reid.   This film is more than just a tale of two families during the Civil War and Reconstruction. This is the film which opened the way for the film industry today. With this film, D. W. Griffith proved the power of storytelling on film. It is a silent picture and should definitely be used in a study of the development of motion pictures. It also has some content that keeps it shown and in the midst of controversy today, namely that of the K.K.K. in a heroic role. This could lead to a study of how they were formed, why they came into existence and what they are today. **V**

Civil War Journal, The *** (A series done by the History Channel). Hosted by Danny

Glover.   This series covers biographies of important people of the war, battles, tactics, weapons, etc. Includes real pictures by Matthew Brady, the famous Civil War photographer. I would urge parents to view these first as some of the real life pictures are somewhat grim. Decide what parts of each segment you can show and what you need to fast forward. However, these are excellent productions with much information not to be found in most texts. Experts, like Ken Burns, are interviewed and give wonderful tidbits about the lives, battles, and times. Mostly for Jr. High and High School. Highly recommended. **V**

Dark Command (1940) **1/2 (See 1800s West)

Friendly Persuasion (1956) **** D: William Wyler. Gary Cooper, Dorothy McGuire, Marjorie Main, Anthony Perkins, Richard Eyre.   From the Jessamyn West novel, this story tells of a Quaker family who try to stay together and make sense of the senselessness of war. Many wonderful opportunities for discussion as the family contends with winning vs. losing, music, church doctrine, to defend their home or welcome the "enemy" and what your family believes and would do in like circumstances. **V**

Gettysburg (1993) **** D: Ronald Maxwell. Tom Berenger, Jeff Daniels, Martin Sheen, Sam Elliot, Maxwell Caulfield, Kevin Conway, C. Thomas Howell, Richard Jordan, Royce C. Applegate and a cast of thousands.   Based upon Michael Shaara's Pulitzer Prize winning book, *The Killer Angels* this is a magnificent recreation of the battle of Gettysburg at the actual site of the battle. Included were over 5,000 Civil War re-enactors who make up the bulk of the battle scenes. See the behind the scenes struggles, based upon the men's own writings. You will see James Longstreet who knew that the South could not win, yet respected Lee and had orders he had to follow. See the famous Pickett's charge and see the hopelessness of the Southern cause at that time. The battle scenes are loud, violent and, at times overwhelming, but I assume the real battle was as well. Parents, watch this to see if you think it appropriate for your children's ages. Try to find a copy with the "making the film" interviews with the re-enactors and actors. The actors, like Sam Elliot, were awed by the re-enactors and stated that there was no way they could have made the film without them. Highly recommended. Parents should preview for content. **[PG]** **V**

Gods and Generals (2003) **** D: Ron Maxwell. Jeff Daniels, Stephen Lang, Robert Duvall, Mira Sorvino, Kali Rocha.   Based on the book by Jeffrey M. Shaara, this is the prequel to *Gettysburg,* above and is best seen on video where you can stop and start it as it is a very long film. This also allows you to edit any parts you feel are inappropriate for your children. While I'm sure that it is in no way as realistic as this war, neither does a parent *have* to expose young children to gory scenes. That said, it is generally a *wonderful* film and one that all history lovers and believers should support in order to let Hollywood know we'd like more films of this ilk. This film begins in early 1861 and continues through 1863, ending with the Battle of Chancellorsville. The central character in this story is Thomas "Stonewall" Jackson and his part in the war. He is shown exactly as he was, a man of incredible faith, a man who loved God, loved his wife, loved his home. I *loved* the scene where he is walking the hills and praying on what is about to become a battlefield dressed in shirtsleeves and a shawl. It reminded me of Bible stories of praying under a prayer shawl and the symbolism of being "hidden under His "wings," a Biblical metaphor for the prayer shawl or *talit.* I think that most families will definitely want to see this film. **[PG-13]** **V, DVD**

Great Locomotive Chase, The (1956) *** D: Francis D. Lyon. Fess Parker, Jeffrey Hunter, Jeff York, John Lupton.   The Disney made, true story of Andrew's Raiders who crept into Confederate territory and stole a locomotive engine and the chase that ensued as the Confederates try to catch them before they get behind Yankee lines. Lots of action and fun. Originally titled *Andrew's Raiders.* **V**

Guns of Ft. Petticoat, The (1957) *** D: George Marshall. Audie Murphy, Kathryn Grant, Hope Emerson, Jeff Donnell.   Murphy plays a Texan fighting for the Union who comes to Texas to warn the settlers of an impending Indian attack. There are no men due to the war so he trains the women to fight the Indians. Cute surprise ending. You may recognize Kathryn Grant who later became Mrs. Bing Crosby. Thanks to my youngest daughter for watching this and providing the review. She really liked it.

Horse Soldiers, The (1959) *** D: John Ford. John Wayne, William Holden, Constance Towers, Althea Gibson, Hoot Gibson, Anna Lee, Russell Simpson, Ken Curtis, Denver Pyle. Based upon actual incidents, this is the story of a Union colonel (Wayne) who leads a sabotage party deep behind Confederate lines while fighting with his army surgeon and confederate hostage. **V**

Johnny Shiloh (1963) **1/2 D: James Neilson. Kevin Corcoran, Brian Keith, Darryl Hickman. Corcoran (who played Arliss in Old Yeller) tags along with the a troop in the Civil War which is led by Keith. Well acted and first shown in two parts on the old Sunday night Disney T.V. show. **V**

Little Colonel, The (1935) *** (See Music/Arts)

Littlest Rebel, The (1935) *** D: David Butler. Shirley Temple, John Boles, Jack Holt, Karen Morley, Bill "Bojangles" Robinson, Stepin' Fetchit.   Set in the Old South during the Civil War, Shirley dances with Robinson, snares the heart of a Union officer (Holt) and protects her father (Boles) whom Holt is after. **V**

Of Human Hearts (1938) **1/2 (See Family)

Red Badge of Courage, The (1951) *** D: John Huston. Audie Murphy, Bill Mauldin, Douglas Dick, Royal Dano, John Dierkes, Arthur Hunnicutt, Tim Durant, Andy Devine; narrated by James Whitmore. Stephen Crane's novel of a young Yankee soldier who runs under fire and then has to deal with the guilt of his lack of courage. Excellently done film packs quite a punch in its study of the fine line between bravery and cowardice. Includes some intense battle scenes as well as a humorous one in which a general promises to share supper with just about every platoon he meets! Some good discussion information in this film. **V**

Shenandoah (1965) ***1/2 D: Andrew V. McLaglen. James Stewart, Doug McClure, Glenn Corbett, Patrick Wayne, Rosemary Forsyth, Katharine Ross, Tim McIntire, Paul Fix, Denver Pyle, George Kennedy, James Best, Harry Carey, Jr.   Crusty Virginia widower (Stewart) farms in the Shenandoah valley with his family and strives to remain neutral in the war. His wife died giving birth to his youngest son and (like Joseph and Benjamin to Jacob) is very precious to him. The son finds and wears a soldier's cap. When found by the group from the opposing side, he is taken prisoner. Stewart goes after him, trying to find where he has been taken. Definitely shows the heartbreak of the war and to this family in particular. Later made into a Broadway musical of the same title. There is no blatant gore, but one scene suggests it. Depending upon the age of the children, parents may wish to edit that scene. Some parents may find Stewart's prayer at the beginning somewhat objectionable. Though it is certainly not the way we pray (!), it is in keeping with the character he is playing. **V**

Young Mr. Lincoln (1939) ***1/2 D: John Ford. Henry Fonda, Alice Brady, Marjorie Weaver, Donald Meek, Milburne Stone, Ward Bond.   Fonda has the title role as the young attorney proves his ability and honesty. One my children really liked. Look for "Doc" from Gunsmoke, Milburne Stone. **V**

NOTES

1900s

All the President's Men (1976) *** D: Alan J. Pakula. Robert Redford, Dustin Hoffman, Jason Robards, Jack Warden, Martin Balsam, Hal Holbrook, Jane Alexander, Stephen Collins, Meredith Baxter, Ned Beatty, Robert Walden, Polly Holliday, F. Murray Abraham.   Based upon real-life Washington Post reporters Bob Woodward and Carl Bernstein (Redford and Hoffman) who persevered with scraps of information and broke the entire Watergate break-in scandal of the Nixon administration. Perhaps one of the best looks at the tedium and hard work of journalism. Even though this shows an important part of our fairly recent history and covers the rare impeachment of a president (at that time) this is NOT for younger audiences and MUST be taped from T.V. and edited, even for high school students, in my opinion. The language is atrocious. I think the only way you can safely show this film is to obtain a copy and then send it off to have the offensive language removed or have a Guardian on your TV.   [PG]

Anastasia (1956) **** D: Anatole Litvak. Ingrid Bergman, Yul Brynner, Helen Hayes, Akim Tamiroff, Martita Hunt, Felix Aylmer, Natalie Schafer.   Based upon a play by Marcelle Maurette, this film version of the fictional story of the daughter of Tzar Nicholas, supposedly spared from assassination pulls you in and has you yearning with Bergman to find out if she really is Anastasia. Bergman's fine performance earned an Oscar. Not real history, but an interesting look at what might have been if you study the last Russian royal family.   **V**

Anne of Avonlea (1987-Canadian) TVM D: Kevin Sullivan. Megan Follows, Colleen Dewhurst, Frank Converse, Schuyyler Grant, Jonathan Crombie, Patricia Hamilton, Rosemary Dunsmore.   Based on the books by Lucy Maud Montgomery, this sequel is that rare creature that matches the wonderful original. This takes up where *Anne of Green Gables* ends, continuing the story of Anne's adoption by Matthew Cuthbert and his sister, Marilla, and Anne's adventurous escapades. She leaves her island home to go to the city and teach at an all girls school. As usual, there is never a dull moment. Ultimately, she realizes that what she was looking for was really to be found at home. Followed by *The Continuing Story.*   Above average **V, DVD**

Anne of Green Gables (1985-Canadian) TVM D: Kevin Sullivan. Megan Follows, Colleen Dewhurst, Patricia Hamilton, Marilyn Lightstone, Charmion King, Rosemary Radcliffe, Jackie Burroughs, Richard Farnsworth.   Based on the classic children's book by Lucy Maud Montgomery, this wonderful adaptation follows the life of Anne through hard "posts" to her adoption by a bachelor farmer, Matthew Cuthbert and his sister, Marilla and the life she gains in their home, "Green Gables." A wonderful story full of old-time values and lessons. This entire series is a family favorite and sure to become one of yours, too. Above average. Followed by *Anne of Avonlea.* **V, DVD**

Anne of Green Gables: The Continuing Story (2000-Canadian) TVM D: Stefan Scaini. Megan Follows, Jonathan Crombie, Cameron Daddo, Schuyyler Grant.   The finale of this wonderful story finds Gilbert and Anne about to be married at the outbreak of WWI. Now a doctor, Gilbert goes overseas and Anne begins working for a publisher while working on a book of her own. Gil disappears in Europe and Anne goes overseas to find him. Again, a wonderful family film. Above average **V, DVD**

Around the World in Eighty Days (1956) *** (See Literature)

Ballad of Josie, The (1967) **1/2 D: Andrew McLaglen. Doris Day, Peter Graves, George Kennedy, Andy Devine, William Talman, David Hartman, Don Stroud.   This is not a great film but does give an up close look at the western feud between those who raised cattle and those who raised sheep. Doris Day plays a widow who comes up with the idea to raise sheep in cattle country in order to support herself and raise her son. This also has some women's suffrage content. Clean family viewing.

Belles on Their Toes (1952) *** (See Literature)

By the Light of the Silvery Moon (1953) **1/2 D: David Butler. Doris Day, Gordon MacRae, Leon Ames, Rosemary DeCamp, Mary Wickes, Billy Gray.   Set in post WWI, this sequel to *On Moonlight Bay* has MacRae returning to fiancée Day. There is a part where the son (Gray) thinks his father may be involved with another woman. This proves to be his overactive imagination, but parents may wish to view this first and omit that part. **V**

Carbine Williams (1952) *** D: Richard Thorpe. James Stewart, Jean Hagen, Wendell Corey, Paul Stewart, James Arness.   History of the inventor of the carbine rifle who did so from prison. Stewart plays Williams who was charged with murder in a shootout over an illegal still. The hung jury ended with Williams pleading guilty to 2nd degree murder believing he'd get a lighter sentence. While serving his time, he came up with the idea for the carbine rifle and was allowed to experiment with his idea and develop the gun which was used extensively in WWII as it was lighter and easier to carry. Well done film.

Cheaper By the Dozen (1950) *** (See Literature)

China Cry (1990) [NR] D: James Collier. Julia Nickson Soul, Russell Wong.   Set in the 1950s this is the true story of Sung Neng Yee, now known as Nora Lam. She was the child of a wealthy Chinese family who is excited about the promises of the Communists until they took her father prisoner and used him for medical experiments from which he died. She tried to be obscure and fit into the society, but her past comes to light and she is brought in for questioning. As a child, she was educated by Christian missionaries to China and accepted Messiah. Now, she must choose whether or not to reject Him, or stand by her childhood decision. Is He *REALLY* who they told her He was? I think parts of the film need editing so I recommend that parents watch it first, but overall, it's a well done film of an amazing story of God's protection in the midst of persecution. **[PG-13] V**

Christy Video series based on the book by Catherine Marshall about her mother's life as a schoolteacher in the Great Smokies, early 1900. Watch any and all of them! *Excellent.* **V**

Court-Marshall of Billy Mitchell, The (1955) ***1/2 (See WW I, WW II)

Cross Creek (1983) **1/2 D: Martin Ritt. Mary Steenburgen, Rip Torn, Peter Coyote, Dana Hill, Alfre Woodard, Joanna Miles, Ike Eisenmann, Cary Guffey.   The story of Marjorie Kinnan Rawling who wrote *The Yearling* and the story behind the story. Parts need to be edited, so watch it first. [PG] **V, DVD**

Dive Bomber (1941) *** (see Science)

Driving Miss Daisy (1989) **** (See Family Films)

Edison, the Man (1940) ***1/2 D: Clarence Brown. Spencer Tracy, Rita Johnson, Lynne Overman, Charles Coburn, Gene Lockhart.   Sequel to *Young Tom Edison* (later in this section) though not entirely factual, does tell about Edison and his genius and creativity. **V**

Eleanor Roosevelt Story, The (1965) ***1/2 D: Richard Kaplan. Narrated by Archibald Macleish, Eric Sevareid, Francis Cole.   Oscar-winning documentary about the former First Lady. Parents preview. **V**

Exodus (1960) *** D: Otto Preminger. Paul Newman, Eva Marie Saint, Ralph Richardson, Peter Lawford, Lee J. Cobb, Sal Mineo, John Derek, Hugh Griffith, Gregory Ratoff, Felix Aylmer, Jill Haworth, David Opatoshu, Marius Goring. George Maharis.   Based on the Leon Uris' novel of war for an independent Israel at the end of WW2. Included is the conflict between Arabs and Jews for the land the Jews were given by God and which archeology has now confirmed they occupied for centuries but for which archeologists cannot find any evidence of the Philistine occupation through which the Arabs claim the land. (the Philistines were assimilated into conquering Assyria and Babylon and never returned to the land as did the Jews. The term "Palestine" came from a Roman general using this name as a derivation of the word "Philistine" *in reference to the **Jews** as a insult to them by calling them the name of their historical enemies.)* An interesting film covering

the struggle for and birth of a nation which people said didn't and would never exist, yet came to be exactly as foretold in Biblical prophecy– a nation that was born in a day. I think, worth seeing for that aspect, alone. **V**

Farmer's Daughter, The (1947) ***1/2 D: H. C. Potter. Loretta Young, Joseph Cotten, Ethel Barrymore, Charles Bickford, Rose Hobart, Harry Davenport, Lex Barker, James Aurness (Arness).   A comedy for which Young won an Oscar as a Swedish-American girl who isn't afraid of hard work or for standing up for that in which she believes. After trusting the wrong person and losing her tuition for nursing school, she doesn't call home and whine for help. She finds work with an employment agency who place her in the home of a famous and powerful political family, who just happen to be very nice people. She is shown speaking up for her beliefs and not being intimidated by her employers. She is informed about the candidates and publicly and openly disapproves of the chosen party favorite as she tells all about his bad voting record at a political rally. She is then targeted by the opposition for their candidate for Congress! Though this is a fictional film, it is clean and gives a good discussion starter for the political process, the importance of being informed about your candidates and the issue, as well as the movie's view of the United Nations. What is yours? There is a sweet romance between Young and Cotten, the son of the family for whom she works. She marries him at the end of the film. **V**

Gandhi (1982-British) ***1/2 D: Richard Attenborough. Ben Kingsley, Candice Bergen, Edward Fox, John Gielgud, Trevor Howard, John Mills, Martin Sheen, Rohini Hattangandy, Ian Charleson.   Biography of the life of Gandhi (1969-1948) who rose from a simple lawyer to become a world leader for peace. Won eight Oscars, with Kingsley deservedly winning best actor. Has some parts parents may wish to edit due to the culture and violence of the time. View first and decide. **[PG] V, DVD**

Gentleman Jim (1942) ***1/2 D: Raoul Walsh. Errol Flynn, Alexis Smith, Jack Carson, Alan Hale, John Loder, William Frawley, Minor Watson, Ward Bond, Arthur Shields.   Biography of boxer Jim Corbett with Flynn at his best in (reportedly) his favorite role. Parents might wish to preview it first. **V**

Grapes of Wrath, The (1940) **** (See Literature)

Greatest Show on Earth (1952) ***1/2 D: Cecil B. DeMille. Betty Hutton, Charlton Heston, Cornel Wilde, Dorothy Lamour, Gloria Grahame, James Stewart, Henry Wilcoxon.   Big production of the circus, and behind the scenes life. Included are many character sketches of lives of the performers. May have items some parents would find undesirable, so please view this one first. However, if you want a film on circus, this seems to be the best of all the choices. **V**

Hellfighters (1968) **1/2 D: Andrew V. McLaglen. John Wayne, Katharine Ross, Jim Hutton, Vera Miles, Bruce Cabot.   Based upon real-life oil well firefighter Red Adair, this film shows the danger, and skill necessary to fight these fires. This is the only film of any kind about which I know that covers this subject. I highly recommend parents watch this one first as Hutton is shown to be quite a womanizer before he marries the boss's daughter (Ross) and there are other items which may be of concern to some parents, as well. Originally rated [R], though would probably be [PG] today. **V**

Holiday (1938) ***1/2 D: George Cukor. Katharine Hepburn, Cary Grant, Doris Nolan, Lew Ayres, Edward Everett Horton.   This story gives a lot of room for discussion on values, what matters in life, judging other by appearance as well as a look at the times. Another delightful family film. **V**

Houdini (1953) **1/2 D: George Marshall. Tony Curtis, Janet Leigh, Torn Thatcher, Ian Wolfe, Sig Ruman.   Remade for TV with Paul Michael Glaser and Sally Struthers, but avoid it as it is loaded with the occult. This one is more fiction than factual biography of the famed escape artist, but the best film for children. It still covers who he was, what he accomplished, and how he died. **V**

Hunt For Red October, The (1990) ***1/2 D: Dhon McTiernan. Sean Connery, Alec Baldwin, Scott Glenn, Sam Neill, James Earl Jones.   Based upon the Tom Clancy novel, this gives a good look at the cold war, stockpiling of arms, more and more technical warfare, as well as the differing world-views of the United States and the Soviet Union, again called Russia today. Connery plays a Soviet nuclear missile submarine captain who may or may not be planning a defection in the newest, top secret Soviet developed sub. Baldwin plays the CIA agent who has studied the man and is trying to figure out what is happening. The tension mounts as the Soviet navy is sent after their sub and Soviet diplomats begin spinning a story for our government on why their subs may be headed into our waters. A truly fascinating film which requires many watchings to "get it all." Also, a good discussion piece for high school students and parents on the many issues raised in the film. Try to see on TV for the removal of the few bad words. **[PG] V**

Ice Station Zebra (1968) **1/2 D: John Sturges. Rock Hudson, Ernest Borgnine, Patrick McGoohan, Jim Brown, Tony Bill, Lloyd Nolan. Based upon the Alistair MacLean novel, this high tension Cold War film has sub-commander Hudson sailing for the North Pole to await orders, not knowing that something is about to happen. **[G] V**

I'd Climb the Highest Mountain (1951) *** D: Henry King. Susan Hayward, William Lundigan, Rory Calhoun, Gene Lockhart, Ruth Donnelly. Filmed on location in Georgia, this is the story of a country preacher whose bride has to learn a new way of life in the hill country. There are some hard times faced including the death of their child, yet their faith must get them through. There is one scene in which a woman in the church begins to seek out the young pastor, but his wife sees through her and sends her packing! While a potentially sticky subject with younger children, for high school students, this is a good point for women being able to see the motives of other women, and men with men which is why it is a good idea for women to disciple women and men, men. It also could lead to a good discussion of women as helpmates for their husbands and how we complete each other in marriage. **V**

Inherit the Wind (1960) ***1/2 D: Stanley Kramer. Spencer Tracy, Fredric March, Gene Kelly, Florence Eldridge, Dick York, Harry Morgan. From the play based upon the famous Scopes "Monkey Trial" of 1925 in which Clarence Darrow was the defense counsel and William Jennings Bryan the prosecutor of the case. Darwin's *Origin of the Species* was published in 1859. In 1959, a centennial celebration was held in which it was said that Darwinism had conquered the world. This movie was made that year and released the next. I will warn you that the film is slanted toward making the viewer side with the evolutionists. William Jennings Bryan, a Christian, is made to look like a fanatical fool with stereotypical Christian biases but with no real smarts in the "scientific," "real" world and this movie is based upon many plain lies! In it a preacher curses Scopes and is present in the classroom when he is arrested; in reality no such preacher even existed. In fact, Scopes volunteered to be arrested to help the ACLU challenge the law. In the movie his counsel does not want him found guilty; in reality, his counsel *wanted* him convicted so they could appeal to the Supreme Court. In the movie, the city fathers were embarrassed about the publicity; in reality the city father's hatched up the idea to put Dayton on the map. The movie shows Scopes locked up for the duration of the trial and the citizens of Dayton being hateful to Clarence Darrow. In reality, Scopes was free the entire time and the citizens of Dayton were hospitable to Darrow. (Darrow really was an atheist and he said that he'd never been in a town where his beliefs differed as widely "as the great mass." He stated that he came to town a perfect stranger, yet no one treated him with the slightest discourtesy.) In the movie, the people wanted to lynch Scopes and the preacher's daughter, who was in love with Scopes and is "enlightened" about evolution by him. In reality, Scopes was liked by the town and since the preacher is fictitious, so is his daughter. And here's a very drastic bias of the movie in which William Jennings Bryan is shown to be a hateful tyrant who rants and raves when in fact, he was just the opposite and it was Clarence Darrow who ranted and raved.

High school students might wish to read Philip Johnson's *Defeating Darwinism by Opening Minds*, an interesting book written by a man who taught criminal law at UC at Berkley (not your average conservative Christian school) Johnson states that the public should not take individual claims seriously in the evaluation of evidence (like the latest "missing link" find) because these evaluations are a result of the bias and prejudice by the evolutional ide-

ology who've never *considered* that their premise might be false. He states that the purpose of the film was to pit those who believe in God as Creator against those who believe in a system of atoms and molecules as the source of life.

PBS recently did a show called *Monkey Trial* which publicly told the inaccuracies of the film for the first time. Indeed, an eye witness to the trial was interviewed and spoke of her dislike of the film because of it's falsehoods; that it simply had not happened that way. Yet, this film is still shown in classrooms today and Hollywood even did a remake of the film with George C. Scott and Jack Lemmon which again portrayed Bryan not as the eloquent Bible believing man he was, but as a ranting and raving bigot.

Another possible book for high school students to read is Benjamin Wiker's *Moral Darwinism* which indicts Darwinism's destructive influence upon society. He says that the PBS program did not even mention the Darwinian racism of the actual biology text (*A Civic Biology, Presented in Problems* by George William Hunter, PhD) that Scopes had in the classroom. In it, alcoholics, law breakers, the mentally challenged and other so called "true parasites" should be stuffed away in asylums, separated by gender so they cannot "breed." (In the chapter entitled *Parasitism and its Cost to Society)* Hunter stated "The Remedy": "If such people were lower animals, we would probably kill them off to prevent them from spreading." This echoed Darwin's own teachings from *The Descent of Man*, "The civilized races of man will almost certainly exterminate and replace throughout the world the savage races" which he defined to especially mean black Africans. Bryan joined the prosecution team to *oppose* just that kind of Darwinian bigotry, which today is called hate speech. As a Christian, Bryan detested that bigotry.

It might also be interesting to note that German militarism believed these ideas and got much of their inspiration from Darwin, which helped to begin WWII. Also agreeing with this thinking was the heartless version of capitalism. According to Philip Johnson, "Andrew Carnegie and John D. Rockefeller loved Darwinism because it said they were right to amass all the money in the world. If other people didn't have money, it was because they were inferior." Johnson says the movie and evolutionists want you to think evolution is a factual and wonderful philosophy; it's not really against your religion. "You can believe in a watchmaker God who made the laws in the first place and then went away and doesn't bother us anymore; that should satisfy you. So, it's various ways of trying to give you counterfeit in place of the real gold of the doctrine of creation by God." Perhaps this is why the film ends with Spencer Tracy (Darrow) holding the Darwinism book in one hand and the *Bible* in the other, as though they balance each other with no conflict.

I would urge parents to view this one first. For high school students who will soon be facing this attitude of science as "god" and evolution as "truth," this might be a good exercise in looking at how this attitude is presented and how they could more successfully use apologetics to present the real Truth. Because evolutional philosophy really does control the public mindset today, Christians have a vested interest in learning about the Scopes trial and applying that knowledge, which could really influence public policy, especially education. **V**

NOTE: I *HIGHLY* recommend Dr. Kent Hovind's (blue) video series! (See Science/Nature) This video set has done more to strengthen my children's faith in the Bible while exposing the truth about Darwinian evolution as a religion and the bias of the scientific community for evolution vs. Creation than any other one thing I've done for science. I cannot recommend them highly enough. For information, see www.drdino.com

I Remember Mama (1948) ***1/2 D: George Stevens. Irene Dunne, Barbara Bel Geddes, Oscar Homolka, Philip Dorn, Cedric Harwicke, Edgar Bergen, Rudy Vallee, Barbara O'Neil, Florence Bates, Ellen Corby.   Based upon Kathryn Forbes memoirs of growing up in an immigrant Norwegian family in San Francisco. I especially like how Mama trades a secret family recipe in order to get help for her budding author daughter. Beautifully done. **V**

Iron Eagle (1986) *1/2 D: Sidney J. Furie. Louis Gossett, Jr., Jason Gedrick, David Suchet, Tim Thomerson, Larry G.Scott, Caroline Lagerfelt, Jerry Levine.   The story of the son of an air force pilot whose father has been shot down and taken prisoner in the Middle East. I don't show this to my children as a movie, but did use some of the aerial scenes to show them air warfare. View first to see what you think. Needs editing for language. **V**

Iron Will (1994) *** D: Charles Haid. Mackenzie Astin, Kevin Spacey, August Schellenberg, David Ogden Stiers, Brian Cox, George Gerdes, John Terry.   Though this film was dismissed by the critics, I think it deserves a second look. The story is one of a young man living in Canada during WWI whose chance at college is lost when his father is killed in a dog-sledding accident. He finds that he may have a second chance if he can beat the almost impossible odds of winning the Winnipeg-to-St. Paul dog-sled race. Though parents may want to edit some scenes, this is a story of perseverance against incredible odds. [PG] **V**

Joni (1980) **1/2 D: James F. Collier. Joni Eareckson, Bert Remsen, Katherine De Hetre, Cooper Huckabee, John Milford, Michael Mancini, Richard Lineback.   Biography of Joni Eareckson who broke her neck in a diving accident, awoke to life as a quadriplegic, and her journey of faith. [G] **V**

Kentucky (1938) *** (See Horses)

Keys of the Kingdom, The (1944) *** D: John M. Stahl. Gregory Peck, Thomas Mitchell, Vincent Price, Edmund Gwenn, Roddy McDowall, Cedric Hardwicke, Peggy Ann Garner.   Based on A. J. Cronin novel, this is a fine film of the self-sacrifice of a missionary (Peck). Parents may wish to view first. **V**

Knute Rockne, All American (1940) *** (See Sports)

Lean on Me (1989) **1/2 D: John G. Avildsen. Morgan Freeman, Beverly Todd, Robert Guillaume, Alan North, Lynne Thigpen, Robin Bartlett, Michael Beach, Ethan Phillips, Regina Taylor.   Real-life story of principle "Crazy Joe" Clark who single handedly took drastic measures to clean up his New Jersey high-school. See this and you'll be thankful you home school or consider it if you are not currently doing so! Parents should definitely view this one first. [PG-13] **V, DVD**

Life With Father (1947) **** D: Michael Curtiz. William Powell, Irene Dunn, Elizabeth Taylor, Edmund Gwenn, ZaSu Pitts, Jimmy Lydon, Martin Millner.   Adapted from the Broadway play and based upon Clarence Day's story of growing up in New York city at the turn of the century with a very unusual father. This is a delightful film for all, and one with some strong values shown. I especially like the scene in which the boy has been given a "cut down" suit of his father's. He cannot act like himself because he's in his father's suit! **V, DVD**

Magnificent Yankee, The (1950) *** D: John Sturges. Louis Calhern, Ann Harding, Eduard Franz, James Lydon, Philip Ober, Richard Anderson, Hayden Rorke, John Hamilton.   Wonderful story of Oliver Wendell Holmes, Jr., and his loving wife, spanning the years from his move to D. C. in 1902 to begin life as a Supreme Court Justice to his death in 1935. Calhern is wonderful recreating the role he played on Broadway. Don't miss this one. **V**

Man Called Peter, A (1955) *** (See Bible)

Man of a Thousand Faces (1957) ***1/2 D: Joseph Pevney. James Cagney, Dorothy Malone, Jane Greer, Marjorie Rambeau, Jim Backus, Jeanne Cagney, Robert J. Evans, Roger Smith, Jack Albertson, Snub Pollard.   Biography of silent film star Lon Chaney, who probably did more to further incredible makeup for the screen in the early years of film than any other single person. His life had many tragic elements, including the mental illness of his first wife. Watch and edit the parts to which you might object, but see the parts where he did some amazing things. **V, DVD**

Marie (1985) *** D: Roger Donaldson. Sissy Spacek, Jeff Daniels, Keith Szarabajka, Morgan Freeman, Fred (Dalton) Thompson (now a U. S. Senator), Don Hood, John Cullum.   True story of a divorced young mother who goes to work for the Governor of Ten-

nessee in the Department of Correction and discovers corruption. She must decide what to do: blow the whistle and take the heat or turn a blind eye. Thompson (now in Congress) plays himself as Marie's lawyer. View first for content before showing. **[PG] V**

Miracle Worker, The (1962) **** D: Arthur Penn. Anne Bancroft, Patty Duke, Victor Jory, Inga Swenson, Andrew Prine, Beah Richards, Kathleen Comegys.   Fascinating and well done film version of William Gibson's play about Annie Sullivan (Bancroft) who accepts the challenge to try to reach blind, and deaf Helen Keller (Duke). Both of these women had originated the roles on Broadway and won Oscars for them in this film. An incredible film for the entire family. REALLY don't miss this one and don't bother with any remakes. **V, DVD**

Mr. Smith Goes to Washington (1939) **** D: Frank Capra. James Stewart, Jean Arthur, Claude Rains, Edward Arnold, Guy Kibbee, Thomas Mitchell, Eugene Pallette, Beulah Bondi, Harry Carey.   My favorite Frank Capra/Jimmy Stewart movie. Stewart plays an idealistic young Senator who finds nothing but corruption in the U.S. Senate, bringing about his disillusionment, and then his rallying to fight the injustice he sees. Arthur plays the savvy insider who is won over by Mr. Smith and his sincerity. Harry Carey is brilliant as the Vice President (who presides over the Senate). Highly recommended. **V**

My Gal Sal (1942) **12 (See Musicals) Based upon the life of composer Paul Dresser.

My Man Godfrey (1936) ***1/2 D: Gregory La Cava. William Powell, Carole Lombard, Gail Patrick, Alice Brady, Eugene Pallette.   Delightful screwball comedy set during the Great Depression. This offers a lot of opportunity to talk about appearance versus substance, judging others, character, right and wrong, as well as seeing the great differences of the ultra wealthy and ultra poor of the time. A good family film as well as a good discussion piece. **V**

My Side of the Mountain (1969) **1/2 D: James B. Clark. Ted Eccles, Theodore Bikel, Tudi Wiggins, Frank Perry, Peggy Loder.   Based upon the book by the same name, this is the story of a boy who runs away from home to the wilderness and lives by his wits. He makes a home for himself in a hollowed out tree and befriends a bird of prey. Definitely read the book first and then watch the film. Then compare and contrast the two. My two *girls* really enjoyed the book. **V**

Never Let Me Go (1953) **1/2 D: Delmer Davies. Clark Gable, Gene Tierney, Bernard Miles, Richard Haydn, Kenneth More, Belita, Theodore Bikel.   Gable marries a Soviet ballerina and tries to figure out how to smuggle her out of the country. A look at the cold war, iron curtain and how it affected non-military lives. **V**

Never Say Goodbye (1946) *** D: James V. Kern. Errol Flynn, Eleanor Parker, Lucile Watson, S.Z. Sakall, Hattie McDaniel, Forrest Tucker, Donald Woods.   Flynn plays an artist whose wife divorced him because she didn't trust him with the models who were an inherent part of his art. Their child, "Flip" spends half her time with dad and half with mom, but the *entire* time trying to reunite her parents. Cute film of how they get back together. **V**

Next Voice You Hear, The (1950) **1/2 D: William Wellman. James Whitmore, Nancy Davis (Reagan), Lillian Bronson, Jeff Corey.   I remember seeing this as a child and the memory of it still strikes me as the scene in church was shown as the *norm* for that time. How different things are today! The voice of God is heard on the radio and the effects of that transmission is the message of this movie. Preview. **V**

Night to Remember, A (1958-British) **** D: Roy (Ward) Baker. Kenneth More, David McCallum, Jim Dixon, Laurence Naismith, Frank Lawton, Honor Blackman, Alec McCowen, George Rose.   Precisely produced documentary style account of the sinking of the *Titanic*. SO much better than the trashy 1997 version, which I recommend that you skip. Parents may wish to view first. **V, DVD**

On Moonlight Bay (1951) **1/2 D: Roy Del Ruth. Doris Day, Gordon MacRae, Billy Gray, Mary Wickes, Leon Ames, Rosemary DeCamp.   A slice of turn of the century Americana. MacRae goes off to World War I at the end. Sequel: *By the Light of the Silvery Moon*. **V**

Operation Thunderbolt (1977) *** D: Menahem Golan. Yehoram Gaon, Klaus Kinski. True story of famous Israeli commando raid on July 4, 1976 to rescue 104 hijacked passengers from a plane at Entebbe in Uganda. Tense, with mostly Israeli cast, Israel gave its stamp of approval to this. Better than *Raid on Entebbe or Victory at Entebbe*. [**PG**] **V**

Peacemaker (1997) **1/2 D: Mimi Leder. George Clooney, Nicole Kidman, Armin Mueller-Stahl, Marcel Iures, Alexander Baluev, Rene Medvesek, Gary Wernts, Randolph Batin Koff, Michael Boatman. Interesting look at the danger of radicals having nuclear weapons. This is the story a science advisor to the U.S. government and her military advisor who must find missing nuclear weapons from the old Soviet government stores that have disappeared. They find out about this when a nuke blows up in Russia. This film was originally rated [R], so you'll need to tape it from TV and edit it to see it, like we did. Most of the R content has been removed for television and the movie provides an up close look and understanding of why our President is so concerned about Islamic radicals and Saddam Hussein in particular, getting their hands on suitcase nuclear weapons. The premise for this is factual which we are currently watching become a reality. [**R**] **V, DVD**

San Francisco (1936) ***1/2 D: W. S. Van Dyke II. Clark Gable, Jeanette MacDonald, Spencer Tracy, Jack Holt, Jessie Ralph, Ted Healy, Shirley Ross.   Gable is a "bad-boy" who is a childhood chum of Tracy, now a minister. MacDonald comes to Gable's attention and he makes her the star of his show, over Tracy's protests to both. When the San Francisco earthquake hits, Gable sees the light, and sees the treasure he has in the love of MacDonald. A film of redemption with a strong message that God can and will forgive even the lowliest sinner. Very well done.   **V**

Sarah, Plain and Tall (1990) TVM D: Glenn Jordan. Glenn Close, Christopher Walken, Lexi Randall, Margaret Sophie Stein, Jon De Vries, Christopher Bell.   Hallmark Hall of Fame version of Patricia Lachlan's book about a Kansas widower in 1910 who advertises for a wife. The ad is answered by Sarah Wheaton of Maine who comes for a visit to see if she can "make a difference." A beautiful film for the entire family. Sequel: *Skylark*. Above average. **V**

Skylark (1993) TVM D: Joseph Sargent. Glenn Close, Christopher Walken, Lexi Randall, Christopher Bell, Margaret Sophie Stein, Jon De Vries, Teresa Hughes, Elizabeth Wilson.   The sequel to *Sarah, Plain and Tall,* tells the story of the now married Sarah and Jacob during a drought on the prairie. The barn catches on fire and many farmers are leaving their land. Jacob decides to hold on, but sends Sarah and the children to Maine. They see a very different life than they've ever seen before, including Sarah's rather free-spirited aunts. (followed by *Winter's End*) Above average. **V**

Spirit of St. Louis, The (1957) *** (See Science/Nature) About Lindbergh's trans-Atlantic flight.

Stand Up and Cheer (1934) ** (See Music/Arts) Depression Era film with Shirley Temple.

Story of Seabiscuit (1949) **1/2 (See Horses)

Stranger in Town, A (1943) *** D: Roy Rowland. Frank Morgan, Richard Carlson, Jean Rogers, Robert Barrat, Porter Hall, Chill Wills, Donald MacBride, John Hodiak.   *Excellent* Capraesque film has corrupt town officials vs. small town lawyer who defends the "little people" who get in the way of the agenda of the corrupt officials. Morgan stumbles into town on a hunting trip and aids the young lawyer by teaching him some necessary courtroom skills to gain victory over his opponents. Morgan's identity when revealed at the end is quite a surprise to all, especially to the corrupt politicians who feel they have him neatly sewed up! His end speech takes on a new meaning in light of recent history. Don't miss this one!!

Sunrise at Campobello (1960) *** D: Vincent J. Donehue. Ralph Bellamy, Greer Garson, Hume Cronyn Jean Hagen, Ann Shoemaker, Alan Bunce, Tim Considine, Zina Bethune, Frank Ferguson Lyle Talbot.   Well done story of F. D. R., his political battles as well as his physical one against polio. Bellamy successfully recreates his stage role and Garson portrays his wife, Eleanor.

Thousand Heroes, A (1992) TVM Charlton Heston, Richard Thomas, James Coburn, Leon Russom, John M. Jackson.   Based on a true story of a downed passenger plane in Sioux City, Iowa, in 1989. An interesting look at a group of heroic Americans and American ingenuity. Also known as *Crash Landing: The Rescue of Flight 232*. Above average.

Three Days of the Condor (1975) ***1/2 D: Sydney Pollack. Robert Redford, Faye Dunaway, Cliff Robertson, Max von Sydown, John Houseman.   Intriguing story about the intelligence community in which Condor (code name for Redford) who is a reader for the CIA, sends a hypothetical thesis about oil to his faceless superiors which causes an attack upon his office. All are killed except for himself. The rest of the movie is spent with him trying to survive while working to uncover what happened and who is responsible. This is a good film for discussion, but will need to be edited as it is gory in places and to survive and escape detection, Redford kidnaps Dunaway. There is some content here which should be eliminated. Other than that, it is a biting film about who holds the power and what they do with it. Be sure to tape from TV so that most of the bad content will/can be edited. Originally rated [**R**].   **V**

Top Gun (1986) **1/2 D: Tony Scott. Tom Cruise, Kelly McGillis, Val Kilmer, Anthony Edwards, Tom Skeritt, Michael Ironside, John Stockwell, Barry Tubb, Rick Rossovich, Tim Robbins, James Tolkan, Meg Ryan.   The story of a young pilot who gets sent to Top Gun school and comes face to face with himself and his past. There is blatant immorality in this movie so I don't recommend showing this without viewing it first. This is another movie that I did not show my children, but simply excerpted the aerial scenes to show them jet warfare. [**PG**] **V, DVD**

Top Secret Affair (1957) **1/2 (See Family Films)

Torn Curtain (1966) **1/2 D: Alfred Hitchcock. Paul Newman, Julie Andrews, Lila Kedrova, David Opatoshu, Ludwig Donath.   Story of an American scientist (Newman) who has hit a block in his research. He knows that a Professor Lent [behind the iron curtain] is ahead of him, so he defects - but only to get what Lent knows. Andrews plays his fiancée/secretary who has no clue what is going on. This presents an interesting look at the underground system during the Cold War, the atmosphere behind the iron curtain and the race between the Soviets and U.S. Parents, view this first as some cuts show some violent scenes and some do not. Idea: view after reading *God's Smuggler* by Brother Andrew. **V**

Unsinkable Molly Brown (1964) *** (See Musicals)

War Games (1983) **1/2 D: John Badham. Matthew Broadrick, Dabney Coleman, John Wood, Ally Sheedy, Barry Corbin, Juanin Clay, Maury Chaykin.   Young Broadrick plays a computer whiz who hacks his way into the government's early warning system to "play a game" with the computer. The game turns out to be the real thing, which is thermo-nuclear war! The trick is how to get the computer to stop. This requires the help of the computers inventor who is supposedly dead. I believe this movie was done as disarmament propaganda, however, the seriousness of this type of war and the potential devastation is shown without blood and gore. Therefore, to see this could give children an understanding of why adults are so concerned about this issue. **V**

West Point Story (1950) **1/2 (See Music/Arts)

Winter's End (1999) NR D: Glenn Jordan. Glenn Close, Christopher Walken, Jack Palance.   Daughter Anna has become a nurse and is working round the clock during the famous influenza epidemic during WWI. Jacob's father returns home after years of being gone and out of touch and the emotional pain his leaving had upon a young Jacob is shown. Sarah's and Jacob's daughter, Cassie, is included in this one, too. Above average. (Third in *Sarah, Plain and Tall* Series) **V**

Young Tom Edison (1940) *** D: Norman Taurog. Mickey Rooney, Fay Bainter, George Bancroft.   Tells of Edison's early life, his failure in school, his inquisitiveness and how his quick thinking saved his mother's life as well as others. Like Josiah, the boy king, children need to see that they *can* make a difference even while still children. **V**

Blood Alley (1955) **1/2 D: William Wellman. John Wayne, Lauren Bacall, Paul Fix, Mike Mazurki, Anita Ekberg.   Not the most serious of films but it does deal with the Chinese who tried to escape Communism by fleeing to Hong Kong. Parents may wish to view this first. **V**

Born Free (1966) ***1/2 (See Literature)

Hatari! (1962) ***1/2 (See Science/Nature)

Inn of the Sixth Happiness, The (See **Bible**, WWII and Family)

King Solomon's Mines (1950) ***1/2 D: Compton Bennett, Andrew Marton. Deborah Kerr, Stewart Granger, Richard Carlson, Hugo Haas.   Granger is an African guide who is contacted by Carlson to take himself and his sister on a safari into uncharted territory to look for her husband who has disappeared. Intriguing film with lots of good scenery. Parents may wish to edit parts, so preview first.   **V**

Living Free (1972) **1/2 D: Jack Couffer. Susan Hampshire, Nigel Davenport, Geoffrey Keen.   The sequel to *Born Free* with Elsa now grown and with cubs of her own. **[G] V**

Naked Jungle, The (1954) *** D: Byron Haskin. Eleanor Parker, Charlton Heston, Abraham Sofaer, William Conrad.   A tale of life in the jungles of South America and the American (Heston) who carved out an empire with hard work and determination. Included in this movie are mail-order brides, marriage by proxy and fighting an enemy which seems unbeatable- *marabunta* – soldier ants. This is *not* a cheap horror film of killer ants. Instead, it is one of the few movies of which I know that covers anything interesting set in South American. There is a mention of adultery which leads to justice by the jungle people's punishment, a scene where Heston's character is intoxicated and behaves badly, and a scene which shows a shrunken head. These could be edited and still salvage the film. Watch it first and decide what you want to do. **V**

Quiet Man, The (1952) **** D: John Ford. John Wayne, Maureen O'Hara, Barry Fitzgerald, Victor McLaughlin, Mildred Natwick, Arthur Shields, Ward Bond.   *Wonderful* story of Wayne returning to his native Ireland after quitting the boxing ring. He purchases a plot of land which puts him at odds with a native landholder who wanted the land for himself. This complicates Wayne's life because he decides to wed the man's sister. There's lots of fun in watching the Irish courting rituals and Wayne's reaction to them. Thereafter comes a rousing tale of marriage, customs, misunderstanding, Irish tempers and the longest scene ever filmed of a man dragging his wife back home! This is a beautiful movie, filmed on location and is one the entire family will enjoy. Clean family fun for all. **V**

Secret of the Incas (1954) **1/2 D: Jerry Hopper. Charlton Heston, Robert Young, Nicole Maurey, Thomas Mitchell, Glenda Farrell, Yma Sumac.   Adventure tale of an explorer searching for lost treasure. Most noteworthy, the voice and singing performance of the incredible Yma Sumac.

Shadowlands (1993-British) ***1/2 D: Richard Attenborough. Anthony Hopkins, Debra Winger, Edward Hardwicke, Michael Denison, Joseph Mazzello, John Wood, Robert Flemying, Peter Howell, Peter Firth. Excellently done biography of famous author C. S. Lewis (*The Chronicles of Narnia*) who was settled into mid-life as an Oxford scholar in the 1950s and meets an American woman poet, Joy Gresham, who admires his work. Through time, they fall in love and are married only to find out shortly thereafter that she has terminal cancer. **[PG]   V, DVD**

Sound of Music, The (1965) ***1/2 (See Family, Musicals and **WWII**)

World War I

African Queen, The (1951) **** D: John Huston. Katharine Hepburn, Humphrey Bogart, Robert Morley, Peter Bull, Theodore Bikel.   The tale of a river boat captain and a spinster missionary who travel downriver during WWI fighting the elements, the river and in the end, the Germans. Bogart won an Oscar for this role. **V**

Anne of Green Gables, The Continuing Story (2000) TVM (See 1900s)

Court-Marshall of Billy Mitchell, The (1955) ***1/2 D: Otto Preminger. Gary Cooper, Charles Bickford, Ralph Bellamy, Rod Steiger, Elizabeth Montgomery, Fred Clark, James Daly, Jack Lord, Peter Graves, Darren McGavin.   Wonderful film of true story. Mitchell (Cooper) was a flying ace who trained flyers on precision bombing as well as being an aviation visionary. The most fascinating part of this movie is Mitchell's (*correct*) prediction of the Japanese attack on Pearl Harbor, which he made in *1925!* This is a keeper. Don't miss this film! **V**

Fighting 69th, The (1940) **1/2 D: William Keighley. James Cagney, Pat O'Brien, George Brent, Jeffrey Lynn, Alan Hale, Frank McHugh, Dennis Morgan, George Reeves (later TVs "Superman") Fictitious story of real life regiment. Cagney plays a tough guy who finds that he's not tough on the battle field. Indeed, his actions of cowardice get many of his regiment killed. This character study takes one through his fear, his cowardice, his near execution and his encounter with a priest who helps him confront himself. Worth seeing. **V**

For Me and My Gal (1942) **1/2 (See Music/Arts)

Lawrence of Arabia (1962-British) **** D: David Lean. Peter O'Toole, Alec Guiness, Anthony Quayle, Arthur Kennedy, Omar Sharif, Jose Ferrer.   Based upon the book *The Seven Pillars of Wisdom* by T. E. Lawrence this is the epic story of his adventures as a British officer who brings together the various feuding Arab tribes to fight the Turks. The first part of this movie is wonderful and certainly worth seeing for it was filmed on location. However, once Lawrence bombs a train and walks away dressed as a Arab, (in white) with his servant who is dressed in black, you can stop the film. From then on, it goes down. This is a good place to stop and avoid some depressing character issues of Lawrence as well as him being taken by the Turks, beaten and with an implied forced molestation by a homosexual Turkish general (Ferrer). The rest of the film really offers no more to the viewer worth seeing. The first part tells who Lawrence was, the bulk of what he did and shows the scenery of that part of the world. From this, a good discussion could be raised about the Arabs today and then, united and feuding, and how their being united figures into end time prophecy, Christianity vs. Islam and their worldviews including "written" destiny vs. valuing life and much more. This movie won seven Academy Awards including a well deserved Best Score by Maurice Jarre. The theme is hauntingly beautiful. Parents should *definitely* preview this one. **V**

Nurse Edith Cavell (1939) *** D: Herbert Wilcox. Anna Neagle, Edna May Oliver, George Sanders, ZaSu Pitts, May Robson, H. B. Warner, Robert Coote.   The story of a WWI nurse who worked with the Belgium underground to help wounded soldiers escape the Kaiser's troops. She was one of two prisoners executed, and the only woman. The world created such an uproar upon her death that the thirty some-odd other prisoners scheduled for execution were not killed. Parents view first. **V**

Paths of Glory (1957) **** D: Stanley Kubrick. Kirk Douglas, Ralph Meeker, Adolphe Menjou, George Macready, Wayne Morris, Richard Anderson.   Based upon a true story by Humphrey Cobb of the same title, this is set in 1916 France. A General is given the impossible task of taking and holding a strategic hill. He assigns it to a Colonel and his troops, all of whom are exhausted. The General orders the artillery to fire on their own troops. When the mission fails, the General has three soldiers picked to be tried for cowardice in a rigged trial and executed. Shows the hubris of the General and the degenerate thinking of the command staff. One line needs omitting, so preview for this. This film has become a classic on the insanity of war. **V, DVD**

Random Harvest (1942) ***1/2 D: Mervyn LeRoy. Ronald Colman, Greer Garson, Philip Dorn, Susan Peters, Henry Travers, Reginald Owens.   Based upon a novel by James Hilton, this tells the story of a soldier suffering from amnesia who wanders from the hospital and is found by kind-hearted Garson, who takes him under her wing and nurses him back to health. They fall in love and marry, without his memory returning. One day, he goes to the city on business, is involved in an accident and his memory returns, but his memory of the married life he had been living is gone. A touching story of enduring love, near misses, yet triumph in the end. **V**

Sergeant York (1941) ***1/2 D: Howard Hawks. Gary Cooper, Walter Brennan, Joan Leslie, George Tobias, Stanley Ridges, Margaret Wycherly, Ward Bond, Noah Beery, Jr. June Lockhart.   The biography of Alvin York from the backwoods of Tennessee, who lives a wild life and then gets saved. Later, he is drafted for WWI. He tries to dissent for religious reasons, but is not allowed out of service. He ends up seeking the Lord as to how he can fight. He gets his answer and ends up winning the Congressional Medal of Honor. Alvin York was the consultant to Hollywood in the making of this picture. One day, when seeing Gary Cooper smoking, he told him that he couldn't smoke, drink or cuss if Cooper was going to play him! Cooper honored York's request and abstained during the duration of making the film. Fine family viewing. **V**

Stars and Stripes Forever (1952) **1/2 D: Henry Koster. Clifton Webb, Robert Wagner, Ruth Hussey, Debra Paget.   Largely fictionalized account of the life of John Philip Sousa, but still worth watching. Included are the invention of the Sousaphone and many Sousa marches. The Sousa family and band were *very* disappointed in the way this film turned out, but I think it is worth seeing for the music and the story telling about John Philip Sousa, whose music is still played and heard. (see Music/Arts, also) **V**

Wings of Eagles, The (1957) **1/2 D: John Ford. John Wayne, Maureen O'Hara, Dan Dailey, Ward Bond, Ken Curtis, Edmund Lowe, Kenneth Tobey, Sig Ruman.   The biography of Frank "Spig" Wead, a WWI pioneer aviator who suffered an accident and became paralyzed. This tells of his amazing recovery and the dedication of a friend in helping him to walk again. One caution, Wayne and wife, O'Hara fight, drink and behave in a way that would certainly be up for discussion, or editing! View first and decide what you want to do if you show this one.

Winter's End (1999) NR Third in the *Sarah, Plain and Tall* trilogy. Above average. (See 1900s)

Zepplin (1971-British) *** D: Etienne Perier. Michael York, Elke Sommer, Peter Carsten, Marius Goring, Anton Diffring, Andrew Keir.   German born English aviator is torn as to where his loyalty lies during WWI. Good film with interesting special effects. Parents may wish to preview. **[G] V**

NOTES

World War II

There are so many movies from this era, that I have divided them by theatres of operation.

The South Pacific

Air Force (1943) *** D: Howard Hawks. John Garfield, John Ridgely, Gig Young, Arthur Kennedy Charles Drake, Harry Carey, George Tobias, Faye Emerson.   Opens with Gettysburg Address and tells the story of the indomitable crew of a B-17 bomber who were a part of a group of bombers who flew from the mainland to Pearl Harbor as it was being attacked by the Japanese, a true event. They emergency land on Maui, are attacked by snipers and head for Pearl. From there they are sent to Wake Island and ultimately to the Philippines. This movie offers information for further study on many items including the attack on Pearl Harbor, President Roosevelt's address, part of which is heard, Wake Island and what happened there, the attack on Clark airfield in the Philippines, loading bombs, aerial warfare with an unescorted bomber, planes taking off on an aircraft carrier (real footage), Japanese ships sinking after an aerial attack, and of course, the unprovoked attack of the Japanese on Pearl Harbor which brought the U.S. into this war. Compare with recent events of the unprovoked attack on the World Trade center, with no declaration of war for warning by either, the killing of civilians today vs. military instillations being targeted by the Japanese, etc., whatever occurs to you as important to discuss. The politically correct crowd may discount this movie for the slang "Japs" and the attitude of the Americans in the film, but this IS a film of its time, displaying the outrage and attitude of our nation, and how we STILL felt two years later. **V, DVD**

American Guerilla in the Philippines (1950) **1/2 D: Fritz Lang. Tyrone Power, Micheline Prelle (Presle), Tom Ewell, Bob Patten, Tommy Cook, Jack Elam.   Based upon a novel by Ira Wolfert, this tells the story of the resistance to the Japanese after the fall of the Philippines, including the covert acts by trapped American G.I.s. (G. I. stands for "government issue.") Though the story is fiction, the location is authentic, giving a first hand account of the terrain fought for so bitterly. This is the place which General MacArthur left, stating, "I shall return." And he did. There is a romantic angle here that some parents might wish to edit, so I recommend that you preview it first.

Away All Boats (1956) *** D: Joseph Pevney. Jeff Chandler, George Nader, Julie Adams, Lex Barker, Keith Andes, Richard Boone, David Janssen.   Based upon the book by the same title, the Captain (Chandler) of the attack transport Belinda must train his inexperienced men and make them into an efficient crew. This movie has a lot of pluses. It shows the discipline to serve with people you may not like personally, but who are necessary for the job. It shows the ingenuity demanded of a commander and crew under adverse circumstances; it shows dedication to getting the job done. Though this movie didn't rate very high with critics at the time, I think it has a lot to offer about the war effort and the job of this kind of crew. Note: Nader and Adams play a married couple and in letters to each other they reminisce about their courtship. Some parents may object to some of this. I recommend viewing it first. This entire section could easily be cut without harming the rest of the films content. One of my eldest daughter's favorites. **V**

Back to Bataan (1945) *** D: Edward Dmytryk. John Wayne, Anthony Quinn, Beulah Bondi.   Another good flag waver of Wayne leading Filipino guerillas to victory in battle. Mostly factual as far as where they were, the places named, that the Filipino guerillas fought hand in hand with U.S. troops, etc. **V**

Bataan (1943) *** D: Tay Garnett. Robert Taylor, George Murphy, Thomas Mitchell, Lloyd Nolan, Lee Bowman, Robert Walker, Desi Arnaz, Barry Nelson.   Realistic film of famous incident on Pacific Island. Parents might wish to view this first as most everyone dies. However, as an account of the fierceness of fighting in the Pacific Theatre, this is but a mere fraction. **V, DVD**

Court-Marshall of Billy Mitchell, The (1955) ***1/2 (See WWI)

Destination Tokyo (1943) *** D: Delmer Daves. Cary Grant, John Garfield, Alan Hale, John Ridgely, Dane Clark, Warner Anderson, William Prince.   Grant is commander of a U.S. sub that is sent to Japan and is to infiltrate the harbor at Tokyo and send messages with information on enemy movement back to command. Suspenseful tale with fine job by all. **V**

Father Goose (1964) *** D: Ralph Nelson. Cary Grant, Leslie Caron, Trevor Howard, Jack Good, Nicole Felsette.   Grant plays an irascible "bum" who is coerced into playing lookout on a South Seas island for the British navy. He is "paid" for this work in alcohol, so parents may want to view this first, for content. While checking up on his nearest "neighbor," a lookout on the next island, he finds Caron and a group of school girls, all daughters of highly important individuals. He cannot leave them stranded on the island with the Japanese patrolling the area, so is forced into taking them with him as he returns to his own "humble abode." At that point the fun begins. My favorite line is uttered by Trevor Howard, "What, Goody-Two Shoes and the Filthy Beast?" If you feel this is appropriate for your family, there will be laughs and some tense moments as the characters try to learn to get along under tense conditions and stay un-noticed by the Japanese. **V**

Fighting Seabees, The (1944) *** D: Edward Ludwig. John Wayne, Susan Hayward, Dennis O'Keefe, William Frawley.   A flag waver of the personal and professional conflicts of a construction crew boss (Wayne) and naval officer (O'Keefe). Hayward plays a journalist who contributes to their conflict. The major contribution of this film is the information about the naval engineer-sailors, the "Seabees" (stands for Construction Battalion) and how they came to be. **V**

Flying Leathernecks, The (1951) *** D: Nicholas Ray. John Wayne, Robert Ryan, Jay C. Flippen, Janis Carter, Don Taylor, William Harrigan.   Tough Marine Major (Wayne) expects a lot of his Marines. Executive officer (XO) Ryan thinks he's too tough and demands too much. Good flag waver with some nice aerial sequences. **V**

Flying Misfits, The TVM Pilot movie for the television series, *The Black Sheep Squadron.*   This is the story of how this squadron came about under the leadership of Greg "Pappy" Boynton. They were, indeed, a group of screw-up misfits who did some daring deeds during the war in the Pacific. Occasionally, the history channel will show the movie and/or segments from the series and include interviews with real members of this squadron. They comment on their life and missions, and sometimes on the events being shown in the series. Though all the stories may not be accurate, the real life characteristics of the squadron, its commander, and how they operated are factually based. Real life "Pappy" Boynton was the advisor to the movie and T.V. series. May require some editing.

Gallant Hours, The (1960) *** D: Robert Montgomery. James Cagney, Dennis Weaver, Ward Costello, Richard Jaeckel.   Biography of Admiral "Bull" Halsey done in documentary style. Wonderful film of a man whose input and involvement was pivotal to our victory in this war. This is one not to miss. **V**

Guadalcanal Diary (1943) **1/2 D: Lewis Seiler. Preston Foster, Lloyd Nolan, William Bendix, Richard Conte, Anthony Quinn.   True story by war correspondent Richard Tregaskis of the 1st wave of Marines to land on Guadalcanal from August 7-December 10, 1942. Shows the maturation of the troops as well as the intense fighting that took place, and includes real footage. Worth seeing. **V, DVD**

Heaven Knows Mr. Allison (1957) *** D: John Huston. Deborah Kerr, Robert Mitchum.   A sweet tale of a nun (Kerr) and a Marine (Mitchum) who are stranded on an island in the South Pacific which also happens to be inhabited by the Japanese! Mitchum is tenderly chivalrous in his care of Kerr. Though this has nothing in reality to do with the war, it is set in a real time and place and is a movie which I think all families will like. **V**

MacArthur (1977) *** D: Joseph Sargent. Gregory Peck, Dan O'Herlighy, Ed Flanders, Sandy Kenyon, Dick O'Neill.   A good look at the very controversial title figure. Includes his famous, statement, "I shall return" in context. It also shows his "trademark" corn cob pipe. He was the Supreme Commander of the South West Pacific Theatre of Operations.

(I got that straight from my father who served under his command.) **[PG]** **V**

Merrill's Marauders (1962) ****1/2** D: Samuel Fuller. Jeff Chandler, Ty Hardin, Peter Brown, Andrew Duggan, Will Hutchins, Claude Akins, John Hoyt.   True story of Brig. General Frank Merrill, (Chandler in his last role) leader of a band of G.I.s fighting Japanese in the jungles of Burma and the incredible odds under which they continued. The 75th Rangers trace their beginning to Merrill's Marauders. Film is accurate in the near impossibility of the mission and the total exhaustion of the men. **V**

Midway (1976) ***1/2** D: Jack Smight. Charlton Heston, Henry Fonda, James Coburn, Glenn Ford, Hal Holbrook, Robert Mitchum, Cliff Robertson, Toshiro Mifune, Robert Wagner, Edward Albert.   Mostly soap-opera of Heston's son (Albert) in love with a Japanese girl. Does have some good battle scenes, but must be previewed and edited for language and content. Better choice: Wing and a Prayer. **[PG]** **V, DVD**

Mister Roberts (1955) ******* (See Family)

None But the Brave (1965) ****1/2** D: Frank Sinatra. Frank Sinatra, Clint Walker, Tommy Sands, Tony Bill, Brad Dexter.   War drama about the crew of a plane crash who take refuge on a remote island inhabited by a Japanese patrol. Both are stranded on the island and must decide to fight the war or make their own truce for survival. The ending is a message about the futility of war. **V**

Operation Petticoat (1959) *****1/2** (See Family)

Outsider, The (1961) ******* D: Delbert Mann. Tony Curtis, James Franciscus, Bruce Bennett, Gregory Walcott, Vivian Nathan.   Curtis plays Ira Hamilton Hayes, the shy Pima Indian who was one of the marines to raise the U. S. flag on Iwo Jima in this biography.

Pride of the Marines (1945) *****1/2** D: Delmer Davies. John Garfield, Eleanor Parker, Dane Clark, John Ridgely, Rosemary DeCamp, Ann Doran, Ann Todd, Warren Douglas.   Embellished true story of Marines who were blinded during a Japanese attack. Parents may wish to preview.

PT 109 (1963) ****** D: Leslie Martinson. Cliff Robertson, Robert Culp, Ty Hardin, James Gregory, Robert Blake.   Based upon the true story of John F. Kennedy's command during WW2 and the shipwreck which caused him physical problems for the rest of his life. I remember being fascinated with this story as a child and the fact that the President had his own rocking chair. (At times it was his only way of dealing with the pain.) **V**

Sands of Iwo Jima (1949) ******* D: Allan Swan. John Wayne, John Agar, Adele Mara, Forrest Tucker, Arthur Franz, Juilie Bishop, Richard Jaeckel, Wally Cassell, Richard Webb.   Fictional story based upon the true story of the raising of the flag on Iwo Jima. The three surviving Marines who raised the flag have small parts. Worth seeing for this important historical event, and the impact the picture of this event had on our nation. **V, DVD**

So Proudly We Hail (1943) ******* D: Mark Sandrich. Claudette Colbert, Paulette Goddard, Veronica Lake, George Reeves, Sonny Tufts, Barbara Britton, Walter Abel.   Not completely historically accurate. As a matter of fact, the real nurses who lived this adventure were furious over the portrayal of the facts through this film. That said, this is a very entertaining film about army and navy nurses on Bataan and Corregidor in the South Pacific. There is self-sacrifice as Veronica Lake gives her lives for her fellow nurses, (which never really happened), and a sweet romance between Claudette Colbert and future "Superman" George Reeves. With all of it's historical flaws, it still gives a picture of the hardships of service on these islands. Some of the facts which are realistically portrayed are: the first placement on Bataan and then being moved to Corregidor, the underground tunnel hospital on Corregidor, the fact that the nurses were actually in these locales, and the shortage of medicine and medical supplies, to name a few. This is a favorite of my eldest daughter who set me straight on the facts/mistakes in the film. She read the book upon which this information was based, *We Band of Angels* by Elizabeth M. Norman.

South Pacific (1958) *** (See Music/Arts)

They Were Expendable (1945) **** D: John Ford. Robert Montgomery, John Wayne, Donna Reed, Jack Holt, Ward Bond.   Based upon the true story of America's PT boat war in the South Pacific, this is a favorite of my eldest daughter. It shows the tunnels used for the hospital as happened in reality on Corregidor, it shows the Americans burning money and supplies to keep the Japanese from getting them, it shows the indomitable spirit of the Americans in a really tough spot. It ends with MacArthur's famous statement, "I shall return." The screen play was written by Frank "Spig" Wead, who had been a WWI aviator, whose story is told in *The Wings of Eagles*. **V**

Thirty Seconds Over Tokyo (1944) *** D: Mervyn LeRoy. Van Johnson, Robert Walker, Spencer Tracy, Phyllis Thaxter, Scott McKay, Robert Mitchum, Don DeFore, Stephen McNally, Louis Jean Heydt, Leon Ames, Paul Langton, Bill Williams.   Covers the first American attack on Japan in this well crafted film. A crashed airplane crew are taken in by Chinese civilians, who protect and doctor them at the risk of their own lives. Wonderful character study and development. Tracy makes an appearance as General Doolittle. Oscar winner for special effects. **V**

Tora, Tora, Tora (1970) ***1/2 D: Richer Fleisher, Toshio Masuda, Kinji Fukasusu. Martin Balsam, Soh Yamamura, Jason Robards, Joseph Cotten, Tatsuya Mihashi, E. G. Marshall, James Whitmore. Well done documented joint U.S. and Japanese recreation of the events leading up to and the attack upon Pearl Harbor from both point of views. A very good film for the event which brought the United States into the second World War. [PG] **V**

Torpedo Run (1958) **1/2 D: Joseph Pevney. Glenn Ford, Ernest Borgnine, Diane Brewster, Dean Jones.   Story of sub captain (Ford) and XO (Borgnine) who are buddies and serve together on possibly the toughest mission a man can face: destroying the enemy ship carrying your wife and children. Ford has a rough time thereafter and buddy Borgnine sticks by him, even when offered his own command. Sub warfare is covered including taking depth charges, as well as the struggle such a sacrifice requires. **V**

Up Periscope (1959) **1/2 D: Gordon Douglas. James Garner, Edmond O'Brien, Andra Martin, Alan Hale, Carleton Carpenter, Frank Gifford.   Garner plays a Navy Lieutenant who is assigned to a submarine during WW2 as it reconnoiters Japanese held territory. Parents should view first. **V**

Wackiest Ship in the Army, The (1960) *** D: Richard Murphy. Jack Lemmon, Ricky Nelson, John Lund, Chips Rafferty, Tom Tully.   Unique story is a mixture of comedy and drama about the use of a SAILing ship (as in, "with sails") as a decoy in WW2. Fun for the entire family and a nice change from some of the more somber offerings of this period. **V**

Wing and a Prayer (1944) *** D: Henry Hathaway. Don Ameche, Dana Andrews, William Eythe, Charles Bickford, Cedric Hardwicke, Kevin O'Shea, Richard Jaeckel, Henry (Harry) Morgan.   Fine film of life aboard an aircraft carrier just after Pearl Harbor and the military strategy before the Battle of Midway. Real footage is seamlessly woven into the story. A much better choice for Midway than the film by that title. **V, DVD**

Europe

Battleground (1949) *** D: William Wellman. Van Johnson, John Hodiak, Ricardo Montalban, George Murphy, Marshall Thompson, Denise Darcel, Don Taylor, Richard Jaeckel, James Whitmore, James Arness, Scotty Beckett.   Where the Battle of the Bulge (below) gives an overview of the entire maneuver, this is the up close look at the experience of one troop of men. We got a kick out of Johnson and his eggs! See *Bulge* and this for a really good idea of what it was all about. Both recount famous "Nuts" story.   **V**

Battle of the Bulge, The (1965) **1/2 D: Ken Annakin. Henry Fonda, Robert Shaw, Robert Ryan, Telly Savalas, Dana Andrews, George Montgomery, Ty Hardin, Pier Angeli, Charles Bronson, James MacArthur.   Story of this important battle, based on fact. The framework of truth is there, down to the response of Brigadier General Anthony C. McAuliffe who, when given the option of surrender to the Germans, replied, "Nuts." Shaw, the leader of the German Panzers, is shown to be a remarkable strategist and I especially liked Bronson's character, an admirable officer who was willing to sacrifice himself for the sake of his men. I think it is worth seeing. **V**

Betrayed (1954) ** D: Gottfried Reinhardt. Clarke Gable, Lana Turner, Victor Mature, Louis Calhern, O. E. Hasse, Wilfrid Hyde-White, Ian Charmichael.   Filmed on location, this covers part of the war in the Netherlands. Gable, a colonel, falls in love with a resistance fighter, Turner, who may or may not be a double agent. **V**

Chips, the War Dog (1990) TVM D: Ed Kaplan. Brandon Douglas, Ned Vaughn, Paxton Whitehead, Ellie Cornell, Robert Miranda.   Good Disney story of young Army recruit who has a dog phobia being assigned to train a German Shepherd and then they both go to war and accomplish an incredible feat. **V**

Command Decision (1948) **** D: Sam Wood. Clark Gable, Walter Pidgeon, Van Johnson, Brian Donlevy, Charles Bickford, John Hodiak, Edward Arnold, Marshall Thompson, Richard Quine, Cameron Mitchell, John McIntire.   Fabulously done film version of the William Wister Haines stage play with Gable as a Flight Commander who knows the grim fact that most of the men he sends on flight missions over Germany will never return, yet he must to get the job done. Johnson plays his secretary and gives a bit of levity to this well done drama. Highly recommended. **V**

Darby's Rangers (1958) **1/2 D: William Wellman. James Garner, Etchika Choureau, Jack Warden, Edward Byrnes, Venetia Stevenson, Torin Thatcher, Peter Brown, Corey Allen, Stuart Whitman, Murray Hamilton, David Janssen.   Loosely factual account of William O. Darby and the U.S. Army Rangers he developed during WWII, based upon the British commandoes. This tells some facts of his efforts and training along with fiction about his men, their relationships with each other and their sweethearts. The only movie to my knowledge about this important figure in the American military. My father was one of the 6th Ranger Battalion and trained under Darby. My dad set up a sword to be given each year in Darby's honor to the highest standing graduating ROTC student at UGA, which is also my fathers' Alma Mater. It is the highest honor given and the most coveted prize. Darby was the Assistant Division Commander (Executive Officer) of the 10th Mountain Division. He died in combat after having gone on a reconnaissance mission. He was found dead with his driver, but with twenty-five dead German soldiers around him. He was up for promotion to Brigadier General and received the rank and the Congressional Medal of Honor posthumously .

Desperate Journey (1942) *** D: Raoul Walsh. Errol Flynn, Raymond Massey, Ronald Regan, Nancy Coleman, Alan Hale, Arthur Kennedy, Albert Basserman.   Crew of bomber downed in Germany try to escape with important information. Unsure whether they'll succeed, they do as much damage as possible on their way to the border. Includes plenty of comic relief (including a German officer with a "glass jaw") along with some wartime propaganda showing American attitudes of that time. My youngest daughter who doesn't like war films really liked this one.

Diary of Anne Frank (1959) *** D: George Stevens. Millie Perkins, Joseph Schildkraut, Shelly Winters, Richard Beymer, Lou Jacobi, Diane Baker, Ed Wynn.   Film version of Broadway play based on Anne's famous diary, about her family and another Jewish family hiding in Amsterdam during WWII. Read the book first and then compare. Parents should view first. **V**

Enemy Below, The (1957) *** D: Dick Powell. Robert Mitchum, Curt Jurgens, Theodore Bikel, Doug McClure, Russell Collins, David Hedison.   Oscar winner for special effects, this is an immensely intriguing movie about a cat and mouse game between destroyer captain Mitchum and Reich submarine captain Jurgens, which becomes more of a battle between captains than ships. Film portrays courage, dignity, honor, and respect for the warrior ability in each other. Highly recommended by my family. **V**

Escape (1940) *** D: Mervyn LeRoy. Norma Shearer, Robert Taylor, Conrad Veidt, Nazimova, Felix Bressart, Albert Basserman, Philip Dorn, Bonita Granville, Blanche Yurka.   A Countess (Shearer) helps an American (Taylor) get his famous actress mother out of a German concentration camp. Well acted and especially powerful in showing the terror the Nazis generated and their disposal of all who opposed them or by whom they felt threatened in any way. Based on best-seller by Ethel Vance.

Escape From Sobibor (1987) TVM D: Jack Gold. Alan Arkin, Joanna Pacula, Rutger Hauer, Hartmut Becker, Jack Shepherd.   The virtually unknown true story of the largest escape from a WWII Nazi death camp. All German paper work about this camp and its existence were destroyed after the escape, except for a very few overlooked papers. Based upon a book about this camp, this movie tells what happened there, how the Nazi's separated those they could use and destroyed the rest, and shows the plan for and the escape. If you can find it on the history channel, many times an interview with a survivor of the camp is included. This is a very powerful interview and proves, beyond a shadow of a doubt, that the place did exist. There are some scenes included which cause me to strongly recommended it for older children and that parents view it first for content. An amazing film. Above average.   **V**

Foreign Correspondent (1940) ***1/2 D: Alfred Hitchcock. Joel McCrea, Laraine Day, Herbert Marshall, George Sanders, Albert Basserman, Robert Benchley, Edmund Gwenn, Eduardo Ciannelli, Harry Davenport, Martin Kosleck.   McCrea is a reporter caught in the middle of a spy ring and in love with the daughter of a well placed spy. Obviously used to convince America of the need to join the war in Europe, but well done nonetheless. **V**

Four Jills and a Jeep (1944) **1/2 (See Music/Arts)

Glenn Miller Story, The (1954) *** (See Music/Arts)

Go For Broke! (1951) ***.D: Robert Pirosh. Van Johnson, Lane Nakano, Henry Nakamura, George Miki, Henry Oyasato, Warner Anderson.   Excellent WWII drama opens with newly commissioned Johnson assigned to train and lead Japanese-Americans (called Nisei) and his open prejudice against them which they overcome with their dedication. This group, the 442nd Regimental Combat Team actually existed and fought valiantly for the U.S. while many of their relatives lived in the interment camps in the U.S. Highly recommended.   **V, DVD**

Great Escape, The (1963) **** D: John Sturges. Steve McQueen, James Garner, Richard Attenborough, Charles Bronson, James Coburn, David McCallum, Donald Pleasence, James Donald, Gordon Jackson, John Leyton, Angus Lennie, Nigel Stock.   Based upon a true story, this fine film by an all star cast tells the story of a massive escape plan from a Nazi prison camp, the teamwork between Allies from various countries, the planning, the stealth, the teamwork, and of course, Steve McQueen's famous motorcycle ride. For most all ages, but with some of the horror of war included. Parents will need to decide if it is age appropriate for their children. **V**

Guns of Navarone (1961) ***1/2 D: J. Lee Thompson. Gregory Peck, David Niven, Anthony Quinn, Stanley Baker, Anthony Quayle, James Darren, Irene Papas, Gia Scala, James Robertson Justice, Richard Harris, Albert Lieven, Bryan Forbes, Walter Gotell.

Based on the Alistair MacLean novel, this is one action packed film. Allied commandos must infiltrate an impregnable German fortress and destroy huge guns so that Allied fleet can safely pass by. There are a few parts parents may wish to omit.   **V, DVD**

Hiding Place, The (1975) **1/2 D: James F. Collier. Julie Harris, Eileen Heckart, Arthur O'Connell, Jeanette Clift.   Based upon the book by the same title, this is the story of Corrie ten Boom and her family who aided the Jews in Holland during WWII. They made a false wall "hiding place" for the Jews in their home and were ultimately entrapped by the Nazis and taken to a prison camp. Her father and sister, Betsie, die while imprisoned. She was set free "by mistake" a few days before all women her age in the camp were killed. Corrie ten Boom was later very well known as an international speaker for Christ and told of her learning forgiveness, no matter how hard it seems. The movie seems drab and at times depressing due to the hardships of the camp and the overcast days of filming. Read the book (wonderful) and compare. I have been to Haarlem, Holland, to the ten Boom watch shop and stood in the hiding place. It was surprisingly small and cramped. It was also amazing to think of the number of people who hid there and how quickly they could get into the hiding place! I highly recommend reading the book first and then seeing the movie. Don't miss this amazing story.   **V**

Imitation General (1958) **1/2 D: George Marshall. Glenn Ford, Red Buttons, Tina Elg, Dean Jones. My family thinks this is a cute film. A black and white comedy, this tells the story of the American attitude of "take charge" in a crisis. The general is killed and Ford, a sergeant, receives the generals helmet, literally, at his feet. Out of curiosity, he tries on the helmet. Soldiers come upon him, and assume he IS the general! He's caught in a trap – tell the truth and face a possible court marshal, or fill the breach and avert chaos? We found it highly entertaining.

Immortal Battalion (1944-British) ***1/2 D: Carol Reed. David Niven, Stanley Holloway, James Donald, John Laurie, Leslie Dwyer, Hugh Burden, Jimmy Hanley, Billy Hartnell, Raymond Huntley, Reginald Tate, Leo Genn, Penelope Dudley Ward, Renée Asherson, Raymond Lovell, Peter Ustinov, Trevor Howard.   Excellent British wartime film showing how a group of malcontent civilians are brought into a fighting unit who all pull together. Howard's first film. Originally titled *The Way Ahead*. **V, DVD**

Inn of the Sixth Happiness, The (1958) *** (See Bible)

Into the Arms of Strangers: Stories of the Kindertransport (2000) ***1/2 D: Mark Jonathan. Narrated by Judi Dench.   Well done documentary tells the incredible story of the effort to place Jewish children from Germany, Austria, and Czechoslovakia with caring families in England. Largely told by the people who lived this experience along with some rare footage of this period. It won an Oscar for Best Documentary. While it shouldn't be missed, it also needs some editing for children, so parents please preview. **[PG], V, DVD**

Judgment at Nuremberg (1961) **** D: Stanley Kramer. Spencer Tracy, Burt Lancaster, Richard Widmark, Marlene Dietrich, Judy Garland, Maximillian Schell, Montgomery Clift, William Schatner. This is definitely a film for older students and adults, if chosen. The account of the trials and those who were tried is true. The trials covered some very complex issues and the film shows how the insidious rise of evil can slowly warp a person's perception of good and bad, of right and wrong. Real footage of the bombed out city is shown as are scenes of the famous rally grounds used by Hitler. Ironically, Dachau was located nearby. The parent needs to be warned that a film presented as evidence in the courtroom shows real footage of the horrors done in the concentration camps. If you choose to view this, you will understand why General (later President) Eisenhower forced the German citizens who lived near the concentration camps to go inside and view them and the bodies of the Jews there. He wanted to prove to them that the atrocities were real so they would never be able to deny and/or claim ignorance of what happened. Also, several issues the parent might choose to edit are, sterilization of those the Nazi's deemed unworthy to reproduce, (does the government have the right to make this decision for an individual vs. the point of the law?), a insinuated relationship between a man and a 16 year old girl, crematorium ovens, real films of the liberation army and what they saw. Though this is by no means a beautiful sight, it is one which proves that this really did happen and the rumor which arises from time to time by extremists that it is all "Jewish propaganda" can be seen to be false. On the positive side, Lancaster's testimony is noteworthy as we see in order for forgiveness to take place, the confession of wrong-doing is necessary. He admits that Germany did know what was going on with the people disappearing. A good discussion can be had from Maximillian Schell's monologue in which he says the world was not responsible to interfere in Germany's government. If they decided to elect Hitler and wanted to live under his rule that was their decision. Only when he began to invade other countries did it become the world's concern. And also, the closing statement about personal responsibility: if a man is not responsible for his own actions, then who is? He makes a choice from several possibilities, therefore, it IS his responsibility. Since this same attitude prevails in our country, today, I think that this is worth discussing. There are so many issues which may prove questionable for each family therefore this is a film which I feel the parents must view first. Excellent and thought provoking. **V**

Little Boy Lost (1953) *** D: George Seaton. Bing Crosby, Claude Dauphin, Nicole Maurey, Gabrielle Dorziat.   Set in post-WWII France, newspaperman Bing is trying to find his son. Shows the chaos in Europe after the war and the desperation as people tried to locate family members. Parents preview.   **V**

Longest Day, The (1962) **** D: Ken Annakin, Andrew Marton, Berhard Wicki. John Wayne, Rod Steiger, Robert Ryan, Peter Lawford, Henry Fonda, Robert Mitchum, Richard Burton, Richard Beymer, Jeffrey Hunter, Sal Mineo, Roddy McDowall, Eddie Albert, Curt Jurgens, Gert Frobe, Sean Connery, Robert Wagner, Red Buttons, Mel Ferrer, and many more.   All star cast in one of the best WWII films ever made. It tells the story of the Normandy invasion from many points of view including American, British, and German. This is one you don't want to miss. **V**

Miracle of the White Stallions (1963) **1/2 D: Arthur Hiller. Robert Taylor, Lili Palmer, Kurt Jurgens, Eddie Albert, James Franciscus, John Larch.   A Disney movie, this is a good all round family movie showing the determination and the dedication of Robert Taylor's character to protect the famous Lipizzaner stallions and mares. Due to the fighting coming to their location, the horses must be moved and hidden to survive. Continuously, Taylor's character shows cunning and resourcefulness to protect his equine charges. Wonderful performance of these renown horses at the end. **V**

Mortal Storm, The (1940) ***1/2 D: Frank Borzage. Margaret Sullivan, James Stewart, Robert Young, Frank Morgan, Robert Stack, Bonita Granville, Irene Rich, Maria Ouspenskaya, Gene Reynolds, Ward Bond.   Taken from the Phyllis Bottome novel, this film has a lot to recommend it. It begins right before WWII, with a highly respected professor and his admiring students. When Hitler comes to power, the students begin to disdain and fall away from any contact with the professor, including belittling him and disrupting his class. The reason for the change from admiration to disdain for him? He is a Jew. The story goes on to show how the rise of Naziism affects him and his family, with his daughter having to sneak out of the country by skiing through a mountain pass. I think this film gives rise to some really good discussion points for you and the children. Highly recommended. **V**

Mrs. Miniver (1942) ***1/2 D: William Wyler. Greer Garson, Walter Pidgeon, Dame May Whitty, Teresa Wright, Reginald Owen, Henry Travers, Richard Ney, Henry Wilcoxon, Helmut Dantine, Peter Lawford.   Winner of six Academy Awards and a film which wrung American sympathy for the British, this film tells the story of an English family who must learn to cope with war and how it affects all their lives and their town. Though not entirely factual, it is a clean, wonderful family movie which does show the damage, destruction, and even death which England experienced in the Blitz. There are some nice character issues addressed, too. **V**

One Against the Wind (1991) *** D: Larry Elikann. Judy Davis, Sam Neill, Anthony Higgins, Christien Anholt, Kate Beckinsale, Denholm Elliot.   Based upon a true story,

Davis plays an English born Countess who helps Allied flyers escape Germany. For this action she was decorated with military honors including two Croix de Guerre. Very interesting, and excellently done. Worth seeing. **V**

On the Double (1961) *** (See Family)

Operation Crossbow (1965) ***1/2 D: Michael Anderson. George Peppard, Sophia Loren, Trevor Howard, Tom Courtenay, Anthony Quayle, John Mills, Sylvia Syms, Richard Todd, Lilli Palmer.   Fictional story of Allies plan to infiltrate and destroy an underground missile plant in Germany. The story is fictional, but I understand the bomb in question and the underground factory were factual. Preview first.   **V**

Patton (1970) * Though this movie is supposed to be incredible, the language was so bad that I could not salvage enough of it to see. Therefore, I recommend passing on this one or see *only* with a Guardian.

Red Ball Express (1952) **1/2 D: Budd Boetticher. Jeff Chandler, Alex Nicol, Charles Drake, Hugh O'Brien, Jack Kelly, Jacqueline Duval, Sidney Poiter, Jack Warden.   The story of the real-life truck convoys which kept the Army moving with its behind the scenes work. They were created to bring supplies to Patton's army deep in German held territory in France. In actuality, this group was made up largely of blacks who served their country during this terrible war.   **V**

Secret War of Harry Frigg, The (1968) **1/2 D: Jack Smight. Paul Newman, Sylva Koscina, Andrew Duggan, Tom Bosley, John Williams, Vito Scotti, James Gregory.   Newman is a soldier who is in the brig. Because he can break out of anything, he is given the opportunity to escape court marshal if he will go to Italy and rescue five Allied generals who are being held captive. This is a comedy and in no way truly educational, but is a fun movie set during this period. **V**

Son of Lassie (1945) **1/2 (See Family Films)

Sound of Music, The (1965) ***1/2 D: Robert Wise. Julie Andrews, Christopher Plummer, Eleanor Parker, Peggy Wood, Richard Hayden, Anna Lee, Portia Nelson, Norma Varden, Marni Nixon. The Children: Charmain Carr, Nicholas Hammond, Heather Menzies, Duane Chase, Angela Cartright, Debbie Turner, Kym Karath.   Based upon a true story from which came the Broadway musical, and well deserved winner of five Academy Awards, this film tells the story of the Von Trapp family who fled Austria in 1938 to escape Hitler's regime. Hitler wanted to force Captain Von Trapp, a former Austrian naval hero, into the Third Reich's navy, thereby using his involvement as a seal of approval on Austria's joining forces with Hitler's army and agenda. Most of the film is centered around the story of Maria Von Trapp, (who was sent as a novice in the Catholic church to be a governess to the seven Von Trapp children) and the Captain, whom she later marries. She came into their household bringing life, love and helped to heal the rift between a father and his children. A truly lovely, inspirational family movie with many wonderful musical numbers from Rodgers and Hammerstein. The songs "Something Good" and "I Have Confidence" were original to the movie and were not part of the original Broadway score. The Broadway version starred Mary Martin as Maria Von Trapp. Also included is the singing of a chant by the nuns in the opening of the film which you can use to show the children the musical form of Gregorian Chant. Rodgers and Hammerstein include harmonies that would not be of the period, but the children can get the idea. Highly recommended. **V**

Stalag 17 (1953) **** D: Billy Wilder. William Holden, Don Taylor, Otto Preminger, Robert Strauss, Harvey Lembeck, Richard Erdman, Peter Graves, Neville Brand, Sig Rumann, Ross Bagdasarian. Oscar winning film based upon a Broadway play, this is a fabulous film about POW life in a WWII prison camp; its tension, its monotony, and included is an American in the barracks who is actually a German spy. Highly recommended. **V**

To Hell and Back (1956) ***1/2 D: Jesse Hibbs. Audie Murphy, Marshall Thompson, Charles Drake, Jack Kelly, Paul Picerni, Gregg Palmer, Brett Halsey, David Janssen. This is the true story of Audie Murphy, the most decorated soldier in the history of our country, and what led to his receiving the Congressional Medal of Honor. If anything, the movie underplays his heroism. The scene on the tank, shows a very short lapse of time. In actuality, it was over an hour that he single-handedly held off the German advance while standing upon a burning tank. Another incredible aspect of the movie is Audie, himself. He looks terribly young in this film, but when you see pictures of him at the time of these events, you realize how very young he really was when he did these incredible deeds of heroism. Don't miss this movie. Highly recommended. **V**

Tonight and Every Night (1945) *** (See Music/Arts)

Tuskegee Airmen, The (1995) TVM D: Robert Markowitz. Laurence Fishburne, Cuba Gooding, Jr., Andre Braugher, Allen Payne, Malcolm-Jamal Warner, Courtney B. Vance, Christopher McDonald, John Lithgow.   Story of the first squadron of black combat fighters in WWII, the "Fighting 99th," and their battles with prejudice at home, with the enemy, and with their fellow white aviators in Europe. Not a first rate film, but the only one covering this information. Interesting. Average **V**

Von Ryan's Express (1965) *** D: Mark Robson. Frank Sinatra, Trevor Howard, Raffaella Carra, Brad Dexter, Sergio Fantoni, Edward Mulhare, James Brolin.   Sinatra plays a pilot who has been captured by the Germans and delivered to a POW camp where, as a colonel, he is the top ranking officer. After some mistakes, Sinatra leads the men in a daring escape and captures a freight train which is transporting prisoners. A very exciting tale of escape, sacrifice, and daring. One of my eldest daughter's favorite WWII films. **V**

Watch on the Rhine (1943) **** D: Herman Shumlin. Bette Davis, Paul Lukas, Geraldine Fitzgerald, Lucile Watson, Beulah Bondi, George Coulouris, Donald Woods.   Film version of Lillian Helman play of American Davis returning home from Nazi occupied Europe with three children and her German husband who is an important member of the anti-Fascists Resistance. Davis is daughter of a former Associate Supreme Court Justice whose mother is hosting a Romanian refugee who is also a Nazi spy. Incredibly well done film showing the insulation of Americans while Europe lives in fear. Lukas won an Oscar for his performance. Parents, preview first.

Note: I recommend reading Ancient Rome and How it Affects You Today by Richard J. Maybury for more information on fascism.

Where Eagles Dare (1968) ***1/2 D: Brian G. Hutton. Richard Burton, Clint Eastwood, Mary Ure, Michael Hordern, Patrick Wymark, Robert Beatty, Ferdy Mayne, Anton Diffring, Donald Houston, Ingrid Pitt.   A cliff hanger based upon an Alistair MacLean story where an Allied team must go in and pose as Germans to free an American officer who is held captive by the Germans in a supposedly impenetrable mountain castle. Locals with the Resistance, in this case women, work with the team to help them accomplish their goal. There are a few things to which some parents might object, including the team dealing with one of the women who turns out to be a spy. I recommend you view this one first. **V**

Yank in the RAF, A (1941) *** (See Musicals)

NOTES

Other Theatres of War

Above and Beyond (1952) *** D: Melvin Frank, Norman Panama. Robert Taylor, Eleanor Parker, James Whitmore, Jim Backus.   Wonderful account of U.S. pilot who captained the plane and mission of dropping the first atomic bomb on Hiroshima. This shows the stress upon him and the other men involved, as well as the stress upon their families. It shows the fear of this unknown weapon, the naming of the plane, the "Enola Gay" and the *vastly* different attitudes and mores of then and now. When on the ship before taking off, the men pray in Jesus' name; I cried. How far we have fallen as a nation. **V**

Bridge on the River Kwai, The (1957) **** D: David Lean. William Holden, Sir Alec Guiness, Jack Hawkins, Sessue Hayakawa, Geoffrey Horne, James Donald, Andre Morell, Ann Sears.   The story of British P.O.W.s who are interred in a Japanese prison camp for the purpose of building a bridge for the Japanese. Guiness is the officer who will not budge on his principles of how the Japanese will deal with the British. Holden plays an American P.O.W. who escapes the camp and later comes back with British commandoes to blow up the bridge. This is a very intriguing film and one ripe for discussion. Especially good for discussion are the characters of Holden and Guiness, self vs. the greater good, and how it is easy to get involved in a single focus and yet miss the greater purpose. However, I do recommend parents view it first for a few items. Based on fact, but not at all factual as a story. Compare with the truth. **V**

Captains of the Clouds (1942) *** D: Michael Curtiz. James Cagney, Dennis Morgan, Alan Hale, Brenda Marshall, George Tobias.   Cagney and buddies enlist in the Canadian air force as former bush pilots, but are told they are too old to be fighter pilots. Some decide to stay as instructors, others don't. Cagney has trouble fitting into military life, but heroically redeems himself at end. Good flag waver. **V**

Desert Fox (1951) ***1/2 D: Henry Hathaway. James Mason, Cedric Hardwicke, Jessica Tandy, Luther Adler, Everett Sloane, Leo G. Carroll, George Macready, Richard Boone, Robert Coote.   The story of German Field Marshal Rommel, a brilliant strategist and asset to the Third Reich, but also a man of principle. Tells the story of his genius, and his part in the plot to assassinate Hitler after much deliberation and the realization that Hitler was mad, somewhat portrayed in the film. In reality, Rommel was in favor of deposing Hitler, not murdering him. Jessica Tandy, later famous in *Driving Miss Daisy* plays his wife. **V**

Flying Tigers, The (1942) *** D: David Miller. John Wayne, John Carroll, Anna Lee, Paul Kelly, Mae Clarke, Gordon Jones, James "Jimmie" Dodd.   Set in WWII China, this tells the story of the famous "Flying Tigers" with some nice aerial fight scenes. **V**

God Is My Co-Pilot (1945) **1/2 D: Robert Morey. Dennis Morgan, Raymond Massey, Andrea King, Alan Hale, Dane Clark, John Ridgely, Stanley Ridges, Donald Woods.   Flying Tiger pilot Morgan, becomes ace at fighting Japanese from China. Includes information on the Flying Tigers, the war in China, Tokyo Joe, the male counterpart of Tokyo Rose, and some good aerial fighting scenes as well as the understanding that this Macon, GA hero did not and could not have done these deeds of heroism without some heavenly aid. Worth seeing. **V**

North Star (1943) **1/2 D: Lewis Milestone. Anne Baxter, Dana Andrews, Walter Huston, Ann Harding, Eric von Stroheim, Jane Withers, Farley Granger, Walter Brennan.   One of few accounts of war on the Russian front. Largely fictious account of German invasion of Ukraine. Patriotic, anti-fascist film shows some German atrocities which were factual, given through eye-witness accounts given to the screen writer, Lillian Hellman. Later recycled into a more politically correct version *Armoured Attack.* **V**

Objective Burma (1945) ***1/2 D: Raoul Walsh. Errol Flynn, William Prince, James Brown, George Tobias, Henry Hull.   Flynn and a group of paratroopers must go into Burma to wipe out an important Japanese post. Once in, they can't get out. Suspenseful film is very well done and worth seeing. One note, this film was not popular in Britain as it leaves out the British part of this true operation. It wasn't shown in British theatres for seven years! **V**

Best Years of Our Lives, The (1946) *** D: William Wyler. Fredric March, Myrna Loy, Teresa Wright, Dana Andrews, Virginia Mayo, Harold Russell, Hoagy Carmichael.   The story of three WWII veterans returning home; the trials they encounter, the attitude of those they meet, readjusting to civilian life. This supposedly "perfectly captured the mood of postwar U.S." Russell was an actual vet who lost his hands. From this picture, he took home two Oscars, one for Best Picture and another special Oscar for bringing hope and courage to other veterans. Parents definitely need to view this one first. **V, DVD**

Clock, The (1945) ***1/2 D: Vincente Minnelli. Judy Garland, Robert Walker, James Gleason, Keenan Wynn.   Soldier Walker has a two day leave in N.Y.C., and meets Garland. They spend his leave seeing each other and doing some unique things like making deliveries for a milkman. They decide to marry, but have many obstacles to overcome in order to do so before his leave is up. I think this gives a unique look at the desperation of wartime. Clean family fare and well acted. **V**

Eleanor Roosevelt Story, The (1965) ***1/2 D: Richard Kaplan. Narrated by Archibald Macleish, Eric Sevareid, Francis Cole.   Oscar-winning documentary of this famous First Lady who stepped up to the plate to help her husband and her country in an incredibly difficult time. Parents may wish to preview. **V**

Gang's All Here, The (1943) **1/2 (See Music/Arts)

Gangway for Tomorrow (1943) ** D: John H. Auer. Margo, John Carradine, Robert Ryan, Amelita Ward, William Terry, Harry Davenport, James Bell, Charles Arnt, Wally Brown, Alan Carney.   Nice work for the war propaganda department, this covers the lives of five workers in wartime munitions plant told as flashbacks. It shows the moral of the American people and the social mores of the time, unfortunately, so very different from today. A bit dated and perhaps "hokey" for some, but worth seeing for the reflection of the values of the American people of that day.

Give 'Em Hell, Harry! (1975) *** D: Steve Binder. James Whitmore.   Film version of Whitmore's one man play triumph as the 33rd President, who made the monumental decision to drop the atomic bomb on Nagasaki and Hiroshima. His reason? To save American lives. Parents need to view this first. **[PG] V**

Government Girl (1943) **1/2 D: Dudley Nichols. Olivia de Havilland, Sonny Tufts, Anne Shirley, Jess Barker, James Dunn, Paul Stewart, Agnes Moorehead.   WWII flag waver is great family fun as production expert (Tufts) comes to Washington to get a job done and doesn't bother to learn who's important and the ins and outs of D.C. behind-the-scenes politics. He just wants to do the job, but is thwarted until his secretary (de Havilland) takes him to task and teaches him the ropes. Still there's a sticky wicket and a possible trial with some still applicable looks into government bureaucracy. I think this is a wonderful wartime film. Try to tape it from TV since it's not on video.

Hollywood Canteen (1944) **1/2 D: Delmer Daves. Bette Davis, John Garfield, Joan Leslie, Robert Hutton, Dane Clark, Janis Paige, plus a huge array of guest stars including: Eddie Cantor, Jack Carson, Joan Crawford, Ida Lupino, Eleanor Parker, S. Z. Sakall, Alexis Smith, Barbara Stanwyck.   Set in the real Hollywood Canteen, which was a place for servicemen to be entertained by Hollywood's best. It gave them a place to go and they also got to dance with the stars. My father was there in 1943 while training with the 6th Ranger Battalion, danced with Joan Leslie and (two steps) with Betty Grable. Preview. **V**

House on 92nd St., The (1945) ***1/2 D: Henry Hathaway. William Eythe, Lloyd Nolan, Signe Hasso, Gene Lockhart, Leo G. Carroll, Lydia St. Clair.   Based on fact and filmed on actual locations of the story, this documentary style film tells of FBI counterespionage moves during WWII, showing Nazi agents operating in NYC and attempting to get their hands on part of the information about the atomic bomb. An Oscar winner which is different, but informative. Parents may wish to preview. **V**

Human Comedy, The (1943) ***1/2 D: Clarence Brown. Mickey Rooney, Frank Morgan, Jackie "Butch" Jenkins, James Craig, Marsha Hunt, Fay Bainter, Ray Collins, Darryl Hickman, Donna Reed, Van Johnson.   Based on a story by William Saroyan, this paints a picture of Americana during WWII, with Rooney having to take on more and more responsibility as the "man of the house." Parents may wish to view for appropriateness. **V**

Incredible Mr. Limpet, The (1964) ** (See Family Films; to introduce younger children to this subject)

Keeper of the Flame (1943) **** D: George Cukor. Spencer Tracy, Katharine Hepburn, Richard Whorf, Margaret Wycherly, Forrest Tucker.   War correspondent Tracy is back from Europe to write about the death of an American hero, a man he admired. Once he arrives in town he finds something's amiss. Amid tension and intrigue, he uncovers interesting pieces and finally the truth. Though this was obviously made as a commentary on WWII, some of the statements in here are amazingly timely today. Highly recommended. **V**

One for the Book (see Voice of the Turtle)

Since You Went Away (1944) ***1/2 D: John Cromwell. Claudette Colbert, Jennifer Jones, Joseph Cotton, Shirley Temple, Monty Wooley, Hattie McDaniel, Agnes Moorehead, Craig Stephens, Keenan Wynn, Nazimova, Robert Walker, Lionel Barrymore.   Patriotic Selznick [classified 4-F] wanted to contribute to the war effort and serve his country by showing how the average American was affected by the war and how important everyone at home was to the war effort. Based upon Margaret Buell Wilder's book in which a series of letters are exchanged by a wife and her soldier husband, this is the story of a family (all women) who must learn to make it through WWII on their own while husband/father is away fighting the war. This covers some interesting subjects: taking in boarders, economizing on purchases and groceries, doing for self instead of having household help, etc. Parents may wish to view this first, but I think there is enough here to make it worth considering and that most will approve. Selznick talked 16 year old Temple out of a two year retirement for this film.   **V**

Stagedoor Canteen (1943) *** D: Frank Borzage. Cheryl Walker, William Terry, Marjorie Riordan, Lon McCallister, Margaret Early, Michael Harrison (Sunset Carson).   Wartime romance between a soldier and a hostess at N.Y.C. canteen for servicemen is as much a piece of history as entertainment. Includes cameos and speeches for support of the war by Katharine Hepburn, Harpo Marx, Paul Muni, Helen Hayes, Benny Goodman, Count Basie, and Edgar Bergen. Hollywood helped to support the war effort with films like this as well as the stars going out on war bond drives to raise funds for the war. Worth seeing just for the historical perspective. **V, DVD**

Sullivans, The (1944) *** D: Lloyd Bacon. Anne Baxter, Thomas Mitchell, Selena Royle, Ward Bond, Bobby Driscoll, Addison Richards.   Largely fictional story of real-life Sullivan brothers from Waterloo, Iowa, who all enlisted, went off to fight in WWII, and all died when their ship was attacked. Their story brought about the policy that brothers cannot serve in the same unit. A.k.a. *The Fighting Sullivans.* **V**

Sunday Dinner for a Soldier (1944) *** D: Lloyd Bacon. Anne Baxter, John Hodiak, Charles Winninger, Anne Revere, Chill Wills, Bobby Driscoll, Jane Darwell.   Excellent film of a poor family who invite a lonely soldier to dinner and are repaid for their kindness.

This is the Army (1943) *** (see Music/Arts)

Thousands Cheer (1943) **1/2 (See Musicals)

Voice of the Turtle, The (1947) ***1/2 D: Irving Rapper. Ronald Reagan, Eleanor Parker, Eve Arden, Wayne Morris, Kent Smith.   Cute wartime comedy about G.I. (Reagan) who falls for a slightly ditzy girl (Parker). A sweet romance.

Korean War

Battle Hymn (1957) **1/2 D: Douglas Sirk. Rock Hudson, Martha Hyer, Anna Kashfi, Dan Duryea, Don DeFore.   Hudson plays a minister who returns to duty to help train fighter pilots for the war. **V**

Men of the Fighting Lady (1954) *** D: Andrew Marton. Van Johnson, Walter Pidgeon, Louis Calhern, Dewy Martin, Keenan Wynn, Frank Lovejoy, Robert Horton, Bert Freed.   Well done action story of men aboard an aircraft carrier with an especially nail-biting ending. **V**

Pork Chop Hill (1959) ***1/2 D: Lewis Milestone. Gregory Peck, Harry Guardino, Rip Torn, George Peppard, James Edwards, Bob Steele, George Shibata, Biff Elliot, Woody Strode, Robert Blake, Norman Fell, Martin Landau, Bert Remsen, (Harry) Dean Stanton, Gavin McLeod.   Excellent film about men who had to keep a hill at all costs. With scarcely any replacements or ammunition, this film shows true courage and determination. Highly recommended. **V, DVD**

NOTES

Vietnam War

Operation Dumbo Drop (1995) **1/2 D: Simon Wincer. Danny Glover, Ray Liotta, Denis Leary, Doug E. Doug, Corin Nemec, Dinh Thein Le.   In this Disney film a new by-the-book captain arrives to relieve Glover only to find himself having to replace the village elephant, killed by the Viet Cong. Includes information on the Ho Chi Minh Trail, informants for both sides (double agents), as well as scenery and terrain. Parents preview first for at least one spot, edit as needed, and see what you think. Mostly a fun film. **[PG] V**

Agony and the Ecstasy, The (1965) *** D: Carol Reed. Charlton Heston, Rex Harrison, Ciane Cilento. The story of Michelangelo's stormy artistic relationship with Pope Julius II over the painting of the Sistine Chapel. An interesting way to tie in this famous artist, his work and the Catholic church in history. (See Renaissance for more information.) **V**

Alexander's Ragtime Band (1938) *** D: Henry King. Tyrone Power, Alice Faye, Don Ameche, Ethel Merman, Jack Haley, Jean Hersholt, Helen Westley, John Carradine.   Filled with wonderful songs by Irving Berlin, Power is a band-leader, Ameche the piano player, and Faye the singer. It's been years since I've seen this, but cannot remember anything objectionable. Songs include "Easter Parade" and "Blue Skies." **V**

Alice in Wonderland (1951) *** (See Literature)

American In Paris, An (1951) ***1/2 D: Vincente Minnelli. Gene Kelly, Leslie Caron, Oscar Levant, Georges Guetary, Nina Foch.   Centered upon music by George Gershwin, this film broke ground in several ways. This ballet was unique in length (17 minutes) and combined modern dance, tap, "jitterbug," and classical ballet. It was the most expensive sequence ever produced, coming in at $450,000! It also introduced Leslie Caron, (a ballerina in France) whom Gene Kelly "discovered." The plot is of an American artist who is torn between Caron and Foch, but the dancing and music are wonderful. **V**

Anchor's Aweigh (1945) *** D: George Sidney. Gene Kelly, Frank Sinatra, Kathryn Grayson, Jose Iturbi.   Though this might fit better in the Family section, I placed it here because of the ground breaking use of animation with a live actor in the dance scene of Gene Kelly with Jerry the mouse. The studio did not want to let Kelly try this until Kelly consulted with Walt Disney who was working on the same idea for *The Three Caballeros*. The story is about two sailors on leave, with Kelly as a (somewhat) wolf who gets tamed by the lovely Kathryn Grayson. If parents are concerned, view first, but at least show this innovative scene. **V**

Annie (1982) **1/2 D: John Huston. Albert Finney, Carol Burnett, Aileen Quinn, Bernadette Peters, Tim Curry, Ann Reinking, Geoffrey Holder, Edward Herrman.   Film version of the Broadway musical which was based on the comic strip about a much loved orphan during the Depression years. Not as well done as the Broadway version, but acceptable. **[PG] V, DVD**

Annie Get Your Gun (1950) *** D: George Sidney. Betty Hutton, Howard Keel, Louis Calhern, Edward Arnold, Keenan Wynn.   Film version of Irving Berlin's famous Broadway musical based on the life of Annie Oakley. Though I wish they'd let Ethel Merman recreate her Broadway role, Hutton does an okay job, just brace yourself for her overblown, highly energetic performance. (She usually makes me tired!) But, this is still worth seeing for some great American musical theatre songs including "Anything You Can Do," and "There's No Business Like Show Business." **V, DVD**

Anything Goes (1956) ** D: Robert Lewis. Bing Crosby, Jeanmarie, Donald O'Connor, Mitzi Gaynor, Phil Harris, Kurt Kasznar.   Cole Porter's songs are as wonderful as ever in this story of show business partners who go to Europe seeking a fresh face for the leading lady of their next show. The problem is that they both find one! Though this is not the original story from Cole Porter's Broadway show, it's still fun.

April in Paris (1952) **1/2 D: David Butler. Doris Day, Ray Bolger, Claude Dauphin, Eve Miller, George Givot, Paul Harvey.   In a case of mistaken identity, Doris is given an all expense paid trip to Europe to star in a show which is being put on by the state department to improve Franco-American relations. Far fetched, but fun and includes Doris singing the famous "April in Paris" tune. **V**

April Love (1944) **1/2 (See Horses)

Babes in Arms (1939) **1/2 D: Busby Berkeley. Mickey Rooney, Judy Garland, Charles Winninger, Guy Kibbee, June Preisser, Douglas McPhail.   Based upon the Rodgers and Hart show with only one song from the original show preserved. What's left is the familiar "let's start a show" story as a vehicle for Rooney and Garland. Still, clean family fun. **V**

Babes in Toyland (1934) *** D: Gus Meins, Charles R. Rogers. Stan Laurel, Oliver Hardy, Charlotte Henry, Henry Kleinbach (Brandon), Felix Knight, Jean Darling, Johnny Downs, Marie Wilson.   Laurel and Hardy version of Victor Herbert's operetta. Very well done, but perhaps with some scary parts for the very young. View first to see if appropriate for your family. **V**

Babes in Toyland (1961) **1/2 D: Jack Donahue. Ray Bolger, Tommy Sands, Annette Funicello, Henry Calvin, Gene Sheldon, Tommy Kirk, Ed Wynn, Ann Jillian.   Disney version of Victor Herbert's operetta. Colorful and perhaps easier for the young to see.

Babes on Broadway (1941) **1/2 D: Busby Berkeley. Mickey Rooney, Judy Garland, Fay Bainter, Virginia Weidler, Richard Quine, Ray McDonald, Donna Reed.   Another Rooney/Garland film showcasing their talents as young MGM stars. Film debut of Margaret O'Brien who later starred with Judy in *Meet Me in St. Louis.* **V**

Baby Take a Bow (1934) ** D: Harry Lachman. Shirley Temple, James Dunn, Claire Trevor, Alan Dinehart, Ray Walker.   Shirley's first starring role boosted her to stardom, which you can understand; she's adorable. Though dated, it is still charming and one that most little girls will love. **V**

Band Wagon, The (1953) ***1/2 D: Vincente Minnelli. Fred Astaire, Cyd Charisse, Oscar Levant, Nanette Fabray, Jack Buchannan.   The story of a movie star making a come back on Broadway in a musical with a director of classical plays! The results are horrifying until the star and others in the cast take over and breathe life into the show making it what it should be, entertainment instead of a commentary on the state of mankind. Lots of fun song and dance numbers. A fine family film. **V**

Barkleys of Broadway, The (1949) *** D: Charles Walters. Fred Astaire, Ginger Rogers, Oscar Levant, Billie Burke, Gale Robbins.   Married partners are split by a manager who must later reunite them. Good song and dance scenes by Astaire and Rogers, as usual. Songs include: "They Can't Take That Away From Me," "You'd Be Hard to Replace." **V**

Because You're Mine (1952) **1/2 D: Alexander Hall. Mario Lanza, James Whitmore, Doretta Morrow, Dean Miller, Paula Corday, Jeff Donnell, Spring Byington, Don Porter, Eduard Franz, Bobby Van. Lanza, an opera star, is drafted and falls in love with the sister of his sergeant. Not the greatest plot, but fun for those who enjoy Lanza's singing. **V**

Belle of New York (1952) ** D: Charles Walters. Fred Astaire, Vera-Ellen, Marjorie Main, Keenan Wynn, Alice Pearce.   Vera-Ellen is a Salvation Army type of girl who meets Astaire, a playboy type during the "Gay '90s" in New York. **V**

Bells Are Ringing (1960) *** D: Vincente Minnelli. Judy Holliday, Dean Martin, Fred Clark, Eddie Foy, Jr., Jean Stapleton, Ruth Storey, Frank Gorshin, Gerry Mulligan.   Judy recreates her role in the hit Broadway play as an answering service operator who gets personally involved with her clients. Wonderful, generally unknown musical which includes the songs, "The Party's Over," "Just in Time," "Perfect Relationship," "Drop That Name," and "Simple Little System." **V**

Benny Goodman Story, The (1955) *** D: Valentine Davies. Steve Allen, Donna Reed, Herbert Anderson, Herbert Anderson, Hy Averback, Berta Gersten, Robert F. Simon, Sammy Davis, Sr., Gene Krupa, Lionel Hampton, Teddy Wilson, Harry James, Ziggy Elman, Martha Tilton.   Though not entirely factual, this gives the story of Benny Goodman's rise to fame as a musician and his unusual courtship of the woman who became his wife. The music is terrific and the children will get to see some real-life musical greats. **V**

Big Broadcast of 1936, The (1935) **1/2 D: Norman Taurog. Jack Oakie, George Burns, Gracie Allen, Lyda Roberti, Henry Wadsworth, Wendy Barrie, C. Henry Gordon, Ethel Merman, Charlie Ruggles, Mary Boland, Bill "Bojangles" Robinson, The Nicholas Brothers. No plot to speak of, but some show business greats including the original Amos 'n Andy. (Greeman Gosden and Charles Correll, in blackface) Worth more as a piece of history than as a movie. Parents view first and extract what you think important to see.

Billy Rose's Jumbo (1962) ***1/2 D: Charles Walters. Doris Day, Stephen Boyd, Jimmy Durante, Martha Raye, Dean Jagger. Wonderful family film about rival circuses which includes songs by Rodgers and Hart. Durante owns the "Pop Wonder Circus" which is always having a hard time meeting ends due to bad luck and Pop's propensity to gamble. Daughter Doris is constantly trying to second guess Pop and circumvent financial disaster. The main asset of their show: Jumbo the elephant, which the other circus wants badly. Enter Boyd as the agent for the other show, who also carries another secret. Main problem? He falls for Doris. A fun look at the circus for kids and the entire family. **V**

Birth of the Blues (1941) *** D: Victor Schertzinger. Bing Crosby, Brian Donlevy, Carolyn Lee, Eddie (Rochester) Anderson, Mary Martin. Title describes this fictional account of Bing organizing a jazz band in New Orleans (N'Awlins, if you please!) and has some great jazz songs in it, including "St. Louis Blues," "Melancholy Baby," as well as the title song. **V**

Blue Skies (1946) *** D: Stuart Heisler. Fred Astaire, Bing Crosby, Joan Caulfield, Billy De Wolfe, Olga Dan Juan, Frank Faylen. Astaire and Crosby are former show-biz partners with Caulfield in the middle. Lovely Irving Berlin songs make this a joy to watch. Songs include "Puttin' on the Ritz," "A Couple of Song and Dance Men," as well as the title song. **V**

Born to Dance (1936) *** D: Roy Del Ruth. Eleanor Powell, James Stewart, Virginia Bruce, Una Merkel, Sid Silvers, Frances Langford, Raymond Walburn, Buddy Ebsen, Reginald Gardiner. Cole Porter's music with great tap numbers by Powell and Stewart sings! Fine family film. **V**

Boyfriend, The (1971-British) **1/2 D: Ken Russell. Twiggy, Christopher Gable, Moyra Fraser, Max Adrian, Vladke, Sheybal, Georgina Hale, Tommy Tune, cameo by Glenda Jackson. Film version of the stage play, this is a story within a story that recreates some of the Hollywood musicals Busby Berkley style, as well as being a spoof of the 1920s. It's been years since I've seen this, (on stage or the film) so it might be best for parents to preview this one first. **[G] V**

Boys from Syracuse, The (1940) **1/2 D: A. Edward Sutherland. Allan Jones, Joe Penner, Martha Raye, Rosemary Lane, Irene Hervey, Eric Blore. Film version of Rodgers and Hart Broadway musical based upon Shakespeare's *Comedy of Errors* which he based upon *The Menaechmi* by Plautus. This is the only film version of any of these plays (set in Ancient Greece) and gives the basics of the story of two sets of twins separated at birth and the mix-ups that happen when one set comes to the town in which the other set resides. Parents should view this one first. Songs include "Falling in Love With Love," and "This Can't Be Love."

Brigadoon (1954) *** D: Vincente Minnelli. Gene Kelly, Van Johnson, Cyd Charisse, Elaine Stewart, Barry Jones, Hugh Laing. Based upon the Broadway musical by Lerner and Lowe, the story is about a Scottish town which only comes to earth once every hundred years and the American hunters who stumble upon it and cannot understand what they are seeing and experiencing. Though this has some faults, (discussion potential, here), it also has lots of charm and the redeeming qualities of unselfishly laying down one's life for others, how our choices affect others, and some beautiful music and lovely dances. **V**

Broadway Melody of 1938 (1937) **1/2 D: Roy Del Ruth. Robert Taylor, Eleanor Powell, George Murphy, Binnie Barnes, Buddy Ebsen, Judy Garland, Sophie Tucker, Charles Igor Gorin, Raymond Walburn, Robert Benchley, Willie Howard, Billy Gilbert. Worth seeing for Garland's famous, "Dear Mr. Gable" song. Parents should preview first. **V**

Broadway Melody of 1940 (1940) *** D: Norman Taurog. Fred Astaire, Eleanor Powell, George Murphy, Frank Morgan.   Cole Porter's songs set in a light story of dance partner rivalry. Fine footwork by the stars and wonderful dance numbers include Porter's "Begin the Beguine." **V**

Buddy Holly Story, The (1978) *** D: Steve Rash. Gary Busey, Charles Martin Smith, Don Stroud, Maria Richwine, Amy Johnston, Conrad Janis, Dick O'Neill, William Jordan.   Busey does a fine job of portraying legendary Holly and also (along with Smith and Stroud) actually plays and sings! Due to some of the content, parents definitely need to view this one first and decide whether or not it meets with their approval. **[PG] V, DVD**

Bundle of Joy (1956) **1/2 D: Norman Taurog. Eddie Fisher, Debbie Reynolds, Adolphe Menjou, Tommy Noonan.   Musical remake of *Bachelor Mother*. (see Family Films) Made when Fisher and Reynolds were married in real life. **V**

Bye Bye Birdie (1963) *** D: George Sidney. Janet Leigh, Dick Van Dyke, Ann-Margret, Maureen Stapleton, Paul Lynde, Jesse Pearson, Bobby Rydell, Ed Sullivan.   Fun musical about an Elvis type character who comes to small town to deliver "One Last Kiss" (also a song title) to adoring fan (Ann-Margret) before departing for the army via the draft. This causes unforeseen problems with her family, her boyfriend, as well as the songwriter (Van Dyke) who really wants to be a biochemist. Filled with great tunes, this is a film I think most will like. If the subject matter concerns you, view first. Songs include "One Last Kiss," "Put On a Happy Face," "The Telephone Song," "A Lot of Livin'," "One Boy," "Bye, Bye Birdie," "Everything is Rosie," "Lovely to be a Woman." **V, DVD**

Cabin in the Sky (1943) *** D: Vincente Minnelli. Eddie "Rochester" Anderson, Lena Horne, Ethel Waters, Louis Armstrong, Rex Ingram, Duke Ellington and His Orchestra, The Hall Johnson Choir. Dated black musical about good vs. evil in competition for the soul of "Little Joe" with a bit of racism, too. Based on the Broadway play, this is as much filled with the historical great black entertainers as anything else. Preview for content. **V**

Calamity Jane (1953) *** D: David Butler. Doris Day, Howard Keel, Allyn (Ann) McLerie, Philip Carey, Gale Robbins, Dick Wesson, Paul Harvey.   A fun tale of rowdy, boisterous Calamity Jane (Day) and Wild Bill Hickok (Keel), who only realize their feelings for each other when "Ca-lam" decides to spruce up and become more feminine. Lots of fun for the family with the Oscar winning song, "Secret Love." **V**

Call Me Madam (1953) *** D: Walter Lang. Ethel Merman, Donald O'Connor, George Sanders, Vera-Ellen, Billy DeWolfe, Walter Slezak.   Merman recreates her role from the Broadway play which was loosely based upon the life of Perle Mesta, a famous Washington hostess and Liechtenstein ambassador; thus the song, "Hostess With the Mostest." Irving Berlin was a genius with counter-melodies: two independent melodies, when put together, create harmony. This same technique is used in opera. This musical includes my favorite Irving Berlin duet, "You're Just in Love."

Carefree (1938) *** D: Mark Sandrich. Fred Astaire, Ginger Rogers, Ralph Bellamy, Luella Gear, Jack Carson, Franklin Pangborn.   Wacky comedy has Astaire as a psychiatrist who must psychoanalyze Rogers accompanied by Irving Berlin's music. Preview if concerned about the content. Songs include "Change Partners," "I Used to Be Color Blind." **V**

Carnival of the Animals *(Carnival des Animeaux)* **[NR]** PBS video hosted by Gary Burgess (MASH's "Radar") which presents this wonderful musical "zoological fantasy" by Camille Saint-Saën to children. This piece of music is a wonderful one to use to introduce certain instruments of the orchestra to children and also presents musical imagery in a terrific, simple way for children to understand. Saint-Saën used two pianos dueling to portray pianists, the marimba to portray "bones," for example, and richly text painted so that the children can "hear" the animals. Included are a majestic lion, braying mules, a dancing elephant, bouncy kangaroos, a cuckoo, and fish. Even fossils join in with a fast and rattly dance and Anna Pavlova's famous, "The Swan," which is exquisitely beautiful. This does not contain the complete work, so get a copy to hear it in its entirety. HIGHLY recommended! **V**

Carousel (1956) ***1/2 D: Henry King. Gordon MacRae, Shirley Jones, Cameron Mitchell, Barbara Ruick, Claramae Turner, Robert Rounseville, Gene Lockhart.   Wonderful film version of the famous Rodgers and Hammerstein play. Julie Jordan (Jones) works in a mill until one night she meets a barker from a carousel, Billy Bigelow. (MacRae) They marry, but he's no good and lives selfishly. He doesn't "wake up" until Julie tells him they're going to have a baby, whereupon he takes the easy way out and dies in the process of a holdup. The film is done in "heaven time" as the "Star Keeper" (wonderful Lockhart) gives him a chance to go back to earth, help his child and try to straighten out the mess he made. Though this might sound "new agey" or weird, it truly isn't. It is a lovely story and raises some interesting discussion points about prejudice, character, and love along with some great R & H songs. Songs include "If I Loved You," "June is Bustin' Out All Over," "Mister Snow," "Soliloquy," "When You Walk Alone." **V**

Chitty Chitty Bang Bang (1968) **1/2 D: Ken Hughes. Dick Van Dyke, Sally Ann Howes, Lionel Jeffries, Gert Frobe, Anna Quayle, Benny Hill.   My daughters loved this film as young elementary aged children. Van Dyke is an unsuccessful, though highly imaginative widowed inventor whose two children meet a gorgeous lady, the daughter of a sweet-making mogul. The children are in love with a car in a junk yard and in order to finance purchasing it for them Prof. Potts (Van Dyke) comes up with a candy with holes in it, called "Toot Sweets" (also a song). They get the car, Potts refurbishes it and it becomes "Chitty Chitty Bang Bang," which takes them on a marvelous adventure. Songs include "Hush-a-bye Mountain," "Me Ol' Bamboo," "Truly Scrumptious," and the title song. **[G]   V, DVD**

Cinderella (1950) *** (See Family Films) Animated version.

Cinderella (1964) TVM (See Rodgers and Hammerstein's Cinderella in Music/Arts.)

Coal Miner's Daughter (1980) ***1/2 D: Michael Apted. Sissy Spacek, Tommy Lee Jones, Beverly D'Angelo, Levon Helm, Phyllis Boyens, Ernest Tubbs.   Biography of country legend Loretta Lynn MUST be edited for children. The most amazing part of this is that Spacek (who deservedly won an Oscar) did her own singing instead of being dubbed by Lynn! **[PG] V**

Cover Girl (1944) *** D: Charles Vidor. Rita Hayworth, Gene Kelly, Lee Bowman, Phil Silvers, Jinx Falkenburg, Eve Arden, Otto Kruger, Anita Colby.   Rita, Kelly, and Silvers are friends and performers in a small theatre. Rita finds out about a magazine looking for a cover girl so she goes to give it a try and just happens to be the epitome of what the owner wanted—a girl who looked like a girl in his past who got away – and who turns out to be her grandmother! Lovely costumer with great songs by Jerome Kern and Ira Gershwin including "Long Ago and Far Away." **V**

Daddy Long Legs (1955) **1/2 D: Jean Negulesco. Fred Astaire, Leslie Caron, Thelma Ritter, Fred Clark, Terry Moore, Larry Keating.   A wealthy man anonymously sponsors a French orphan's education and she falls in love with him. This is a May-December romance, with some good dance numbers. You'll have to decide if it's appropriate for your family. **V**

Daughter of Rosie O'Grady (1950) **1/2 D: David Butler. June Haver, Gordon MacRae, Debbie Reynolds, Gene Nelson, James Barton, S. Z. Sakall, Jane Darwell.   Period musical with plenty of songs from turn-of–the-century America. Pretty costume film.

Deep in My Heart (1954) *** D: Stanley Donan. Jose Ferrer, Merle Oberon, Helen Traubel, Doe Avedon, Tamara Toumanova, Paul Stewart, Douglas Fowley, Jim Backus; guest stars Walter Pidgeon, Paul Henreid, Rosemary Clooney, Gene and Fred Kelly, Jane Powell, Vic Damone, Ann Miller, Cyd Charisse, Howard Keel, Tony Martin.   Based

upon the life of operetta composer Sigmund Romberg, includes many highlights of his music (much of which you have heard before) and the only film appearance of the Kelly brothers. **V**

Desert Song (1953) **1/2 D: H. Bruce Humberstone. Kathryn Grayson, Gordon McRae, Steve Cochran, Raymond Massey, William Conrad, Dick Wesson. Film version of Romberg's operetta, this tells the story of an American (McRae) who is the secret leader of the good natives (the Riffs) in battle with the evil Arabs. Some lovely music. **V**

Diamond Horseshoe (1945) **1/2 D: George Seaton. Betty Grable, Dick Haymes, Phil Silvers, William Gaxton, Beatrice Kay, Carmen Cavallaro, Margaret Dumont. Colorful costume musical about Grable making the difficult choice of a life of wealth and ease or love and financial struggle. Songs include "The More I See of You," and "I Wish I Knew."

Dixie (1943) *** D: A. Edward Sutherland. Bing Crosby, Dorothy Lamour, Billy De Wolfe, Marjorie Reynolds, Lynne Overman, Raymond Walburn, Eddie Foy, Jr., Grant Mitchell. Supposed biography of famous pioneer minstrel Dan Emmett, composer of the title song. (who was black!) Parents preview.

Doctor Doolittle (1967) **1/2 D: Richard Fleischer. Rex Harrison, Samantha Eggar, Anthony Newley, Richard Attenborough, Pieter Bull, Geoffrey Holder. The story of the doctor who can talk to the animals and the Oscar winning song are included in this lovely, colorful costumer for children. Clean and fun for the entire family and *definitely* the version you want to see over the Eddie Murphy one. **V, DVD**

Dolly Sister, The (1945) **1/2 D: Irving Cummings. Betty Grable, John Payne, June Haver, S. Z. Sakall, Reginald Gardiner, Frank Latimore. About a sister vaudeville act set during the period of WWI. Lovely revival of old songs with the angle of the meeting and marrying of each sister's mate included. **V**

Down Argentine Way (1940) *** D: Irving Cummings. Don Ameche, Betty Grable, Carmen Miranda, Charlotte Greenwood, J. Carrol Naish, Henry Stephenson, Leonid Kinskey. One of the best 20th Century Fox musicals ever made. This film boosted Grable to stardom in the story that has her falling in love with Ameche, who plays an Argentine horse breeder. Miranda is at her best in this one, wild hats, platform shoes and all. Watch for the amazing Nicholas Brothers dance. A beautiful costumer. **V**

Do You Love Me? (1946) **1/2 D: Gregory Ratoff. Maureen O'Hara, Dick Haymes, Harry James, Reginald Gardiner, Alma Kruger. Cinderella story of plain O'Hara as dean of a Music School en route to New York when she meets band leader James who insults her, awakening her femininity. She undergoes a transformation to a beauty and then meets Haymes when she wishes to "show" James that he was wrong about her. Both men court her and the best man wins her in the end. Fun and sweet.

DuBarry Was a Lady (1943) *** D: Roy Del Rio. Red Skelton, Lucille Ball, Gene Kelly, Virginia O'Brien, Rags Ragland, Zero Mostel, Donald Meek, George Givot, Louise Beavers, Tommy Dorsey and His Orchestra. Nightclub worker Skelton loves Ball from afar. He drinks a Mickey Finn and dreams he's back in time as Louis XVI and has to deal with Madame DuBarry (Ball). Colorful costume film with title of Cole Porter's Broadway show, but only one of the songs remains intact ("Friendship"). Does include the Dorsey band and the amazing Buddy Rich on the drums doing "Well Git It." Part is done like a vaudeville show giving the opportunity for several cameos. Generally a fun film. Does include Mostel as "Rami the Swami," who looks into his crystal ball and tells fortunes. Preview if concerned. **V**

Easter Parade (1948) ***1/2 D: Charles Walters. Judy Garland, Fred Astaire, Peter Law ford, Ann Miller, Jules Munshin. Wonderful Irving Berlin musical about dancer Astaire, who is ditched by his partner (Miller) and picks Garland to be the new partner whom he must train. Music includes "Stepping Out with My Baby," "Shaking the Blues Away," "A Couple of Swells," and the title song. Clean family fun. **V**

Eddie Duchin Story, The (1956) ** D: George Sidney. Tyrone Power, Kim Novak, Victoria Shaw, James Whitmore. *Bio of Hollywood pianist-bandleader of the 1930s and*

40s, with tragic ending. **V**

Emperor's Waltz, The (1948) **1/2 D: Billy Wilder. Bing Crosby, Joan Fontaine, Roland Culver, Lucile Watson, Richard Haydn, Sig Ruman. Bing sells record players to royalty in Franz Joseph's Austria. Parents might wish to preview. **V**

Everything I Have Is Yours (1952) ** D: Robert Z. Leonard. Marge and Gower Champion, Dennis O'Keefe, Eduard Franz. Champions play a dance team who have finally gotten their big break and then discover that they are expecting. **V**

Fabulous Dorseys, The (1947) ** D: Alfred E. Green. Tommy Dorsey, Jimmy Dorsey, Janet Blair, Paul Whiteman, William Lundigan. Supposed "biography" of famous band leading brothers. Does have some nice music and highlights of famous musicians. Parents might wish to preview. **V**

Fancy Pants (1950) *** D: George Marshall. Mr. Robert Hope (formerly Bob), Lucille Ball, Bruce Cabot, Jack Kirkwood, Lea Pennman, Eric Blore. Musical remake of *Ruggles of Red Gap* (see Family) with Bob playing the English valet and Lucy the nouveau riche wildcat heading to her western home. **V**

Fantasia (1940) ***1/2 D: Ben Sharpteen. Leo Stokowski and the Philadelphia Orchestra. Narrated by Deems Taylor. Walt Disney's groundbreaking film of eight animated vignettes accompanied by music. I do want to caution parents to view this first. This film is always highly recommended and when one understands the technical advancements made in this one film, it is understandable. However, content wise, this film has some items that parents should view first. (The Sorcerer's Apprentice, A Night on Bald Mountain, for example) Parts have been know to give nightmares to small children. If you wish to use it, it is easy to edit and show just the vignettes you wish as it is a composite film. **V**

Fiddler on the Roof (1971) ***1/2 D: Norman Jewison. Topol, Norma Crane, Leonard Frey, Molly Picon, Paul Mann, Rosalind Harris, Michele Marsh, Neva Small, Candice Bonstein, Paul (Michael) Glaser. Wonderful film adaptation of the Broadway play with choreography by Jerome Robbins and violin by Issac Stern. This is the story of Tevye, a Jewish man who lives in a small Russian village of Anatevka. He has a very difficult wife, and three daughters of marriageable age. Covers the life of this family during the time of the Russian Revolution, their Jewish community and customs, and some unexpected things, too. This is a dark and somewhat depressing story, but the customs, treatment of the Jews and history seem fairly accurate. Worth seeing at least once. **V**

Finian's Rainbow (1968) ***1/2 D: Francis Ford Coppola. Fred Astaire, Petula Clark, Tommy Steele, Keenan Wynn, Al Freeman, Jr., Don Francks, Barbara Hancock. Burton Lane-E.Y. Harburg ("Over the Rainbow") musical about an Irishman and his daughter, who come to the southern part of the U.S. in possession of a leprechaun's pot of gold. Somewhat dated today, but still a wonderful handling of material in film which was way ahead of its day - racial prejudice. A fun, lively story with some great musical numbers. There is one scene in which Og, the leprechaun uses a "spell." We easily edit this and the film still views well. Family fun and good discussion material. **[G]** **V**

Five Pennies, The (1959) **1/2 D: Melville Shavelson. Danny Kaye, Barbara Bel Geddes, Tuesday Weld, Louis Armstrong, Bob Crosby (Bing's brother), Harry Guardino, Ray Anthony, Shelley Manne, Bobby Troup. Biography of coronet player and band leader, Red Nichols. Good music with some great trumpet work by Louis Armstrong. A family film and one of my 17 year old's favorites. **V**

Flower Drum Song (1961) ** D: Henry Koster. Nancy Kwan, James Shigeta, Miyoshi Umeki, Juanita Hall, Benson Fong. Rogers and Hammerstein musical from the Broadway version. Nice songs and good choreography tell the story of San Francisco's Chinatown and the problem of transitioning between tradition and current society. **V**

Follow the Fleet (1936) *** D: Mark Sandrich. Fred Astaire, Ginger Rogers, Randolph Scott, Harriet Hilliard (Nelson), Astrid Allwyn, Betty Grable. Sisters Rogers and Hilliard

are trying to save their father's boat. Sailors Astaire and Scott help them by putting on a show, but also falling in love with them. Wonderful Irving Berlin songs are part of this fun. Scott is a bit of a stinker, but Hilliard reforms him. **V**

Footlight Serenade (1942) *** D: Gregory Ratoff. Betty Grable, Victor Mature, John Payne, Jane Wyman, Phil Silvers, James Gleason, Mantan Moreland, Cobina Wright, Jr.   Boxer Mature, who is cocky and a bit arrogant woos Grable not knowing that she's engaged to Payne. Twists and turns and lots of backstage fun. **V**

For Me and My Gal (1942) **1/2 D: Busby Berkeley. Judy Garland, Gene Kelly, Marta Eggerth, Ben Blue, Horace McNally, Keenan Wynn.   Musical story of vaudevillians who want to play the Palace Theatre, circa WWI. This was Kelly's film debut. Clean family film. **V**

For the First Time (1959) **1/2 D: Rudolph Maté. Mario Lanza, Johanna Von Koszlan,. Kurt Kasznar, Zsa Zsa Gabor, Hans Sohnker.   Lanza plays an opera star who falls in love with a deaf girl and takes her to doctor after doctor to find someone to help her hear. Lanza's last film appearance, though he later did the singing for *The Student Prince.* **V**

42nd Street (1933) **** D: Lloyd Bacon. Warner Baxter, Ruby Keeler, George Brent, Bebe Daniels, Dick Powell, Guy Kibbee, Una Merkel, Ginger Rogers, Ned Sparks, George E. Stone.   THE definitive backstage musical that has experienced a comeback on Broadway in recent years. Old story of director with everything to lose when leading lady (Daniels) sprains ankle and novice (Keeler) has to fill in for "the show to go on." Filled with (then) innovative Busby Berkeley production numbers, which are still amazing to behold. Songs include "Young and Healthy," "You're Getting to Be a Habit With Me," and "Shuffle Off to Buffalo." Parents may wish to cut parts, so view first. **V, DVD**

Four Jills in a Jeep (1944) **1/2 D: William A. Seiter. Kay Francis, Carole Landis, Martha Raye, Mitzi Mayfair, Phil Silvers, Dick Haymes, Jimmy Dorsey and His Orchestra: guest stars Betty Grable, Alice Faye, Carmen Miranda, George Jessel.   The reenactment of the four leading ladies actual experiences entertaining G.I.s overseas during WWII. Clean, inspiring, family fun. **V**

Funny Face (1957) ***1/2 D: Stanley Donan. Audrey Hepburn, Fred Astaire, Kay Thompson, Michel Auclair, Suzy Parker, Ruta Lee.   Show with wonderful Gershwin tunes about a bookworm (Hepburn) who is "discovered" by a fashion photographer (Astaire) and offered a trip to Paris to be a model for a magazine spread. She takes them up on the offer only to meet a philosopher of existentialism, in which she is interested. (a good topic for discussion, as it's still around) She finds that he's not all she thought him to be, while Astaire is. Songs include, "How Long Has This Been Going On," " 'S Wonderful," "He Loves and She Loves," and the title tune. **V**

Funny Girl (1968) **** D: William Wyler. Barbra Streisand, Omar Sharif, Kay Medford, Anne Francis, Walter Pidgeon, Lee Allen, Gerald Mohr.   Streisand recreates her Broadway role and won an Oscar in her film debut as Fanny Brice, singer-comedienne, who was very successful on stage, but whose private life was not. Not a great biography, but a wonderful musical with fine songs by Jule Styne ("People," "Don't Rain on My Parade," "The Greatest Star") and "Second Hand Rose," which is from the period of Brice's life. ("My Man," Brice's theme song is mysteriously missing as a real number in the film.) Parents should watch this first as there are some scenes and at least one song which should be edited. **[G] V**

Gang's All Here, The (1943) **1/2 D: Busby Berkeley. Alice Faye, Carmen Miranda, Phil Baker, Benny Goodman and Orchestra, Eugene Pallette, Charlotte Greenwood, Edward Everett Horton, Tony DeMarco, James Ellison, Sheila Ryan.   Wartime musical with Baker headed off to war while both Faye and Ryan believe that he's engaged to them. Some great Berkeley styled musical numbers include the classic "The Lady With the Tutti-Frutti Hat," as well as "The Polka Dot Polka," "No Love, No Nothin'."

George Balanchine's The Nutcracker (1993) **1/2 D: Emile Ardolino. Darci Kistler,

Damian Woetzel, Kyra Nichols, Bart Robinson Cook, Macaulay Culkiin, Jessica Lynn Cohen; narrated by Kevin Kline.   Based upon the famous Hans Christian Anderson tale, this film includes Balanchine's beautiful choreography. [G] **V**

Girl Crazy (1943) ***1/2 D: Norman Taurog. Mickey Rooney, Judy Garland, Gil Stratton, Robert E. Strickland, "Rags" Ragland, June Allyson, Nancy Walker, Guy Kibbee, Tommy Dorsey and his Orchestra.   Great Gershwin stage show comes to film with songs intermingled in tale of Rooney being sent west to forget girls. He and Garland pal up and the rest is about fun song and dance numbers. Score includes, "I Got Rhythm," "Embraceable You," "But Not For Me." **V**

Girl Most Likely, The (1957) **1/2 D: Mitchell Leisen. Jane Powell, Cliff Robertson, Keith Andes, Tommy Noonan, Kaye Ballard, Una Merkel.   Powell is courted and proposed to by three guys and must decide which one she'll marry. Bright and breezy costumer with energetic choreography by Gower Champion. **V**

Girl of the Golden West, The (1938) **1/2 D: Robert Z. Leonard. Jeanette MacDonald, Nelson Eddy, Walter Pidgeon, Leo Carrillo, Buddy Ebsen, Leonard Penn.   Film version of Romberg operetta with predictable romance between good girl MacDonald and outlaw Eddy. **V**

Give a Girl a Break (1953) **1/2 D: Stanley Donan. Marge and Gower Champion, Debbie Reynolds, Helen Wood, Bob Fosse, Kurt Kasznar, Richard Anderson, William Ching, Larry Keating.   Three young women compete for starring Broadway role. Highlight is getting to see choreography greats Gower Champion and Bob Fosse dancing together. Music By Ira Gershwin and Burton Lane. **V**

Glass Slipper, The (1955) **1/2 D: Charles Walters. Leslie Caron, Michael Wilding, Keenan Wynn, Estelle Winwood, Elsa Lancaster, Amanda Blake.   Off-beat version of the Cinderella story still has its own charm. See what you think. **V**

Glenn Miller Story, The (1954) *** D: Anthony Mann. James Stewart, June Allyson, Charles Drake, George Tobias, Harry Morgan, Frances Langford, Louis Armstrong, Gene Krupa.   A somewhat fictionalized story of this great big band leader with plenty of his wonderful music. The end is true, the plane he was taking during WWII was lost at sea. **V**

Godspell (1973) *** D: David Greene. Victor Garber, David Haskell, Jerry Sroka, Lynne Thigpen, Katie Hanley, Robin Lamont.   Based upon the play, this puts into modern day settings the story of Yeshua, (Jesus) his disciples and includes some fine music ("Day by Day," "Beautiful City," "All For The Best," "Turn Back, Oh Man," "On The Willows") by Stephen Schwartz. Though confusing at times, there is still enough to redeem it and make it worth seeing. There are only three things I really dislike: the double casting of John the Baptist/Judas Iscariot, a superman emblem on Yeshua's shirt and the last scene in which Yeshua is not shown as risen, though it is implied. One item of note is that both Broadway and Hollywood produced this musical which is based upon the gospel of Matthew! [G]   **V**

Good News (1947) *** D: Charles Walters. June Allyson, Peter Lawford, Patricia Marshall, Joan McCracken, Ray McDonald, Mel Torme.   College musical of bookworm Allyson catching the star football player, Lawford. Songs include "Varsity Drag," "The Best Things in Life are Free," and "Just Imagine." Nice costumer by MGM. **V**

Great Caruso, The (1951) *** D: Richard Thorpe. Mario Lanza, Ann Blyth, Jarmila Novotna, Dorothy Kirsten.   Based loosely upon the life of the legendary tenor, this film is very fun and includes some great music. A good way to introduce the world of opera to your children. **V**

Great Ziegfeld, The (1936) *** D: Robert Z. Leonard. William Powell, Myrna Loy, Luise Rainer, Frank Morgan, Fanny Brice, Virginia Bruce, Reginald Owen, Ray Bolger, Stanley Morner (Dennis Morgan).   Well done biography of the flamboyant impresario (played by Powell), who wanted a show which was spectacular in every way. Includes Seeing the real Fanny Brice who really performed in the Ziegfeld Follies. **V**

Guys and Dolls (1955) ***1/2 D: Joseph L. Mankiewicz. Marlon Brando, Jean Simmons, Frank Sinatra, Vivian Blaine, Stubby Kaye.   Film version of the hit Broadway play based upon characters by Damon Runyon. Brando is blatantly miscast, but was a top box office draw at the time and thus, landed the role. Simmons was also not the best choice for the female lead, but such are the politics of Hollywood. This is the story of Sister Sarah Brown and the Save A Soul Mission, who are trying to bring salvation to the people in their area of New York. These characters are mostly gamblers, con men and show girls. Sinatra plays Nathan Detroit, who runs a floating crap-game and has been engaged to Adelaide (Blaine) for 14 years! Though this could lend itself to the seamy, this show is NOT that way. It is filled with good triumphing over evil and Sister Sarah reforming the gambler of ALL gamblers, Sky Masterson (Brando). The leads were all Hollywood stars except for Vivian Blaine, who beautifully recreates her Broadway roll as Adelaide, as does Stubby Kaye as "Nicely Nicely" (thank you!). The music from this show is well known, and tuneful. Songs include "Luck Be a Lady," "Sit Down, You're Rockin' the Boat," "If I Were a Bell," "Guys and Dolls," "Fugue for Tinhorns," and the famous "Adelaide's Lament," though the most famous hit from the Broadway version, "A Bushel and a Peck" was mysteriously omitted. **V, DVD**

Hans Christian Anderson (1952) *** D: Charles Vidor. Danny Kaye, Farley Granger, Jeanmaire, Roland Petit.   This charming film is a great one for the entire family. It has wonderful Frank Loesser (*Guys and Dolls*) songs including "Inchworm" (All children should know this for help with math. It helped both of mine.) "Ugly Duckling," "Thumbelina," "Copenhagen," etc. **V**

Happiest Millionaire, The (1967) **1/2 D: Norman Tokar. Fred MacMurray, Tommy Steele, Greer Garson, Geraldine Page, Gladys Cooper, Hermione Bradley, Lesley Ann Warren, John Davidson.   Wacky Disney musical about the household of eccentric millionaire MacMurray who runs a boxing school and *Bible* class, *and* he keeps pet alligators in the conservatory! His daughter (Warren) knows more about boxing than about being a young lady and is sent off to school for polish where she meets and falls for Davidson. My favorite is Tommy Steele, who plays the intrepid and lively butler. A family film with lots of unusual content and the last film Walt Disney personally oversaw. **V, DVD**

Harvey Girls, The (1946) ***1/2 D: George Sidney. Judy Garland, Ray Bolger, John Hodiak, Angela Lansbury, Preston Foster, Virginia O'Brien, Marjorie Main, Cyd Charisse.   Judy and the virtuous Harvey Girls come with the railroad as it expands West in order to open railroad cafés and also bring the standards of civilization to the rowdy frontier. Lansbury plays the opposing side of saloon girls, and virtue meets "bad girls" head on, though this is highly stylized as most all MGM musicals were. Includes Oscar winning song "On the Atchison, Topeka and the Santa Fe." Good fun for the family. **V**

Hello Dolly! (1969) *** D: Gene Kelly. Barbra Streisand, Walter Matthau, Michael Crawford, E. J. Peaker, Marianne McAndrew, Tommy Tune, Louis Armstrong, Danny Lockin.   From the Thornton Wilder story *The Matchmaker* upon which the Broadway play was based. (in which Carol Channing had the title role) The Jerry Herman score has some changes, but most songs are intact. Dolly Levi (Streisand) plays a matchmaker who ends up getting herself matched. Some may not recognize the head clerk in Horace Vandegelder's store as the "Phantom of the Opera," but it is the same Michael Crawford, just much younger. Perhaps the most incongruent part of the film is the end scene in which Jewish Dolly is seen entering a protestant church! Still, a fun film for the family. **V**

Hello Frisco, Hello (1943) ** D: H. Bruce Humberstone. Alice Faye, John Payne, Jack Oakie, Lynn Bari, Laird Cregar, June Havoc, Ward Bond.   Payne gets too big for his britches as a Barbary Coast entrepreneur, causing pain to those who care about him and try to open his eyes to what he's doing. Includes Oscar winning song, "You'll Never Know." **V**

Here Come the Waves (1944) *** D: Mark Sandrich. Bing Crosby, Betty Hutton, Sonny Tufts.   Wartime musical with Crosby as a popular crooner who wants to serve in the Navy like his father. Hutton plays twin sisters, one of whom is crazy about him, the other whom he is crazy about. When the first one finds out that he is supposed to ship out, she sends a letter to command suggesting using him in a show to recruit for the Waves! He isn't happy and decides to work fast and furious to get the show up and film his parts so he can join his unit at sea. There follows a series of mishaps and music by the famous team of Harold Arlen-Johnny Mercer, including "Old Black Magic," "Ac-cent-u-ate the Positive," which is performed in (now illegal) blackface. Fun film for the family. **V**

Higher and Higher (1943) **1/2 D: Tim Whelan. Michele Morgan, Jack Haley, Frank Sinatra, Leon Errol, Marcy McGuire, Victor Borge, Mary Wickes, Mel Torme.   Once wealthy Errol informs servants that he is now broke. They come up with a plan to raise money by launching one of them into society as Errol's relative, recently arrived in town. Morgan is elected, but has a crush on next door neighbor Sinatra, playing himself in his film debut. Interesting twists and clean fun for all with an neat solution for the problems facing Errol's household. **V**

High Society (1956) *** D: Charles Walters. Bing Crosby, Grace Kelly, Frank Sinatra, Celeste Holm, John Lund, Louis Calhern, Louis Armstrong.   Musical remake of *The Philadelphia Story*. Kelly was never lovelier as a socialite who is planning to remarry when ex-husband (Crosby) reenters her life. Sinatra and Holm play a reporter and photographer who are there to cover her wedding. Very up and up production with some alcohol and inference to immorality, but nothing happens or is shown. Includes some wonderful Cole Porter songs, "True Love," "Did You Evah?" as well as "Now You Has Jazz" with Crosby and Armstrong. This was Kelly's last role before becoming the Princess of Monaco. Preview.   **V**

Hit the Deck (1955) **1/2 D: Roy Rowland. Jane Powell, Tony Martin, Debbie Reynolds, Ann Miller, Vic Damone, Russ Tamblyn, Walter Pidgeon, Kay Armen, Gene Raymond.   Technicolor remake of *Follow the Fleet* most famous for Vincent Youman's song, "Hallelujah." Nice costume film. **V**

Hitting a New High (1937) **1/2 D: Raoul Walsh. Lily Pons, Jack Oakie, Edward Everett Horton, Lucille Ball, Eric Blore, Eduardo Ciannelli.   Not a great story, but worth watching just to hear the amazing coloratura Lily Pons sing. (See *I Dream Too Much*, below, for explanation.) The title refers to her voice, not the story, which is a musical romance. Parents may wish to preview first.

Holiday in Mexico (1946) **1/2 D: George Sidney. Walter Pidgeon, Ilona Massey, Roddy McDowall, Jose Iturbi, Xavier Cugat, Jane Powell.   Powell plays the daughter of an ambassador who is falling in love while her father finds love himself. Lovely songs by a very young Powell. Pretty costume film. **V**

Holiday Inn (1942) ***1/2 D: Mark Sandrick. Bing Crosby, Fred Astaire, Marjorie Reynolds, Virginia Dale, Walter Abel, Louise Beavers.   Lots of Irving Berlin songs revolving around the holidays. The story is about a man (Crosby) who leaves show business to move to the country and run an Inn which is only open on Holidays. Astaire is his dancer buddy who is looking for a new partner and thinks he may have found her at the Inn. Crosby doesn't want to lose her, and tries to keep Astaire from stealing his partner. There's an Irving Berlin song for every holiday you'd think of and some you wouldn't. **V**

Hollywood Canteen (1944) **1/2 (See WWII, The Home Front)

Hollywood Hotel (1937) **1/2 D: Busby Berkley. Dick Powell, Rosemary Lane, Lola Lane, Ted Healy, Johnnie "Scat" Davis, "Alan Mowbray, Frances Langford, Louella Parsons.   Routine musical of Powell winning a talent contest and pursuing Hollywood stardom. Worth viewing for look at real-life Parsons, Benny Goodman and band playing famous "Sing, Sing, Sing," as well as showing the famous Goodman Quartet (with Gene Krupa, Lionel Hampton and Teddy Wilson). For an opportunity to see the REAL musicians of the Goodman band makes this one worth seeing. Also includes song "Hooray for Hollywood." Parents might wish to preview.

I Dream of Jeanie (1952) ** (See 1800s)

I Dream Too Much (1935) **1/2 D: John Cromwell. Lily Pons, Henry Fonda, Eric Blore, Osgood Perkins.   Though the sound is not the best and the picture is dated, this film is

worth seeing to hear the magnificent Lily Pons who was an opera star of her era and an incredibly good coloratura (high, light soprano, very flexible vocally, known for some incredible "vocal gymnastics"). In this, her Hollywood debut, she and Fonda are a struggling young married couple. Set in Paris. **V**

I'll See You in My Dreams (1951) **1/2 D: Michael Curtiz. Doris Day, Danny Thomas, Frank Lovejoy, Patrice Wymore, James Gleason.   Largely fictional biography of lyricist Gus Kahn (Thomas) with Day as his wife. There is a hussy who makes a play for him, but gets nowhere. Songs include "Ain't We Got Fun," "It Had to Be You."   **V**

I Love Melvin (1953) **1/2 D: Don Weis. Donald O'Connor, Debbie Reynolds, Una Merkel, Allyn Joslyn, Jim Backus, Richard Anderson, Noreen Corcoran.   Cute musical has O'Connor trying to impress Reynolds by telling her he can get her on the cover of *Look* magazine. **V**

I Married an Angel (1942) ** D: W. S. Van Dyke II. Jeanette MacDonald, Nelson Eddy, Edward Everett Horton, Binnie Barnes, Reginald Owen, Douglass Dumbrille.   Based upon the Rogers and Hart musical, Eddy dreams he married an angel (MacDonald). **V**

Incendiary Blonde (1945) **1/2 D: George Marshall. Betty Hutton, Arturo de Cordova, Charlie Ruggles, Albert Dekker, Barry Fitzgerald, Mary Phillips, Bill Goodwin.   Flashy biography of 1920s nightclub owner and entertainer Texas Guinan. Colorful costume film. Parents preview first.

Interrupted Melody (1955) ***1/2 D: Curtis Bernhardt. Eleanor Parker, Glenn Ford, Roger Moore, Cecil Kellaway, Ann Codee Stephan Bekassy.   A wonderful biography of the Australian Wagnerian opera singer Marjorie Lawrence, who was stricken with polio and with the help of her M.D. husband, makes a comeback to sing at the Metropolitan Opera. The superb Eileen Farrell sings for Parker, who does a credible job of portraying an opera singer. There are some struggles she faces in deciding to continue living, but her ultimate strength of character comes through. This should appeal even to those who are not opera fans. Highly recommended. **V**

In the Good Old Summertime (1949) *** D: Robert Z. Leonard. Judy Garland, Van Johnson, S. Z. "Cuddles" Sakall, Spring Byington, Clinton Sundberg, Buster Keaton.   Musical remake of *The Shop Around the Corner* casts Judy and Van as the unsuspecting pen pals who work with and hate each other. Good family fun and plenty of good music. Liza Minnelli's film debut in the last scene. **V**

Invitation to the Dance (1956) **1/2 D: Gene Kelly. Gene Kelly, Igor Youskevitch, Claire Sombert, David Paltenghi, Daphne Dale, Claude Bessy, Tommy Rall, Carol Haney, Tamara Toumanova, Belita. This was the film Kelly fought to make for years and eventually went to Europe to do so. It is three vignettes of stories told entirely through dance. The final segment "Sinbad" is the best with Kelly in a Hanna-Barbera cartoon world, dancing with multiple cartoon characters. (reminiscent of Anchors Aweigh where he danced with Jerry Mouse) Music by Jacques Ibert, Andre Previn and Rimsky-Korsakov.

Irish Eyes Are Smiling (1944) **1/2 D: Gregory Ratoff. Monty Wooley, June Haver, Dick Haymes, Anthony Quinn, Maxie Rosenbloom, Veda Ann Borg, Maeve McGrail.   Loose biography of composer Ernest R. Ball who wrote "When Irish Eyes Are Smiling," "Mother Machree" and others which are included.

It Happened in Brooklyn (1947) **1/2 D: Richard Whorf. Frank Sinatra, Kathryn Grayson, Jimmy Durante, Peter Lawford, Gloria Grahame.   Musical of G.I. (Sinatra) who returns to Brooklyn. Always fun to watch top performers and especially memorable is the Sinatra-Durante duet "The Song's Gotta Have Heart." Also Grayson sings "The Bell Song" from *Lakmé* by Delibes. It's a very tough operatic coloratura aria. **V**

I Wonder Who's Kissing Her Now (1947) **1/2 D: Lloyd Bacon. June Haver, Mark Stevens, Martha Stewart, Reginald Gardiner, Lenore Aubert, William Frawley.   Recreation of the life and loves of songwriter Joseph E. Howard.

Jazz Singer, The (1927) **1/2 (See Science/Nature for innovation in films.)

Jupiter's Darling (1955) ** D: George Sidney. Esther Williams, Howard Keel, George Sanders, Marge and Gower Champion, Norma Varden.   Musical spoof of Hannibal's attack on Rome. **V**

Just For You (1952) *** D: Elliott Nugent. Bing Crosby, Jane Wyman, Ethel Barrymore, Bob Arthur, Natalie Wood, Cora Witherspoon, Regis Toomey.   Story of widowed musical producer (Crosby) whose son is away at school to avoid the show business scene, and whose daughter is at home under the care and tutelage of a impoverished socialite. Imagine Crosby's shock when he finds out that the socialite drinks and that his son is planning to enter show business as a songwriter! Generally a fun and wacky film with great Harry Warren-Leo Robin score including the fun song, "Zing a Little Zong." **V**

King and I, The (1956) ***1/2 D: Walter Lang. Deborah Kerr, Yul Brynner, Rita Moreno, Martin Benson, Terry Saunders, Rex Thompson, Alan Mowbray.   The film version of the famous Rogers and Hammerstein Broadway musical in which Gertrude Lawrence starred before her fight with cancer. Based upon the well known story of *Anna and the King of Siam* (See 1800s World) which tells the real life story of a widowed English schoolteacher (Kerr) who travels with her son to Siam to teach the children of the King. Brynner recreates his Broadway role and won an Oscar for it. Some scenes may concern some people, but could be easily eliminated. The King has many children by wives and concubines (as did Solomon) and Moreno's character has been given to the King by the King of Burma as a peace keeping measure. She is in love with the young ambassador who delivered her to Siam. Generally a wonderful film.   **V**

Note: For a fun history fact, Yul Brynner showed up for the audition for the Broadway play, read for the King and was turned down! He went home, shaved his head, returned to audition again, and was hired. Sometimes they just can't see you if you don't have the look they imagine, so he helped them along. He said that he *knew* that the role was for him. It was the definitive role of his career.

Kismet (1955) **1/2 D: Vincente Minnelli. Howard Keel, Ann Blyth, Dolores Gray, Monty Wooley, Sebastian Cabot, Vic Damone.   From the Broadway musical which tells of a beggar who has a lovely daughter and wishes only the best for her. What he doesn't know is that she is in love with the ruler of the land (whom she knows as a poor man) and he's in love with her. The father's scheming almost gets them in trouble, but it comes out alright in the end. An Arabian Nights kind of story with some lovely music. Three songs "And This Is My Beloved," Stranger in Paradise," and "Baubles, Bangles and Beads," are based upon themes from String Quartet No. 2 in D Major by Borodin (1833-1887). An interesting way to introduce classical music: show the movie and then play the quartet upon which it is based. **V**

Kiss Me Kate (1953) *** 1/2 D: George Sidney. Kathryn Grayson, Howard Keel, Ann Miller, Bobby Van, Keenan Wynn, James Whitmore, Bob Fosse, Tommy Rall, Kurt Kasznar, Ron Randell.   Film version of Cole Porter's Broadway musical which was loosely based upon Shakespeare's *Taming of the Shrew.* (See Renaissance) Grayson and Keel play a formerly married couple who fight off stage and onstage as Kate and Petruchio. Some wonderful songs include "So In Love," "Brush Up Your Shakespeare" (wonderfully done by Wynn and Whitmore), "From This Moment On," "I Hate Men." A fun way to introduce Shakespeare to kids. There is some room to discuss how people handle relationships with this film, in more ways than one! **V**

Lady Be Good (1944) *** D: Norman Z. McLeod. Eleanor Powell, Ann Sothern, Robert Young, Lionel Barrymore, John Carroll, Red Skelton, Virginia O'Brien, Dan Dailey, Jimmy Dorsey and His Orchestra. Musical of married songwriters with plenty of good "hoofin'." Songs include: "Lady Be Good," "Fascinating Rhythm," "You'll Never Know," and the Oscar winning, "Last Time I Saw Paris." **V**

La Traviata (1982-Italian) **** D: Franco Zeffirelli. Teresa Stratas, Placido Domingo, Cornell MacNeil, Alan Monk, Axelle Gail.   Verdi's opera (which was adapted from Alexandre Dumas' *Camille)* translates very well to film. Beautifully done and a good introduction to this medium if you approve of the subject matter. Parents should preview.   **[G] V, DVD**

Let's Dance (1950) **1/2 D: Norman Z. McLeod. Betty Hutton, Fred Astaire, Roland Young, Ruth Warrick, Shepperd Strudwick, Lucile Watson, Barton MacLane, Melville Cooper.   War widow Hutton desperately tries to keep her young son out of the clutches of his wealthy great-grandmother and returns to dancing with her former partner in this lesser known Astaire musical. **V**

Lili (1953) ***1/2 D: Charles Walters. Leslie Caron, Mel Ferrer, Zsa Zsa Gabor, Jean-Pierre Aumont, Amanda Blake, Kurt Kasznar.   Charming musical of young orphan girl who comes to the city looking for work and finds work with a carnival in which she interacts with puppets as her job. She becomes enamored with another performer with Gabor as the "other woman." Innocent, but parents might wish to edit parts. Oscar winning score includes song, "Hi Lili, Hi Lo." **V**

Listen, Darling (1938) **1/2 D: Edwin L. Marin. Judy Garland, Freddie Bartholomew, Mary Astor, Walter Pidgeon, Alan Hale, Scotty Beckett.   Judy and Freddie plot to land Astor with a husband. Judy sings, "Zing Went the Strings of My Heart." **V**

Little Colonel, The (1935) *** D: David Butler. Shirley Temple, Lionel Barrymore, Evelyn Venable, John Lodge, Sidney Blackmer, Bill "Bojangles" Robinson.   Set during Reconstruction, Shirley tries to play peacemaker between her mother and grandfather. This is the film which contains her famous step dance with Robinson, who was her favorite dancing partner. **V**

Little Nelly Kelly (1940) **1/2 D: Norman Taurog. Judy Garland, George Murphy, Charles Winninger, Douglas McPhail.   Cute musical based on George M. Cohan play with Judy patching up a family feud. **V**

Littlest Rebel, The (1935) *** (See Civil War)

Look For the Silver Lining (1949) **1/2 D: David Butler. June Haver, Ray Bolger, Gordon MacRae, Charles Ruggles, Rosemary DeCamp.   Surface bio of Marilyn Miller, famous star of Broadway. Still, clean family film, nice music and dancing. Find a good biography about her to complete this film. **V**

Louisiana Purchase (1941) **1/2 D: Irving Cummings. Bob Hope, Vera Zorina, Victor Moore, Irene Bordoni, Dona Drake.   Film version of Irving Berlin's musical. Typical Hope silliness, with Moore as worried, nervous statesman. Hope's filibuster scene is a classic. **V**

Lovely to Look At (1952) **1/2 D: Mervyn LeRoy. Kathryn Grayson, Red Skelton, Howard Keel, Ann Miller, Marge and Gower Champion, Zsa Zsa Gabor.   Remake of Jerome Kern's *Roberta* with Technicolor facelift. Skelton is at his zany best and the songs are still lovely. **V**

Lust For Life (1956) **1/2 D: Vincente Minnelli. Kurt Douglas, Anthony Quinn, James Donald, Pamela Brown, Everett Sloane, Niall MacGinnis, Noel Purcell, Henry Daniell.   Film adaptation of Irving Stone's biography of Vincent Van Gogh, played by Douglass. Quinn won an Oscar for his portrayal of Gauguin. I did not like this film, but it does show the tortured life of Van Gogh, who was supposed to be a minister, but became a painter instead, making this a film ripe for discussion. Please view this one first, parents as it is very dark and depressing. You need to decide if it is right for your family. **V**

Magnificent Rebel (1962) *** D: Georg Tressler. Karl Boehm, Ernst Nadhering, Ivan Desny, Gabriele Porks.   European Disney film about the life of Beethoven. Beautiful scenery, great music with a powerful scene at the end where Beethoven stands onstage, holding the score to his music, hearing it in his head, yet unable to hear it with his ears or the applause when it is over. A much better choice than *Immortal Beloved* which is rated "R".

Make Mine Music (1946) **1/2 D: Joe Grant. Voices of Nelson Eddy, Dinah Shore, Jerry Colonna, The Andrews Sisters, Andy Russell, Sterling Holloway and music by the Benny Goodman Quartet.   A ten part Disney animated feature with some wonderful music. I have only seen some of these as excerpts so cannot comment on the entire film but what I have seen, I thought was well done. Segments include: "Johnny Fedora and Alice Blue Bonnet,"

"Casey at the Bat," "The Whale Who Wanted to Sing at the Met," "After You've Gone," and "Peter and the Wolf" (by Prokofiev) which is a wonderful introduction to using an instrument and a musical theme to represent a character or action in the story. Try to find it on the Disney channel and tape it.

Mary Poppins (1963) **** D: Robert Stevenson. Julie Andrews, Dick Van Dyke, David Tomlinson, Glynis Johns, Ed Wynn, Hermione Baddeley, Karen Dotrice, Matthew Garber, Arthur Treacher, Reginald Owen.   The classic children's story by P. I. Travers comes to life in this Disney musical with Oscar winning score by the Sherman brothers. Mary Poppins is the "perfect nanny" and has come to straighten out the problems in the Banks household. Andrews won the Oscar for Best Actress for this film and thanked Warner brothers for not casting her in the role she created on the London and later Broadway stages as Eliza Doolittle in *My Fair Lady!* Warner didn't think she had the star power to carry the film and cast Audrey Hepburn instead and dubbed her voice. Disney picked Andrews up for this film and she beat Hepburn for the Best Actress award. Songs include: "Chim-Chim-Cheree," "A Spoonful of Sugar," "Super-cali-fragil-istic-expi-ali-docious," "Jolly Holiday," "I Love to Laugh," "Let's Go Fly a Kite," "Feed the Birds." A family and children's classic movie. **V, DVD**

Maytime (1937) *** D: Robert Z. Leonard. Jeanette MacDonald, Nelson Eddy, John Barrymore, Herman Bing, Tom Brown, Lynne Carver, Rafaela Ottiano, Paul Porcasi, Sig Ruman, Walter Kingsford, Harry Davenport.   MacDonald is an opera star who falls in love with poor young singer, Eddy. Problem is, she has a marriage of convenience to her mentor, Barrymore. Only one song survived the transition from Sigmund Romberg's stage version to screen, "Will You Remember." **V**

Meet Me in St. Louis (1944) **** D: Vincente Minnelli. Judy Garland, Margaret O'Brien, Lucille Bremer, Tom Drake, Mary Astor, Leon Ames, Marjorie Main, June Lockhart, Harry Davenport, Joan Carroll, Hugh Marlowe.   Wonderful Americana movie of a family who lives in St. Louis in 1903, the time of the World's Fair and who find out that their father has been transferred to New York and they will have to leave their beloved home. Songs include, "The Boy Next Door," "The Trolley Song," "Have Yourself a Merry Little Christmas." O'Brien steals all the scenes she's in, for which she won a special Oscar as the year's best child actress. Don't miss this enchanting film. **V**

Merry Andrew (1958) **1/2 D: Michael Kidd. Danny Kaye, Pier Angeli, Baccaloni, Robert Coote. Cute movie of Kaye as a teacher at a British boy's prep-school, but who wants to become an archeologist. The circus comes to the area and Kaye, who is engaged, falls in love with Angeli, a circus aerialist. There is a song about the Pythagorean theory which was very helpful to my oldest daughter when it came to geometry. Fun for all.

Merry Widow, The (1934) *** D: Ernst Lubitsch. Maurice Chevalier, Jeanette MacDonald, Una Merkel, Edward Everett Horton, George Barbier, Herman Bing.   A lot of fun but not absolutely true to the Franz Lehar operetta which tells the story of a widow who falls in love with a prince, Danillo. My favorite line is in the opening scene (of the play) when the Prince's servant is asked to identify himself, he responds that he is "Nish." The other party doesn't understand and he replies, "That's 'N' as in Napolean, 'I' as in myself and 'SH' as in sssssshhhhhh!" Wonderful, tuneful score. Even those who don't like grand opera should like this. Try to see the real operetta on the stage. **V**

Mikado, The (1939) *** D: Victor Schertzinger. Kenny Baker, John Barclay, Martyn Green, Jean Colin, Constance Wills.   Color version of the Gilbert and Sullivan operetta. Includes, "Three Little Maids." Parents should preview.

Moon Over Miami (1941) *** D: Walter Lang. Don Ameche, Betty Grable, Robert Cummings, Carole Landis, Charlotte Greenwood, Jack Haley.   Grable and sisters go to Miami on a shoestring in hopes of snaring a rich husband. Colorful and tuneful. **V**

Music for Millions (1944) **1/2 D: Henry Koster. Margaret O'Brien, Jimmy Durante,

June Allyson, Marsha Hunt, Hugh Herbert, Jose Iturbi, Connie Gilchrist, Harry Davenport, Marie Wilson, Larry Adler, Ethel Griffies.   Kid sister of war-bride Allyson comes to stay with her while she plays in an all female orchestra under the baton of Iturbi. She's not supposed to have a kid in the room or a baby, who will be coming soon. Lots of classical music is included in this sweet film.

Music Man, The (1962) ***1/2 D: Morton Da Costa. Robert Preston, Shirley Jones, Buddy Hackett, Hermione Gingold, Paul Ford, Pert Kelton, Ronny Howard.   Preston reprises his Broadway role as Professor Harold Hill who uses the "think" method to teach bands to play. Shirley Jones plays the local music teacher/librarian who can expose him. Some really fun scenes are the barbershop quartet who can't agree on anything but can always be diverted into song, the ladies auxiliary who become a Grecian dance group, and the famous "Trouble" number. Other songs include, "Lida Rose," "Good Night My Someone," "Seventy-Six Trombones," "'Til There Was You," and "The Wells Fargo Wagon." Some parents may want to watch this first as there may be some things to which they might object or wish to edit. **V**

Music of the Heart (1999) *** D: Wes Craven. Meryl Streep, Aidan Quinn, Anglea Bassett, Gloria Estefan, Jane Leeves, Cloris Leachman, Kieran Culkin, Charlie Hofheimer, Jay O. Sanders.   Based upon a true story, a divorced woman moves to East Harlem and starts a Suzuki violin program against all the odds and makes it work. She requires dedication, discipline and the children blossom. The climax is a concert at Carnegie Hall with the children playing alongside the world's top violinists including Issac Stern, Itzhak Perlman, and many others. I stumbled upon the concert on TV one weekend and then learned about the movie, which does need some parental editing for immorality, so view first. **[PG] V, DVD**

My Dream Is Yours (1949) **1/2 D: Michael Curtiz. Jack Carson, Doris Day, Lee Bowman, Adolphe Menjou, Eve Arden.   Carson boosts Day to radio stardom. Highlight: Bugs Bunny dream sequence. Cute film with plenty of singing by Day. **V**

My Fair Lady (1964) ***1/2 D: George Cukor. Rex Harrison, Audrey Hepburn, Stanley Holloway, Wilfred Hyde-White, Gladys Cooper, Jeremy Brett, Theodore Bikel, Henry Daniell, Mona Washbourne, Isobel Elsom.   Film version of the Learner and Lowe musical from Bernard Shaw's *Pygmalion*. Professor Henry Higgins (Harrison) takes a bet to transform cockney flower girl (Hepburn) into a lady. He can place anyone within a few blocks of the place they were born from the way they speak. ("Why Can't the English Teach Their Children How to Speak?") Songs include "The Rain in Spain," "I Could Have Danced All Night," "On the Street Where You Live," "Just You Wait," "Get Me to the Church on Time," and "Show Me." Film won 8 Oscars. The original London version starred Julie Andrews as Eliza Doolittle, the flower girl. When it came time to make a movie of it, she was turned down to recreate the role because she was an unknown. Hepburn's voice had to be dubbed and Julie went on to be cast as Mary Poppins, for which she won a Best Actress Oscar that same year. In her acceptance speech, she thanked Fox for not casting her as Eliza. I'm sure they lived to regret it. **V**

My Gal Sal (1942) *** D: Irving Cummings. Rita Hayworth, Victor Mature, John Sutton, Carole Landis, James Gleason, Phil Silvers, Mona Maris, Walter Catlett.   Set in the Gay '90s, this musical is about songwriter Paul Dresser (Mature) who wrote *On the Banks of the Wabash,* and who's in love with Hayworth's character, a well known singer. A colorful costume film.

My Sister Eileen (1955) ***1/2 D: Richard Quine. Betty Garrett, Janet Leigh, Jack Lemmon, Kurt Kaszner, Dick York, Horace McMahon, Bob Fosse.   Based upon the same story as the Broadway musical *Wonderful Town,* this tells of sisters from Ohio who move to New York seeking success. They find an apartment in Greenwich Village with an eccentric landlord and some unusual neighbors. Some fun numbers are involved. This was Bob Fosse's first effort to choreograph on his own. He plays the soda jerk in love with Eileen. (Leigh) Ruth (Garrett) is a want-to-be writer who meets publisher Lemmon. If there is anything which could be considered objectionable it would be that the apartment was previously owned by a woman of questionable virtue and because of that strange people walk in and out of their apartment, and the young married couple upstairs (who haven't told her mother they've married), who are due for a visit from mom. One of the most fun scenes is when Ruth is sent on a wild goose chase to interview the sailors of a foreign country. They don't understand English and follow her home. The only thing they can do to keep them entertained is to Congo! (See Family Films for the original version, [same title] which is also very good.) **V**

My Wild Irish Rose (1947) ** D: David Butler. Dennis Morgan, Andrea King, Arlene Dahl, Alan Hale, George Tobias.   Loosely based biography of songwriter Chauncey Olcott includes plenty of Irish songs.

Naughty But Nice (1939) **1/2 D: Ray Enright. Dick Powell, Ann Sheridan, Gale Page, Helen Broderick, Ronald Regan, Allen Jenkins, ZaSu Pitts.   Powell plays a music professor who inadvertently writes a hit popular song, which leads to complications and mix-ups. Worth seeing to here songs based upon classical composers Wagner, Liszt, Mozart and Bach. A nice musical challenge is to figure out what the original pieces were and which composer wrote it. Parents might wish to preview first.

Naughty Marietta (1935) **1/2 D: W. S. Van Dyke II. Jeanette MacDonald, Nelson Eddy, Frank Morgan, Elsa Lancaster, Douglass Dumbrille, Cecilia Parker.   First film in which MacDonald and Eddy were partnered. She plays a French princess running off to America who falls in love with Indian Scout Eddy. Victor Herbert's operetta includes "The Italian Street Song," "Tramp, Tramp, Tramp," and "Ah, Sweet Mystery of Life." Somewhat dated, but still worth seeing. . **V**

Neptune's Daughter (1949) *** D: Edward Buzzell. Esther Williams, Red Skelton, Keenan Wynn, Betty Garrett, Ricardo Montalban, Mel Blanc.   Musical romance has Esther as a swim suit designer who is out to protect her crush-prone younger sister (Garrett) from a South American polo-playing playboy (Montalban) not knowing that the man whom her sister thinks is the polo player is Skelton! Esther struggles with her own attraction to Montalban, who sees a good thing and goes after it. Includes Academy Award winning duet, "Baby, It's Cold Outside." **V**

New Moon (1940) *** D: Robert Z. Leonard. Jeanette MacDonald, Nelson Eddy, Mary Boland George Zucco, H. B. Warner, Grant Mitchell, Stanley Fields.   Hammerstein-Romberg operetta set in old Louisiana includes "One Kiss," "Softly as in Morning Sunrise," "Lover Come Back to Me," "Stout-Hearted Men." One of my daughters' favorite Nelson Eddy-Jeanette MacDonald films. **V**

New Orleans (1947) **1/2 D: Arthur Lubin. Arturo de Cordova, Dorothy Patrick, Billie Holliday, Louis Armstrong, Woody Herman and Band, Meade Lux Lewis, other jazz stars.   Fictionalized birth of jazz includes appearances by some early jazz greats. Worth watching to see them. **V, DVD**

Nice Girl? (1941) *** D: William A. Seiter. Deana Durbin, Franchot Tone, Walter Brennan, Robert Stack, Robert Benchley.   Durbin, a child vocal prodigy, is shown as a young woman with Tone and Stack both vying for her. Durbin and Judy Garland were at MGM at the same time. MGM kept Judy and let Deanna's option drop. Judy was a pop singer and Deanna was classically trained. Both were amazing singers as children, just in different areas of music. **V**

Night and Day (1946) **1/2 D: Michael Curtiz. Cary Grant, Alexis Smith, Monty Wooley, Ginny Simms, Jane Wyman, Eve Arden, Mary Martin, Victor Francen, Alan Hale, Dorothy Malone.   Loosely based biography on the life of songwriter Cole Porter. The scene with Mary Martin being brought to Porter's attention and singing "My Heart Belongs to Daddy," is true. Songs include "You're the Top," "Night and Day." **V**

Oh, You Beautiful Doll (1949) **1/2 D: John M. Stahl. June Haver, Mark Stevens, S. Z. Sakall, Charlotte Greenwood, Gale Robbins.   Based upon the true story of composer Fred Fisher, ("Peg o' My Heart") this is the story of a serious composer's work becoming popular music. Bright, cheery costumer.

Oklahoma! (1955) ***1/2 D: Fred Zinnemann. Gordon MacRae, Shirley Jones, Charlotte Greenwood, Rod Steiger, Gloria Grahame, Eddie Albert, James Whitmore, Gene Nelson, Barabara Lawrence, Jay C. Flippen.   Film version of landmark 1943 Rodgers and Hammerstein Broadway play of the same title. This play is hailed as THE play which began modern musical theatre. One item of note, this was the first play to use dance to forward the plot. Previously, dance was either interjected and all action stopped, or the dance was a rehearsal or performance in the plot. With Oklahoma!, dance was used to tell part of the story so the dance *became* part of the plot, a very new idea in its day. Agnes de Mille's groundbreaking Broadway choreography can also be seen in the movie version. The score includes many familiar tunes including "Oh, What a Beautiful Mornin'," "The Surrey With the Fringe on Top," "People Will Say We're In Love," "Kansas City," "The Farmer and the Cowman," and the title song. When filmed, two takes were done of each scene, one after the other. One version is in Cinemascope, the other is in Todd-AO. The video version is in Cinemascope and the laserdisc version is in Todd-AO. Some feel the latter is superior. Rent both and judge for yourself! If the child is interested, investigate the two processes and their differences. **V**

Oliver! (1968) ***1/2 D: Carol Reed. Ron Moody, Oliver Reed, Shani Wallis, Mark Lester, Jack Wild, Harry Secombe, Hugh Griffith, Shelia White.   From the Broadway play, this musical version of Dickens' *Oliver Twist* is a fun way to introduce children to this famous story of a young boy who meets the Artful Dodger and is taken into a gang of boy thieves whose leader is the crafty Fagin. As with the book, the movie has its light and dark spots. Parents may wish to view it first for suitability. Tuneful score includes "Consider Yourself," "Who Will Buy?," "As Long As He Needs Me," "Oom Pah Pah," and the title song. This film won six Academy Awards, including special prize to Onna White for her energetic choreography. **[G] V**

One and Only Genuine, Original Family Band, The (1968) **1/2 D: Michael O'Herlihy. Walter Brennan, Buddy Ebsen, Leslie Ann Warren, John Davidson, Janet Blair, Kurt Russell.   The story revolves around a musical family who are involved in the debate of the 1888 Presidential campaign and the question of statehood for the Dakota territory, which eventually ended up as North and South Dakota. Good, clean family fun. **[G] V**

One Night of Love (1934) ***1/2 D:Victor Schertzinger. Grace Moore, Tullio Carminati, Lyle Talbot, Mona Barrie, Luis Alberni, Jessie Ralph.   Classic story of a young girl who wants to be an opera singer and goes to Europe where she comes under the tutelage of a famous and demanding impresario. Worth seeing just to hear Moore (a famous opera star of her day) sing. Even with the primitive sound equipment of the day, you can still tell that she had quite a voice. **V**

On Moonlight Bay (1951) **1/2 D: Roy Del Ruth. Doris Day, Gordon MacRae.   Based upon Booth Tarkington's Penrod stories of a tomboy (Day) and next door neighbor (MacRae). A good family film with a sequel, *By the Light of the Silvery Moon*. (Also see 1900s) **V**

On the Town (1949) **** D: Gene Kelly and Stanely Donen. Gene Kelly, Frank Sinatra, Vera-Ellen, Betty Garrett, Ann Miller, Jules Munshin, Alice Pearce, Florence Bates.   An innovative film shot on location (not then the norm) and telling the story of three sailors on 24 hour leave in New York City. Based upon the Broadway play by Betty Comden, Adolphe Green and Leonard Bernstein, this movie is considered a classic, yet dropped some of the best songs of the Broadway version. Some parents may not like some situations in this film so I recommend parents viewing it first. **V**

Orchestra Wives (1942) **1/2 D: Archie Mayo. George Montgomery, Ann Rutherford, Glenn Miller and his Band, Lynn Bari, Carole Landis, Cesar Romero, Virginia Gilmore, Mary Beth Hughes, The Nicholas Brothers, Jackie Gleason, Henry (Harry Morgan).   I don't recommend this as a film to view but I do recommend that the parents take out the scenes with the band and give the children the opportunity to see the Glenn Miller band with Glenn at the helm. Also worth seeing are the fabulously athletic Nicholas Brother's dances. **V**

Oscar (1991) **1/2 D: John Landis. Sylvester Stallone, Ornella Muti, Don Ameche, Peter Rigert, Tim Curry, Vincent Spano, Marisa Tomei, Eddie Bracken, Linda Gray, Chazz Palminteri, Kurtwood Smith, Yvonne De Carlo, Ken Howard, William Atherton, Martin Ferrero, Harry Shearer, Richard Romanus, Kirk Douglas.   *I am not recommending this film for children.* However the *credits* are worth watching! Sounds strange, I know, but the opening credit has a cute puppet figure singing Figaro's *Largo al factotum,* from Rossini's *Barber of Seville* (*Il Barbiere di Siviglia*) which fits in nicely with a study of music from the Romantic period. It's about a barber who is telling us how indispensable he is and how everyone is always calling for him. The opening section, while fun to watch, is incomplete. To hear the entire aria, listen to the *closing* credits! Once they've seen the cute puppet, they should listen to the recording at the end with no problem. Other than these two things, you'll have to decide if you want to show the movie, which discusses immorality several times. [**PG**]   **V**

Otello (1986-Italian) ***1/2 D: Franco Zefferilli. Placido Domingo, Katia Ricciarelli, Justino Diaz, Petra Malakova, Urbano Barberini.   A wonderful film version of Verdi's opera based upon the story made famous by Shakespeare. If you have studied the story and wish to expose your children to opera, you can hardly do better than Domingo. By the way, in English, this is pronounced O-thel-o. In Italian, and thus throughout this movie, you will hear O-tell-o. [**PG**]   **V**

Pajama Game, The (1957) *** D: George Abbott, Stanely Donen. Doris Day, John Raitt, Carol Haney, Eddie Foy, Jr., Barbara Nichols, Reta Shaw.   Film version of the hit Broadway play containing most of the original cast. This is the story of a pajama factory which is the center of a battle between labor and management over labor unions. Day is the head of the grievance committee who falls in love with the new foreman who is considered management. Famous songs include, "Hernando's Hideaway," "Hey, There," "I'm Not at All in Love," and "There Once Was a Man." "Steam Heat" features Bob Fosse's unique chorographical style of white socks and tight, controlled movements. There is a song called "I Would Trust Her" done by Eddie Foy, Jr. and Reta Shaw which mentions some situations to which some parents might not approve, as does "Once a Year Day" at the company picnic and in the fashion show at the end. Parents, watch these scenes and see if you'd like to omit them. However, if you want a good picture showing the disagreements of labor and management, this is the best one for children, so don't throw out the baby with the bath water. Just omit what you find objectionable and keep the rest. **V**

Paramount on Parade (1930) **1/2 D: Dorothy Arzner, Otto Brower, Edmund Goulding, Victor Heerman, Edwin Knopf, Rowland V. Lee, Ernst Lubitsch, Lothar Mendes, Victor Schertzinger, A. Edward Sutherland, Frank Tuttle. Jean Arthur, Clara Bow, Maurice Chevalier, Gary Cooper, Nancy Carroll, Leon Errol, Stuart Erwin, Kay Francis, Fredric March, Helen Kane, Jack Oakie, William Powell, Buddy Rogers, and more.   As much a piece of film history as anything, this was a feature that was designed to show off Paramount stars. See what you think. Parents should preview first.

Perils of Pauline, The (1947) *** D: George Marshall. Betty Hutton, John Lund, Constance Collier, Billy de Wolfe, William Demarest.   Fun musical-comedy loosely based on silent film star Pearl White. Hutton is as revved up as ever and some of the bits are quite humorous, especially how she gets a job in pictures. **V, DVD**

Peter and the Wolf (1946) In 1938 Sergei Prokofieff played his musical work for Walt Disney who was working on *Fantasia* and *Pinocchio* at that time. Then WWII intervened and called on Disney studios to make training films for the war. It wasn't until after the war that this animated film was produced, but it was worth the wait. In this wonderful cartoon version of Prokofieff's work, each character has a musical theme, which is played for the child and explained before the actual story begins. This way, the child recognizes the entrance of the characters when their musical theme is played. Peter, a little boy, disobeys his grandfather and goes out to hunt the wolf. He is represented by a string quartet. Sache, the bird's theme is played on the flute. Sonya the duck's theme is played on the oboe. Ivan the cat is played by a clarinet, Grandpapa's theme is played by the bassoon.

The hunter's theme (gunshots) is played by the timpani (or kettle drums). And the wolf is depicted with brass and cymbals. Narrated by Sterling Holloway, it is a fun way to introduce children to musical instruments and the idea of musical themes, also known as *leitmotifs* for whom Wagner is most famous. Try to find on the Disney channel and tape it.

Peter Pan (1953) *** D: Hamilton Luske, Clyde Geronimi, Wilfred Jackson. Voices of Bobby Driscoll, Kathryn Beaumont, Hans Conried, Bill Thompson, Heather Angel, Paul Collins, Candy Candido, Tom Conway.   Disney animated feature of classic story by James M. Barrie about a young girl who meets a boy who's lost his shadow only to find that he never grows up. He takes her and her two brothers with him to "Never Land" where they battle the evil Captain Hook and his band of pirates. Parents: "Pan" was a Greek god so you'll need to decide whether or not this is okay for your family. **V, DVD**

Peter Pan (1960) TVM D: Vincent J. Donahue. Mary Martin, Cyril Richard, Margalo Gilmore, Sondra Lee; narrated by Lynn Fontanne.   In 1954, Jerome Robbins decided to produce a new musical version of the children's story, Peter Pan. Traditionally, the role of Peter is played by a woman and Mary Martin was chosen. She wowed audiences for 150 performances and even won a Tony award. This TV version is a wonderful recreation of the Broadway play with Jerome Robbins choreography and songs by Styne, Comden, and Green intact. Classic story comes to life including great songs for children, "I Gotta Crow," "I Won't Grow Up," "Never Land," "I'm Flying" and more. My youngest loved this when she was little.

Peter Rabbit and Tales of Beatrix Potter (1971-British) ***1/2 D: Reginald Mills.   At the time of this writing, I have been unable to locate a version of this in my area. However, this is a film ballet done by the Royal Ballet Company telling stories of Beatrix Potter's characters. Since it is done by this fabulous Ballet Company, I didn't want to omit a mention of it. I hope you can find a version of it in your area. Since I couldn't review it for you, I recommend parents watch it first and then show it to the children. **V**

Pete's Dragon (1977) ** D: Don Chaffey. Helen Reddy, Jim Dale, Mickey Rooney, Red Buttons, Shelley Winters, Sean Marshal, Jane Kean, Jim Backus, Jeff Conaway, voice of Charlie Callas.   Disney musical of an orphaned boy and his only friend, a dragon who is (most of the time) invisible. **[G] V, DVD**

Phantom of the Opera, The (1943) *** D: Arthur Lubin. Claude Rains, Susanna Foster, Nelson Eddy, Edgar Barrier, Jane Farrar, Miles, Mander, J. Edward Bromberg, Hume Cronyn.   The only acceptable version of this famous tale, in my opinion. However, I still recommend parents view this first and exercise caution when showing this to younger children, whose very active imaginations could still make this too scary. This is a more musical version than scary, telling the story of a violinist with the Paris opera orchestra who can no longer play and turns to composing while worshipping the young Christine from afar. He is disfigured in an accident and turns into the "Phantom" of the opera who wishes for young Christine to be heard and to replace the current Prima Donna (top female singer). He begins to threaten the management and the Prima Donna to get his way. Lots of lovely music in this version. I would avoid all other films of this story and use this one with caution and with older children. If you wish to hear some truly beautiful music around this story, I recommend obtaining or borrowing a copy of the recording of Andrew Lloyd Webber's Broadway musical by the same name, starring Sarah Brightman as Christine and the wonderful Michael Crawford as the Phantom. Webber's score is hauntingly beautiful. **V**

Pigskin Parade (1936) *** D: David Butler. Stuart Erwin, Patsy Kelly, Jack Haley, Johnny Downs, Betty Grable, Arline Judge, Dixie Dunbar, Judy Garland, Anthony (Tony) Martin, Elisha Cook, Jr. Grady Sutton, The Yacht Club Boys.   College football musical-comedy with Erwin the country-bumpkin who becomes a hero on the field. Kelly's amusing as the coach's wife who's more knowledgeable about the game than he! Garland sings, "It's Love I'm After" in her feature debut. **V**

Pinocchio (1940) **1/2 D: Ben Sharpsteen, Hamilton Luske. Voices of Dickie Jones, Christain Rub, Cliff Edwards, Evelyn Venable, Walter Catlett, Frankie Darro.   Disney film of puppet who becomes a boy by undergoing various trials is too scary for children, in my opinion. You'll have to preview and see what you think. Includes Oscar winning song

"When You Wish Upon a Star." **V, DVD**

Pirate, The (1948) ***1/2 D: Vincente Minelli. Judy Garland, Gene Kelly, Walter Slezak, Gladys Cooper, Reginald Owens, George Zucco, The Nicholas Brothers.   A case of mistaken identity when Judy thinks that Gene is a famous pirate when in reality he is a circus clown. Songs include the famous "Be A Clown" by Cole Porter. Gene's dances are breathtaking especially the one where he swings on a huge rope several stories in the air! He helped to come up with the special effects and the way to shoot this scene. Fine family fun. **V**

Pirates of Penzance, The (1983) **** D: Wilford Leach. Kevin Kline, Angela Lansbury, Linda Ronstadt, George Rose, Rex Smith, Tony Azito.   Joseph Papp's hit Broadway revival of Gilbert and Sullivan's musical took the theatrical world by storm when Linda Ronstadt proved she could sing operetta AND very well, thank you. NO one knew the belting country rock Ronstadt had high Cs! An additional surprise was the inclusion of pop singer Rex Smith. The inimitable Kevin Kline, as the Pirate King, steals every scene he's in. This fun film version was made in a very theatrical style which works wonderfully. It is one of mine and my children's all time favorites. Perhaps best G & S on film. Highly recommended. **[G] V**

A note of interest: you might obtain a copy of Linda Ronstadt's recording in her known field and compare her singing to what she does in this film. Ask the children to describe the differences they hear and be sure to note that while her high notes are pure and wonderful, her diction is terrible! You cannot understand what she is saying. But, in the scene with the "Keystone Cops" you can see the difference when she sings in her "chest voice" (the one for which she is known) where every word is understandable, as opposed to her "head voice" in which she cannot be understood. Good diction is a challenge for all singers, especially those in operetta, opera and chamber music. (classical music)

Pleasure of His Company, The (1961) *** D: George Seaton. Fred Astaire, Lilli Palmer, Debbie Reynolds, Tab Hunter, Gary Merrill, Charlie Ruggles.   Lesser known comedy of wanderer Astaire, who comes to visit his daughter before her wedding, charming her and creating chaos for his former wife and her husband. Parents should preview first.

Poor Little Rich Girl (1936) *** D: Irving Cummings. Shirley Temple, Alice Faye, Jack Haley, Gloria Stuart, Michael Whalen, Jane Darwell, Claude Gillingwater, Henry Armetta.   Shirley runs away from home and joins vaudeville team (Faye and Haley) and wins over crusty sponsor Gillingwater and is ultimately reunited with her father. One of Shirley's best. **V**

Porgy and Bess (1959) **1/2 D: Otto Preminger. Sidney Poitier, Dorothy Dandridge, Pearl Bailey, Sammy Davis, Jr., Brock Peters, Diahann Carroll, Ivan Dixon, Clarence Muse.   Gershwin's wonderful opera of life on Catfish Row among the poor. Hollywood chose their black stars of the day and though credibly done, I still wish that Cab Calloway had been allowed to recreate his Broadway role as "Sportin' Life." I had the pleasure of seeing him do the role on stage while I was in college. He was phenomenal. Songs include, "Summertime," "It Ain't Necessarily So," "I Got Plenty of Nothin," "There's a Boat That's Leavin' Soon."

Red Shoes, The (1948-British) **** D: Michael Powell. Emeric Pressburger, Anton Walbrook, Marius Goring, Moira Shearer, Robert Helpman, Leonide Massine, Albert Basserman, Ludmilla Tcherina, Esmond Knight.   Oscar winning tale of a young ballerina (the exquisite Moira Shearer) who is torn between two men, one the young composer whom she loves and the other the dance impresario who carries the keys for her future as a dancer and her love for the ballet. Highly stylized film contains some wonderful dancing and has become a favorite for dancers and lovers of the ballet. Due to the subject matter, parents may wish to view this before showing it to their children. **V**

Rhapsody in Blue (1945) *** D: Irving Rapper. Robert Alda, Joan Leslie, Alexis Smith, Oscar Levant, Charles Coburn, Julie Bishop, Albert Basserman, Morris Charnovsky,

Herbert Rudley, Rosemary DeCamp, Paul Whiteman, Hazel Scott.   Though mostly fictional, this film does give a look at George Gershwin and his love for his work, (writing songs) and some of the conflicts he dealt with within himself. The culmination of the film is Oscar Levant beautifully playing the title work. **V**

Rigoletto (1993) NR D: Leo Paur. Joseph Paur, Ivey Lloyd, John Huntington, Ryan Healy, Alyson Breinholt.   Made by Feature Films for Families (www.familytv.com/index_usa.asp) in an attempt to make clean, family films with nothing parents have to edit, this story is an allegory of the life of Messiah, put into the early 1900s. A mysterious man has moved into the town mansion. Suddenly, strange things begin to happen. In the meantime, young Bonnie is offered a job to work in the mansion and her family desperately needs the money. While there she befriends the reclusive Rigoletto, who shares with her his knowledge of music and singing. A wonderful film that families will love. Just have the hankies ready for the end.   **V**

Roberta (1935) *** D: William A Seiter. Irene Dunne, Fred Astaire, Ginger Rogers, Randolph Scott, Helen Westley, Claire Dodd, Victor Varconi.   Famous Jerome Kern musical brought to film is a bit dated, but still has its charm. Scott visits his aunt, the famous fashion designer "Roberta" while in Europe with a band. He meets and is puzzled by her assistant an impoverished noblewoman, Dunne, who runs more and more of his aunt's business. Astaire and Rogers have never been better. The lovely songs include: "I Won't Dance," "Lovely to Look At," and "Smoke Gets in Your Eyes." **V**

Rodger's and Hammerstein's Cinderella (1964) TVM D: Charles S. Durbin. Ginger Rogers, Walter Pidgeon, Celeste Holm, Jo Van Fleet, Stuart Damon, introducing Lesley Ann Warren.   Originally written for Julie Andrews, this colorful costume version of the classic tale is filled with great R & H songs including, "Ten Minutes Ago," "In My Own Little Corner," "A Lovely Night," "Impossible," and "Do I Love You." Tape from TV. Don't bother with the newer version of this.

Romeo and Juliet (1966-British) *** D: Paul Czinner. Margot Fonteyn, Rudolf Nureyev, David Blair, Desmond Doyle, Julia Farron, Michael Somes.   Royal Ballet dances classic Tchaikovsky ballet with famous stars Fonteyn and Nureyev. Not as slick as dance films today, but worth seeing for the famous leads and amazing when one realizes that Fonteyn was 47 when she danced this. **V, DVD**

Rose Marie (1936) *** D: W. S. Van Dyke II. Jeanette MacDonald, Nelson Eddy, Reginald Owens, Allan Jones, James Stewart, Alan Mowbray, Gilda Gray.   This version isn't true to the original operetta, but is worth seeing if you are a fan of the stars. The famous "Indian Love Call" is included. **V**
(1954) **1/2 D: Mervyn LeRoy. Ann Blyth, Howard Keel, Fernando Lamas, Bert Lahar, Marjorie Main, Joan Taylor, Ray Collins.   This version is more faithful to the original operetta, but lacks the enthusiasm of the above version. Keel tries to tame tomboy Blyth, but instead falls in love with her. As there must always be conflict in a story, Lamas provides it by also falling for Blyth. Personally, I prefer the voices of this cast. Children might enjoy seeing "the Cowardly Lion" without all the makeup. His song, "I'm the Mountie Who Never Got His Man" is one of the films highlights.

Rose of Washington Square, The (1939) **1/2 D: Gregory Ratoff. Tyrone Power, Alice Faye, Al Jolson, William Frawley, Joyce Compton, Hobart Cavanaugh, Louis Prima.   Faye plays a thinly disguised Fanny Brice, whose life was made famous in the later Broadway play and film, *Funny Girl.* Power plays gambler Arnstein. Best thing about this is that Faye gets to sing Brice's signature song, "My Man" which was totally omitted from the score of *Funny Girl.* In sequel film *Funny Lady,* this was corrected, but I don't recommend that film for children. Parents would be wise to preview first. **V**

Royal Wedding (1951) *** D: Stanley Donen. Fred Astaire, Jane Powell, Peter Lawford, Sarah Churchill Keenan Wynn, Albert Sharpe.   The story of a brother and sister song and dance team who go to London at the time of Queen Elizabeth II's wedding and find their own mates as well. Score was written by Alan Jay Lerner (of *My Fair Lady* fame) and Burton Lane. The scene in which Fred Astaire dances on the walls and ceiling still cause awe and wonder. Other highlights are his dance with a coat rack and his duet with Powell, "How Could You

Believe Me When I Said That I Loved You (When You Know I've Been a Liar All My Life?)." **V**

Seven Brides for Seven Brothers (1954) **** D: Stanley Donen. Howard Keel, Jane Powell, Jeff Richards, Russ Tamblyn, Tommy Rall, Virginia Gibson, Julie Newmeyer (Newmar–of Cat Woman/Batman fame), Ruta Kilmonis (Lee), Matt Mattox, Jacques D'Amboise.   Wonderful family musical set around the turn of the century. Keel comes down from the mountains with one agenda: to find a wife in a day and marry her. When he finds her (Powell) and brings her to the family farm, his brothers are inspired to do the same. Their new sister takes them in hand to teach them a few manners about courting, leading to the song, "Goin' Courtin'." Shortly thereafter, they get to try out what they've learned at a neighbor's barn raising which provides the background for some incredible dancing and a war between the brothers and the town men. (Michael Kidd's choreography is wonderful) Later, heart sore and bruised, the brothers are calf-eyed over the girls and Keel (who is reading the classics!) suggests that they kidnap the girls in order to marry them, just like the "Sobbin' Women." Powell is appalled and the girls move into the house and the boys into the barn. There is one scene in which the girls are in their "unmentionables" and a mention is made of wondering which boy slept in which bed. That is the only real possibility of an "objectionable" item I can find in the entire film. This is one the entire family can enjoy with good lessons, great music and dance. See in letterbox format if at all possible. Lots of fun for all. **V**

Seven Hill of Rome (1958) **1/2 D: Roy Rowland. Mario Lanza, Peggie Castle, Marisa Allasio, Renato Rascel, Rosella Como.   Singer Lanza retreats to Rome for a rest and falls in love. Not a great plot, but nice music, clean fun and great singing by Lanza. **V**

Seven Little Foys, The (1955) **1/2 D: Melville Shavelson. Bob Hope, Milly Vitale, George Tobias, Billy Gray, James Cagney.   Fun biography of vaudeville entertainer Eddie Foy and the inclusion of his children in his act when his wife passes away. Cagney does a cameo as George M. Cohan. Cagney got started in show business on Broadway and Mr. Cohan was instrumental in his success. To repay George M. in a small way, Cagney would only agree to do the role if they would NOT pay him for it. The dance scene between Hope as Foy and Cagney as Cohan is a highlight of the film. **V, DVD**

Shall We Dance? (1937) ***1/2 D: Mark Sandrich. Fred Astaire, Ginger Rogers, Eric Blore, Edward Everett Horton.   Dance team of Astaire and Rogers pretend to be wed in this one. Wonderful Gershwin tunes "Let's Call The Whole Thing Off," "They All Laughed," and "They Can't Take That Away From Me." **V**

Shine On Harvest Moon (1944) **1/2 D: David Butler. Ann Sheridan, Jack Carson, Dennis Morgan, Irene Manning, S. Z. Sakall.   Pleasant family musical covering the lives of Nora Bayes and Jack Norworth who were great entertainers. Black and white with finale in color.

Shocking Miss Pilgrim, The (1947) **1/2 D: George Seaton. Betty Grable, Dick Haymes, Anne Revere, Allyn Joslyn, Gene Lockhart, Elizabeth Patterson.   Cute story set in the 1870s of woman typewriter operator who seeks a job in the world of business, a world which at that time was a man's world. She finds a place to stay in a house of "misfits," all of whom hate Boston, the town in which they reside! Included in this film is the suffragette movement. For a film on this subject, (other than *Mary Poppins*) this is a good, clean family film. Also included is a score by Gershwin.

Showboat (1939) *** D: James Whale. Irene Dunn, Allan Jones, Helen Morgan, Paul Robeson, Hattie McDaniel. **V**
(1951)*** D: George Sidney. Kathryn Grayson, Ava Gardner, Howard Keel, Joe E. Brown, Marge and Gower Champion, Robert Sterling, Agnes Morehead, Lief Erickson, William Warfield. **V, DVD**   This musical was very innovative for its time and is a legend in musical theatre history. (See 1800s, East for more information.)

Silk Stockings (1957) *** D: Rouben Mamoulian. Fred Astaire, Cyd Charisse, Janis Page,

Peter Lorre, George Tobias, Jules Munshin, Joseph Buloff, Barrie Chase.   A musical re-make of *Ninotchka* with Cyd as the Russian who is in Paris on a mission and who tries to stay emotionally unmoved by the romantic city. Fred plays a movie producer who helps her to see that there is more to life than being an automaton of the state. Includes wonderful dance numbers and musical score by Cole Porter. I especially like the "Stereophonic Sound" number. For a look at the differences in view between capitalism and communism, on a light note, this is the film. **V**

Singin' in the Rain (1952) **** D: Gene Kelly, Stanley Donen. Gene Kelly, Debbie Reynolds, Donald O'Connor, Jean Hagen, Cyd Charisse, Milard Mitchell, Douglas Fowley, Madge Blake, Rita Moreno. Considered by many as *the* definitive movie musical, this film takes a look at the transition from silent film to "talkies" and the impact this transition had on the movie industry. Through the fabulous perform-ance of Jean Hagen as "Lena," we can see why many film stars from the silent era were unable to make the transition to "talkies." Many had accents which made them unable to be understood, others either overacted vocally or were just plain terrible, and some, like "Lena" had voices which could shatter glass. This was a momentous time in the film industry which not only changed the way films were made, but also made and broke careers. Another challenge the film shows is HOW to make sound work. One of my favorite scenes in the film is when the film and audio get out of sync and the characters are saying, "No, no, no" to the action of "Yes, yes, yes!" and vice versa. This one is one that I think the entire family can enjoy and just might inspire some investigation into the history of the film industry, if you have a child who is so inclined. Film highlights include the title song, "Good Morning," and the infamous "Make 'Em Laugh" by Donald O'Connor. **V**

Slipper and the Rose, The (1976-British) *** D: Bryan Forbes. Richard Chamberlain, Gemma Craven, Annette Crosbie, Michael Horden, Margaret Lockwook, Christopher Gable, Kenneth Moore, Edith Evans. The Cinderella story as a musical, written by the Sherman brothers of *Mary Poppins* fame. A good pro-duction and good family fun. **[G] V**

Small Town Girl (1953) **1/2 D: Leslie Kardos. Jane Powell, Farley Granger, Ann Miller, S. Z. Sakall, Billie Burke, Bobby Van, Robert Keith, Nat King Cole.   Typical MGM musical with small town Powell meeting playboy Granger, a spoiled rich boy who gets a lesson when he is jailed for speeding through town. If you don't watch anything else, watch Bobby Van's number as a human pogo stick. It's the only dance on film of simply jumping for minutes on end. Also noteworthy is Ann Miller's tap number staged by the infamous Busby Berkeley showing an orchestra with no bodies. (Their limbs come out of the floor!) **V**

So Dear to My Heart (1949) ***1/2 D: Harold Schuster. Burl Ives, Beulah Bondi, Bobby Driscoll, Luana Patten, Harry Carey.   Sweet, warm Disney film about a boy who is determined to raise a black sheep and bring him to the competition at the State Fair. This includes scenes of farm life and the use of a HUGE spinning wheel. Based upon the book, *Midnight and Jeremiah* by Sterling North, this one is a keeper for fine family films. Includes Ives' famous song, "Lavender Blue (Dilly Dilly)." **V, DVD**

Song is Born, A (1948) **1/2 D: Howard Hawks. Danny Kaye, Virginia Mayo, Hugh Herbert, Steve Cochran, Felix Bressart; guest stars Benny Goodman, Louis Armstrong, Charlie Barnet, Lionel Hampton, Tommy Dorsey.   Musical remake of *Ball of Fire* (See Family) is worth seeing just to see the real-life jazz greats, especially Goodman who's one of the brainy scholars. A group of scholars are writing an en-cyclopedia and need to learn about jazz in order to write intelligently about it. **V**

Song of Love (1947) **1/2 (See 1800s Europe)

Song of Scherazade (1947) ** D: Walter Reisch. Yvonne De Carlo, Brian Donlevy, Jean-Pierre Aumont, Eve Arden, Philip Reed.   Musical is fantasy as far as the plot line goes, but does give a nice setting to hear and learn to identify Rimsky-Korsakov's famous work. According to the film, supposedly it came from dancer De Carlo. **V**

Song of the South (1946) ***1/2 D: Wilfred Jackson (animation), Harve Foster (live-action). Ruth Warrick, James Baskett, Bobby Driscoll, Luana Patten, Lucile Watson, Hattie McDaniel, Glenn Leedy.   This film has always been a favorite of mine since it tells about Uncle Remus and the tales of Joel Chandler Harris, who happens to be one of my kin. This tells the story of a young boy who lives on a plantation and is befriended by Uncle Remus, who tells him wonderful stories about Brer Rabbit, Brer Fox, and Brer Bear, which in turn sets up the film for some great action and animation. Included is the Oscar winning song, "Zip a Dee Doo Dah." At this time this is only available on Japanese imported laserdisc. Let's hope Disney corrects this in the future.

So This is Love (1953) **1/2 D: Gordon Douglas. Kathryn Grayson, Merv Griffin, Walter Abel, Rosemary DeCamp, Jeff Donnell.   Biography of opera star Grace Moore. **V** [To see the real Moore, see *One Night of Love* in this section.]

Sound of Music, The (1965) ***1/2 (See WWII, Europe)

South Pacific (1958) *** D: Joshua Logan. Rossano Brazzi, Mitzi Gaynor, John Kerr, Ray Walston, Juanita Hall, France Nuyen, Tom Laughlin.   Film version of Rodgers and Hammerstein's Broadway play of a young Army nurse who comes to the South Pacific during WWII, meets a French planter on the island upon which she is stationed and falls in love. This was the first major hit to deal with a May-December romance. For educational value, I think this film covers racial prejudice in a way with which children can deal and understand. Nellie falls in love with Emile, who has half-Polynesian children; Lt. Joe Cable falls in love with Liat, who is Tonkinese. This dilemma is covered in the song, "Carefully Taught." What does the Bible say about the races? From where did they come? Is any race shown by God to be "better than" or "less than?" Where do these opinions come from? Why are they still around? Are there advantages/disadvantages to different races? What about them marrying? If you wish to address this topic, this (and West Side Story) might be a good place to bring the topic into focus. Includes: "There is Nothin' Like a Dame," "Some Enchanted Evening," "Bali H'ai," "Happy Talk," "Honey Bun." **V**

Springtime in the Rockies (1942) *** D: Irving Cummings. Betty Grable, John Payne, Carmen Miranda, Cesar Romero, Charlotte Greenwood, Edward Everett Horton, Jackie Gleason.   Broadway duo bicker, split and wish to rejoin, but pride and "saving face" get in the way. Close to being *the* definitive Fox musical of the 1940s. Included are Harry James (Grable's real life husband) and his band, Carmen Miranda, complete with platform shoes and wacky headdress, and Helen Forrest singing "I Had the Craziest Dream." **V**

Stand Up and Cheer (1934) ** D: Hamilton MacFadden. Warner Baxter, Madge Evans, James Dunn, Sylvia Froos, John boles, Shirley Temple, Ralph Morgan, Aunt Jemima, Mitchell and Durant, Nick (Dick) Foran, Nigel Bruce, Stepin Fetchit.   President hires a big-time producer to be Secretary of Amusement to help the country out of their slump from the Depression. Highlight of film is Shirley Temple's star making appearance with James Dunn singing, "Baby Take a Bow." **V**

Star is Born, A (1954) ****1/2 D: George Cukor. Judy Garland, James Mason, Charles Bickford, Jack Carson, Tom Noonan.   Musical remake of the original 1937 Janet Gaynor, Fredric March film is better than the original and certainly better than the 1976 Streisand remake. This film is a classic in musical movie history, which is why I'm including it. Parents will need to view first to see if they approve of the subject matter for their children. The story is of a famous movie actor (Mason) who is on the decline from alcoholism who crosses paths with a young singer (Garland) who intrigues him. He still knows the business and goes about to successfully make her a star. (The makeup scene for her screen test is a ball!) They marry, against his better judgment, as he watches her career take off and his go down the tubes. Includes some of Garland's most famous songs which she later used in her live concerts, "The Man That Got Away," "It's a New World," and the famous and show-stopping "Born in a Trunk" medley. **V, DVD**

Stars and Stripes Forever (1952) **1/2 (See WWI) Biography of John Philip Sousa.

Star Spangled Rhythm (1942) *** D: George Marshall. Bing Crosby, Ray Milland, Bob Hope, Veronica Lake, Dorothy Lamour, Susan Hayward, Dick Powell, Mary Martin, Alan Ladd, Paulette Goddard, Cecil B. DeMille, Arthur Treacher, Preston Sturges, Eddie Anderson, Robert Preston, William Bendix & more.   Paramount's effort to raise wartime spirits is filled with songs and sketches woven around a loose plot of a studio switchboard operator (Betty Hutton) and gate guard (Victor Moore) who told his sailor son that he's the studio boss! **V, DVD**

State Fair (1945) *** D: Walter Lang. Jeanne Crane, Dana Andrews, Dick Haymes, Vivian Blaine, Charles Winninger, Fay Bainter.   A remake of an earlier film, this contains the only film score done by Rodgers and Hammerstein. The story is about a family who go to the state fair and have their lives changed. Jeanne Crane plays a wholesome girl who meets a newspaper man who surprises himself by falling in love with her. Her brother, (Haymes) meets a girl who sings with a band at the fair, but comes to learn that the girl he's always known back home is the real jewel. Good clean family fun with some wonderful R & H tunes including "It's a Grand Night For Singing," and the Oscar winning, "It Might as Well Be Spring." Remade in 1962 starring Pat Boone and Ann Margret, this first version is the best. **V**

St. Louis Blues (1958) **1/2 D: Allen Reisner. Nat "King" Cole, Eartha Kitt, Ruby Dee, Pearl Bailey, Juano Hernandez, Cab Calloway, Ella Fitzgerald.   Worth seeing for the wonderful cast, alone. This is a supposed biography of W. C. Handy, a black composer of the early 1900s. In the film Handy, the son of a preacher, wrestles with the talent he knows God has given him and his desire to please his father versus the need to express his talent in the way God gave it to him – an innovative style of music in his day. A good opportunity for discussion with your children. What do THEY (and you!) think is right?

Stormy Weather (1943) **1/2 D: Andrew L. Stone. Lena Horne, Bill (Bojangles) Robinson, Cab Calloway and His Band, Katherine Dunham, Fats Waller, Dooley Wilson, The Nicholson Brothers. This film is a parade of black performers of the day around a rather silly plot, but worth seeing to see the who's who on the roster of black artists. **V**

Story of Vernon and Irene Castle, The (1939) *** D: H. C. Potter. Fred Astaire, Ginger Rogers, Edna May Oliver, Walter Brennan, Lew Fields.   Story of real life husband and wife dance team who were famous in the early 20th century. Included are authentic song and dance. A wonderful family film with an ending of self-sacrifice. **V**

Strictly Ballroom (1992-Australian) **1/2 D: Baz Luhrmann. Paul Mercurio, Tara Morice, Bill Hunter, Barry Otto, Pat Thompson, Gia Carides, Peter Whitford, Antonio Vargas.   Poor film, but worth seeing if you are at all interested in ballroom dancing. The process by which the dance is broken down, taking risks by being different, standing up in the face of adversity are all in this film. Parents should view it first and just show the dance scenes, especially the final dance which is well worth seeing. Famous Spanish flamenco dancer and choreographer, Vargas, is featured in the film as female lead's father. **[PG-13] V**

Strike Up the Band (1940) **1/2 D: Busby Berkley. Mickey Rooney, Judy Garland, Paul Whiteman, June Preisser, William Tracy.   Typical Mickey/Judy plot with kids trying to get into show-biz. Clean family fun with some unique numbers including a symphony which is performed by animated pieces of fruit! **V**

Student Prince, The (1954) **1/2 D: Richard Thorpe. Ann Blyth, Edmond Purdom, John Ericson, Louis Callhern, Edmund Gwenn.   Film version of Romberg's operetta with the main draw being the voices of Blyth and Mario Lanza, who dubbed the singing for Purdom. The plot is about a young prince who does not know how to be a man and is thus sent (undercover) to a school in order to learn how *not* to be a stuffed shirt. There he falls in love with a sweet girl who works in her family's inn/tavern and ultimately faces the dilemma of duty over love. Beautiful music including, "Summertime in Heidelberg," "Glaudeamus Igitur," and the famous "Serenade." **V**

Summer Stock (1950) *** D: Charles Walters. Judy Garland, Gene Kelly, Eddie Bracken, Marjorie Main, Gloria De Haven, Phil Silvers, Hans Conried.   Judy holds down family farm against all odds and is set to marry Orville (Bracken) when self-centered younger sister (De Haven) brings her theatrical group (and her "big break") to the farm to rehearse due to shortage of funds for a rehearsal hall. In order to stay, Judy requires the city slickers to pitch in, help, and work the farm. Of course, this leads to disaster after disaster. Inevitably, flighty younger sister takes off and Judy has to step in and fill the void from which she begins to understand the draw of show business. Included are Kelly's famous dance with a newspaper and Judy's famous "Get Happy" number. Fun for all. **V**

Note: It took a lot of research, trial and error to find just the right aged paper to achieve what Gene Kelly wanted in his dance. Even the "little things" are sometimes not so little.

Sun Valley Serenade (1941) *** D: H. Bruce Humberstone. Sonja Henie, John Payne, Glenn Miller and His Orchestra, Milton Berle, Lynn Bari, Joan Davis, Dorothy Dandridge, The Nicholas Brothers.   Real life Olympic skating champion Henie plays a war refugee who is traveling with her guardian (Payne) and the Miller band to Sun Valley. Songs include "Chattanooga Choo Choo" and "In the Mood." A nice look at the Glenn Miller band with Glenn at the helm and at Henie in her element as a skater. You can see how skating styles have changed since this was made. If interested, read her biography. **V**

Swanee River (1939) **1/2 D: Sidney Lanfield. Don Ameche, Al Jolson, Andrea Leeds, Felix Bressart, Russell Hicks.   Biography of composer Stephen Foster (Ameche) includes Jolson portraying E. P. Christy, the famous minstrel. Parents might wish to preview.

Sweet and Low Down (1944) **1/2 D: Archie Mayo. Benny Goodman and His Band, Linda Darnell, Jack Oakie, Lynn Bari, James Cardwell, Allyn Joslyn, Dickie Moore.   Another film that is worth watching as much for the history as for the rather thin plot of a trombonist who makes it big in the Goodman Band. Worth watching to see the real life Benny Goodman and his band as for the movie; the jam session is a particular highlight. Parents might wish to preview.

Sweethearts (1938) **1/2 D: W. S. Van Dyke II. Jeanette MacDonald, Nelson Eddy, Frank Morgan, Florence Rice, Ray Bolger.   Stars are part of a Victor Herbert operetta who are manipulated apart. Plot is trite, but music is nice. If studying operetta or Victor Herbert, this one should be included. **V**

Swingtime (1936) **** D: George Stevens. Fred Astaire, Ginger Rogers, Victor Moore, Helen Broderick, Eric Blore, Betty Furness.   Fine pairing of Astaire and Rogers as dance partners who fall in love with the complication of Astaire's fiancée back home. Wonderful music by Jerome Kern with lyrics by Dorothy Fields (see *Deep in My Heart* for info on her) include "A Fine Romance," and "The Way You Look Tonight." **V**

Take Me Out to the Ball Game (1949) *** D: Busby Berkley. Frank Sinatra, Esther Williams, Gene Kelly, Betty Garrett, Edward Arnold, Jules Munshin, Richard Lane, Tom Dugan.   Williams takes over baseball team of Sinatra and Kelly in this generally fun musical around baseball. **V**

Tea for Two (1940) *** D: David Butler. Doris Day, Gordon MacRae, Gene Nelson, Patrice Wymore, Eve Arden, Billy De Wolfe, S.Z. Sakall.   Based upon stage play *No, No, Nanette,* Day has the opportunity to star in a Broadway show which just needs a little backing. Unknown to her, her uncle (Sakall) has lost her fortune in the stock market crash of 1929. Her uncle gets her to bet that she cannot answer every question with "No" over the period of a weekend, thinking this will keep his secret. The film covers the many mishaps of the weekend with some lovely tunes, including the title one. Great musical numbers are included. **[G] V**

That Lady in Ermine (1948) **1/2 D: Ernst Lubitsch. Betty Grable, Douglas Fairbanks, Jr., Cesar Romero, Walter Abel, Reginald Gardiner, Harry Davenport.   Cute fantasy musical of mythical European kingdom in which Grable is a princess who's just been married. Her ancestors come to life from paintings as Fairbank's army descends upon her castle.

That Midnight Kiss **1/2 (1949) D: Norman Taurog. Kathryn Grayson, Mario Lanza, Jose Iturbi, Ethel Barrymore, Keenan Wynn, J. Carrol Naish, Jules Munshin.   Socialite Grayson has aspirations of becoming an opera singer and Grandmother intends to help. Grayson meets Lanza who is working to purchase his own truck and falls for him. Iturbi plays himself, as the maestro of the opera company in question. Grayson brings Lanza along, he sings for Iturbi and replaces the stereotypical fat, egotistical tenor Grayson can't stand. There are complications to overcome, but it all comes right in the end. **V**

That's Entertainment **** (1974), **II** ***1/2 (1976), **and III** ***1/2 (1994)   Each of these films is hosted by former MGM stars and shows clips and excerpts of famous MGM musicals of the past. III shows some never before seen clips. Each is rated **[G]**. **V**

There's No Business Like Show Business (1954) *** D: Walter Lang. Ethel Merman, Dan Dailey, Donald O'Connor, Marilyn Monroe, Johnnie Ray, Mitzi Gaynor, Hugh O'Brian, Frank McHugh.   Great Irving Berlin songs make up the score to this story of the ups and downs of a show business family. Included are Monroe's "Heat Wave" and the title song for which Merman was very famous. Preview. **V**

This is the Army (1943) *** D: Michael Curtiz. George Murphy, Joan Leslie, Lt. Ronald Reagan, Sgt. Joe Louis, Kate Smith, George Tobias, Alan Hale, Charles Butterworth, Dolores Costello, Una Merkel, Stanley Ridges, Rosemary DeCamp, Frances Langford, Irving Berlin and more.   Hollywood stars in the service, soldiers, and others join Irving Berlin in a WWII version of his famous WWI Broadway show *Yip Yip Yaphank*. Many songs and skits of the 1940s included. Parents may wish to preview. **V**

Thoroughbreds Don't Cry (1937) **1/2 D: Alfred E. Green. Judy Garland, Mickey Rooney, Ronald Sinclair, Sophie Tucker, C. Aubrey Smith, Frankie Darro, Henry Kolker, Helen Troy.   Musical racetrack story with Rooney as a jockey who's mixed up in crooked dealings. First Garland/Rooney film. **V**

Thoroughly Modern Millie (1967) **1/2 D: George Roy Hill. Julie Andrews, James Fox, Mary Tyler Moore, Carol Channing, Beatrice Lillie, John Gavin, Jack Soo, Pat Morita, Philip Ahn.   1920s setting has Andrews a modern working girl living in a boarding house into which southern belle Moore moves. Strange happenings are going on in this place culminating in the disappearance of Moore. Cute film is very different, but still fun. Channing is wonderful as the singing, glass breaking matriarch of a wealthy family. Oscar winner for the Elmer Bernstein score, this later became a Broadway play. Preview. **V**

Thousands Cheer (1943) **1/2 D: George Sidney. Mickey Rooney, Judy Garland, Gene Kelly, Red Skelton, Eleanor Powell, Ann Sothern, Lucille Ball, Virginia O'Brien, Frank Morgan, Kathryn Grayson, Lena Horne and many others.   Grayson comes to live with officer-father at an army base and falls for private Kelly. She prepares an all star show for the men giving MGM an opportunity to parade some of its stars while boosting wartime morale. **V**

Three Caballeros, The (1945) *** D: Norman Ferguson. Aurora Miranda, Carmen Molina, Dora Luz, voices of Sterling Holloway, Clarence Nash, Jose Oliveira, Joaquin Garay.   Rousing Disney salute following the Good Neighbor policy by showing Latin America through Donald Duck's eyes. Filled with wonderful music, great cartoon sequences and clever blending of animation and real life, it's a great film for old and young alike. **V, DVD**

Three Little Words (1950) *** D: Richard Thorpe. Fred Astaire, Vera-Ellen, Red Skelton, Arlene Dahl, Keenan Wynn, Gloria De Haven, Debbie Reynolds, Carleton Carpenter.   Musical about songwriters Kalmar and Ruby, their partnership and rise to fame. Many fine tunes including, "Who's Sorry Now," "Thinking of You," and the title song. Debbie Reynolds plays Helen Kane, but the real Helen dubbed "I Wanna Be Loved By You." **V**

Till the Clouds Roll By (1946) **1/2 D: Richard Whorf. Robert Walker, Van Heflin, Lucille Bremer, Dorothy Patrick. Guest stars: Judy Garland, Kathryn Grayson, Lena Horne, Tony Martin, Dinah Shore, Frank Sinatra, June Allyson, Angela Landsbury, Cyd

Charisse, Virginia O'Brien.   Biography of songwriter Jerome Kern. Strongest points are numbers by guest stars and a mini-production of Kern's famous *Showboat*. Highlights include Lena's "Why Was I Born?" and Judy's "Look For the Silver Lining."   **V**

Tin Pan Alley (1940) ******* D: Walter Lang. Alice Faye, Betty Grable, Jack Oakie, John Payne, Esther Ralston, Allen Jenkins, Nicholas Brothers, John Loder, Elisha Cook, Jr.   Tells of songwriters trying to get a break. Interesting for a look at the importance of Tin Pan Alley in the world of music publishing in the early part of the 20ᵗʰ century. Clean family fun.   **V**

Toast of New Orleans ****1/2** (1950) D: Norman Taurog. Kathryn Grayson, Mario Lanza, David Niven, Rita Moreno, J. Carrol Naish.   Grayson is a famous singer who comes to the Bayou only to be joined in song by an uninvited fisherman! The rest of the film is spent transforming Lanza into an opera singer with the typical romance between the leads. Lanza's famous "Be My Love" is included.   **V**

Tonight and Every Night (1945) ******* D: Victor Saville. Rita Hayworth, Janet Blair, Lee Bowman, Marc Platt, Leslie Brooks. Professor Lamberti, Florence Bates.   The epitome of "The show must go on!" A theatre group in wartime England perform amidst bombings, hazards, personal sacrifice and never miss a performance. A lighter look at the "Blitz" of London.   **V**

Too Many Girls ****1/2** (1940) D: George Abbott. Lucille Ball, Richard Carlson, Eddie Bracken, Ann Miller, Hal LeRoy, Desi Arnaz, Frances Langford.   Rogers and Hart comedy brings Lucy to the west to college at "Pottawatomie" in Stopgap, New Mexico. Typical college hijinks. Film debut of later famous Van Johnson, as well as Bracken and Arnaz. This was where Lucy and Desi met.   **V**

Too Young to Kiss (1951) ****1/2** D: Robert Z. Leonard. June Allyson, Van Johnson, Gig Young, Paula Corday, Hans Conried.   Allyson is a concert pianist who can't get an interview with the big "starmaker" Johnson. She finds out he's auditioning children and masquerades as a child just to get to audition for him. It turns into a never ending situation with some real comic moments, ending with her falling for him.

Top Hat (1935) ******** D: Mark Sandrich. Fred Astaire, Ginger Rogers, Edward Everett Horton, Helen Broderick, Eric Blore, Erik Rhodes.   One of *the* best Astaire/Rogers musicals filled with great music and wonderful dance numbers including "Check to Cheek," "Isn't This a Lovely Day to Be Caught in the Rain," "Top Hat, White Tie and Tails," along with other greats by Irving Berlin. Rogers mistakes Astaire for the husband of her friend (Broderick) when really Horton is her husband's friend. One mistake leads to another until it all works out in the end.   **V**

Turning Point, The (1977) ****1/2** D: Herbert Ross. Anne Bancroft, Shirley MacLaine, Mikhail Baryshnikov, Leslie Browne, Tom Skerritt, Martha Scott, Marshall Thompson.   Do *NOT* show this entire movie! However, DO excerpt the dance scenes; they are wonderful. The chance to see Baryshnikov dance *Le Corsaire* is worth the rental price. Added bonuses are seeing the Pas de Deux of Baryshnikov and Browne, and Browne's contemporary solo to Duke Ellington's music. If you have one who loves dance and particularly the ballet, excerpting the dance scenes in this will be a wonderful treat. [**PG**]   **V**

Two Tickets to Broadway (1951) ****1/2** D: James V. Kern. Tony Martin, Janet Leigh, Gloria De Haven, Eddie Bracken, Ann Miller, Barbara Lawrence, Smith and Dale, Bob Crosby.   Leigh, a county girl who comes to the big city, meets De Haven and Miller on the bus and they work together with Martin to get on Crosby's TV show. Bracken has scammed them by telling them they have a spot on the show. Leigh finds out the truth and through a series of events Bracken *does* get them on the show. Some good numbers, including Crosby's spoof of brother, Bing.   **V**

Two Weeks With Love ****1/2** (1950) D: Roy Rowland. Jane Powell, Ricardo Montalban, Louis Calhern, Ann Harding, Debbie Reynolds, Carleton Carpenter.   Powell is out to prove to her parents how grown up she has become. Most famous for Reynolds-Carpenter's "Abba Dabba Honeymoon."   **V**

Unfinished Dance (1947) ******* D: Henry Koster. Margaret O'Brien, Cyd Charisse, Karin

Booth, Danny Thomas, Esther Dale.   This film originally didn't receive great reviews but charmed both myself and my daughters. Charsse is the leading ballerina with a ballet company and young O'Brien has a huge case of hero worship for her, missing class in the ballet school to admire Charisse from afar. The company brings in a big named Prima Ballerina and O'Brien comes to Charisse's defense in a most alarming way. This story is a tale of love, wrong actions, repentance, and forgiveness, as well as a character study of the two ballerinas. Ask your children who was the REAL Prima ballerina? If you cannot find it, have someone tape it for you. You'll treasure your copy if you have little girls who love the ballet. I think it's a jewel of a movie. Highly recommended.

Unsinkable Molly Brown (1964) *** D: Charles Walters. Debbie Reynolds, Harve Presnell Ed Begley, Jack Kruschen, Hermione Baddeley.   The film version of the Broadway play based upon real life Molly Brown who lived in Denver in the late 1800s, sailed on the Titanic (which sank April 14-15, 1912) and with her unwavering courage, calmed people and kept them going until help arrived and they were rescued. Perhaps not 100% accurate, but still gives a good look at the lady who was reportedly very down to earth and somewhat larger than life. **V**

Vagabond King (1956) ** D: Michael Curtiz. Kathryn Grayson, Oreste, Rita Moreno, Cedric Hardwicke, Walter Hampden, Leslie Nielsen; narrated by Vincent Price.   Remake of Rudolf Friml's operetta about François Villon, who matches wits with King Louis XI. Filmed before without music as *If I Were King*. (See Middle Ages)

Waltz King, The (1963) **1/2 D: Steve Previn. Kerwin Matthews, Brain Aherne, Senta Berger, Peter Kraus, Fritz Eckhardt.   Disney bio of Johann Strauss, Jr. (the Younger) whose father (Aherne) doesn't want him following in his footsteps as a composer/orchestra leader and of Jr's determination to do just that. Thankfully, he did and we have beautiful waltzes such as the Blue Danube because he did. Includes lots of good music. Filmed in Germany, was originally shown in U.S. in two parts for the TV show. **V**

We're Not Dressing (1934) *** D: Norman Taurog. Bing Crosby, Carole Lombard, George Burns, Gracie Allen, Ethel Merman, Leon Errol, Ray Milland.   Rich girl (Lombard) is fascinated with sailor (Crosby) on her yacht, but turns up her nose at him. When shipwrecked, the entire rich ensemble becomes dependent upon the skills of commoner Crosby. Dated film but still fun and brings up some interesting discussion points as snobbery of this type still exists. Movie is also worth seeing for a peek at Burns and Allen in the flesh and at their best. This is on record in my family as the first film my father ever saw.   **V**

West Point Story (1950) **1/2 D: Roy Del Ruth. James Cagney, Virginia Mayo, Doris Day, Gordon MacRae, Gene Nelson, Alan Hale, Jr., Jack Kelly, Roland Winters.   Cagney, an abrasive director, is sent to West Point by a producer friend to break his nephew out of West Point under the guise of putting on the annual West Point show. Cagney imports Mayo and Day to help. Cagney gets in trouble with WP as he ignores their rules in order to accomplish his agenda. To combat this, the WP administration makes him a cadet so that he has to follow the same rules as the boys! Songs include "The Military Polka" and "The Kissing Rock." **V**

West Side Story (1961) **** D: Robert Wise, Jerome Robbins. Natalie Wood, Richard Beymer, George Chakiris, Rita Moreno, Russ Tamblyn, Tucker Smith, David Winters, Tony Mordente, Simon Oakland, John Astin.   Winner of ten Academy Awards, this groundbreaking film version of the Broadway play of *Romeo and Juliet* style story set in 1950s New York city has just about everything going for it. Bernstein originally wrote this to be black vs. white, but didn't think it would succeed, so changed it to Hispanics vs. whites. The choice of the stars is a bit of a mystery, for the original Broadway cast was quite something, but everything still clicks. Bernstein's score is brilliant, as is Robbins choreography. Songs include "Maria," "Tonight, "Somewhere," "America," and the jazzy opening, "Jets and Sharks." **V**

96

White Christmas (1954) *** D: Michael Curtiz. Bing Crosby, Danny Kaye, Rosemary

Clooney, Vera-Ellen, Dean Jagger, Mary Wickes.   Two army buddies, (Crosby and Kaye) now back in show biz and big producers, get a letter from a fellow in their outfit asking them to check on his sisters (Clooney and Vera-Ellen) who are trying to break into "the biz." In a comedy of mishaps, they all end up together on a train to Vermont and discover that the guys former General (Jagger) owns a ski lodge that's in trouble. All four pitch in to help and a show is on. Included in the show is a recreation of an old minstrel show. These were done in a semi-circle fashion with "Mr. Tambo" on one end and "Mr. Bones" on the other. The "moderator" was called "Mr. Interlocutor." Watch for this scene and see if you can figure out who plays whom! Songs include: "Sisters," "Mandy," "Count Your Blessings," and the title song. Great, *fun* family film. **V**

Wizard of Oz (1939) **** D: Victor Fleming. Judy Garland, Ray Bolger, Bert Lahr, Jack Haley, Frank Morgan, Billie Burke, Margaret Hamilton, Charley Grapewin, Clara Blandick, The Singer Midgets. Famous film of the classic children's book by L. Frank Baum has become an American classic. A girl from Kansas gets a bump on the head and travels to far away Oz, where she must find a "wizard" in order to return home. There are some scary elements in this so edit it for your children if you choose to see it. Most famous song from the film, "Over the Rainbow," as well as the score won an Oscar. **V, DVD**

Words and Music (1948) **1/2 D: Norman Taurog. Mickey Rooney, Tom Drake, June Allyson, Ann Sothern, Judy Garland, Gene Kelly, Lena Horne, Vera-Ellen, Cyd Charisse, Allyn Ann McLerie, Mel Torme', Betty Garrett, Perry Como, Janet Leigh.   Somewhat accurate biography of songwriter Larry Hart and his partnership with (young) Richard Rodgers. Included are some great song and dance numbers by some of Hollywood's best, including the famous "Slaughter on Tenth Avenue." **V**

Yankee Doodle Dandy (1942) **** D: Michael Curtiz. James Cagney, Joan Leslie, Walter Huston, Irene Manning, Rosemary DeCamp, Richard Whorf, Jeanne Cagney, S.Z. Sakall, Walter Catlett, Frances Langford, Eddie Foy, Jr., George Tobias.   In his own inimitable fashion, Cagney plays the famous songwriter and Vaudevillian entertainer George M. Cohan, for which he won an Oscar. Filled with Cohan's music and good dance numbers, it's just an unbeatable musical film. No doubt the flag waving only helped in the war effort. Songs include: "Only Forty-five Minutes from Broadway," "Mary," "Over There," and the title song. Beware edited versions. The one you want runs 126 minutes. **V**

Yank in the RAF, A (1941) **1/2 D: Henry King. Tyrone Power, Betty Grable, John Sutton, Reginald Gardiner, Donald Stuart, Richard Fraser.   Power's fighting with the RAF in WWII while Betty sings and entertains. **V, DVD**

You'll Never Get Rich (1941) *** D: Sidney Lanfield. Fred Astaire, Rita Hayworth, John Hubbard, Robert Benchley, Osa Massen.   Astaire is in a show and gets drafted. The show must go on and he must go to camp. Benchley brings show to the Army, and Astaire tries to romance Rita away from a captain and straighten out his philandering friend. Cole Porter's music includes "So Near and Yet So Far." **V**

Young Man With a Horn (1950) **1/2 D: Michael Curtiz. Kirk Douglas, Lauren Bacall, Doris Day, Juano Hernandez, Hoagy Carmichael, Mary Beth Hughes.   Drama of trumpet player (Douglas) inspired by Bix Beiderbecke's life. Bacall plays the bad girl and Day the wholesome one. Harry James dubbed the trumpet playing. Interesting story of the ups and downs of a performer's life. Preview. **V**

Young People (1940) **1/2 D: Allan Dwan. Shirley Temple, Jack Oakie, Charlotte Greenwood, Arleen Whelan, George Montgomery, Kathleen Howard.   Show-biz couple decides to retire from the footlights and move to a small town to give their daughter a "regular life." Problem is, they've no idea how to fit in! They are shunned by the majority, but make a few friends and are eventually accepted when they save the day in a crisis situation. Clean family fun with song and dance, too. **V**

You Were Meant for Me (1948) **1/2 D: Lloyd Bacon. Jeanne Crain, Dan Dailey, Oscar Levant.   Nice costume film of a band leader and his wife during the Depression.

You Were Never Lovelier (1942) *** D: William A. Seiter. Fred Astaire, Rita Hayworth, Adolphe Menjou, Leslie Brooks, Adele Mara, Xavier Cugat.   Rita's simply not interested in men, but is waiting for fairy tale knight on a white charger. No one measures up. Father (Menjou) takes matters into his own hands and begins writing romantic letters to her to prove she IS romantic while seeking a young man for her. Astaire is trying to get a job dancing at Menjou's establishment, meets Rita and through circumstances, becomes the man of the letters. Includes some great songs by Jerome Kern with lyrics by the inimitable Johnny Mercer *and* the knight on the white charger.   **V**

Ziegfeld Follies (1946) *** D: Vincente Minelli. William Powell, Judy Garland, Lucille Ball, Fred Astaire, Fanny Brice, Lena Horne, Red Skelton, Victor Moore, Virginia O'Brien, Cyd Charisse, Gene Kelly, Edward Arnold, Esther Williams.   All star film with vignettes throughout. Highlights are Astaire/Kelly dance (their only in a film until That's Entertainment II), and seeing the *real* Fanny Brice in action, who was given her "big break" by the *real* Ziegfeld!   **V**

NOTES

Biographies

Abe Lincoln in Illinois (1940) **** (See 1800s-Civil War)

Adventures of Mark Twain, The (1944) *** (See 1800s-East)

Adventures of Robin Hood, The (1938) **** (See Middle Ages) Real-life or legend has yet to be definitely established. Also includes Richard the Lion-heart and his weasely brother, Prince John.

Agony and the Ecstasy, The (1965) **1/2 (See Renaissance) About Michelangelo painting the Sistine Chapel

Anna and the King of Siam (1946) ***1/2 (See 1800s-The World) About Anna Leonowens

Anne of the Thousand Days (1969) *** (See Reformation) About Queen Anne Boleyn

Annie Oakley (1935) *** (See 1800s-West) About famous sharp shooter

Autobiography of Miss. Jane Pittman, The (1974) TVM Above average. (See 1800s-Civil War)

Babe Ruth Story, The (1948) ** (See Sports) About famous ball player

Barretts of Wimpole Street, The (1957) *** (See Literature)

Beau Brummell (1954) **1/2 (See 1800s-Europe)

Becket (1964) **** (See Middle Ages) About Thomas á Becket and King Henry II of England

Belle Starr (1941) **1/2 (See 1800s-Civil War) About famous female Confederate spy

Ben and Me NR (See 1700s) About Ben Franklin and a mouse named Amos

Benny Goodman Story, The (1955) *** (See Music/Arts) About famous Big Band leader

Brian's Song (1971) TVM Above average (See Sports) About Chicago Bears' Brian Piccolo

Broken Arrow (1950) *** (See 1800s-West) About Cochise

Buccaneer, The (1958) *** (See 1800s-East) About General Andrew Jackson, Pirate Jean Lafitte and the Battle of 1812.

Buddy Holly Story, The (1978) ***1/2 (See Musicals) About famous musician

Buffalo Bill (1944) **1/2 (See 1800s-West)

Caesar and Cleopatra (1946-British) **

Calamity Jane (1953) *** (See 1800s-West)

Captain From Castille (1947) *** (See Renaissance) Includes Cortez's conquest of Mexico

Carbine Williams (1952) *** (See 1900s) About the development of the carbine rifle

Chisum (1970) **1/2 (See 1800s-West) Includes Billy the Kid

Cleopatra (1934) ***1/2 (See Ancient Egypt)

Coal Miner's Daughter (1980) ***1/2 (See Music/Arts) About country singer Loretta Lynn

Court-Marshall of Billy Mitchell, The (1955) ***1/2 (See WWI) About aviation pioneer

Cross Creek (1983) *** (See 1900s) About author Marjorie Kinnan Rawling

Crusades, The (1935) *** (See Middle Ages) About Richard the Lion-heart

David (1997) [NR] (See Bible) About King David of the Bible

Davy Crockett, King of the Wild Frontier (1955) *** (See 1800s-East)

Desert Fox (1951) *** (See WWII-Other Theatres of War) About German General Romell

Diamond Jim (1935) *** (See 1800s-East) About Diamond Jim Brady

Eddie Duchin Story, The (1956) ** (See Music/Arts) About pianist-bandleader

Edison, the Man (1940) *** (See 1900s) About Thomas Edison

Eleanor Roosevelt Story, The (1965) ***1/2 (See WWII, The Home Front)

Esther (2000) [NR] (See Bible) About Queen Esther of the Bible

Fabulous Dorseys, The (1947) ** About famous bandleaders of the 1940s

Far Horizons (1955) **1/2 (See 1800s-West) About Lewis and Clark

Flying Misfits, The [NR] (See WWII-South Pacific) About "Pappy" Boyington, leader of the "Black Sheep" fighter squadron.

Gentleman Jim (1942) ***1/2 (See 1900s) About boxer Jim Corbett

Girl in White, The (1952) ** (See Medicine) About first woman ambulance surgeon

Glenn Miller Story, The (1954) *** (See Music/Arts) About famous bandleader

Gorillas in the Mist (1988) *** (See Science/Nature) About Dian Fossey, researcher on gorilla life

Greatest Story Ever Told (1965) **1/2 (See Bible) About Jesus

Great Moment, The (1944) ** (See 1800s-East) About William Morton, anesthesia inventor

Hellfighters (1968) ** (See 1900s) Based on life of oil well fire fighter Red Adair

Hiding Place, The (1975) **1/2 (See WWII-Europe) About Corrie ten Boom

Houdini (1953) **1/2 (See 1900s)

I Dream of Jeanie (1952) ** (See 1800s East) About composer Stephen Foster

If I Were A King (1938) *** (See Middle Ages) About King Louis XI

I'll See You in My Dreams (1951) **1/2 (See Music/Arts) About lyricist Gus Kahn

Incendiary Blonde (1945) *** (See Music/Arts) About entertainer Texas Guinan

Inn of the Sixth Happiness (1958) *** (See Bible) About missionary to China, Gladys Aleward

I Remember Mama (1948) *** (See 1900s) About writer Kathryn Forbes' family

Irish Eyes Are Smiling (1944) **1/2 (See Music/Arts) About composer Ernest R. Ball

Iron Mistress (1952) **1/2 (See 1800s-West) About Jim Bowie

I Wonder Who's Kissing Her Now (1947) **1/2 (See Music/Arts) About songwriter Joseph E. Howard

Jackie Robinson Story, The (1950) *** (See Sports)

Jeremiah (2000) [NR] (See Bible) About biblical prophet

Jesus [NR] (See Bible)

Jim Thorpe-All-American (1951) **1/2 (See Sports) About famous athlete

Joan of Arc (1948) **1/2 (See Middle Ages)

Joni (1980) **1/2 (See 1900s) About quadriplegic Joni Eareckson Tada

Joseph (1995) [NR] (See Bible) About biblical Joseph

Juarez (1939) **1/2 (See 1800s World) About writer of Mexico's Constitution

King of Kings (1961) ***1/2 (See Bible) About Jesus

Knute Rockne, All American (1940) *** (See 1900s) About famous Notre Dame football coach

Lawrence of Arabia (1962-British) **** (See WWI) About T. E. Lawrence

Life of Emile Zola, The (1937) *** (See 1800s World) About famous French writer

Luther (1974) **1/2 (See Reformation) About Martin Luther

MacArthur (1977) *** (See WWII-South Pacific) About General Douglas MacArthur

Magnificent Rebel (1962) **1/2 (See 1800s-Europe) About Beethoven

Man Called Peter, A (1955) *** (See Bible) About Senate Chaplain Peter Marshall

Man For All Seasons, A (1966-British) **** (See Reformation) About Sir Thomas More and King Henry VIII

Man of a Thousand Faces (1957) ***1/2 (See 1900s) About silent film legend, Lon Chaney

Merrill's Marauders (1962) **1/2 (See WWII-South Pacific) About Brigadier General Frank Merrill

Miracle Worker, The (1962) ***1/2 (See 1900s) About Annie Sullivan and Helen Keller

My Wild Irish Rose (1947) ** (See Music/Arts) About songwriter Chauncey Olcott

Northwest Passage (Book I—Roger's Rangers) (1940) *** (See 1700s) About Roger's Rangers

One Against the Wind (1991) TVM (See WWII-Europe) About Countess Mary Lindell who smuggled Allied soldiers out of France

Other Side of the Mountain, The (1975) **1/2 (See Sports) About skier Jill Kinmont

Outsider, The (1961) *** About Ira Hamilton Hayes, the Pima Indian who was one of the Marines who raised the U. S. flag on Iwo Jima

Pride of St. Louis, The (1952) **1/2 (See Sports) About baseball player Dizzy Dean

Pride of the Yankees, The (1942) **** (See Sports) About baseball player Lou Gehrig

Prince of Foxes (1949) **1/2 (See Renaissance) Includes Cesare Borgia

PT 109 (1963) ** (See WWII-South Pacific) About President John F. Kennedy

Sergeant York (1941) ***1/2 (See WWI) About Sergeant Alvin York, winner of Congressional Medal of Honor

Seven Little Foys, The (1955) *** (See Music/Arts) About vaudeville entertainer Eddie Foy

Shadowlands (1993-British) ***1/2 (See 1900s) About author C. S. Lewis

Shine On Harvest Moon (1944) **1/2 (See Music/Arts) About entertainers Nora Bayes and Jack Norworth

Song of Love (1947) **1/2 (See 1800s Europe) About composer Robert Schumann

So This is Love (1953) **1/2 (See Music/Arts) About opera star Grace Moore

Sound and the Silence, The (1992) TVM (See 1800's East) About Alexander Graham Bell

Sound of Music, The (1965) ***1/2 (See WWII-Europe) About Maria von Trapp

Spirit of St. Louis, The (1957) *** (See Science/Nature) About Charles Lindbergh's trans-Atlantic flight

Stanley and Livingstone (1939) *** (See 1800s-The World)

Stars and Stripes Forever (1952) **1/2 (See WWI) About John Philip Sousa

Story of Ruth, The (1960) **1/2 (See Bible) About Ruth of the Biblical book of Ruth

Story of Seabiscuit (1944) *** (See Horses) About the famous racehorse, Seabiscuit

Story of Vernon and Irene Castle, The (1939) *** (See Music/Arts) About famous dancing couple

Story of Will Rogers, The (1952) *** (See Family) About famous humorist

Stratton Story, The (1949) ***1/2 (See Sports) About baseball player Monty Stratton

Sunrise at Campobello (1960) *** (See 1900s) About Franklin Delano Roosevelt

Ten Commandments, The (1956) **** (See Ancient Egypt) Story of Moses and the children of Israel

Tennessee Johnson (1942) **1/2 (See 1800s-East) About President Andrew Johnson

To Hell and Back (1956) *** (See WWII-Europe) About Audie Murphy, the most highly decorated soldier in American history (so far)

Unsinkable Molly Brown (1964) *** (See Music/Arts) About Molly Brown, the heroine of the Titanic.

Virgin Queen, The (1955) *** (See Reformation) About Elizabeth I.

Waltz King, The (1963) ** (See 1800s-Europe) About Johann Strauss, the Younger.

White Angel, The (1936) ** Story of Florence Nightingale. (See 1800s Europe)

Wings of Eagles, The (1957) **1/2 (See WWI) About Frank "Spig" Weed

Young Bess (1953) *** (See Reformation) About Elizabeth I.

Young Mr. Lincoln (1939) ***1/2 (See 1800s-Civil War)

Young Tom Edison (1940) *** (See 1900s)

NOTES

Family Films

Note: Any film from the other categories is also eligible as a family film if it appeals to you and your family. Don't think that these are the only family films. This section is mostly full of fun films which don't necessarily fit in the other categories.

Absent Minded Professor, The (1961) *** D: Robert Stevenson. Fred MacMurray, Nancy Olsen, Keenan Wynn, Tommy Kirk, Ed Wynn, Leon Ames, Elliot Reid.   Disney classic of MacMurray working in his garage and secretly discovering "flubber." (flying rubber) He tries it out on himself and then the basketball team. This results in the rest of the shenanigans. Fun, clean family film. Remade and updated as *Flubber* in 1997. **V**

Adventure in Baltimore (1949) **1/2 D: Richard Wallace. Shirley Temple, John Agar, Robert Young, Josephine Hutchinson.   Set around the turn of the century, this show teamed then married Temple and Agar as neighbors. Temple is a pastor's daughter and artist who is constantly finding trouble without trying. Agar somehow seems to always fall in with her plans. The real corker comes when he agrees to pose for a portrait that doesn't turn out quite like he expected. I think the entire family will like this one.

Adventures of Bullwhip Griffin, The (1967) *** D: James Neilson. Roddy McDowell, Suzanne Pleshette, Karl Malden, Harry Guardino, Richard Hayden, Hermione Bradley, Bryan Russell.   Clean family fun in this Disney spoof of the gold-rush. A fine Boston family has fallen on hard times. The young "heir" has gone west to the gold fields along with his butler. The butler "Bullwhip" and his young charge have some amazing adventures and scrapes. The kids will enjoy this one. **V**

Adventures of Ichabod and Mr. Toad, The (1949) *** (See Literature)

Adventures of Milo and Otis, The (1989—Japanese) **1/2 D: Masanori Hata. Narrated by Dudley Moore.   Fun film of what happens to a cat and a dog when they stray from their farm home. **[G] V**

Adventures of Robin Hood (1938) ****1/2 (See Middle Ages)

Adventures of the Wilderness Family, The (1975) *** D: Stewart Raffill. Robert F. Logan, Susan Damante Shaw, Hollye Holmes, Ham Larsen, Buck Flower, William Cornford.   A couple decide to abandon big city life due to frustration with a child's asthma which is exacerbated by smog. They move to the Rocky Mountains and home school. They build a cabin, live off the land and encounter various trials and dangers along the way. Clean family fun. **[G] V**

Adventures of Tom Sawyer, The (1938) ***1/2 D: Norman Taurog. Tommy Kelly, Jackie Moran, Ann Gillis, May Robson, Walter Brennan, Victor Jory, Spring Byington, Margaret Hamilton.   Unique version of the Mark Twain story including a memorable sequence in the cave with Injun Joe. View first to make sure this won't scare your children.

Affairs of Dobie Gillis, The (1953) *** D: Don Wies. Debbie Reynolds, Bobby Van, Hans Conreid, Lurene Tuttle, Bob Fosse.   Debbie goes to school, meets Dobie and suddenly sees school in a different light, much to the displeasure of her parents. Good look at consequences and opportunity for discussion of goofing off or buckling down. Clean B & W film upon which a later TV program was based. **V**

Air Bud (1977) **1/2 D: Charles Martin Smith. Kevin Zegers, Michael Jeter, Wendy Makkena, Bill Cobbs, Erick Christmas.   Making friends with a dog helps the new boy in town, who discovers that the dog has an uncanny ability to shoot baskets. This brings media attention, causing the abusive former owner to want him back. My children reviewed this film and felt that it would be acceptable to most families. **V, DVD**

Air Bud: Golden Receiver (1998) **1/2 D: Richard Martin. Kevin Zegers, Gregory Harrison, Shayn Solberg, Cynthia Conway, Dick Martin.   In this sequel, Buddy catches footballs instead of making hoops. He and Zegers join the football team and try to match up mom with the local vet, (Harrison) while villains try to steal Buddy for their circus. **V, DVD**

Alaska (1996) **1/2 D: Fraser C. Heston. Thora Birch, Vincent Kartheiser, Dirk Benedict, Charlton Heston, Duncan Fraser, Gordon Tootoosis.   Feuding brother and sister take off into the wilds of Alaska to find their missing aviator father (Benedict). They help and befriend a polar bear cub and try to out fox the poachers who are after it and now, them. Heston is cast as one of the poachers. My children reviewed this and liked it; perhaps your will, too. **[PG]   V**

Alias Jesse James (1959) *** D: Norman McLeod. Bob Hope, Rhonda Fleming, Wendell Corey, Jim Davis, Gloria Talbott.   Zany story has nothing to do with the story of the real Jesse James. Hope is an insurance salesman who comes west and is taken for a sharpshooter. Filled with typical Hope comedy, this is another film in which I can't remember anything objectionable, but it's been a while. Perhaps it would be better to preview it to make sure. **V**

All Creatures Great and Small (1974 U. S.—British) TVM D: Claude Whatham. Simon Ward, Anthony Hopkins, Lisa Harrow, Brian Stirner, Freddie Jones, T. P. McKenna.   Based upon the book of the same title by James Herriot. Ward plays the author as a young veterinarian who has come to work with an eccentric established vet named Siegfried (Hopkins). Not as good as the book, but a great way to introduce children to·these great books or use it to compare to the book after reading it. These are books NOT to be missed! Read them as family read-alouds if you must, but by all means, read it and the sequel. (*All Things Bright and Beautiful*) You'll laugh until you cry. Above average.

All Mine to Give (1957) **1/2 D: Allen Reisner. Cameron Mitchell, Glynis Johns, Patty McCormack, Hope Emerson, Rita Shaw.   Moving story of a Scot who comes to America with his bride to make a new life for himself. They are blessed with a wonderful brood until diphtheria hits. Then the story takes an unusual turn. Worth seeing and talking about this disease and the communication of it as well as the responsibility and sacrifices made. Don't miss it! **V**

Amazing Panda Adventure, The (1995– U.S.-China) **1/2 D: Christopher Cain. Ryan Slater, Stephen Lang, Yi Ding, Huang Fei, Zhou Jiugou, Yao Erga.   A young boy goes to visit his dad in China while he is conducting research on Pandas. The boy gets in over his head when he discovers poachers who have taken a baby panda. The boy along with a Chinese girl, run from the poachers with the cub trying to get back to the boy's father. Filmed on location in China, the scenery is spectacular. **[PG]   V**

American Tail, An (1986) **1/2 D: Don Bluth. Voices of Dom DeLuise, Christopher Plummer, Nehemiah Persoff, Madeline Kahn, Phillip Glasser, John Finnegan, Cathianne Blore, Will Ryan.   Thinking they can escape cats, a Russian mouse family immigrates to America. During a storm (the scariest part of the film) the young mouse son is separated from his family and befriended by a vegetarian cat named "Tiger!" (DeLuise) The film is cute, charming, and funny as the family searches for Fievel and he for his family. The song "Somewhere Out There" was made famous by Linda Ronstadt and James Ingram. For the most part, a winner of a film. I love the part when Madeline Kahn says, "We need a wowee!" (rally) Produced by Steven Spielberg. **[G]   V**

American Tail: Fievel Goes West (1991) **1/2 D: Phil Nebbelink, Simon Wells. Voices of Philip Glasser, James Stewart, Erica Yohn, Cathy Cavadini, Nehemiah Persoff, Dom DeLuise, Amy Irving, John Clesse, Jon Lovitz.   The Mousekewitz family heads west and Fievel continues to find trouble. Biggest treats are Dom DeLuise ("Tiger") and James Stewart's Sheriff Wylie Burp who is armed with "the lazy eye!" The kids will love it. Produced by Steven Spielberg. **[G]   V**

Andy Hardy films These films were made from 1937 to 1958, with Mickey Rooney playing the title role. These are warm, family films which are somewhat dated now, but always containing family values. Indeed, the series won a special Oscar in 1942 "for its achievement in representing the American Way of Life." This is the way we wish were still present in our nation; a belief in God, in doing right even when it cost you something, the importance of family, etc. Though not everyone may agree with everything in these films, I think that overall, any one of these will be considered an appropriate family film. Below you will find them listed in the order of their release. Question marks are by those I feel might be less liked.

A Family Affair
You're Only Young Once
Judge Hardy's Children
Love Finds Andy Hardy
Out West With the Hardys
The Hardys Ride High
Andy Hardy Gets Spring Fever
Judge Hardy and Son

Andy Hardy Meets Debutante
Andy Hardy's Private Secretary
Life Begins for Andy Hardy (?)
The Courtship of Andy Hardy (?)
Andy Hardy's Double Life
Andy Hardy's Blonde Trouble
Love Laughs at Andy Hardy
Andy Hardy Comes Home

Angel and the Badman (1947) *** (See 1800s West)

Angels in the Outfield (1951) *** D: Clarence Brown. Paul Douglas, Janet Leigh, Keenan Wynn, Donna Corcoran, Spring Byington, Ellen Corby, Lewis Stone, Bruce Bennett, voice of James Whitmore. Douglas plays the hot-tempered manager of the Pittsburgh Pirates who gets a new look at baseball and life when angels intervene in his ball club! There are some cameos from baseball and show business. Remade in 1994, but not as well done as this one. **V**

Anne of Avonlea (1987-Canadian) TVM Above Average (see 1900s)

Anne of Green Gables (1985-Canadian) TVM Above Average (see 1900s)

Anything Can Happen (1952) **1/2 D: George Seaton. Jose Ferrer, Kim Hunter, Kurt Kasznar, Eugenie Leontovich, Oscar Beregi, Nick Dennis.   A fun story of a Russian émigré who finds himself in court for picking flowers in the park. There he meets a court reporter who is also a student of folk music and wants recordings of songs from his native area of Russia. Through the film, he falls in love with her and follows her to her home in California. I think this is a sweet story and one everyone can enjoy. I especially like the scene with the "duff."

Apollo 13 (1995) ***1/2 (See Science/Nature)

Aristocats, The (1970) *** D: Wolfgang Reitherman. Voices of Eva Gabor, Phil Harris, Sterling Hollo-way, Scatman Crothers, Paul Winchell, Lord Tim Hudson, Vito Scotti, Thurl Ravenscroft, Nancy Kulp, Pat Buttram, George Lindsey, Monica Evans, Carole Shelley.   Fun story of a cat and kittens of a wealthy owner who stand to inherit a fortune. Not, however, if the butler can stop it! Fun animated film. **[G] V, DVD**

Around the World in 80 Days (1950) *** (See Literature)

Artists and Models (1955) *** D: Frank Tashlin. Dean Martin Jerry Lewis, Shirley MacLaine, Dorothy Malone, Eva Gabor, Anita Ekberg.   Goofy tale of Martin, a cartoonist, who takes ideas from friend and roomie Lewis's outlandish dreams. Interesting commentary on the good or evil of comic books, yet lots of family fun. **V**

At War With the Army (1950) **1/2 D: Hal Walker. Dean Martin, Jerry Lewis, Polly Bergen, Angela Greene, Mike Kellin.   In their starring roles, Martin is a sergeant and Lewis is a PFC. Martin doesn't make life easy for Lewis with Lewis's usual silliness. The Coke machine scene is unforgettable. Cute twist at end. **V, DVD**

Babe (1995-U.S.-Australiian) *** D: Chris Noonan, James Cromwell, Magda Szubanski. Voices of Christine Cavanaugh, Miriam Margolyes, Danny Mann, Hugo Weaving, Miriam Flynn, Russi Taylor, Evelyn Krape; narrated by Roscoe Lee Brown.   Based on the book *The Sheep-Pig* by Dick King-Smith, this is the tale of a pig who thinks he's a sheep herding

dog. The animals converse with one another, which allows you to know what is happening. Babe ends up winning a contest for sheep herding! This is a fun family film with lots of laughs, especially from the singing mice. **[G]** **V, DVD**

Bachelor and the Bobby-Soxer (1947) *** D: Irving Reis. Cary Grant, Myrna Loy, Shirley Temple, Rudy Vallee, Ray Collins, Harry Davenport.   Shirley plays the younger sister of Loy, a Judge. Grant appears before the Judge who does not form a favorable opinion of him, but she orders him to go out with Shirley with the express purpose of disenchanting her crush upon him. Meanwhile, she fights falling for him herself! My girls picked up the word "sconklish" (who *knows* how it's spelled?!) from this movie. **V**

Bachelor Mother (1939) ***1/2 D: Garson Kanin. Ginger Rogers, David Niven, Charles Coburn, Frank Anderson, Ernest Truex.   While walking home from her job in a department store, Rogers sees a baby on a doorstep. When trying to get the baby with the appropriate authorities, she is mistaken for the mother, which leads from one comedy of errors to another. Cute film which was later remade as a musical called *Bundle of Joy*. This one is my pick of the two. **V**

Back to the Future (1985) ***1/2 D: Robert Zemeckis. Michael J. Fox, Christopher Lloyd, Crispin Glover, Lea Thompson, Wendie Jo Sperber, Marc McClure, Claudia Wells, Thomas F. Wilson, James Tolkan, Casey Siemaszko, Billy Zane, Jason Hervey.   Sci-fi comes to life as teenager Fox is transported from the 1980s to the 1950s by the invention of his weird scientist friend (Lloyd). While out of time, he messes up the "space-time continuum" and realizes that unless he can fix things between his parents, he will cease to exist. There are a few questionable scenes, so parents should view it first, but overall, this is a wild and wacky look at the 1950s and how times have changed. Try to see on television so language is edited. **[PG]** **V** (Followed by *Back to the Future II* which I don't recommend as it is depressing and very dark in tone and character.)

Back to the Future III (1990) ***1/2 D: Robert Zemeckis. Michael J. Fox, Christopher Lloyd, Mary Steenburgen, Thomas F. Wilson, Lea Thompson, Elizabeth Shue, Matt Clark, Richard Dysart, Pat Buttram, Harey Carey, Jr., Dub Taylor, James Tolkan.   Finale of the trilogy has Fox transported this time to the Old West, circa 1885 to find Lloyd, his wacky scientist friend and prevent his death. From then on, buckle your seatbelt! **[PG]** **V**

Ball of Fire (1941) ***1/2 D: Howard Hawks. Gary Cooper, Barbara Stanwyck, Oscar Homolka, Dana Andrews, Dan Duryea, S. Z. Sakall, Richard Haydn, Henry Travers, Tully Marshall, Gene Krupa.   Cute comedy of Cooper and other professors who are "holed up" and out of touch with society while working on a new encyclopedia. A chance encounter with a delivery man shows Cooper that his entire section on slang is out of date and so he goes out to find those who can help him with the up-to-date version. He meets a night club entertainer (Stanwyck) whom he invites (along with others) to a round-table discussion on slang. She is the girl-friend of a gangster and needs a place to hide for a while and decides to take up the professor on his offer, but a bit *more* than the offer included; namely, a place to stay. I suggest parents view this one first as some might not approve of parts of this and wish to either skip it or edit it. However, there are some interesting glimpses into our ever changing language. **V, DVD**

Balto (1995) **1/2 D: Simon Wells. Voices of Kevin Bacon, Bob Hoskins, Bridget Fonda, Jim Cummings, Phil Collins, Miriam Margolyes, Lola Bats-Campbell.   Story about a dog that loves his child-owner who comes down with dreaded influenza. He risks his life to get needed medicine through a terrible storm. Good story of courage and loyalty. Does contain some Indian legend/mysticism in a couple of places. Reviewed by my children. **[G]** **V**

Bambi (1942) **** D: David Hand.   Disney's lovely tale of a young deer prince and his life in the forest. Guaranteed to make you cry. **V**

Barefoot Executive, The (1971) ** D: Robert Butler. Kurt Russell, Joe Flynn, Harry Morgan, Wally Cox, Heather North, Alan Hewitt, John Ritter.   Disney film of a kid (Russell)

who discovers a chimp with the ability to faultlessly pick winning TV series, gaining Russell a vice-presidency with the company. Not as well done as some other Disney films, but entertaining for children. **[G] V**

Batman (1966) ** D: Leslie Martinson. Adam West, Burt Ward, Burgess Meredith, Cesar Romero, Frank Gorshin, Lee Meriwether, Neil Hamilton, Madge Blake, Reginald Denny.   Not great filmmaking, but a cleaner choice for the story of Batman than the more recently made versions. Includes the Penguin, Joker, Riddler and Cat Woman all joining forces to defeat the "Caped Crusader." This one is based upon the TV series of the '60s. **V, DVD**

Beauty and the Beast (1991) ***1/2 (See Literature)

Bedtime for Bonzo (1951) **1/2 D: Frederick de Cordova. Ronald Reagan, Diana Lynn, Walter Slezak, Jesse White, Lucille Barkley.   Fun, clean family film of Reagan bringing home a chimp to raise like a child for a scientific experiment. Lynn is hired to help with the chimp. **V**

Beethoven (1992) **1/2 D: Brian Levant, Charles Grodin, Bonnie Hunt, Dean Jones, Oliver Platt, Stanley Tucci, Nicholle Tom, Christopher Castile, Sarah Rose Karr.   Fun film of tightly wound Grodin, owner of a sachet/deodorizing company and family who discover a puppy and then talk him into keeping it. Puppy grows up to be *huge* St. Bernard, who constantly challenges Dad's stress-level. There are a few things parents might not approve of, so view first if concerned. Generally, a funny family film. **V, DVD**

Beethoven's 2nd (1993) **1/2 D: Rod Daniel. Charles Grodin, Bonnie Hunt, Nicholle Tom, Christopher Castile, Sara Rose Karr, Debi Mazar, Chris Penn.   Beethoven falls in love with "Missy" and there are puppies, which the kids have to keep from Dad. A villainess tries to steal and then kill the puppies, so the kids (and parents) come to the rescue. Again, there are a few items some parents may not approve, so preview first. **[PG] V**

Belles on Their Toes (1952) *** (See Literature)

Bells of St. Mary's, The (1945) *** D: Leo McCarey. Bing Crosby, Ingrid Bergman, Henry Travers, William Gargan, Ruth Donnelly, Joan Carroll, Martha Sleeper, Rhys Williams.   Fun film with Bing re-creating his role as Father O'Malley" from *Going My Way*. Here, he joins a parochial school which needs major financial help to survive. God does, indeed, work in mysterious ways in order to fix their problems. Bergman is wonderful as Sister Superior. I especially liked the part where she taught a boy to box! Sure to be a family favorite. **V, DVD**

Benji (1974) ***1/2 D: Joe Camp. Peter Breck, Deborah Walley, Edgar Buchanan, Frances Bavier, Pasty Garret.   Wonderful family film of a amazing dog who saves two kidnapped children. Sequel: *For the Love of Benji*. **[G] V, DVD**

Big Red (1962) *** (See Literature)

Blindfold (1966) **1/2 D: Philip Dunne. Rock Hudson, Claudia Cardinale, Jack Warden, Guy Stockwell, Anne Seymour.   Hudson is a psychiatrist who is asked by a General (Warden) to help de-brainwash a former patient. For security, he is blindfolded each time he is taken to the patient. Hudson gets involved with the patient's sister (Cardinale) as intrigue abounds and discovers that a security breach has taken place. It's then up to the two of them to find where her brother is and save the day. The part of this I always enjoyed was the reconstruction of his blindfolded journey.

Blue Bird, The (1940) ** D: Walter Lang. Shirley Temple, Spring Byington, Nigel Bruce, Gale Sondergaard, Eddie Collins.   Film version of the Maurice Maeterlinck play, Fox's answer to *The Wizard of Oz* leaves something to be desired, but still tells the story in lavish Technicolor. Mostly for children. **V**

Born Free (1966-British) ***1/2 (See Literature)

Boy Named Charlie Brown, A (1969) *** D: Bill Melendez. Voices of Peter Robbins,

Pamelyn Ferdin, Glenn Gilger, Andy Pforsich.   C. Schultz's Peanuts gang's feature film debut. Clean family fun. [G] **V**

Brewster's Millions (1945) **1/2 D: Allan Dwan. Dennis O'Keefe, Helen Walker, Eddie "Rochester" Anderson, June Havoc.   Comedy film about a returning G.I. who must spend $1 million in one month in order to inherit a sizable fortune and the misadventures into which he gets. Remade in 1985, but not as well done as this one. **V**

Bright Eyes (1934) **1/2 D: David Butler. Shirley Temple, James Dunn, Judith Allen, Jane Withers, Lois Wilson, Charles Sellon.   Rich, crusty old man has want-to-be-rich relatives living with him. Orphaned Shirley brings him joy; couple's child, mean Withers, does not. Includes "On the Good Ship Lollipop." **V, DVD**

Bringing Up Baby (1938) ****1/2 D: Howard Hawks. Cary Grant, Katharine Hepburn, Charlie Ruggles, May Robson, Barry Fitzgerald, Walter Catlett, Fritz Feld, Ward Bond.   One of my all time favorite films is now considered "THE" definitive screwball comedy. Hepburn is an heiress (with a pet leopard named "Baby") who falls for zoologist Grant, and makes a shambles of his life. Sit back, watch the masters at work and enjoy! You may become like us and begin calling, "George! George!" **V**

bug's life, a (1998) ***1/2 D: John Lasseter, Andrew Stanton. Voices of Dave Foley, Julia Louis-Dreyfus, Kevin Spacey, Phyllis Diller, David Hyde Pierce, Denis Leary, Richard Kind, John Ratzenberger, Roddy McDowall, Madeline Kahn, Bonnie Hunt, Edie McClurg, Alex Rocco.   Sweet computer-animated film of a young ant Flik, who is a screw-up. Wishing to prove himself to the colony, he takes on the dangerous task of finding help for the colony against plundering grasshoppers. Meaning to hire mercenaries, he hires a group of circus bugs, instead! Fun for young and old. [G] **V, DVD**

By the Light of the Silvery Moon (1953) **1/2 (See 1900s)

Captain January (1936) **1/2 D: David Butler. Shirley Temple, Guy Kibbee, Slim Summerville, Buddy Ebsen, June Lang, Sara Haden.   Sweet tale of orphaned tyke (Shirley) who has been adopted by lighthouse keeper Kibbee. A new truant officer arrives and tries to separate them. With Shirley, Ebsen is seen for the song and dance man he originally was in "The Codfish Ball." He was even supposed to be the Tin Man in *The Wizard of Oz* before Jack Haley, Jr. **V**

Cat Ballou (1965) ***1/2 D: Elliot Silverstein. Jane Fonda, Lee Marvin, Michael Callan, Dwayne Hicman, Tom Nardini, John Marley, Reginald Denny, Jay C. Flippen, Arthur Hunnicutt, Bruce Cabot. Western spoof with Fonda as a school-teacher who turns outlaw when her father is murdered. Marvin won an Oscar for his portrayal of a drunken dime-novel hero fast-gun. Parents may wish to watch this first and decide if it's right for your family. There are a few things that need editing, but mainly it's lots of fun. Nat King Cole and Stubby Kaye narrate in song as strolling minstrels. **V, DVD**

Champagne for Caesar (1950) *** D: Richard Whorf. Ronald Coleman, Celeste Holm, Vincent Price, Barbara Britton, Art Linkletter.   Coleman is a genius who becomes a celebrity on a TV quiz show reminiscent of "The $64,000 Question." Lots of fun as I remember it, but it's been years since I've seen it. Preview if concerned. **V**

Charlotte's Web (1973) *** (See Literature)

China Cry (1990) [NR] (See 1900s)

Christy Series based on the life of Catherine Marshall's mother, a schoolteacher in the Great Smoky mountains in the early 1900s. Worth collecting. *Excellent.* **V**

Computer Wore Tennis Shoes, The (1970) **1/2 D: Robert Butler. Kurt Russell, Cesar Romero, Joe Flynn, Willim Schallert, Alan Hewitt, Richard Bakalyan.   Russell is a an average college kid named Dexter who get shocked by a computer and all the computer's data base gets fed into him! He then becomes unstoppable academically and the big wheel on the College Knowledge team. Unknown to anyone, the computer which was donated by an upstanding citizen (Romero) who in actuality owns gambling joints, also has info from his operations, so now gangsters are after Dexter to keep him from spilling the beans. Family fun for all in this Disney film. **[G] V**

Connecticut Yankee in King Arthur's Court, A (1949) **1/2 (See Middle Ages)

Conspiracy Theory (1997) ***1/2 D: Richard Donner. Mel Gibson, Julia Roberts, Patrick Stewart, Cylk Cozart, Stephan Kahn, Terry Alexander, Troy Garity.   Intriguing story of a bizarre N.Y.C. cabbie fixated on Roberts, who works for the Justice Department. She is investigating the murder of her father, a judge, and trying to find the truth behind it. Unknown to her and the cabbie, he holds the key. Through him, she is drawn into a tangled web of a conspiracy theory which she can only unravel if they can unravel his confused mind. Sounds gruesome, but is totally engrossing and very well acted. This has been all over the television for the last year or so. SEE ON TV as it was originally rated **[R]** and TV apparently cut out whatever made it receive this rating. **V, DVD**

Cowboy and the Lady, The (1938) ** D: H. C. Potter. Gary Cooper, Merle Oberon, Patsy Kelly, Walter Brennan, Fuzzy Knight, Harry Davenport.   Clean fun film of socialite Oberon who meets cowboy Cooper, falls in love and marries him and the complications that ensue. Cute. **V**

Cross and the Switchblade (1972) **1/2 D: Don Murray. Pat Boone, Erik Estrada, Jackie Giroux, Jo-Ann Robinson.   The true story of David Wilkerson who was called by God to N.Y.C. to work with gang members and drug addicts. He was a preacher of a small town church and saw a news report about N.Y.C. gang members who had committed murder. God moved his heart to go to N.Y.C., meet them and tell them about Messiah. I recommend you read the book to your children (parts will need editing) and then see the movie about this amazing man whom God used to reach a lost generation. He also founded Teen Challenge which helped drug addicts kick heroin with the help of God. He is now the pastor of Times Square Church in N.Y.C. Choose from the many books written by David Wilkerson for an insight into his ministry in N.Y.C. and for faith building. The testimonies are incredible. **[PG] V**

Curly Top (1935) **1/2 D: Irving Cummings. Shirley Temple, John Boles, Rochelle Hudson, Jane Darwell, Rafaela Ottiano, Arthur Treacher.   Shirley and sister (Hudson) are orphans who come to the attention of one of the patrons of the orphanage when he sees Shirley singing and falls in love with her. He decides to adopt them and give them a new life. Songs include the famous "Animal Crackers in My Soup." A film for the whole family. **V**

Dimples (1936) **1/2 D: William Seiter. Shirley Temple, Frank Morgan, Helen Westley, Robert Kent, Stepin' Fetchit, Astrid Allwyn.   Shirley tries to save her down-and-out father (Morgan). Songs include "Oh, Mister Man Up In The Moon," "What Did the Bluebird Say." **V, DVD**

Donovan's Reef (1963) *** D: John Ford. John Wayne, Lee Marvin, Elizabeth Allen, Jack Warden, Cesar Romero, Dorothy Lamour, Mike Mazurki.   Fun film of a tropical island and its inhabitants, several of whom are Americans who settled there after WWII. Warden is a widowed doctor who had married an island Princess and has three children. His daughter from his first marriage is coming to the island from Boston for a visit, totally unaware of his second marriage and her half-siblings. Wayne is the doctor's friend who believes she will be a stuffed shirt since she's from Boston and claims the kids for his own during the doctor's absence and her arrival. The fun unrolls from there. There is a unique presentation of the Luke 2 account of Messiah's birth! I think most families will find this a fun film. **V, DVD**

Don't Give Up the Ship (1959) *** D: Norman Taurog. Jerry Lewis, Dina Merrill, Diana Spencer, Mickey Shaughnessy, Robert Middleton, Gale Gordon, Claude Akins.   Probably Lewis' best film without Martin, in which he has "misplaced" a U. S. battleship during the war, and can't remember how he lost it! Fun for all. **V**

Dreamboat (1952) **1/2 D: Claude Binyon. Ginger Rogers, Clifton Webb, Jeffrey Hunter,

Anne Francis, Elsa Lancaster.   Funny film of silent-star Rogers, who cashes in on TV late night showings of her old movies, to the utter horror of her former co-star (Webb) who is now a respected professor. Preview if concerned; it's been years since I've seen this.

Driving Miss Daisy (1989) ****1/2 D: Bruce Beresford. Morgan Freeman, Jessica Tandy, Dan Aykroyd, Patti LuPone, Esther Rolle.   Film version of Alfred Uhry's stage play about a southern Jewish lady (Tandy) who can no longer drive herself and the black man (Freeman) her son (Aykroyd) hires to drive her. This is a delightful film with unique characters and a sweet friendship that develops between the most unlikely people over a period of years. This touches on the subjects of segregation, prejudice, and the way life was in the south at this time. This was set and filmed in Atlanta, Georgia, which is about an hour from my home. Only detraction, Aykroyd's obviously fake southern accent. Don't miss this one and have the tissues ready for the ending! **V, DVD**

Easy Living (1937) *** D: Mitchell Leisen. Jean Arthur, Edward Arnold, Ray Milland, Franklin Pangborn, William Demarest, Mary Nash.   Comedy with working girl (Arthur) having a mink coat dropped on her when it was tossed out a window by millionaire Arnold in response to his spoiled wife. **V**

Egg and I, The (1947) *** D: Chester Erskine. Claudette Colbert, Fred MacMurray, Marjorie Main, Louise Allbritton, Percy Kilbride, Richard Long, Donald MacBride, Samuel S. Hinds.   Colbert is a city girl who marries chicken farmer MacMurray and struggles to figure out how to fit in and be a good "country wife." Lots of fun. **V**

Everybody Does It (1949) *** D: Edmund Goulding. Paul Douglas, Linda Darnell, Celeste Holm, Charles Coburn, Millard Mitchell, Lucile Watson, John Hoyt, George Tobias.   Funny tale of wife (Holm) who wants to be a singer and harassed husband (Douglas) who ends up being "discovered" and getting the vocal career instead.

Everybody's Baby: The Jessica McClure Story (1989) TVM D: Mel Damski. Patty Duke Astin, Beau Bridges, Tom Christopher, Pat Hingle, Roxana Zal, Laura and Jennifer Loesch.   Jessica is the 18-month-old Texas girl who fell down an abandoned well in October of 1987. As the world looks on in anguish, the local fire chief (Pat Hingle) and police chief (Bridges) supervise the efforts to rescue Jessica from her 22-foot-deep prison. The film effectively squeezes the 58 hours of the original incident into two, allotting plenty of time for a surface-level subplot involving the efforts of a Victim's Assistance Program volunteer (Patty Duke) to reassure Jessica's parents. **V**

Every Girl Should Be Married (1948) **1/2 D: Don Hartman. Cary Grant, Franchot Tone, Diana Lynn, Betsy Drake, Alan Mowbray, Eddie Albert.   Comedy of all-America girl (Drake) setting out to trap bachelor (Grant) into marriage. He's smarter than she thinks! **V**

Faithful in My Fashion (1946) ** D: Sidney Salkow. Donna Reed, Tom Drake, Edward Everett Horton, Spring Byington, Sig Ruman.   Comedy-romance of a soldier home on leave excited to see "his girl" who isn't even aware that she is "his girl" and is engaged to someone else! Clean, black and white film.

Farmer's Daughter, The (1947) ***1/2 (See 1900s)

Father of the Bride (1950) **** D: Vincente Minnelli. Spencer Tracy, Elizabeth Taylor, Joan Bennett, Billie Burke, Leo G. Carroll, Don Taylor, Rusty (Russ) Tamblyn.   Liz is engaged to Taylor and the ups and downs as well as the fiasco of our wedding traditions are seen. Tracy as the father, gets all the headaches our wedding rituals bring, especially the financial ones. Sequel, *Father's Little Dividend.* **V** (remade with Steve Martin in 1991. Skip it and watch this one, it's much better.)

Father's Little Dividend (1951) *** D: Vincente Minnelli. Spencer Tracy, Joan Bennett, Elizabeth Taylor, Don Taylor, Billie Burke, Rusty (Russ) Tamblyn.   Tracy's going to be a grandfather and is not looking forward to it! Humorous and done in Tracy's own fabulous style. **V, DVD**

Father Was a Fullback (1949) **1/2 D: John M. Stahl. Fred MacMurray, Maureen

O'Hara, Betty Lynn, Rudy Vallee, Thelma Ritter, Natalie Wood.   Set in MacMurray's household, this covers the problems of a football coach and more besides! Clean family comedy.   **V**

FBI Story, The (1959) *** D: Mervyn LeRoy. James Stewart, Vera Miles, Murray Hamilton, Larry Pennell, Nich Adams, Diane Jergens, Joyce Taylor.   Fabricated history of FBI but still full of action. Perhaps a good way to compare truth with fiction. My eldest daughter recommends reading the Landmark book entitled *The FBI,* from which she copied this quote from J. Edgar Hoover, "When a young man files an application with the F.B.I., we do not ask if he was the smartest boy in his class. We want to know if he was truthful, dependable, and if he played the game fair. We want to know if he respects his parents, reveres God, honors his flag and loves his country. We can teach the new recruit many things, but we must have a substantial individual to begin with in order to make a G-man." Don't we all wish this was the criteria for government jobs, today! Don't you think it would make a huge difference in our society and how our government was run?   **V**

Fitzwilly (1967) **1/2 D: Delbert Mann. Dick Van Dyke, Barbara Feldon, Edith Evans, John McGiver, Harry Townes, John Fiedler, Norman Fell, Cecil Kellaway, Sam Waterston.   Unusual comedy about butler, Fitzwilly (Van Dyke) who robs in order to protect his dearly beloved and eccentric employer. (Evans) Though some parents may not find this humorous, this fit our family's funny bone.   **V**

Flipper (1963) **1/2 D: James Clark. Chuck Conners, Luke Halpin, Kathleen Maguire, Connie Scott. The movie, which later spun off into the TV series, is a clean family tale of a boy who befriends a dolphin.   **V**

Flubber (1997) **1/2 D: Les Mayfield. Robin Williams, Marcia Gay Harden, Christopher McDonald, Raymond J. Barry, Clancy Brown, Ted Levine, Wil Wheaton, Edie McClurg, and the voice of Jodi Benson.   Updated version of Disney's *Absentminded Professor* with high-tech additions, this version has it's points but would need to be previewed by the parents as it contains some crude comedy. This one will have to be "the parent's call."   **V, DVD**

Fluffy (1965) **1/2 D: Earl Bellamy. Tony Randall, Shirley Jones, Edward Andrews, Ernest Truex, Howard Morris, Dick Sargent.   Goofy tale of scientist, Randall, who "goes on the lam" with "his cat," who just happens to be a lion! Though nothing happens, a few eyebrows are raised in the film when Jones loans her apartment to Randall. Overall, a goofy movie.

Follow Me, Boys! (1966) *** D: Norman Tokar. Fred MacMurray, Vera Miles, Lillian Gish, Charlie Ruggles, Elliott Reid, Kurt Russell.   Heartwarming Disney film of a man who settles down in a small town in the 1930s, starts a Boy Scout troop, and gives his life to the boys. He and his wife have no children of their own, so the boys become their family. Sweet and fun, with a great scene where the boy scouts defeat the army!   **V**

Follow That Dream (1962) **1/2 D: Gordon Douglas. Elvis Presley, Arthur O'Connell, Anne Helm, Joanna Moore, Jack Kruschen, Simon Oakland.   Though I'm not a huge Elvis fan, I really like this movie because of the character he plays. His father (O'Connell) decides to homestead in Florida along a newly opened highway. The family includes Presley and other orphans whom the father has taken in. The courtroom scene is a classic in showing how honesty and kindness can overcome the wiles of more unscrupulous characters, as is the theme in the rest of the film. Parents may wish to view first for the romantic element included. Based on a book by Richard Powell entitled, *Pioneer Go Home.*   **V**

For the Love of Benji (1977) *** D: Joe Camp. Benji, Patsy Garrett, Cynthia Smith, Allen Fiuzat, Ed Nelson, Peter Bowles, Bridget Armstrong.   Benji, a mini-Lassie, must outsmart spies who are after the formula tattooed on his paw. Fun family film.   **[G] V, DVD**

Fox and the Hound, The (1981) *** D: Art Stevens, Ted Berman, Richard Rich. Voices of Mickey Rooney, Kurt Russell, Pearl Bailey, Jack Albertson, Sandy Duncan, Jeanette Nolan,

Pat Buttram, John Fiedler, John McIntire, Paul Winchell, Corey Feldman.   Sweet Disney animated feature of the friendship between two natural enemies and how growing up puts their relationship to the test. Clean family film, more like the classic Disney "keepers" of the past. [G] **V, DVD**

Foxfire (1955) **1/2 D: Joseph Pevney. Jane Russell, Jeff Chandler, Dan Duryea, Mara Corday, Barton MacLane.   Russell plays a socialite who marries an Indian mining engineer. Parents need to view this one first as some may not approve of the content, but this film does show the differences in cultures and the prejudice towards a different culture, an attitude which still exists today.

Francis (the Talking Mule) From 1949-1956, these movies entertained many. I was introduced to them as a child through TV and loved them. They are funny, clean and silly, which children love. Francis is a mule who only talks to the somewhat gullible G.I. he befriends, Donald O'Connor, but like Mr. Ed, this only seems to get O'Connor into trouble when he tries to explain HOW he knows what he knows! Francis voice was dubbed by the inimitable Chill Wills. Any of these should be a fun film for a family night.

Francis (1949)
Francis Goes to the Races (1951)
Francis Goes to West Point (1952)

Francis Covers the Big Town (1953)
Francis Joins the Wacs (1954)
Francis in the Navy (1955)

Free Willy (1993) **1/2 D: Simon Wincer. Jason James Richter, Lori Petty, Michael Madsen, Jayne Atkinson, Michael Ironside, Richard Riehle, August Schellenberg. Myklti Williamson.   A young boy who is in the foster children's program is made to return to the aquarium he vandalized in order to remove his handiwork and to work off his debt for the restoration. While there, he becomes fascinated with an orca whale and discovers that the owner is trying to kill "Willy." There is some Indian mysticism parents might wish to omit as well as some heated arguments between the boy and his (caring) foster parents. [PG] **V**

Fugitive, The (1993) ***1/2 D: Andrew Davis. Harrison Ford, Tommy Lee Jones, Sela Ward, Julianne Moore, Joe Pantoliano, Jeroen Krabbe, Andreas Katsulas, Daniel Roebuck, L. Scott Caldwell.   Though this movie would have to be edited from television, I find it an intriguing movie of puzzles. Ford plays a doctor wrongly accused of his wife's murder. In transportation to prison, an escape attempt is made causing the prison bus to collide with a train. Ford escapes and returns to "the scene of the crime" trying to solve the case the police never looked for because they blamed him. Jones plays the U. S. Marshall trailing Ford and the interaction between these two men is fascinating. Parents definitely need to preview from TV version to decide whether this is something of which you approve. [PG] **V**

Full of Life (1956) *** D: Richard Quine. Judy Holliday, Richard Conte, Salvatore Baccaloni, Esther Minciotti.   Holliday and Baccaloni are full of surprises as a first time expectant wife and her overreacting father-in-law. Lots of fun. **V**

Further Adventures of the Wilderness Family, The (1978) *** D: Frank Zuniga. Robert Logan, Susan D. Shaw, Heather Rattray, Ham Larsen, George (Buck) Flower, Brian Cutler.   More about the family who moved to the wilderness for their children's health and for the good of the family. AKA *The Wilderness Family, Part 2*. Followed by *Mountain Family Robinson*. Clean family film. **V**

Gay Purr-ee (1962) **1/2 D: Abe Levitow. Voices of Judy Garland, Robert Goulet, Red Buttons, Hermione Gingold, Paul Frees, Morey Amsterdam.   Animated feature of a cat's experiences in Paris. Best features are the voices of the character's famous actors. **V**

George of the Jungle (1997) **1/2 D: Sam Weisman. Brendan Fraser, Leslie Mann, Thomas Haden Church, Holland Taylor, John Bennett Perry, Abraham Benrubi, Greg Cruttwell, Richard Roundtree, voice of John Clesse; narrated by Keith Scott.   Disney feature based on the 1960s cartoon about a clumsy jungle king. A bit silly for adults but kids love it. [PG] **V, DVD**

Gidget (1959) **1/2 D: Paul Wendkos. Sandra Dee, James Darren, Cliff Robertson, Arthur O'Connell, Joby Baker, Yvonne Craig, Doug McClure, Tom Laughlin.   Though some parents may wonder why I've included this, I love this movie for the moral it gives, that a *good* girl can have a *very* powerful influence. The story is of a late-blooming teenage girl who discovers surfing and wants to be just one of the crowd and how her basic values affect those around her. Parents do need to view this first to see if you approve and watch it with your children and discuss the mind-set/attitude/actions of the teens on screen. Followed by *Gidget Goes Hawaiian, Gidget Goes to Rome, Gidget Grows Up* which are okay films, but not with the message of this one.   **V**

Glass Bottom Boat, The (1966) *** D: Frank Tashlin. Doris Day, Rod Taylor, Arthur Godfrey, Paul Lynde, Eric Fleming, Alice Pearce, Ellen Corby, John McGiver, Edward Andrews, Don De Luis, Dick Martin.   Day is a widow who has been hired by scientist Taylor as his biographer. She's mistaken for a Russian spy and the fun begins. There are some sexual innuendoes parents will want to edit, but this is salvageable and is overall a goofy story with a classic scene with Day and De Luis as a serviceman installing a sound system. Includes famous title song. **V**

Going My Way (1944) **** D: Leo McCarey. Bing Crosby, Barry Fitzgerald, Rise Stevens, Frank McHugh, James Brown, Gene Lockhart.   Father O'Malley (Crosby) comes to work under aging superior (Fitzgerald) who doesn't care for new ways of doing things. After some clashes, Crosby wins him over while working wonders with the street kids of his day. Oscars went to Crosby, Fitzgerald, director McCarey, Best Picture and song, "Swinging on a Star." Also a way to hear famous opera star Rise Stevens.   **V**

Good Morning, Miss Dove (1955) *** D: Henry Koster. Jennifer Jones, Robert Stack, Kipp Hamilton, Robert Douglas, Peggy Knudsen, Marshall Thompson, Chuck Connors, Biff Elliot, Jerry Paris, Mary Wickes, Richard Deacon.   Wonderful family film showing how one life can have a great impact upon many. Jones plays a schoolteacher who is hospitalized and relives her life in flashbacks showing why she was a spinster and how she came to teach school as well as the many lives she touched and even transformed. Find it on TV and tape it. Don't miss this one.

Government Girl (1943) **1/2 (See WWII, The Home Front)

Greyfriars Bobby (1961) **1/2 D: Don Chaffey. Donald Crisp, Laurence Naismith, Alex Mackenzie, Kay Walsh, Duncan Macrae, Gordon Jackson.   Based on a true story this is a British Disney film of a Skye terrier who became the pet of an entire neighborhood due to unusual circumstances. This takes place in the 1800s in Edinburgh and is a wonderful family film. **V**

Grounds for Marriage (1950) **1/2 D: Robert Z. Leonard. Van Johnson, Kathryn Grayson, Paula Raymond, Barry Sullivan, Lewis Stone.   Cute story of opera star and the ex-husband whom she wants to win back.

Gus (1976) *** D: Vincent McEveety. Edward Asner, Don Knotts, Gary Grimes, Tim Conway, Liberty Williams, Dick Van Patten, Dick Butkus.   Disney comedy of a mule whose ability to kick a football boosts last-place team to first place. Crooks try to grab him with predictable Disney results. [G] **V**

Has Anybody Seen My Gal? (1952) **1/2 D: Douglas Sirk. Charles Coburn, Piper Laurie, Rock Hudson, Gigi Perreau, Lynn Bari, William Reynolds, Larry Gates, Skip Homeier.   Clean film of 1920s family who find they've inherited a large sum of money and what it does to their family. Unknown to them, their benefactor is in their midst to watch and see how they handle their windfall. Good discussion material here about what's truly important.

Having Wonderful Time (1938) **1/2 D: Alfred Santell. Ginger Rogers, Douglas Fairbanks, Jr., Peggy Conklin, Lucille Ball, Lee Bowman, Eve Arden, Dorothea Kent, Richard (Red) Skelton, Donald Meek, Jack Carson, Allan Lane, Grady Sutton.   Star studded cast (before they were stars) about a girl who goes on vacation to the Catskills looking for culture and meets Fairbanks, instead. Cute and clean, as I remember it. **V**

Herbie Rides Again (1974) **1/2 D: Robert Stevenson. Helen Hayes, Ken Berry, Stefanie Powers, Keenan Wynn, John McIntire.   Disney sequel to *The Love Bug* has Herbie coming to the rescue of Hayes as she holds off greedy Alonzo Hawk (Wynn). Parents preview as Hayes' character believes in the personification of objects, played out by the "character" of the VW Herbie. [G] **V**

Her 12 Men (1954) **1/2 D: Robert Z. Leonard. Greer Garson, Robert Ryan, Barry Sullivan, Richard Haydn, James Arness, Tim Considine, David Stollery, Frances Bergen.   Garson is a widow who has come to a boys school to be a teacher. She and her students learn some valuable lessons. Sweet.

High Time (1960) **1/2 D: Blake Edwards. Bing Crosby, Fabian, Tuesday Weld, Nicole Maurey. Widower and successful businessman Bing returns to college and teams with a group of kids and getting involved in some of their antics, as well as falling for one of his teachers.

His Girl Friday (1940) **** D: Howard Hawks. Cary Grant, Rosalind Russell, Ralph Bellamy, Gene Lockhart, Helen Mack, Ernest Truex, Clarence Kolb, Porter Hall, Roscoe Karns, Abner Biberman, Cliff Edwards, John Qualen, Frank Jenks, Billy Gilbert.   Fast paced, fast talking remake of *The Front Page* with star reporter Russell coming into the paper to quit and inform her ex-husband (Grant) that she is re-marrying. Trouble is the breaking murder story and Grant's conniving get in her way. **V, DVD**

Holiday (1938) ***1/2 D: George Cukor. Katharine Hepburn, Cary Grant, Doris Nolan, Lew Ayers, Edward Everett Horton, Henry Kolker, Binnie Barnes, Jean Dixon, Henry Daniell.   Well done film adaptation of Philip Barry's play about a young man who meets a girl, only to discover that they want different things out of life. He wants to make enough money to have fun, she wants society and position and all the things to which she is used. She and her father don't understand him or her sister, who thinks much the same way. Wonderful film. **V**

Hollywood Hotel (1937) **1/2 D: Busby Berkeley. Dick Powell, Rosemary Lane, Lola Lane, Ted Healy, Johnny "Scat" Davis, Alan Mowbray, Frances Langford, Louella Parsons, Hugh Herbert, Glenda Farrell, Edgar Kennedy.   Thin plot of Powell as winner of Hollywood talent contest but can't quite "make it." Highlights: seeing the real Louella Parsons and the Benny Goodman band. Songs include "Hooray for Hollywood" and Goodman's famous "Sing, Sing, Sing." Parents should preview this one.

Home Alone 3 (1997) *** D: Raja Gosnell. Alex D. Linz, Olek Krupa, Rya Kihlstedt, Lenny von Dohlen, David Thornton, Haviland Morris, Kevin Kilner, Marian Seldes.   This is my pick of all the Home Alone films. I found the others offensive and mean. In this one, a young boy is defending his home, his family, his neighbors and neighborhood against the "bad guys." Though this is definitely fantasy, the values in this one make it worthwhile to me. I love the little boy's character enough to overlook his older brother and sister's somewhat obnoxious attitudes, even though they redeem themselves in the end. One note: there is a picture of a swimsuit model or something in the brother's room that has post-it notes all over it. Parents might want to buzz that frame and some others. **V**

Homeward Bound: The Incredible Journey (1983) *** D: DuWayne Dunham. Robert Hays, Kim Greist, Jean Smart, Benj Thall, Veronica Lauren, Kevin Chevalia; voices of Michael J. Fox, Sally Field, Don Ameche.   Disney film of three family pets who traverse unfamiliar and untamed terrain to reunite with their owners. With the help of some famous voices, we are allowed to hear the animals thoughts as well as their conversation with each other. Fox's Chance is the youngster (dog) who is always energetic and attracts trouble; Field's Sassy is a finicky cat who is always complaining; Ameche's Shadow is the eldest pet (dog) and the one who keeps a level head and leads the others back home. [G] **V**

Homeward Bound II: Lost in San Francisco (1996) **1/2 D: David R. Ellis. Robert Hays, Kim Greist, Veronica Lauren, Kein Chaevalia, Benj Thall, Michale Rispoli, Max Perlich; voices of Michael J. Fox, Sally Field, Ralph Waite, Sinbad, Jon Polito.   In this sequel, the pet's family goes on vacation and the pets get lost in San Francisco. They have to fight man and dog to reunite with their family. [G] V

Honey, I Blew Up the Kid (1992) *** D: Randal Kleiser. Rick Moranis, Marcia Strassman, Robert Oliveri, Daniel and Joshua Shalikar, Lloyd Bridges, John Shea, Keri Russell, Ron Canada, Gregory Sierra, Julia Sweeney, Ken Tobey.   Sequel to Disney's *Honey, I Shrunk the Kids* has absentminded scientist Moranis accidentally enlarging his toddler son to gigantic proportions. Lots of fun with a final showdown between the "giant" and officials in Las Vegas. Followed by *Honey, We Shrunk Ourselves.* **[PG]** V

Honey, I Shrunk the Kids (1989) *** D: Joe Johnston. Rick Moranis, Marcia Strassman, Kristine Sutherland, Thomas Brown, Jared Rushton, Amy O'Neill, Robert Oliveri.   A scientist who's considered "weird" and a "quack" invents a machine which doesn't work until his son's baseball accidentally hits it, miniaturizing the son, his sister and two neighbor children. They are removed from the house to the backyard, (now a jungle at their present size) by the absentminded inventor who sweeps up and thereby removes them from the house to the garbage. The rest of the film deals with their bickering relationship resolving as they figure out a way to get back to the house and to their folks so they can be enlarged to their normal size. Cute film that most families should enjoy. **[PG]** V

Honey, We Shrunk Ourselves (1997) **1/2 D: Dean Cundey. Rick Moranis, Eve Gordon, Robin Bartlett, Allison Mack, Jack Richardson, Stuart Pankin, Bug Hall.   This time, inventor Moranis manages to shrink himself, his wife and the neighbors leaving the children to resolve the problem. **[PG]** V

Horn Blows at Midnight (1945) *** D: Raoul Walsh. Jack Benny, Alexis Smith, Dolores Moran, Allyn Joslyn, Reginald Gardiner, Guy Kibbee, John Alexander, Margaret Dumont, Franklin Pangborn, Bobby (Robert) Blake.   Somewhat satirical look at mankind not being ready for the trumpet of the Lord to sound as Benny plays an angel sent by God to sound the trumpet to destroy earth. V

Horse in the Gray Flannel Suit (1968) *** (See Horses)

Horsemasters, The (1961) ** (See Horses)

I'd Rather Be Rich (1964) **1/2 D: Jack Smight. Sandra Dee, Maurice Chevalier, Andy Williams, Robert Goulet, Gene Raymond, Charles Ruggles, Hermione Gingold, Allen Jenkins, Rip Taylor.   Dee is engaged to singer Williams, but is called home to see dying grandfather and must produce a fiancé to ease his passing. Williams isn't there, so she grabs Goulet and the fun begins.

I Love You Again (1940) ***1/2 D: W. S. Van Dyke, II. William Powell, Myrna Loy, Frank McHugh, Edmund Love, Donald Douglas, Nella Walker.   Funny story of solid citizen Powell getting knocked out at sea, and coming to as the con man he had been before a previous bump on the head! Loy plays his wife whom he learns is divorcing him (he's too boring) and he tries to stall it. V

Incredible Mr. Limpet, The (1964) ** D: Arthur Lubin. Don Knotts, Jack Weston, Carole Cook, Andrew Duggan, Larry Keating.   Knotts loves fish and dreams of becoming one, only to get his wish and become an animated fish who helps the Navy spot Nazi subs during WWII. Perhaps an easy way to familiarize younger children with the subject of this war. V

Indiana Jones and the Last Crusade (1989) *** D: Steven Spielberg. Harrison Ford, Sean Connery, Denholm Elliot, Alison Doody, John Rhys-Davies, Julian Glover, River Phoenix, Michael Byrne, Alex Hyde-White.   Fun film, the last in the *Raiders of the Lost Ark* trilogy, finds Jones searching for his father who has disappeared. This leads him back to Europe and into contact with the Germans once again. There is at least one scene that needs to be edited and an innuendo that needs to be cut, so view first. Then you can decide if this one meets your standards. In my opinion, this one is not for younger children. For adults, the byplay between Ford and Connery makes the film. You will also have a look at the time of the Crusaders and have the opportunity from this film to discuss salvation by works or by grace. Avoid the second film of the trilogy, *Temple of Doom* as it is too occultic. **[PG]** V

Inheritance, The (1997) [NR] (See Literature)

In Old California (1942) ** D: William McGann. John Wayne, Binnie Barnes, Albert Dekker, Helen Parrish, Patsy Kelly, Edgar Kennedy, Dick Purcell, Harry Shannon. Wayne moves to a western town run by town boss (Dekker) and takes him on. **V, DVD**

In Old Kentucky (1935) **1/2 D: George Marshall. Will Rogers, Dorothy Wilson, Bill "Bojangles" Robinson, Russell Hardie, Louise Henry, Charles Sellon. Old story of family feud but worth seeing the real Will Rogers and Robinson's dancing is always a delight. (See Horses for more information.)

In Old Oklahoma (1943) **1/2 D: Albert S. Rogell. John Wayne, Martha Scott, Albert Dekker, Gabby Hayes, Marjorie Rambeau, Sidney Blackmer, Dale Evans. Action film of Wayne being in the oil business and going up against impossible odds. AKA *War of the Wildcats.* **V**

In Search of the Castaways (1962) ** D: Robert Stevenson. Hayley Mills, Maurice Chevalier, George Sanders, Wilfred Hyde-White, Michael Anderson, Jr., Keith Hamshire. Disney adaptation of Jules Verne story is okay for kids, but parents might wish to preview for some scary parts. **V**

Inspector General, The (1949) *** D: Henry Koster. Danny Kaye, Walter Slezak, Barbara Bates, Elsa Lancaster, Gene Lockhart, Alan Hale, Walter Catlett. Kaye is a buffoon who works with a con-artist gypsy (Slezak) and gets mistaken as a visiting Inspector General and then the fun begins. If you like Danny Kaye's humor, you'll love this one. Most kids do, too. **V, DVD**

I.Q. (1994) *** D: Fred Schepisi. Tim Robbins, Meg Ryan, Walter Matthau, Lou Jacobi, Gene Saks, Joseph Maher, Stephen Fry, Tony Shalhoub, Frank Whaley, Keene Curtis, Charles Durning. Cute comedy about a garage mechanic who falls for a girl at first sight only to find out that she's Einstein's niece. He meets Einstein (Matthau) who likes him and decides to help him in his romantic quest. Parents need to preview for a few things, but it's a salvageable and funny film overall. [PG] **V**

Iron Will (1994) *** (See 1900s)

It Had To Be You (1947) **1/2 D: Don Hartman, Rudolph Maté. Ginger Rogers, Cornel Wilde, Percy Waram, Spring Byington, Ron Randell. Ginger has been engaged multiple times and even to the altar, but can never say the all important words. Now engaged again, her fiancé's family wants to be sure it history doesn't repeat itself. But while on a train, she meets a mysterious figure who leads her to the reason she hasn't been able to commit. Fun, wacky film.

It Happened One Night (1934) **** D: Frank Capra. Clark Gable, Claudette Colbert, Walter Connolly, Roscoe Karnes, Alan Hale, Ward Bond. Society girl Colbert runs away from her wedding and reporter Gable latches on to her without letting her know that he knows who she is. They fall in love amongst many misadventures. Winner of 5 Oscars, it was the first film to do so winning Best Picture, Actor, Actress, Director and Screenplay. The hitchhiking and the blanket "Walls of Jericho" scenes are classics. **V**

It Happened to Jane (1959) **1/2 D: Richard Quine. Doris Day, Jack Lemmon, Ernie Kovacs, Steve Forrest, Teddy Rooney, Russ Brown, Mary Wickes, Parker Fennelly. Cute comedy of widow Day who runs a lobstery in Maine and finds herself in trouble with crooked Kovacs. Lemmon is her long-time friend and lawyer who is also in love with her. Fun scene of running an old train to meet their deadline. Ought to please entire family.

It's a Wonderful World (1939) *** D: W. S. Van Dyke II. Claudette Colbert, James Stewart, Guy Kibbee, Nat Pendleton, Frances Drake, Edgar Kennedy Ernest Truex, Sidney Blackmer, Hans Conried. Screwball comedy with Colbert as a runaway poetess and Stewart a fugitive running from the police. Scene of them in the woods and Stewart dressed as a Boy Scout leader in stolen clothes trying to see through coke-bottle glasses is a classic. Fun family film.

It Should Happen to You (1954) *** D: George Cukor. Judy Holliday, Peter Lawford, Jack Lemmon, Michael O'Shea, Vaughn Taylor. Holliday as average working girl obsessed with seeing her name "up in lights." She gets idea to rent a billboard, put her name

on it, leading to a tangle of things. Interesting look at/discussion piece for the need to be "famous." Great job all, including Lemmon in first film. **V**

It Takes Two (1995) **1/2 D: Andy Tennant. Kirstie Alley, Steve Guttenberg, Mary-Kate Olsen, Ashely Olsen, Philip Bosco, Jane Sibbet, Michelle Grison, Desmond Roberts, Ernie Grunwald, Lawrence Kane. Story line is somewhat based on *The Prince and the Pauper* of two look-a-likes whose paths cross and they decide to trade lives. One is the child of a millionaire the other a poor orphan who has come to summer camp near the other girl's summer home. The wealthy girl's father is about to marry "the wicked witch" and the girls put their heads together to stop the wedding and at the same time interest him in the counselor (Alley) whom they think is great. Cute family film and one my girls really liked. **[PG] V, DVD**

Journey to the Center of the Earth (1959) *** (See Literature)

Jumping Jacks (1952) **1/2 D: Norman Taurog. Dean Martin, Jerry Lewis, Mona Freeman, Don De-Fore, Robert Strauss.   Lots of Martin and Lewis slapstick in this one. Sure to please the kids. **V**

June Bride (1948) *** D: Bretaigne Windust. Bette Davis, Robert Montgomery, Fay Bainter, Tom Tully, Barbara Bates, Jerome Cowan, Mary Wickes.   Cute comedy of magazine writer/editor Davis who must get out the June bride issue and wedding in the dead of winter and the antics this brings about. The bride is a young girl from a small town requiring the magazine to go to them. Montgomery, a top writer, goes along as well as more of the staff. The magazine people pound the bride's Mom into shape, remodel their home and generally causes havoc in their life and home all the while in chaos themselves. Ultimately it comes to a showdown between Davis and Montgomery: who's going to wear the pants. Fun film. **V**

Jungle Book (1967) *** D: Wolfgang Reitherman. Voices of Phil Harris, Sebastian Cabot, Louis Prima, George Sanders, Sterling Holloway, J. Pat O'Malley, Verna Felton, Bruce Reitherman.   Wonderful animated version of classic Kipling tale of young boy, Mowgli, who is raised by wolves and befriended by jungle creatures, most especially Baloo (Harris). Fabulous vocal characterizations by some top notch actors, kooky buzzards and a good score. Songs include, "Bare Necessities," "I Wanna Be Like You," "Trust in Me." Sit back and enjoy this one with your children. **V, DVD**

Just Around the Corner (1938) ** D: Irving Cummings. Shirley Temple, Joan Davis, Charles Farrell, Amanda Duff, Bill Robinson, Bert Lahr, Claude Gillingwater.   Shirley ends the Depression by manipulating Gillingwater to create new jobs. Best feature: musical numbers with Bill Robinson. Sure to delight little girls. **V**

Karate Kid (1984) ***1/2 D: John G. Avidsen. Ralph Macchio, Noriyuki (Pat) Morita, Elisabeth Shue, Randee Heller, Martin Kove, William Zabka, Chad McQueen, Tony O'Dell, Larry Drake.   Macchio is the new kid at school who is a bit of a misfit and has come into the sites of karate-savvy bullies. He is rescued by the janitor of his apartment complex who finally agrees to tutor him in karate. The redeeming points of this movie are the lessons he gets in discipline, following through until completion, etc. There are a few ideologies of eastern culture that might need discussion, but I believe most will like this for a family film and root for the kid at the end as he-the underdog-takes on the bullies in a karate championship match. This film was originally rated R, but I have only seen it from TV, where it has been cleaned up from any bad language or objectionable material. **V**

Kid From Brooklyn, The (1946) *** D: Norman Z. McLeod. Danny Kaye, Virginia Mayo, Vera-Ellen, Steve Cochran, Eve Arden, Walter Abel, Lionel Stander, Fay Bainter.   Zany comedy has Kaye as a milkman who is mistaken for and then turned into a prizefighter. Clean family fun, Kaye style. **V**

Kiss and Tell (1945) **1/2 D: Richard Wallace. Shirley Temple, Jerome Courtland, Walter Abel, Katherine Alexander, Robert Benchley, Porter Hall.   Based on a Broadway play, this has Shirley as a wacky teenager.

Kisses For My President (1964) **1/2 D: Curtis Bernhardt. Fred MacMurray, Polly

Bergen, Arlene Dahl, Edward Andrews, Eli Wallach.   Thirties style comedy has Bergen as the President and Mac-Murray trying to figure out how to fill the role of "first ___?" can't be lady! **V**

Kiss in the Dark, A (1949) ****1/2 D: Delmer Daves. David Niven, Jane Wyman, Victor Moore, Wayne Morris, Broderick Crawford, Joseph Buloff, Maria Ouspenskaya.   Concert pianist Niven learns from business manager of an apartment building he owns as an investment. When he decides to take a closer look, he runs into model Wyman and decides to hang around a bit. Cute comedy with boorish Crawford run out by hours of piano practicing.

Lad: A Dog (1962) ****1/2 (See Literature)

Lady and the Tramp (1955) *****1/2 D: Hamilton Luske, Clyde Geronimi, Wilfred Jackson. Voices of Peggy Lee, Barbara Luddy, Bill Thompson, Bill Baucon, Stan Freberg, Verna Felton, Alan Reed.   One of Disney's best animated features about a pedigreed dog who is rescued and then befriended by a mongrel who introduces her to a whole new world in the streets. Wonderful songs including "He's a Tramp" by the wonderful Peggy Lee, who also does the voices of Darling and the Siamese cats. Sure to enchant children and parents, alike. **V, DVD**

Lady Takes a Chance, The (1943) ***** D: William A. Seiter. Jean Arthur, John Wayne, Charles Winninger, Phil Silvers, Mary Field, Don Costello.   Arthur meets real-life cowboy Wayne while on a bus trip and falls for him. Wacky comedy is lots of fun. **V**

Lady Wants a Mink (1953) ****1/2 D: William A. Seiter. Even Arden, Ruth Hussey, Dennis O'Keefe, William Demarest, Gene Lockhart.   Wife (Hussey) decides that she wants a mink coat, but hubby (O'Keefe) says they can't afford it so she decides to raise her own minks for a coat!

Land Before Time, The (1988) ****1/2 D: Don Bluth. Voices of Pat Hingle, Gabriel Damon, Helen-Shaver, Candace Hutson, Judith Barsi, Will Ryan, Burke Barnes.   I worried about allowing my children to see this when they were young due to the rating. While it is a charming film, the T-Rex in it could be scary for the younger ones, so you decide if it's appropriate for your family. The story is of a young dinosaur who gets separated from his family and must find a particular lush valley. Along the way, he meets up with other junior dinosaurs and they make the trek together. I particularly like Duckie's "Yep, yep, yep!" [PG] **V, DVD**

Lassie, Come Home (1943) *****1/2 D: Fred M. Wilcox. Roddy McDowell, Donald Crisp, Dame May Whitty, Edmund Gwenn, Nigel Bruce, Elsa Lanchester, Elizabeth Taylor and Pal (Lassie).   Wonderful, classic film of Eric Knight's book about a poor family who are forced to sell their beloved pet who then undertakes a nearly impossible journey to return to them. Remade in 1978 as the *Magic of Lassie* starring Jimmy Stewart, Mickey Rooney and Alice Faye. Both versions are available on video. **V**

Last of the Mohicans, The (1936) ***** (See 1700s)

Laura (1944) *****1/2 D: Otto Preminger. Gene Tierney, Dana Andrews, Clifton Webb, Vincent Price, Judith Anderson, Grant Mitchell, Lane Chandler, Dorothy Adams.   Unusual murder mystery where the investigating detective falls in love with the subject of a portrait. Intriguing story, well acted by the leads and a truly clever puzzle of a plot, no horror included. Parents may wish to view first for content. **V, DVD**

Lemon Drop Kid, The (1951) ***** D: Sidney Lanfield. Bob Hope, Marilyn Maxwell, Lloyd Nolan, Jane Darwell, William Frawley.   Based on a Damon Runyon story, Hope portrays a race track gambler who owes big money or else. See if it fits your taste. **V, DVD**

Little Miss Broadway (1938) **** D: Irving Cummings. Shirley Temple, George Murphy, Jimmy Durante, Phyllis Brooks, Edna May Oliver, George Barbier.   Shirley sheds her magic-touch of goodness on Oliver's boarding house in this one. **V**

Little Miss Marker (1934) ***** D: Alexander Hall. Adolphe Menjou, Shirley Temple, Dorothy Dell, Charles Bickford, Lynne Overman, Warren Hymer.   Wonderful version of Damon Runyon tale of a gambler who leaves his daughter as his "marker" (IOU) while he goes to collect the money he owes, she instruct the gamblers about King Arthur and his Knights of the Round Table. This one's lots of fun. **V**

Little Princess, The (1939) *** D: Walter Lang. Shirley Temple, Richard Greene, Anita Louise, Ian Hunger, Cesar Romero, Arthur Treacher, Marcia Mae Jones, Sybil Jason.   Shirley's dad goes off to war and leaves her at a boarding school. Word arrives that he's been killed and Shirley goes from the most privileged student to a servant. She is determined that her father isn't dead and when she can slip away, searches for him in the hospitals and has some interesting adventures along the way.   **V**

Littlest Rebel, The (1935) *** (See Civil War)

Little Women (1933) **** (1949) **1/2 (See Literature)

Living It Up (1954) *** D: Norman Taurog. Dean Martin, Jerry Lewis, Janet Leigh, Edward Arnold, Fred Clark, Sheree North, Sig Ruman.   Remake of *Nothing Sacred* has Jerry supposedly dying from radiation poisoning and Dean as his doctor. Reporter Leigh picks up the story and pitches it to her editor as a way to boost circulation. One of Martin and Lewis' best.

Love Bug, The (1969) ***1/2 D: Robert Stevens. Dean Jones, Michele Lee, Buddy Hackett, David Tomlinson, Joe Flynn, Benson Fong, Iris Adrian.   Wonderful Disney comedy of a man who wants to race and must do so in a VW bug with a mind of its own. Lots of stuff for the kids and plenty of laughs. Any parent who objects to the personification of objects in a story will need to view this first.   **V**

Lt. Robin Crusoe, USN (1966) ** D: Byron Paul. Dick Van Dyke, Nancy Kwan, Akim Tamiroff, Arthur Malet, Tyler McVey.   Disney comedy based on the story of Robinson Crusoe has Navy pilot Van Dyke bail out in a life raft with instructions given by the voice of "Mel" from the DVD show! Crusoe lands on an island where he builds a place to live until rescued. The story covers the basics of the classic story, but with some very different comedic twists. Not classic literature. It is what it is: simple children's fun.   **V**

Luck of the Irish, The (1948) **1/2 D: Henry Koster. Tyrone Power, Anne Baxter, Cecil Kellaway, Lee J. Cobb, Jayne Meadows.   A charming movie of a reporter engaged to the daughter of a powerful man in what is known as a "good match," but not one of love or even great affection. He travels abroad and meets a sweet Irish colleen (Baxter) to whom he's drawn. He also picks up a guardian in the form of a leprechaun, who comes back with him to the U. S. to try save him from making the wrong choice. Some parents may object to the inclusion of a leprechaun, so I suggest you view it first and see if its alright with you. Generally cute. **V**

Magic of Lassie, The (1978) **1/2 D: Don Chaffey. James Stewart, Lassie, Mickey Roonie, Alice Faye, Stephanie Zimbalist, Pernell Roberts, Michael Sharrett, Mike Mazurki.   Remake of *Lassie Come Home* has Stewart cast as the grandfather of Zimbalist and Sharrett, who've been forced to turn their beloved dog over to mean Parnell. Preview. **[G] V**

Magnificent Seven, The (1960) ***1/2 D: John Sturges. Yul Brynner, Steve McQueen, Eli Wallach, Horst Buchholz, James Coburn, Charles Bronson, Robert Vaughn, Brad Dexter.   Story of paid gun-slingers who are intrigued by the offer of a small Mexican village in need of their protection. They've all been paid big money, but never before have they been offered everything someone has. For a small price, but all, they come to the aid of the town. This is a typical, "shoot-em-up" western, so watch first. **V, DVD**

Male Animal, The (1942) ***1/2 D: Elliott Nugent. Henry Fonda, Olivia de Haviland, Joan Leslie, Jack Carson, Herbert Anderson, Don DeFore, Hattie McDaniel, Eugene Pallette.   Cute comedy of a college professor (Fonda) standing up for his principles while it seems that his old rival, back in town for the football game, will make off with the affection of his wife. This is all done "above board" which was the only way the Hayes code would allow it. Watch first if subject matter concerns you.

Man Called Peter, A (1955) *** (See Bible) About Senate Chaplain Peter Marshall.

Man From Snowy River, The (1982-Australian) ***1/2 D: George Miller. Kirk Douglas,

Tom Burlinson, Sigrid Thornton, Jack Thompson, Lorraine Bayly, Tommy Dysart, Bruce Kerr.   Based on an Australian poem, this is a wonderful tale of a young man coming of age. After his father is killed in an accident, young Tom must find work in order to save his "place." He leaves the mountains to go to work for a wealthy man, ultimately falling in love with his daughter. The story includes a wild stallion, a mysterious secret, gorgeous scenery and one of the most astonishing feats of horsemanship ever put on film. Parents should view first. **[PG] V**

Man With a Million (1954-British) **1/2 (See Literature)

Margie (1946) **1/2 D: Henry King. Jeanne Crain, Glenn Langan, Lynn Bari, Alan Young, Barbara Lawrence, Conrad Janis, Esther Dale, Horbart Cavanaugh, Ann Todd, Hattie McDaniel.   Sweet story of a teenager in the 1920s who lives with her grandmother and rarely gets to see her widowed father, though an event happens to close that gap. She has a crush on her new French teacher, who sees her crush and is very kind to her, though the actions he takes would most likely not be seen as innocent in the eyes of today's society. View first and see what you think. Overall, a cute film.

Mark of Zorro, The (1940) ***1/2 (See 1800s, West)

Mask of Zorro, The (1998) *** (See 1800s, West)

Mating Game, The (1959) *** D: George Marshall. Debbie Reynolds, Tony Randall, Paul Douglas, Fred Clark, Una Merkel, Philip Ober, Charles Lane.   Comedy of farm family more interested in relationships and friends than money. Government sends tax-agent (Randall) to look into their unpaid taxes, who falls for daughter Reynolds. He discovers that the U.S. government took horses from this family during the Civil War and never paid for them, therefore the government really owes them! **V**

Mating Season, The (1951) *** D: Mitchell Leisen. Gene Tierney, John Lund, Miriam Hopkins, Thelma Ritter, Jan Sterling, Larry Keating, James Lorimer.   Insightful comedy of a working young man (Lund) who marries a socialite (Tierney) and the financial problems this brings. Unknown to him, his mother (Ritter) comes for a visit and is taken for the housekeeper for which the young bride advertised. Ritter doesn't inform her of the mistake and decides to take on the task of helping her manage on a budget and get a grip on reality. Ritter is my favorite character actress and is fabulous in this film. A really good discussion could be had on the expectations in marriage, different backgrounds and dealing with money.

McHale's Navy (1964) **1/2 D: Edward J. Montagne. Ernest Borgnine, Joe Flynn, Tim Conway, George Kennedy, Claudine Longet, Bob Hastings, Carl Ballantine, Billy Sands, Gavin McLeod, Jean Willes. Movie spin-off from popular TV series has the crew of PT-73 doing all they can to pay off gambling debts and keep Lt. Bingham in the dark. **V**

McHale's Navy Joins the Air Force (1965) **1/2 D: Edward J. Montagne. Tim Conway, Joe Flynn, Bob Hastings, Ted Bessell, Susan Silo, Henry Beckman, Billy Sands, Gavin McLeod, Tom Tully, Jacques Aubuchon.   No McHale in this one, but instead Ensign Parker (Conway) is mistaken for an Air Force up-and-comer and given assignment after assignment which he screws up, but each screw-up somehow results in his promotion. **V**

McLintock! (1963) ***1/2 (See 1800s West)

Meet John Doe (1941) *** D: Frank Capra. Gary Cooper, Barbara Stanwyck, Edward Arnold, Walter Brennan, Spring Byington, James Gleason, Gene Lockhart.   Wonderful film about corruption and the people behind the scenes who'll do just about anything for power. Good film to spark some lively discussions done with the inimitable Capra touch. **V, DVD**

Merry Andrew (1958) **1/2 (See Music/Arts)

Mighty Joe Young (1998) *** D: Ron Underwood. Bill Paxton, Charlize Theron, David Paymer, Regina King, Rade Sherbedgia (Serbedzija), Peter Firth, Linds Purl, Robert Wisdom, Lawrence Pressman, John Alexander.   Paxton comes to Africa to get the truth about a famous legend, does or does it not exist? Theron is a young woman who has been raised with the giant gorilla, Joe, and who was given the duty to protect him. Poachers are after him and in order to protect him, she agrees to transport him to an animal habitat in L. A. where problems ensue as Joe is unfamiliar with all he sees and the well-meaning people at the habitat are, understandably, nervous about him. Only Theron can "control" him, which becomes a big issue when the poachers come after him again. **[PG] V, DVD**

Milkman, The (1950) **1/2 D: Charles T. Barton. Donald O'Connor, Jimmy Durante, Piper Laurie, Joyce Holden, William Conrad, Henry O'Neill, Jess Barker, Frank Nelson.   War veteran O'Connor's father owns a dairy. When his father refuses to hire him, O'Connor goes to work for the competition with his friend, Durante. O'Connor gets in lots of scrapes, falls in love with the boss's daughter and also runs across crooks. Because he suffers from shell-shock, when under pressure he blanks out and quacks like a duck! This leads to many wild and wacky situations. Fun film for the family.

Million Dollar Mermaid (1952) **1/2 D: Mervyn LeRoy. Esther Williams, Victor Mature, Walter Pidgeon, David Brian, Donna Corcoran, Jesse White, Maria Tallchief.   Esther swims in a side-show type of set-up as real life aquatic star Annette Kellerman. Some production numbers by Busby Berkeley. **V**

Miracle Worker, The (1962) ***1/2 (See 1900s) About Annie Sullivan and Helen Keller.

Misadventures of Merlin Jones, The (1964) ** D: Robert Stevenson. Tommy Kirk, Annette Funicello, Leon Ames, Stuart Erwin, Alan Hewitt, Connie Gilchrist.   Disney comedy of brainy Jones (Kirk) and the trouble he gets in with his various bright ideas. Definitely a kid's movie. Sequel: *The Monkey's Uncle*. **V**

Mister Roberts (1955) **1/2 D: John Ford, Mervyn LeRoy. Henry Fonda, James Cagney, William Powell, Jack Lemmon, Betsy Palmer, Ward Bond, Nick Adams, Philip Carey, Harry Carey, Jr., Ken Curtis, Martin Milner, Jack Pennick, Perry Lopez, Pat Wayne.   Fonda recreates his famous (and favorite) stage role in this comedy-drama of an officer on a WWII cargo ship who badly wants active combat duty, but the cantankerous captain won't release him because Fonda is necessary to make him look good. Though now a classic, parents will need to preview first. **V, DVD**

Mister Scoutmaster (1953) *** D: Henry Levin. Clifton Webb, Edmund Gwenn, George Winslow, Frances Dee, Veda Ann Borg.   Webb (as only he can) plays a scoutmaster who hates kids! Wacky film.

Model and the Marriage Broker, The (1951) *** D: George Cukor. Jeanne Crain, Scott Brady, Thelma Ritter, Zero Mostel, Michael O'Shea, Frank Fontaine, Nancy Kulp.   Perhaps I like this film because of my favorite character actress, Ritter. But in the day of "beautiful people" and so many people having a hard time accepting themselves in comparison to air-brushed pictures of those we've deemed as our ideal, I think this film has a lot of insight into what is truly important and how we, as a society, view those who are less than model perfect. Parents, view first; see if you think it's worth-while for your family.

Money From Home (1953) **1/2 D: George Marshall. Dean Martin, Jerry Lewis, Pat Crowley, Robert Strauss, Jack Kruschen.   Martin and Lewis are at their best in this Damon Runyon story of horses and steeplechase races, gamblers who want to fix the race and Lewis, who wants to be a vet and can talk to horses! My youngest daughter really liked this one.

Monkey Business (1952) *** D: Howard Hawks. Ginger Rogers, Cary Grant, Charles Coburn, Marilyn Monroe, Hugh Marlowe.   Grant discovers a serum that makes one feel young again-about 6 years old! Without knowing he's created it, he ingests it along with his wife (Rogers) and boss, (Coburn) and the boss's secretary (Monroe) and the fun begins. **V, DVD**

Monkeys, Go Home! (1967) ** D: Andrew V. McLaglen. Maurice Chevalier, Dean Jones, Yvette Mimieux, Bernard Woringer, Clement Harari, Yvonne Constant.   Disney film about a man (Jones) who inherits an olive farm in France and trains monkeys to pick his crop. Best for kids. **V, DVD**

Monkey's Uncle, The (1965) ** D: Robert Stevenson. Tommy Kirk, Annette Funicello, Leon Ames, Frank Faylen, Arthur O'Connell, Norman Grabowski.   Disney comedy has genius Merlin Jones (Kirk) sleep training a monkey, building a flying machine, and generally getting into trouble. Sequel to: *The Misadventures of Merlin Jones.* **V**

Moon-Spinners, The (1964) **1/2 D: James Neilson. Hayley Mills, Eli Wallach, Pola Negri, Peter McEnery, Joan Greenwood, Irene Papas.   Hayley is on vacation with her aunt on Crete when she stumbles into intrigue and jewelry smuggling. Disney film with a few tense moments, but still clean for kids. **V**

Mother is a Freshman (1949) **1/2 D: Lloyd Bacon. Loretta Young, Van Johnson, Rudy Vallee, Barbara Lawrence, Robert Arthur, Betty Lynn.   Innocent story of a young widow with a college age daughter who is informed that she hasn't any money. The only way she can live and keep her daughter in school is to take advantage of a scholarship one of her ancestors instituted at the college her daughter attends. Only someone with the mother's name can use the scholarship. So, mother and daughter attend the same school, with daughter a bit of a spoiled brat who must grow up, especially when she realizes the teacher upon whom she has a crush is interested in her mother. View it and see what you think.

Mother Wore Tights (1947) *** D: Walter Lang. Betty Grable, Dan Dailey, Mona Freeman, Connie Marshall, Vanessa Brown, Veda Ann Borg.   One of Grable's most popular films about a vaudeville family with Dan Dailey at her side. Score won an Oscar. Usual colorful Grable fluff. **V**

Mountain Family Robinson (1979) **1/2 D: John Cotter. Robert F. Logan, Susan Damante Shaw, William Bryant, Heather Rattray, Ham Larsen, George (Buck) Flower.   Sequel to *The Adventures of the Wilderness Family.* Clean family film of life in the mountains as modern day homesteaders. **[G] V**

Mr. and Mrs. Smith (1941) *** D: Alfred Hitchcock. Carole Lombard, Robert Montgomery, Gene Raymond, Jack Carson, Philip Merivale, Betty Compson, Lucile Watson.   Screwball comedy of a couple who find out that their marriage wasn't legal. Don't let the director fool you, this one is not a typical Hitchcock film. **V**

Mr. Belvedere Goes to College (1949) ** D: Elliot Nugent. Clifton Webb, Shirley Temple, Tom Drake, Alan Young, Jessie Royce Landis, Kathleen Hughes.   The acerbic Mr. Belvedere first seen in *Sitting Pretty* enrolls in college and the fur flies.

Mr. Belvedere Rings the Bell (1951) **1/2 D: Henry Koster. Clifton Webb, Joanne Dru, Hugh Marlowe, Zero Mostel, Doro Merande, Billy Lynn.   I love this film because of the message it gives. In this one, Mr. Belvedere infiltrates an old-folks home in order to prove his theory that age has nothing to do with the value of life.

Mr. Blandings Builds His Dream House (1948) *** D: H. C. Potter. Cary Grant, Myna Loy, Melvyn Douglas, Reginald Denny, Sharyn Moffett, Connie Marshall, Louise Beavers, Ian Wolfe, Lurene Luttle, Lex Barker.   Fun comedy of an apartment dwelling couple who are cramped to the gills and decide to build a home of their own. Everything goes wrong that can go wrong, bringing us a lot of fun. **V**

Mr. Deeds Goes to Town (1936) **** D: Frank Capra. Gary Cooper, Jean Arthur, George Bancroft, Lionel Stander, Douglass Dumbrille, Mayo Methot, Raymond Walburn, Walter Catlett, H. B. Warner. Cooper plays a man named Longfellow Deeds who inherits 20 million dollars and is deemed crazy because he wants to give it away. Arthur is the cynical reporter who tries to figure him out. Capra won a second Oscar for this endearing film. **V, DVD**

Mr. Holland's Opus (1995) ***1/2 D: Stephen Herek. Richard Dreyfuss, Glenne Headly, Jay Thomas, Olympia Dukakis, W. (William) H. Macy, Alicai Witt, Jean Louisa Kelly, Nicholas John Renner, Joseph Anderson, Anthony Natale, Joanna Gleason.   Disney movie of a musician who turns to teaching school intending to do so only long enough to write a major work, but ends up teaching for thirty years is generally grand. It is really worth seeing, but definitely need some editing before the children see it. Mostly it's about a life lived in sacrifice and given to others. [PG] **V, DVD**

Mr. Lucky (1943) *** D: H. C. Potter. Cary Grant, Laraine Day, Charles Bickford, Gladys Cooper, Alan Carney, Henry Stephenson, Paul Stewart, Kay Johnson, Florence Bates.   Wonderful tale of a gambling ship owner (Grant) who decides to use the war relief effort to fund his needs. Instead, he falls for Day and acquires a conscience. Lots of old fun slang terms are included as Grant instructs upper-crust Day in his way of communicating. Sweet film. **V**

Mr. Smith Goes to Washington (1939) ****1/2 (See 1900s)

My Favorite Blonde (1942) *** D: Sidney Lanfield. Bob Hope, Madeleine Carroll, Gale Sondergaard, George Zucco, Victor Varconi.   Bob and his penguin become targets for spies when they are used to deliver a secret message. Hope at his wackiest. **V, DVD**

My Favorite Brunette (1947) *** D: Elliott Nugent. Bob Hope, Dorothy Lamour, Peter Lorre, Lon Chaney, John Hoyt, Reginald Denny.   Bob plays a photographer in this one who gets mixed up with gangsters. Lorre you probably know, the infamous Lon Chaney you may not know, but should. [*Man of a Thousand Faces* tells his story.] Two surprise cameos are included at beginning and end of film. **V, DVD**

My Favorite Spy (1951) *** D: Norman Z. McLeod. Bob Hope, Hedy Lamarr, Francis L. Sullivan, Mike Mazurki, John Archer, Iris Adrian, Arnold Moss.   Bob is the ringer for a murdered spy and finds himself involved in international espionage. Another zany Hope film.

My Favorite Wife (1940) *** D: Garson Kanin. Cary Grant, Irene Dunne, Gail Patrick, Randolph Scott, Ann Shoemaker, Scotty Beckett, Donald MacBride.   Dunne returns home after being lost at sea and missing for seven years only to find that her husband has just (that day) married another woman! May sound sordid, but due to the time in which it was made, is innocent and funny instead. **V**

My Friend Irma (1949) ** D: George Marshall. Marie Wilson, John Lund, Diana Lynn, Don DeFore, Dean Martin, Jerry Lewis, Hans Conreid.   Goofy film based on a radio series about a blonde who was, undoubtedly, the source of all dumb blonde jokes. Lunn is her common sense friend with Martin and Lewis in their first film appearance. **V**

My Friend Irma Goes West (1950) **1/2 D: Hal Walker. John Lund, Marie Wilson, Dean Martin, Jerry Lewis, Corinne Calvet, Diana Lynn, Lloyd Corrigan, Donald Porter, Kenneth Toby.   All the gang goes to Hollywood.

My Love Came Back (1940) **1/2 D: Kurt Bernhardt. Olivia de Haviland, Jeffrey Lynn, Eddie Albert, Jane Wyman, Charles Winniger, Spring Byington.   From a story by Walter Reisch, Classical violinist de Haviland joins a swing band upon losing her scholarship because she taught lessons. Her scholarship is reinstated by businessman/boardmember Winniger and is administered by Winniger's manager, who falls for de Haviland and vice versa. Misunderstanding throws a wedge in the works, but it all works out in the end. Some parents may object to Winniger's interest in de Haviland, so view first.

My Man Godfrey (1936) ***1/2 (See 1900s)

My Sister Eileen (1942) **1/2 D: Alexander Hall. Rosalind Russell, Brian Aherne, Janet Blair, George Tobias, Allyn Joslyn, Elizabeth Patterson, June Havoc.   Funny story of two girls from Ohio who come to the big city and get an apartment in Greenwich Village with a kooky group of people. See Music/Arts for the musical version. Both are very good, each in their own way. **V**

My Six Loves (1963) **1/2 D: Gower Champion. Debbie Reynolds, Cliff Robertson, David Janssen, Eileen Heckart, Hans Conreid, Alice Pearce, Jim Backus.   Reynolds is a stage star who has retired to her country home for a much needed rest, only to find that six orphans have moved into an old shack in the woods on her property. She takes them in until something can be arranged for them and with the help of the local minister (Robertson) decides to keep them. The youngest doesn't speak and steals her heart, but disappears when she goes back to the city to do a new (controversial) play. This is a charming film that shows the importance of parents, moms in particular. Cute song, "It's A Darn Good Thing" included.

New Adventures of Pippi Longstocking, The (1988) ** (See Literature)

Night of the Grizzly (1966) **1/2 D: Joseph Pevney. Clint Walker, Martha Hyer, Keenan Wynn, Nancy Kulp, Ron Ely, Regis Toomey, Jack Elam.   Western story of a rancher (Walker) who overcomes the odds, including a vicious bear, to live in the wild. **V**

North by Northwest (1959) **** D: Alfred Hitchcock. Cary Grant, Eva Marie Saint, James Mason, Leo G. Carroll, Martin Landau, Jessie Royce Landis, Philip Ober, Adam Williams, Josephine Hutchinson, Edward Platt.   Now classic Hitchcock suspense film of an ad-man who stumbles into espionage and intrigue as he is played by two sets of spies for information because they think he's a double agent, while he's running from the police who think he's an assassin. Tense scene on Mt. Rushmore is quite famous. Parents should preview this. **V, DVD**

North to Alaska (1960) *** (See 1800s West)

Nothing Sacred (1937) ***1/2 D: William Wellman. Carole Lombard, Fredric March, Walter Connolly, Charles Winninger, Sig Rumann, Frank Fay.   Comedy about a reporter (March) who exploits a Vermont girl's diagnosis of pending death from radium poisoning for the circulation of papers. Remade as *Living It Up* with Martin and Lewis. Parents preview. **V, DVD**

No Time For Sergeants (1958) ***1/2 D: Mervyn LeRoy. Andy Griffith, Myron McCormick, Nick Adams, Murray Hamilton, Don Knotts.   Hilarious film version of the Broadway play about a well meaning country bumpkin (Griffith) who is inducted into the service and drives his sergeant nuts. The scene with Griffith as the PLO (permanent latrine orderly) is a scream! If you want lots of laughs, this is a good choice. **V**

Off Limits (1953) **1/2 D: George Marshall. Bob Hope, Mickey Rooney, Marilyn Maxwell, Eddie Mayehoff, Stanley Clements Jack Dempsey.   Hope plays a fight manager (of boxers) who gets drafted in the Army. This is a typical Hope comedy, with shenanigans and a romantic interest in Maxwell. **V**

Of Human Hearts (1938) **1/2 D: Clarence Brown. Walter Huston, James Stewart, Gene Reynolds, Beulah Bondi, Guy Kibbee, Charles Coburn, John Carradine, Ann Rutherford.   The story of a misunderstood child (by his father) who grows up to be self absorbed, like his father, and the effect this has on his life and his loving and forbearing mother. In the end, President Lincoln talks to him about the choices he has made. We found this to be a touching film containing some nice family lessons for discussion. **V**

One Hundred and One Dalmatians *** D: Wolfgang Reitherman, Hamilton Luske, Clyde Geronimi. Voices of Rod Taylor, Lisa Davis, Cate Bauer, Ben Wright, Fred Warlock, J. Pat O'Malley, Betty Lou Gerson.   Animated (and original) version of the story of two Dalmatians who bring together their owners, Anita and Roger, in wedlock (as well as themselves) and who later have puppies. Enter Anita's college classmate, Cruella De Vil, who loves furs and wants the puppies to make a coat of them. The dogs have to save their puppies and all the rest (a total of 99), outwitting Cruella and her henchmen. Might be a bit scary for the younger ones, so view first to see if appropriate for your children. **V**

101 Dalmatians (1996) **1/2 D: Stephen Herek. Glenn Close, Jeff Daniels, Joely Richardson, Joan Plowright, Hugh Laurie, Mark Williams, John Shrapnel.   The remake of the above movie, this time with real people. This one contains some physical comedy to which some parents might object, so view first. **V**

102 Dalmatians (2000) ** D: Kevin Lima. Glenn Close, Gerard Depardieu, Ioan Gruffudd, Alice Evans, Tim McInnerny, Ben Crompton, Carol Macready, Ian Richardson, Timothy West; voice of Eric Idle.   Sequel to the above story about the rehabilitation of Cruella de Vil which quickly falls apart upon her release from confinement and her continued quest for a Dalmatian-skin coat. A bit gruesome and without the charm of the one above. [G] **V, DVD**

One in a Million (1930) *** D: Sidney Lanfield. Sonja Henie, Adolphe Menjou, Don Ameche, Ned Sparks, Jean Hersholt, The Ritz Brothers. Film debut of Olympic skater Henie has story revolving around her and the question of her admission to the Winter Olympics. Old black and white is still interesting to see and to compare how the sport of figure skating has developed through the years. If doing a unit of study on the Olympics or the history of figure skating, seeing the real Sonja Henie skate will be a unique experience. **V**

On the Double (1961) *** D: Melville Shavelson. Danny Kaye, Dana Wynter, Wilfrid Hyde-White, Margaret Rutherford, Diana Dors. Kaye's imitation of a British general and his uncanny resemblance brings him to the attention of British intelligence during WWII. They want him to imitate the general to avoid (unbeknownst to him) an assassination attempt on the general's life. Lots of fun Kaye "frolics" and gags. The general he is to imitate is a bit of a rounder, so I recommend seeing this first and omitting the parts with this information. The story can easily be salvaged without it.

Operation Petticoat (1959) ***1/2 D: Blake Edwards. Cary Grant, Tony Curtis, Dina Merrill, Gene Evans, Arthur O'Connell, Richard Sargent, Virginia Gregg, Gavin McLeod. Comedy about a sub-commander (Grant) who is determined to get his ship seaworthy after being sunk and get back in the war. Included is a message from "Tokyo Rose" (who actually existed and transmitted demoralizing radio messages to the U.S troops), as well as about every imaginable mishap, including the taking on of stranded nurses and village people, the birth of a baby on board as well as the transportation of a pig! Curtis plays a pretty-boy officer whose idea of military service is done behind the scenes and in dress whites. He turns out to be a crafty addition to the crew who uses unusual, highly imaginative, and definitely non-military channels to acquire the needed equipment to outfit the sub. There are a few encounters with the nurses some parents might wish to edit. Overall, a funny film. **V**

Other Side of the Mountain, The (1975) **1/2 (See Sports)

Our Hearts Were Young and Gay (1944) *** D: Lewis Allen. Gail Russell, Diana Lynn, Charlie Ruggles, Dorothy Gish, James Brown, Bill Edwards, Beulah Bondi. Based upon the book by Cornelia Otis Skinner, this tells the tale of her trip to Europe as a young woman, along with her friend Emily Kimbrough and the mishaps they had along the way. Set in the 1920s, this one will make you laugh.

Our Little Girl (1935) **1/2 D: John Robertson. Shirley Temple, Rosemary Ames, Joel McCrea, Lyle Talbot. Shirley brings together her separated parents. Wonderful family fun. **V**

Our Miss Brooks (1956) **1/2 D: Al Lewis. Eve Arden, Gale Gordon, Nick Adams, Robert Rockwell, Richard Crenna, Don Porter, Jane Morgan. Based on TV series of the same name, this has some of those ol' timey values we all cherish in our memories. Cute film of Miss. Brooks, a teacher who meets two men who want to marry her and of her boss, who wants to use her brains to run for office. See if you can stand to watch Richard Crenna kill "It's Magic." **V**

Painted Hills, The (1951) **1/2 D: Harold Kress. Lassie, Paul Kelly, Bruce Cowling, Gary Gray, Art Smith, Ann Doran. Set in the West during the 1870s, Lassie plays Shep, a dog who takes care of her owner, a prospector, and the greed that comes with the discovery of gold. Preview. **V, DVD**

Paleface, The (1948) *** D: Norman Z. McLeod. Bob Hope, Jane Russell, Robert Armstrong. Western comedy spoof of "The Virginian," Hope plays timid, bumbling idiot to Russell's savvy sharpshooter. Won an Oscar for the song, "Buttons and Bows." **V**

Pardners (1956) **1/2 D: Norman Taurog. Dean Martin, Jerry Lewis, Lori Nelson, Jackie Loughery, John Baragrey, Agnes Moorehead, Jeff Morrow, Lon Chaney, Jr. Typical Martin and Lewis goofiness has Jerry as a millionaire who cleans up a Western town in Lewis style. **V**

Parent Trap, The (1961) *** D: David Swift. Hayley Mills, Maureen O'Hara, Brian Keith, Charlie Ruggles, Una Merkel, Leo G. Carroll, Joanna Barnes, Cathleen Nesbitt, Nancy Kulp,

Frank DeVol. Innovative for its time, Mills plays twins separated by parent's divorce when infants. One lives in Boston, the other in California and neither knows of the other's existence until they happen to attend the same summer camp. Once the discovery is made, they decide to switch places to meet the parent they don't know. There are some crazy mishaps along the way of getting their parents reunited. All in all, a fun family film. **V**

Parent Trap, The (1998) *** D: Nancy Myers. Lindsay Lohan, Dennis Quaid, Natasha Richardson, Elaine Hendrix, Lisa Ann Walter, Simon Kunz, Polly Holliday, Maggie Wheeler, Ronnie Stevens. Remake of the above film, updating it to the '90s. Rarely do I favor a remake over the original or even think that it's a fraction as good; this one is. The plot differences include mom living in London instead of Boston. There is one scene in which the butler appears in a too brief swimsuit, which can easily be buzzed forward. View first to see if you have any other objections. **V, DVD**

People Will Talk (1951) *** D: Joseph l. Mankiewicz. Cary Grant, Jeanne Crain, Finlay Currie, Walter Slezak, Hume Cronyn, Sidney Blackmer, Margaret Hamilton.   Comedy-drama involving a doctor (Grant) who must tell his widowed patient (Crain) that she is expecting. She decides to end it all rather than be a burden to her father and Grant steps in with a solution: marry him. He comes with a unique and virtually silent companion who holds quite a key to the good doctor and only really opens his mouth when Grant is accused of medical misconduct by Cronyn for treating his patients as human beings. You may want to view this first to see if it's okay for you, but I love the "trial" and the clear message given about "small men." **V**

Pocketful of Miracles (1961) *** D: Frank Capra. Bette Davis, Glenn Ford, Hope Lange, Arthur O'Connell, Thomas Mitchell, Peter Falk, Edward Everett Horton, Ann-Margret, Mickey Shaughnessy, David Brian, Sheldon Leonard, Barton MacLane, John Litel, Jerome Cowan, Fritz Feld, Jack Elam, Ellen Corby. Based on a Damon Runyon story, Davis is Apple Annie who is necessary to supply good luck apples to Dave the Dude (Ford). When circumstances prevent her from supplying his apple-a-day, he gets involved to fix everything. To do that, he must turn her (the modern day equivalent of a bag-lady) into a lady. I love the part where Ford is trying to teach his hoods to dance and behave like gentlemen! Cute, clean film. **V, DVD**

Pollyanna (1960) ***1/2 (See Literature)

Princess and the Pirate, The (1944) *** D: David Butler. Bob Hope, Virginia Mayo, Walter Slezak, Walter Brennan, Victor McLaglen, Hugo Haas, Marc Lawrence.   Wacky comedy of Hope and Mayo on-the run from pirate McLaglen, but trapped by Slezak. **V, DVD**

Princess Bride, The (1987) **1/2 (See Literature)

Princess Diaries, The (2001) **1/2 D: Garry Marshall. Julie Andrews, Anne Hathaway, Hector Elizondo, Heather Matarazzo, Mandy Moore, Caroline Goodall, Robert Schwartzman, Erik Von Detten, Patrick Flueger, Sandra Oh, Mindy Burbano.   Gawky high school student learns that her deceased father was a prince and that with the death of all her family but her grandmother, she is needed to fill the monarchy for the country. She meets her grandmother (Andrews) and has to decide whether or not to take the job. There are some things that need to be edited, so preview it. **[G]** **V, DVD**

Princess O'Rourke (1943) **1/2 D: Norman Krasna. Olivia de Haviland, Robert Cummings, Charles Coburn, Jack Carson, Jane Wyman, Harry Davenport, Gladys Cooper.   Charming film of a princess traveling incognito who is nervous about flying at night and is given too many sleeping pills. When she arrives, no one can wake her up, nor does anyone know who she is. The pilot (Cummings) decides to take her to friends to take care of her. When she awakens, she takes advantage of her escape to get away from her duties and interact with "normal" people. She and Cummings fall for each other and then the powers that be get involved since she's a princess and he's a commoner. Cute film for all. Won an Oscar for Best Screenplay.

Prince Who Was a Thief, The (1951) **1/2 D: Rudolph Maté. Tony Curtis, Piper Laurie, Everett Sloane, Jeff Corey, Betty Garde.   Curtis is an Islamic prince who was spared from the assassin's knife by the assassin (!) who raised him as his own son. Now the time has come for him to retrieve his throne from an evil ruler. Colorful costumer with a different view of the middle east than we've recently received.

Prisoner of Zenda, The (1937) **** D: John Cromwell. Ronald Colman, Madeleine Carroll, Douglas Fairbanks, Jr., C. Aubrey Smith, Raymond Massey, Mary Astor, David Niven, Montagu Love, Alexander D'Arcy. Parents might wish to preview first. **V**
(1952) **1/2 D: Richard Thorpe. Stewart Granger, Deborah Kerr, Jane Greer, Louis Calhern, Lewis Stone, James Mason, Robert Douglas, Robert Coote. **V**
The story of a man who goes to Europe on vacation only to be asked to fill in for a distant cousin, a king in jeopardy for whom he's a dead ringer! He faces the danger and his cousin's fiancée with whom he falls in love. A lovely film.

Private War of Major Benson, The (1955) **1/2 D: Jerry Hopper. Charlton Heston, Julie Adams, William Demarest, Tim Hovey, Sal Mineo, David Janssen Tim Considine, Milburn Stone.   Cute family film of tough Major (Heston) who is assigned to a boys military academy to learn something. Hovey is darling as the little boy who wins his heart. **V**

Quiet Man, The (1952) **** (See 1900s)

Raiders of the Lost Ark (1981) **** D: Steven Spielberg. Harrison Ford, Karen Allen, Wolf Kahler, Paul Freeman, Ronald Lacey, John Rhys-Davies, Denholm Elliot, Anthony Higgins, Alfred Molina.   A roller coaster ride of a movie. Spielberg wanted this movie to have the flavor of the old Saturday matinees he'd watched as a kid. Indiana Jones (Ford) is an professor of archaeology/treasure hunter for a museum. A team of government agents come to him to get help on an intercepted Nazi message they don't understand. They then recruit Jones to go after what they have learned the Nazi's believe to be the location of the lost Ark of the Covenant. From there, the action just keeps rolling. Jones is reunited with an old love. Some parents may wish to buzz some of the dialogue. The only other thing that is "scary" involves a lot of snakes where the ark is located, and the angel of death when the Nazi's try to "use" the ark. Parents might wish to view this first if they haven't seen it, and determine what is appropriate for their children. **[PG] V**

Note: The first in a trilogy, this is followed by *Temple of Doom* which I suggest you skip due to its heavy occult theme. It was so controversial when it was released with a [PG] rating that it was solely responsible for the creation of the [PG-13] rating. The third in the trilogy is *Indiana Jones and the Last Crusade*.

Rebecca of Sunnybrook Farm (1938) **1/2 D: Allan Swan. Shirley Temple, Randolph Scott, Jack Haley, Gloria Stuart, Phyllis Brooks, Helen Westley, Slim Summerville, William Demarest.   No relation to the Kat Douglas Wiggin's book, this has Scott trying to make Shirley into a radio star. Still, a typical clean fun Shirley Temple movie. **V**

Reluctant Debutante, The **1/2 (1958) D: Vincente Minelli. Rex Harrison, Kay Kendall, John Saxon, Sandra Dee, Angela Lansbury.   Dee is Harrison's American daughter who comes to stay with him and his wife (Kendall) during the last English "season" of presenting debutantes to society and the whirlwind of balls night after night. This should be viewed by parents first for a few items which can be easily omitted, but it is worth seeing as Kendall and Harrison make this drawing-room comedy hilarious. Just a note: Kay Kendall *was* Mrs. Rex Harrison when this film was made. She died from cancer shortly after this film. **V**

Reluctant Dragon, The (1941) *** D: Alfred L. Werker (live-action).   Robert Benchley tours the Walt Disney studios in this film which includes some well done cartoon sequences (*Baby Weems, The Reluctant Dragon*) and offers an interesting view into the studio at work.

Mine liked the latter one. **V**

Rescuers, The (1977) *** D: Wolfgang Reitherman, John Lounsbery, Art Stevens, Voices of Bob Newhart, Eva Gabor, Geraldine Page, Joe Flynn, Jeanette Nolan, Pat Buttram, Jim Jordan, John McIntire.   A little girl is kidnapped from an orphanage because of her small stature to retrieve a diamond for villains. It's up to Bernard and Bianca of the all-mouse Rescue Aid Society to save her. Preview first as some parts can be scary. [G] **V**

Rescuers Down Under, The (1990) *** D: Hendel Butoy, Mike Gabriel. Voices of John Candy, Tristan Rogers, Adam Ryen, Frank Welker.   Bernard and Bianca of the all-mouse Rescue Aid Society go to Australia this time to rescue a small boy who has been taken captive by a poacher. Like the first one, parent should view this first for anything scary. [G] **V, DVD**

Return to Snowy River (1988-Australian) **1/2 D: Geoff Burrowes. Tom Burlinson, Sigrid Thornton, Brian Dennehy, Nicholas Eadie, Bryan Marshall.   In the sequel to *The Man From Snowy River,* Jim has returned for Jessica now that he has a good start for their married life. Her father still objects (played this time by Dennehy) and so Jim must again prove himself against those who consider themselves "better," but whose character proves they are not. Parents might wish to preview first for a few items. [PG] **V**

Rookie, The (2002) *** (See Sports)

Rosie! (1967) *** D: David Lowell Rich. Rosalind Russell, Sandra Dee, Brian Aherne, Audrey Meadows, James Farentino, Vanessa Brown, Leslie Neilsen, Margaret Hamilton.   Russell is Dee's well-to-do grandmother, but she is *anything but* the typical grandmother. She is full of life, spirit, and fun as she drags Dee into life with her. Eventually, her children take her to court for mental incompetence as a cover to get her money and to stop her less than stately influence on Dee. Well done film.

Ruggles of Red Gap (1935) **** D: Leo McCarey. Charles Laughton, Mary Boland, Charlie Ruggles, ZaSu Pitts, Roland Young, Leila Hyams.   Fabulous film of English butler (Laughton) who was won in a poker game by loud and unpolished westerner Ruggles and socialite want-to-be Boland. A absolute gem of a film. Don't miss it! **V**

Sabrina (1954) ***1/2 D: Billy Wider. Humphrey Bogart, Audrey Hepburn, William Holden, John Williams, Francis X. Bushman, Martha Hyer, Nancy Kulp.   Based upon the Samuel Taylor play *Sabrina Fair*, this version is charmingly done. See it before you see the newer version for comparisons sake. Each has their own particular brand of charm and strengths. Sabrina is the chauffeur's daughter who goes to Paris to become a chef and to forget David (Holden) the son of the family for whom her father works. When she returns, David is entranced with the chic, Paris-made-over Sabrina to the dismay of his family, who is counting on his engagement to the girl of another powerful industrial family. David's older brother, Linus (Bogart) steps in to do damage control and falls for Sabrina, himself. A sweet story of unexpected love. **V**

Sabrina (1995) *** D: Sydney Pollack. Harrison Ford, Julia Ormond, Greg Kinnear, Nancy Marchand, John Wood, Richard Crenna, Angie Dickinson, Lauren Holly.   Remake of the Bogart/Hepburn film, this one has an updated, '90s version charm. Linus (Harrison) is made much more human and humorous, David (Kinnear) is made much less the stereotypical "playboy." As with the remake of *The Parent Trap* I did not think that this movie could be redone successfully. Well, I was wrong! They did. Parents might wish to preview this to make sure all parts are acceptable to their family, but I think most will find it okay. By the way, the beautiful song by composer John Williams, "In the Moonlight" is sung by none other than rock star, Sting! I think he should switch to jazz, as he has a perfect voice for it. [PG] **V**

Sailor Beware! (1951) *** D: Hal Walker. Dean Martin, Jerry Lewis, Corinne Calvet, Marion Marshall, Robert Strauss, Vince Edwards; guest, Betty Hutton.   Hilarious movie of the misadventures of M & L in the Navy. One of their best films.

Scaramouche (1952) ***1/2 (See 1700s—Europe)

Sea Hawk, The (1940) **** (See Reformation)

Searching For Bobby Fischer (1993) ***1/2 D: Steven Zaillian. Joe Mantegna, Max Pomeranc, Joan Allen, Ben Kingsley, Laurence Fishburne.   Based upon a true story by Fred Waitzkin, this tells of a father whose wife discovers that their son is a chess genius and tells the father. The father seeks help for his son and meets Kingsley, who was a former chess whiz, now sometimes coach. The father enters the child in chess competitions, not understanding the pressure this puts on his son. A wonderful, heart-rending tale for the entire family. There are a few words which need to be edited, but if taped this could easily be done. [PG]   V

Secret War of Harry Frigg, The (1968) **1/2 (See WWII, Europe)

Seven Alone (1975) **1/2 D: Earl Bellamy. Dewey Martin, Aldo Ray, Anne Collings, Dean Smith, Stewart Petersen.   True story of seven children who make a dangerous 2,000 mile journey West in the 1800s after their parents die on the way. An amazing story to watch realizing that this is not someone's imagination, but a recreation of a real-life event. [G]   V, DVD

She Couldn't Say No (1954) **1/2 D: Lloyd Bacon. Robert Mitchum, Jean Simmons, Arthur Hunnicutt, Edgar Buchanan, Wallace Ford, Raymond Walburn, Pinky Tomlin.   Simmons plays a young Englishwoman who returns to give gifts to the townspeople who unselfishly gave to her when she was a very ill child. No one knows who she is, nor does she disclose her identity. She then spends time getting to know the people who lived there when she was a child and how she can best help them. Her well-meaning efforts cause mass chaos. Mitchum plays the local doctor for whom she falls. My family thinks this is charming . V

Shop Around the Corner, The (1940) *** D: Ernst Lubitsch. Margaret Sullavan, James Stewart, Frank Morgan, Joseph Schildkraut, Sara Haden, Felix Bressart, William Tracy, Charles Smith.   Sweet story of two lonely people who by day work side by side in a Budapest notions shop, despising each other when they are, unknowingly, each other secret pen pals. Remade as a musical in *The Good Old Summertime.* V

Sinbad the Sailor (1947) *** D: Richard Wallace. Douglas Fairbanks, Jr., Maureen O'Hara, Anthony Quinn, Walter Slezak, George Tobias, Jane Greer, Mike Mazurki, Sheldon Leonard.   Wonderful tale of Sinbad the Sailor with Fairbanks at his most swashbuckling, and connivingly charming. O'Hara at her loveliest in this beautiful Technicolor costumer in the vein of the Arabian Nights. A highly romanticized view of the middle east. Great fun. V

Sitting Pretty (1948) ***1/2 D: Harry Joe Brown. Robert Young, Maureen O'Hara, Clifton Webb, Richard Haydn, Louise Allbritton, Ed Begley.   Webb is excellent as the eccentric genius, Lynn Belvedere, who applies for a job baby-sitting the children of Young and O'Hara; they were expecting a woman. He not only does a great, though unusual job with their children, but also uniquely deals with the plague of suburbia, gossip. For some fun and laughter, see this one. It was the spin-off film for the Mr. Belvedere series. V

Snoopy, Come Home (1972) *** D: Bill Melendez. Voices of Chad Webber, David Carey, Stephen Shea, Bill Melendez.   Cute second *Peanuts* film centers around the well loved and independent Snoopy. [G] V

Snowball Express (1972) ** D: Norman Tokar. Dean Jones, Nancy Olson, Harry Morgan, Keenan Wynn, Johnny Whitaker, Michael McGreevey.   Jones plays an accountant who inherits a run-down hotel in the Rocky Mountains and decides to try to turn it into a ski resort. He has many hurdles to overcome in this Disney film. Ski chase scene is a film highlight. [G]   V

Snow White and the Seven Dwarfs (1937) **** (See Science/Nature)

Son of Flubber (1963) **1/2 D: Robert Stevenson. Fred MacMurray, Nancy Olsen, Keenan Wynn, Tommy Kirk, Elliott Reid, Joanna Moore, Leon Ames, Ed Wynn, Charlie Ruggles, Paul Lynde, Jack Albertson.   Sequel to the *Absentminded Professor* covers the next set of adventures and inventions involving flubber. **V**

Son of Lassie (1945) ****1/2** D: S. Sylvan Simon. Peter Lawford, Donald Crisp, June Lockhart, Nigel Bruce, William Severn, Leon Ames, Fay Helm, Donald Curtis.   Sequel to *Lassie Come Home* set during WWII with dogs trained for the war effort. Lassie's son goes into Nazi held Norway with Lawford. **V**

Son of Paleface (1952) *****1/2** D: Frank Tashlin. Bob Hope, Jane Russell, Roy Rogers, Douglass Dumbrille, Bill Williams, Harry Von Zell, Iron Eyes Cody.   In the same vein as the prequel, *The Paleface*, this one includes real-life western star Rogers and his faithful sidekick, Trigger. The scene with Trigger and Hope sharing a bed is a comedy classic. **V, DVD**

Spencer's Mountain (1963) ****1/2** D: Delmer Davies. Henry Fonda, Maureen O'Hara, James MacArthur, Donald Crisp, Wally Cox, Veronica Cartwright, Victor French.   Lovely movie which was the basis for the later TV series, *The Waltons*. Fonda's dream is to build a bigger house for his family, but circumstances don't lend themselves to this goal. This is an interesting character study of a man and the choices he makes. A nice family film. **V**

Stanley and Livingstone (1939) ******* (See 1800s-The World)

Stars in My Crown (1950) ****1/2** D: Jacques Tourneur. Joel McCrea, Ellen Drew, Dean Stockwell, Alan Hale, Lewis Stone, Ed Begley, Amanda Blake, James Arness.   Sweet story of a rural minister who quietly and persuasively affects those in his town in 19th century America. Clean, family film. **V**

Story of Will Rogers, The (1952) ******* D: Michael Curtiz. Will Rogers, Jr., Jane Wyman, Carl Benton Reid, James Gleason, Mary Wickes, Eddie Cantor.   Will Jr., portrays his famous father in this film biography of the humorist who stated that he'd never met a man he didn't like. Wyman is his devoted wife, Cantor plays himself.

Stowaway (1936) ****1/2** D: William A. Seiter. Robert Young, Alice Faye, Shirley Temple, Eugene Palette, Helen Westley, Arthur Treacher.   Shirley is a stowaway in this romance involving Young and Faye. Cute Temple film. **V**

Stranger Among Us, A (1992) ****1/2** D: Sidney Lumet. Melanie Griffith, Eric Thal, John Pankow, Tracy Pollan, Lee Richardson, Mia Sara, Jamey Sheridan, Jake Weber, Burtt Harris.   This is not the type of film I normally recommend, but this one has a very interesting difference making it worth including. The story is of a N.Y.C. cop (Griffith) who is sent to the Hasidic Jewish community to investigate a disappearance. She quickly uncovers that a murder has occurred and that it had to be the work of an insider; someone within the community. To uncover what's happened and find the murderer, she must go undercover into this community, which gives us an informative and intriguing look at the customs, food, dress, and way of life of the Hasidic Jews. This film is *definitely* one that **must** be previewed first and edited, but I feel that there is no other film I've seen which gives such insight and respect for the people who are the descendents of Abraham, with whom God made an eternal covenant. Their way of life even changes the hard-boiled character Griffith plays. Try to tape it from TV, where much of the language and objectionable material has already been edited. For older students. **[PG-13]** **V**

Note: Reportedly, Napoleon once asked one of his generals for proof of God's existence to which this general answered: "The existence of the Jewish people." If there were no God, then the Jews would not exist since for most of history they have been a people without a homeland, disseminated into other lands and cultures, yet have been able to remain a distinct people. No other group has done so.

Stranger in Town, A (1943) ******* D: Roy Rowland. Frank Morgan, Richard Carlson, Jean Rogers, Robert Barrat, Porter Hall, Chill Wills, Donald MacBride, John Hodiak.   *Excellent* Capraesque film has corrupt town officials vs. small town lawyer who defends the "little people" and gets in the way of the agenda of the corrupt officials. Morgan stumbles into town on a hunting trip and aids the young lawyer by teaching him some necessary

courtroom skills to gain victory over his opponents. Morgan's identity when revealed at the end is quite a surprise to all, especially to the corrupt politicians who feel they have him neatly sewed up. His end speech takes on a new meaning in light of recent history. Don't miss this one!!

Strongest Man in the World, The (1975) ** D: Vincent McEveety. Kurt Russell, Joe Flynn, Eve Arden, Cesar Romero, Phil Silvers, Dick Van Patten, Harold Gould, James Gregory.   Third in the Disney trilogy of campus comedies has Russell and pals discovering a magic formula for super-strength and battling the crooks who want it. Film is aimed at kids. [G]

Summer Magic (1963) **1/2 D: James Neilson. Hayley Mills, Burl Ives, Dorothy McGuire, Deborah Walley, Eddie Hodges, Una Merkel.   Disney film of widow who raises her family on a shoestring and in a rented house whose owner doesn't know it's rented. Sweet family film. **V**

Sun Comes Up, The (1949) ** D: Richard Thorpe. Jeanette MacDonald, Lloyd Nolan, Claude Jarman, Jr., Lewis Stone, Dwayne Hickman.   MacDonald is a widow whose son has been killed for which she blames his dog. She moves to the country to recover and encounters a young orphan boy whom she first ignores, but who ultimately wins her heart and helps to bring her back to life. **V**

Support Your Local Gunfighter (1971) ** D: Burt Kennedy. James Garner, Suzanne Pleshette, Jack Elam, Harry Morgan, John Dehner, Joan Blondell, Dub Taylor, Ellen Corby, Henry Jones, Marie Windsor, Dick Curtis, Chuck Connors, Grady Sutton.   Con artist Garner tries to cash in on the rivalry and mining dispute by passing Elam off as a notorious gunslinger. Great fun for all and not a sequel to the film below, in spite of similar title and cast. [G] **V, DVD**

Support Your Local Sheriff (1969) ***1/2 D: Burt Kennedy. James Garner, Joan Hackett, Walter Brennan, Harry Morgan, Jack Elam, Bruce Dern, Henry Jones, Gene Evans.   Outrageous comedy of a guy passing through a mining town, becoming sheriff and taming the town with his quick wittedness and unique approach to problems. Hackett is great as the mayor's wacky daughter, Brennan spoofs his character from *My Darling Clementine* and Elam's off-beat deputy are also fun. Full of laughs. [G] **V, DVD**

Susannah of the Mounties (1939) **1/2 D: William A. Seiter. Shirley Temple, Randolph Scott, Margaret Lockwood, J. Farrell MacDonald, Moroni Olsen, Victor Jory.   Mountie Scott raises a mini-mountie in orphan Temple in another Temple feature. **V**

Swan, The (1956) *** D: Charles Vidor. Grace Kelly, Alec Guiness, Louis Jourdan, Agnes Moorehead, Jessie Royce Landis, Brian Aherne, Leo G. Carroll.   Comedy of manners with Kelly as a princess who is promised to a prince/distant cousin whom she has met, but really doesn't know or love. The ring on her finger is her real engagement ring to Prince Rainier of Monaco. **V**

Swiss Family Robinson, The (1960) ***1/2 (See Literature)

Take a Letter, Darling (1942) *** D: Mitchell Liesen. Rosalind Russell, Fred MacMurray, Constance Moore, Robert Benchley, Macdonald Carey, Dooley Wilson, Cecil Kellaway.   Fun and fast paced film of executive Russell who hires MacMurray for her secretary. That just gets the ball rolling! MacMurray doesn't do well being dictated to so takes matters into his own hands when it comes to a particular account. Entertaining film with a touch of romance.

Talk of the Town (1942) **** D: George Stevens. Jean Arthur, Ronald Colman, Cary Grant, Glenda Farrell, Edgar Buchanan, Charles Dingle, Rex Ingram, Emma Dunn, Tom Tyler, Lloyd Bridges.   Fascinating comedy with outstanding cast about a fugitive from justice (Grant) who hides out in the rented country home of an unsuspecting law professor who is in line for a Supreme Court nomination. He tries to convince Colman by the letter of the law that there's a human side to all laws. Arthur tries to protect them both. Intriguing film, is excellently done. **V**

Tammy and the Bachelor (1957) *** D: Joseph Pevney. Debbie Reynolds, Walter Brennan, Leslie Nielsen, Mala Powers, Fay Wray, Sidney Blackmer, Mildred Natwick.   Country girl Tammy (Reynolds) lives on a riverboat, and meets young pilot Nielsen, when she and her grandfather (Brennan) rescue him from a crash in the river. When Brennan is taken to jail for making corn liquor, he sends Tammy to Neilsen to protect until he can return. This film is charming as Tammy, with all her simplicity and honesty, comes face to face with the pretensions of society. A clean family film. It has several sequels, but this one is the best. **V**

Tammy and the Doctor (1963) **1/2 D: Harry Keller. Sandra Dee, Peter Fonda, Macdonald Carey, Beulah Bondi, Margaret Lindsay, Reginald Owen, Adam West.   This time Tammy (Dee) has accompanied "Miz Call" to a hospital for heart surgery. In order to stay, she must work and there the mishaps begin. Along the way, she falls for a young doctor (Fonda). Some parents might wish to edit a scene or two from this one, dealing with some of her mishaps in the medical arena. **V**

Tammy Tell Me True (1961) **1/2 D: Harry Keller. Sandra Dee, John Gavin, Virginia Grey, Beulah Bondi, Cecil Kellaway, Edgar Buchanan.   Tammy (Dee) comes to college, falls for her professor (Gavin) and effects everyone she meets. Most interesting is her friendship with a cantankerous old woman (Bondi) and her babysitting experience with the children of two intellectuals who don't believe in disciplining their children.

Tarzan (1999) **1/2 D: Kevin Lima, Chris Buck. Voices of Tony Goldwyn, Minnie Driver, Glenn Close, Rosie O'Donnell, Brian Blessed, Nigel Hawthorne, Lance Henriksen, Wayne Knight.   Disney animated film of Edgar Rice Burroughs' classic tale includes some great Phil Collins songs. Preview and see if it meets with your approval. **[G] V, DVD**

That Darn Cat! (1965) *** D: Robert Stevenson. Hayley Mills, Dean Jones, Dorothy Provine, Roddy McDowall, Neville Brand, Elsa Lanchester, William Demarest, Frank Gorshin, Ed Wynn.   Disney comedy/drama of a cat who leads FBI investigators to bank robbers holding a hostage. Great family fun. Don't bother with the remake. **V**

This Happy Feeling (1958) *** D: Blake Edwards. Debbie Reynolds, Curt Jurgens, John Saxon, Alexis Smith, Estelle Winwood, Mary Astor, Troy Donahue, Joe Flynn.   Cute film of a young woman (Reynolds) who is taken with an actor who offers her a job as his secretary while his next door neighbor, (handsome Saxon) wants her attention. Winwood is hilarious as the imbibing, eccentric Mrs. Early and I chuckle at Jurgens calling for her to play chiropractor to his bad back. Parents will wish to preview this to see if it's okay for your family. **V**

Three Cheers for the Irish (1940) ** D: Lloyd Bacon. Thomas Mitchell, Dennis Morgan, Priscilla Lane, Alan Hale, Virginia Grey, Irene Hervey, Frank Jenks, William Lundigan.   Mitchell plays a beat walking Irish cop who is facing retirement with dread, only to find out that his replacement's a Scotsman for whom his daughter falls. Cute film.

3 Ninjas (1992) ** D: Jon Turteltaub. Victor Wong, Michael Treanor, Max Elliott Slade, Chad Power, Rand Kingsley, Alan McRae, Margarita Franco, Patrick Laborteaux.   Disney film of three young brothers who learn ninja skills from their grandfather. Their skills get put to good use when they are kidnapped by the enemy and archrival of their grandfather. Filled with hilarious bits that kept my children thoroughly entertained. **[PG] V**

3 Ninjas High Noon at Mega Mountain (1998) ** D: Sean McNamara. Loni Anderson, Hulk Hogan, Jim Varney, Victor Wong, Mathew Botuchis, Michael J. O'Laskey II, J. P. Roeske II, Chelsey Earlywine, Alan McRae.   Last of 3 Ninjas movies where terrorists take over a theme park and the 3 Ninjas and a friend, along with Hulk Hogan must save the day. **[PG] V**

3 Ninjas Knuckle Up (1995) *1/2 D: Simon S. Sheen. Victor Wong, Charles Napier, Michael Treanor, Max Elliot Slade, Chad Power, Crystle Lightning, Patrick Kirkpatrick. Grandfather and 3 Ninjas help an Indian tribe whose land is being poisoned by a dump leased by a crooked tycoon. The ninjas must help Jo find her father, who has been kidnapped and save the day once more. **[PG-13] V, DVD**

Ticklish Affair, A (1963) ** D: George Sidney. Shirley Jones, Gig Young, Red Buttons, Carolyn Jones, Edgar Buchanan.   Navy commander Young responds to a distress call and finds it's the result of the inquisitive children of Jones, a Navy widow. Buttons plays Jones' brother, who gets the kids involved in "moon walking" using weather balloons to give them the effect of weightlessness. (A good study!) This brings about the film's climax when the youngest child drifts out to sea.

Toby Tyler, or Ten Weeks with a Circus (1960) **1/2 (See Literature)

To Catch a Thief (1955) *** D: Alfred Hitchcock. Grace Kelly, Cary Grant, Jessie Royce Landis, John Williams, Charles Vanel, Brigette Auber.   Grant is a reformed cat burglar who is suspected of a new string of robberies which mimic his M. O. Kelly is the daughter of a wealthy woman who is expected to be the next target. **V**   [While making this film, Grace Kelly first met her prince and later became Princess Grace of Monaco.]

Top Secret Affair (1957) **1/2 D: H. C. Potter. Susan Hayward, Kirk Douglas, Paul Stewart, Jim Backus, John Cromwell.   Douglas is an Army general who is ordered to visit a magazine publisher in her home against his wishes and better judgment. A tangled mess ensues as she tries to get some dirt on him by attempting to get him drunk. The plan backfires on her and she ends up falling for the general but in a moment of pique, leaks information damaging to him which brings him before a senate hearing. However, nothing is as it seems. You can learn the Army song (*The Caisson Go Rolling Along*) from this film as well as have some laughs.

Toy Tiger (1956) **1/2 D: Jerry Hopper. Jeff Chandler, Laraine Day, Tim Hovey, Cecil Kellaway, Richard Haydn, David Janssen.   Cute film about a young boy in a boarding school while his widowed mother tries to earn enough money as a driven N. Y. magazine editor to eventually quit and be with her son. Chandler is an artist for the magazine who doesn't understand her drive since she's chosen to keep her son a secret. He quits and ends up in the town in which her son attends school. The son has told everyone that his father is a famous explorer who's arriving that day. When Chandler steps off the bus, he's chosen to "be" the father! Cute family film about what's really important in life.

Treasure of Matecumbe (1976) **1/2 D: Vincente McEveety. Robert Foxworthy, Joan Hackett, Peter Ustinov, Vic Morrow, Jane Wyatt, Johnny Doran, Billy "Pop" Attmore.   A young boy must outwit a ruthless captain to retrieve hidden gold to save his family home. He is helped by a runaway bride (Hackett), a "snake oil" salesman (Ustinov) and his black sheep uncle (Foxworthy). Ustinov is particularly entertaining in this Disney film. **[G] V**

Trouble Along the Way (1953) **1/2 D: Michael Curtiz. John Wayne, Donna Reed, Charles Coburn, Sherry Jackson, Marie Windsor, Tom Tully, Leif Erickson, Chuck Connors.   Perhaps one of the most unusual John Wayne movies ever made, this casts him as a divorced father who is trying to maintain custody of his young daughter. His self-respect returns when he begins coaching a football team for a small Catholic school. **V**

Ugly Dachshund, The (1966) **1/2 D: Norman Tokar. Dean Jones, Suzanne Pleshette, Charlie Ruggles, Kelly Thordsen, Parley Baer.   Cute Disney comedy of a houseful of Dachshunds (owned by the wife) while the husbands longs for a Great Dane! He gets one and oh, the chaos that ensues! My children really enjoyed this when they were small. **V**

Voyage to the Bottom of the Sea (1961) *** D: Irwin Allen. Walter Pidgeon, Joan Fontaine, Robert Sterling, Barbara Eden, Michael Ansara, Peter Lorre, Frankie Avalon, Henry Daniell, Regis Toomey. Fun sci-fi which will enable you to show your children (or grandchildren) the "high tech" stuff of your day! Pidgeon is an admiral aboard an atomic submarine trying to prevent the earth from being fried by a radiation belt. **V, DVD**

Wackiest Ship in the Army, The (1960) *** (See WWII, South Pacific)

Walk to Remember, A (2002) **1/2 D: Adam Shankman. Mandy Moore, Shane West, Peter Coyote, Daryl Hannah, Lauren German, Clayne Crawford, Al Thompson, Paz de la Huerta.   Based on the popular book by Nicholas Sparks, this film is about a high school aged girl, daughter of a widowed minister, who changes a boy's life. She's a Christian, he isn't. This is not as strongly portrayed as in the book, but it is there, as long as you understand that the scene of him driving along the road is his spiritual "rebirth." Due to some of the content, especially in the opening scene, parents need to view this first and edit it. Mostly for older children, but it does show how one person's life, lived with integrity, can change someone else's life. Have your hankies ready. [PG] V, DVD

Wee Willie Winkie (1937) *** D: John Ford. Shirley Temple, Victor McLaglen, C. Aubrey Smith, June Lange, Michael Whalen, Cesar Romero, Constance Collier, Douglas Scott.   Shirley and her mom come to India to live with her Grandfather (Smith) and she is taken under the wing of a sergeant (McLaglen) in one of her best films. The film states that the story was inspired by Rudyard Kipling's story. V

We're No Angels (1955) **1/2 D: Michael Curtiz. Humphrey Bogart, Aldo Ray, Peter Ustinov, Joan Bennett, Basil Rathbone, Leo G. Carroll.   Three convicts from Devil's Island become involved with a French family and help them out of some sticky situations. A different comedy, featuring Bogart in a more off-beat way than normal. You'll have to decide if it's for you. V

We're Not Dressing (1934) *** (See Music/Arts)

What About Bob? (1991) *** D: Frank Oz. Bill Murray, Richard Dreyfuss, Julie Haggerty, Charlie Korsmo, Kathryn Erbe, Tom Aldredge, Susan Willis, Roger Bowen, Fran Brill, Doris Belack.   Hysterically funny (I think) film of a neurotic man who manages to become the worst nightmare of pompous psychiatrist Dreyfuss and shows up on his family's vacation! Intolerable to the Dr., but the family thinks Bob is great and can't understand why dear old dad doesn't think so, too. He ultimately drives Dreyfuss crazy, while he's cured. I'm not normally a fan of Murray's humor, but this film is genuinely funny. V, DVD

Wheeler Dealers (1963) *** D: Arthur Hiller. Lee Remick, James Garner, Jim Backus, Phil Harris, Shelley Nye.   Cute spoof of Texas millionaires includes a girl on Wall Street who means to make good and Garner's just the Texan to help her. My husband loves the part in the posh French restaurant when Garner tells the waiter to have the chef burn his steak. V

Where the Red Fern Grows (1974) ***D: Norman Toker. James Whitmore, Beverly Garland, Jack Ging, Lonny Chapman, Stewart Peterson.   Based upon the novel by Wilson Rawls, this is a wonderful family film set in Oklahoma during the 1930s and of a boy who desperately wants a hunting dog. The film is loaded with chances for good character to shine through and the film doesn't disappoint. Well done, but with a teary ending. [G] V

Willy Wonka and the Chocolate Factory (1971) **1/2 D: Mel Stuart. Gene Wilder, Jack Albertson, Peter Ostrum, Roy Kinnear, Aubrey Woods, Michael Bollner, Ursula Reit.   Film adaptation of Ronald Dahl's *Charlie and the Chocolate Factory* has some moral lessons to teach, but is a bit rough at times. A young impoverished boy purchases a candy bar and is one of five lucky winners who get to see inside the top secret and mysterious Wonka Candy Factory. See what you think for your children. Mine liked it when they were little. Includes hit song, "Candy Man." [G] V,DVD

Without Reservations (1946) *** D: Mervyn LeRoy. Claudette Colbert, John Wayne, Don DeFore, Anne Triola, Frank Puglia, Phil Brown, Thurston Hall, Louella Parsons, Dona Drake.   One of my favorite movies, Colbert is an author who has written a run-away best seller. While on a train trip to L.A. for the making of the movie based on her book, she meets the spitting mental image she has of the leading man. You guessed it, John Wayne. Wayne's a soldier traveling with buddy Defore, and in order to not lose him, she travels with them without telling them who she is. One situation after another arises causing lots of viewing fun along with some cute comments about Hollywood. V

Woman of the Year (1942) ***1/2 D: George Stevens. Spencer Tracy, Katharine Hepburn, Fay Bainter, Dan Tobin, Reginald Owen, Roscoe Karns, William Bendix.   First teaming of now legendary Tracy and Hepburn. Kate's a polished, upper crust political commentator who meets a regular Joe in sports reporter Tracy, and they wed. Kate's first baseball game being explained to her by Tracy in the press box is a treat. **V, DVD**

World in His Arms, The (1952) *** D: Raoul Walsh. Gregory Peck, Ann Blyth, John McIntire, Anthony Quinn, Andrea King, Eugenie Leontovich, Sig Ruman.   Peck is a sea captain who meets Blyth and falls in love with her without knowing that she's a Russian countess. Information about the purchase of Alaska from Russia is included, as well as the "harvesting" of seals. Set in 1850s San Francisco. (Also see 1800s, West)

Yours, Mine and Ours (1968) *** D: Melville Shavelson. Lucille Ball, Henry Fonda, Van Johnson, Tom Bosley, Tim Matheson.   Based on a true story, a Navy nurse who's widowed with eight children meets a Navy Lieutenant widower with TEN children and they fall in love and decide to marry. Blending their families is an adventure, to say the least, along with an amazing shopping expedition and breakfast making experience. You've just got to see it to believe it! Fonda is deployed for sea duty and finds out in a crayon picture that they're about to become a family of TWENTY-ONE!! Generally cute and family oriented, there is one scene of Fonda's kids spiking Lucy's drink and she gets drunk. Other than that, I can't think of anything that would make this film objectionable to anyone. **V, DVD**

Babe Ruth Story, The (1948) ** D: Roy Del Ruth. William Bendix, Claire Trevor, Charles Bickford, Sam Levene, William Frawley, Mark Koenig, Mel Allen, Harry Wismer, H. V. Kaltenborn.   Though nowhere near fact, I feel that this is easily watchable and still gives kids a way to learn about Babe Ruth through the medium of film while also allowing them to have fun comparing it to the facts they learn. It is definitely preferable to the newer version which is not suitable for children. *Pride of the Yankees* features the REAL Babe Ruth. **V**

Brian's Song (1971) TVM D: Buzz Kulik. James Caan, Billy Dee Williams, Jack Warden, Judy Pace, Shelley Fabares.   Based upon *I Am Third* by Gale Sayers, (God first, others second, I am third) this is a wonderful movie about the relationship between Sayers and Brain Piccolo who both played for the Chicago Bears. Piccolo was a guy with a sense of fun while Sayers was quiet and shy. They were the first black and white players to room together, ground breaking in itself, but the movie is about friendship, determination, perseverance, and courage in the face of an overwhelming foe—cancer. According to Sayers, Brian cheered up his team mates when they visited him in the hospital. He said, "He never gave up hope. Brian impacted my life, the Chicago Bears at that time, to focus on family, life, what's important, not just football." Filmed during the Bear's training camp at St. Joseph's college in Indiana, just a few years after Piccolo's death to cancer, it includes real life Chicago Bears who knew and played with both of these men. Nominated for 11 Emmys, including outstanding single program, it won 5 as it was "a mile-stone of excellence in made-for-TV movies." NFL and movie critics raved over Caan's performance which also brought the real Joy Piccolo (Brian's wife) to tears. It was screened by the Chicago Bears who knew "Pic" and when it ended there was total silence in the room and many eyes were not dry. Dick Butkus, NFL Hall of Fame honoree and former team mate of Brian Piccolo's said, "When the movie came out, *Brian's Song,* it was kind of interesting just to see how they put it all together because you were involved in it a bit (he had a bit part playing himself). Then when it came on it was a tear jerker and like all movies, they try to do about something living in the past or whatever, they're always not quite true...But in this case, it was so ...*close."* "Finally, a sports football movie we can be proud of " said Paul Hornung, NFL Hall of Fame honoree. Mike Malone, of ESPN and a former pro-football player said, "(Brian's Song is the) greatest sports movie of all time." This unifying movie has been used by schools to teach racial harmony. It was also used by U.S. Army Colonel Henry Emmersen in S. Korea in 1975 when he took over a 1/2 black, 1/2 white infantry unit that was suffering from racial tension. Every year the Chicago Bears give an award to a rookie and veteran who best exemplify the courage, loyalty, and teamwork of Brian Piccolo. There are numerous awards given in remembrance of Brian Piccolo, who has also had the Brian Piccolo Cancer Fund for cancer research named in his honor. "Pic's death has brought new life to millions of others." Remade by Disney in 2002 as a 2 hour movie instead of 74 minutes, it has more inaccuracies than the original. Those who knew Brian Piccolo only talk about the original version, which is my choice of the two. The original also includes NFL footage of the real Sayers and Piccolo, which also adds a touch of reality to the film. By all means get this film and see it. The whole family will enjoy it. **[G] V**

D2: The Mighty Ducks (1994) ** D: Sam Weisman. Emilio Estevez, Kathryn Erbe, Michael Tucker, Jan Rubes, Carsten Norgaard, Maria Ellingsen, Joshua Jackson, Elden Ryan Ratliff (Hansen), Shaun Weiss, Matt Doherty.   Story of an underdog hockey team who has previously won a championship. This gives the coach the chance to coach his former team as Team USA in the Junior Goodwill Games, and the opportunity is also there for him to make major bucks for endorsing. This Disney film is one my children liked. View first for content. We have only seen this from TV and so I don't know whether the video version is okay or not. (First one: *The Mighty Ducks*) **[PG] V**

D3: The Mighty Ducks (1996) ** D: Robert Lieberman. Emilio Estevez, Jeffrey Nordling, Joshua Jackson, David Selby, Heidi Kling, Joss Ackland, Elden Ryan Ratliff

(Hansen), Shaun Weiss, Vincent A. Larusso, Matt Doherty, Columbe Jacobsen, Aaron Lohr.　　Last of the trilogy, this time the ducks have won scholarships to an exclusive private school where they are treated as outsiders by the snobby kids. They have a new coach (Nordling) but Estevez returns at the end to bail them out of trouble. **[PG] V**

It Happens Every Spring (1949) ***1/2 D: Lloyd Bacon. Ray Milland, Jean Peters, Paul Douglas, Ed Begley, Ted de Corsia, Ray Collins, Jessie Royce Landis, Alan Hale, Jr., Debra Paget.　　Cute comedy of chemistry professor (Milland) who discovers a formula which causes objects to repel wood. He leaves academia and begins a baseball career as a pitcher, using his secret weapon to rise to fame. Cute story, lots of fun for all. **V**

Jackie Robinson Story, The (1950) *** D: Aubrey E. Green. Jackie Robinson, Ruby Dee, Minor Watson, Louise Beavers, Richard Lane, Harry Shannon, Ben Lessy, Joe Fluellen.　　Biography of Robinson, the first black man to play major-league baseball. Shows the prejudice and social issues of the time. Parents may wish to preview. **V, DVD**

Jim Thorpe-All-American (1951) **1/2 D: Michael Curtiz. Burt Lancaster, Charles Bickford, Steve Cochran, Phyllis Thaxter, Dick Wesson.　　Biography of the famous Native American Olympic runner who was stripped of his medals for playing professional baseball and the circumstances leading up to this. Not as tawdry as it may seem. The pro-ball incident was very innocent and many feel Thorpe should have been able to keep his medals. **V**

Knute Rockne, All American (1940) *** D: Lloyd Bacon. Pat O'Brien, Gale Page, Donald Crisp, Ronald Reagan, Albert Bassermann, John Qualen.　　Biography of famous Notre Dame football coach with Reagan as star player George Gipp, as in "win just one for the Gipper".

Mighty Ducks, The (1992) ** D: Stephen Herek. Emilio Estevez, Joss Ackland, Lane Smith, Heidi Kling, Josef Sommer, Joshua Jackson, Elden Ratliff (Hansen), Shaun Weiss, Matt Doherty.　　The first in a Disney trilogy about a inner-city peewee hockey team and the self-absorbed, arrogant lawyer who gets assigned to be their coach as part of a community service sentencing for drunk driving. This is one film you *must* tape and preview from TV where the bad language has been edited. Followed by D2 and D3, listed above. **[PG] V, DVD**

One in a Million (1930) *** (See Family Films)

Other Side of the Mountain, The (1975) **1/2 D: Larry Peerce. Marilyn Hassett, Beau Bridges, Belinda J. Montgomery, Nan Martin, William Bryant, Dabney Coleman, Dori Brenner, Griffin Dunne.　　True-life story of Olympic hopeful skier Jill Kinmont and the accident that left her paralyzed. **[PG] V**

Pride of St. Louis, The (1952) **1/2 D: Harmon Jones. Dan Dailey, Joanne Dru, Richard Crenna, Hugh Sanders, Richard Hylton, James Brown.　　Biography of Hall of Fame pitcher Dizzy Dean. **V**

Pride of the Yankees, The (1942) **** D: Sam Wood. Gary Cooper, Teresa Wright, Babe Ruth, Walter Brennan, Dan Duryea, Ludwig Stossel, Addison Richards, Hardie Albright.　　Outstanding biography of baseball star Lou Gehrig (Cooper) including his famous speech. Film of the real Babe Ruth, too. **V, DVD**

Remember the Titans (2000) *** D: Boaz Yakin. Denzel Washington, Will Patton, Donald Faison, Wood Harris, Ryan Hurst, Ethan Suplee, Nichole Air Parker, Hayden Panettiere, Kip Pardue, Craig Kirkwood.　　Fabulous film based on a true story of a black coach who is brought in to replace a popular white coach during the 1970s and who must bring the black and white kids together as a team to fight the opponent and not each other. Preview first as some content needs to be edited, especially one scene in the locker room. Overall, an excellent film. **[PG] V, DVD**

Rookie, The (2002) ***1/2 D: John Lee Hancock. Dennis Quaid, Rachel Griffiths, Jay Hernandex, Beth Grant, Angus T. Jones, Brian Cox, Rick Gonzales, Royce D. Applegate. True life story of Jim Morris, a high-school science teacher/baseball coach who had washed out of a pro-career due to injuries. While working with his high school team one day, he is amazed to find that he can pitch again. He talks to the boys of having dreams for their future and they challenge him to follow his dreams back to pro-ball at age 35. This is a clean, family movie from Disney which I believe most families will applaud. [G] **V**

Something for Joey (1977) TVM D: Lou Antonio. Geraldine Page, Gerald S. O'Loughlin, Marc Singer, Jeff Lynas, Linda Kelsey, Steven Guttenberg, Paul Picerni, Kathleen Beller.   This film opens in the fall of 1971 and covers a two and a half year period in the loving and tight relationship of Heisman trophy winner John Cappelletti, a running back for Penn State, and his younger brother Joey. When "Cappy" won the Heisman, he dedicated it to his brother in a speech that is "unique in the history of the Heisman." It has also been called "a speech from the heart" for Joey had leukemia. There is wonderful music included by David Shire. Highly recommended. Above average. **V**

Story of Seabiscuit (1949) **1/2 (See Horses)

Stratton Story, The (1949) ***1/2 D: Sam Wood. James Stewart, June Allyson, Frank Morgan, Agnes Moorehead, Bill Williams, Jimmy Dykes, Bill Dickey.   Stewart plays Monty Stratton, the baseball player who lost a leg in a hunting accident in this Oscar winning film. **V**

NOTES

Science/Nature

Anchors Aweigh (1945) **1/2 (See Music/Arts)

Apollo 13 (1995) ***1/2 D: Ron Howard. Tom Hanks, Bill Paxton, Kevin Bacon, Gary Sinise, Ed Harris, Kathleen Quinlan, Miko Hughes, David Andres, Chris Ellis, Joe Spano, Xander Berkeley, Marc McClure, Tracy Reiner, Brett Cullen; opening narration by Walter Cronkite.   Story of the ill-fated mission to the moon and the tense time as NASA tries to figure out how to bring the disabled craft and astronauts home and the effect on the astronaut's families as they all wait and pray. The real commander of the Apollo 13 mission, Jim Lovell, has a bit part as an officer on the aircraft carrier in the final sequence. Read about him and his mission and then look for him when you watch and compare the movie to history. Tense and very well done. Parents *must* preview this first for language. [PG]   V, DVD

Arrow, The (1997) ***1/2 D: Don McBrearty. Dan Aykroyd, Sara Botsford, Ron White, Aidan Devine. Canadian designed plane, the world's fastest fighter interceptor jet developed in the 1950s, able to break Mach 2, and why it was scuttled. Parts have *very* bad language, so tape and preview. Best bet, use a Guardian.

Birth of a Nation, The (1915) **** (See Civil War)

Born Free (1966-British) (See Literature)

Carbine Williams (1952) *** (See 1900s) About the development of the carbine rifle.

Cheetah (1989) *** D: Jeff Blyth, Keith Coogan, Lucy Deakins, Collin Mothupi, Timothy Landfield, Breon Gorman, Ka Vundia, Kuldeep Bhakoo.   Disney film about two kids who come to Kenya for a few months to join their parents, make friends with a Masai and adopt a cheetah cub as a pet. Great scenery and nature covered. Parents might wish to preview. [G]   V, DVD

Clarence the Cross-eyed Lion (1965) ** 1/2 D: Andrew Marton. Marshall Thompson, Betsy Drake, Cheryl Miller, Richard Haydn, Alan Caillou.   Film which later became the TV show *Daktari* is fun family comedy set in Africa. V

Creation Science Evangelism Videos Dr. Kent Hovind has come up with the most fascinating, attention keeping, fun and highly rememberable seminar videos I've ever seen. They will make you laugh, help you and your children understand how science and the Word of God are *totally* compatible and build their faith in the *Bible* as God's infallible word like nothing else I've seen. My children love these and have learned tons of good science from them. Because of the humor, they have surprised me with how much they remember. They even quote Dr. Hovind when something comes up that applies to one of his "Hovindisms." Don't miss these wonderful videos. They are more than worth the investment. You want the blue set with the workbook found at: www.drdino.com He even tells you to make copies! V, DVD

Dive Bomber (1941) *** D: Michael Curtiz. Errol Flynn, Fred MacMurray, Ralph Bellamy, Alexis Smith, Robert Armstrong, Regis Toomey, Craig Stevens.   Well done film covering the dangers and stress encountered by test pilots. In this film the challenge of finding the cause of blacking out at high altitude is undertaken by medical doctors played by Bellamy and Flynn, the latter also being a pilot. Most incongruous thing: medical doctors smoking cigarettes! V

Gorillas in the Mist (1988) *** D: Michael Apted. Sigourney Weaver, Bryan Brown, Julie Harris, John Omirah Miluwi, Iain Cuthbertson, Constantin Alexandrov, Waigwa Wachira.   Based on the life and research of Dian Fossey, who went to Africa in 1967 with no prior experience and set out to document the vanishing mountain gorillas for *National Geographic*; her consuming obsession with the gorillas, her feud with poachers, and her tragic murder. All true, but parents should preview this one first. [PG]   V, DVD

Hatari! (1962) ***1/2 D: Howard Hawks. John Wayne, Elsa Martinelli, Red Buttons,

Hardy Kruger, Gerard Blain, Bruce Cabot.   Wonderful adventure/comedy tale of wild animal trappers in Africa with plenty of fun, scenery, adventure, comedy and danger. Filmed on location, this is an up close and personal look at the animals and habitat of Africa, some of the animals seen in zoos and what can make them dangerous when trying to catch them. Don't miss Red Button's trapping the monkeys and Martinelli becoming "Mama" to the baby elephants! Famous "Baby Elephant Walk" by Mancini is from this movie. There might be some subject matter parents would wish to edit, so view it first. Title is Swahili for "Danger!" **V, DVD**

Jazz Singer, The (1927) **1/2 D: Alan Crosland. Al Jolson, May McAvoy, Warner Oland, Eugenie Besserer, Otto Lederer, William Demarest, Rosco Karns.   You may be wondering why this film is here. It stands out in movie history and needs to be here for the innovation of sound in film as it is the first film to incorporate sound. Also, compare the film quality of then and now. Story is about a Jewish Cantor who wishes for his son to be a Cantor, too, but the son has dreams of show business. Songs include "My Mammy," "Toot Toot Tootsie Goodbye," "Blue Skies." **V**

Jungle Cat (1960) **1/2 D: James Algar. Narrated by Winston Hibler.   A Disney True-Life Adventure with wonderful wildlife footage. The jungle cat is a jaguar. **V**

Jurassic Park (1993) ***1/2 D: Steven Spielberg. Sam Neill, Laura Dern, Jeff Goldblum, Richard Attenborough, Bob Peck, Martin Ferrero. B. D. Wong, Joseph Mazzello, Ariana Richards, Samuel L. Jackson, Wayne Knight.   *I recommend parents view this one first before showing to your children.* It is filled with computer generated dinosaurs, making it interesting to see them move and roam the earth, but is also quite violent and could lead to nightmares. My children and husband saw this and the sequels, I did not so they wrote this review. Adventure about a doctor who takes DNA from a mosquito caught in amber and recreates dinosaurs. All is great until dinosaurs get loose. Then it becomes a battle for the life of man vs. the dinosaurs. **[PG-13] V, DVD**

Kon-Tiki (1951) *** No director credited. Narrated by Ben Grauer, Thor Heyerdahl.   Oscar winning documentary of Heyerdahl's trip from Peru to Tahiti thus proving his theory that ancient boats crossed the Pacific. Parents, preview. **V, DVD**

Living Desert, The (1953) *** D: James Algar. Narrated by Winstone Hibler.   Disney's first True-Life Adventure film covers what lives in the American desert along with some fabulous scenery. Worth seeing for the wild-life and scenery, alone. An Academy Award winner. Parents, preview. **V**

Living Free (1972-British) **1/2 D: Jack Couffer. Susan Hampshire, Nigel Davenport, Geoffrey Keen. Sequel to *Born Free* picks up the life of Elsa the lioness and her three cubs. **[G] V**

Lost World: Jurassic Park, The (1997) **1/2 D: Steven Spielberg. Jeff Goldblum, Julianne Moore, Pete Postlethwaite, Arliss Howard, Richard Attenborough, Vince Vaughn, Vanessa Lee Chester, Peter Stormare, Harvey Jason, Richard Schiff, Thomas F. Duffy, Jospeh Mazzello, Ariana Richards.   *I recommend parents view this one first before showing to your children.* It is filled with computer generated dinosaurs, making it interesting to see them move and roam the earth, but is also quite violent and could lead to nightmares. My children and husband saw this, I did not so they wrote this review. Many years after the first incident, the scientist who recreated the dinosaurs lets other scientists know that there is another island inhabited by dinosaurs. He sends one of the men from the original fiasco to the second island with a group of people who, after a series of events, capture a tyrannosaurus Rex and bring him to the U. S. Havoc one again reigns when the T-Rex gets loose in N.Y.C. Followed by *Jurassic Park III,* which my family suggests you skip. **[PG-13] V, DVD**

October Sky (1999) ***1/2 D: Joe Johnston. Jake Byllenhaal. Chris Cooper, Laura Dern, Chris Owen, William Lee Scott, Chad Lindberg, Natalie Canerday, Scott Miles.   Based on a true story, this touching drama tells about Homer Hickam, Jr., (Gyllenhaal) who sees Sputnik soaring across the nighttime sky in 1957 and becomes fascinated with the idea of building his own rocket with his friends and also has the dream of getting out of his West Virginia coal mining hometown. Father disapproves of all of this as the mine foreman, who wants his son to be just like him. Homer pursues his dream with encouragement from his mother and his teacher. This does need editing for some bad words, but other than that, is an excellent film. Why can't they just leave that stuff out and make good family films? **[PG]** **V, DVD**

Rascal (1969) **1/2 (See Literature)

Secrets of Life (1956) *** D: James Algar. Narrated by Winston Hibbler.   Disney True-Life Adventure takes a close-up look at plant life, insect life, sea creatures, and nature wonders, including volcanoes. Excellent film view of all of these and more.   **V**

Snow White and the Seven Dwarfs (1937) **** D: David Hand. Voices of Adrianna Caselotti, Harry Stockwell, Lucille LaVerne, Scotty Mattraw, Roy Atwell, Pinto Colvig, Otis Harlan, Billy Gilbert, Monroni Olsen.   I put this film here because of its groundbreaking use of animation. First, you'll need to preview this to see if it meets with your approval to show because it does include the occult. If you feel you can edit it and show it, then you can see first hand the amazing feats that were undertaken by Walt Disney studios in producing this full feature animated film when none had existed before. Every animated film made since this time built upon the technology of this one, making this worthwhile in the annals of animated motion picture science. Includes some famous songs like, "Heigh Ho," "Whistle While You Work," and "Some Day My Prince Will Come."   **V, DVD**

Spirit of St. Louis, The (1957) *** D: Billy Wilder. James Stewart, Patricia Smith, Murray Hamilton, Marc Connelly.   Interesting story of preparation for the first trans-Atlantic flight, with Stewart's excellent portrayal of Charles Lindberg.   **V**

Twister (1996) *** D: Jan DeBont. Helen Hunt, Bill Paxton, Cary Elwes, Jami Gertz, Lois Smith, Alan Ruck, Philip Seymour Hoffman, Jeremy Davies, Todd Field, Zach Grenier, Jake Busey.   This movie *must* be edited before allowing children to see it, but it is the only rentable movie with which I am familiar covering this subject and showing tornadoes (though computer generated) and the damage they can do. The story is about storm-chasers who are trying to get a machine named "Dorothy" up *into* a tornado in order to get data back from the inside of the funnel. See what you think. **[PG-13]** **V, DVD**

Vanishing Prairie, The (1954) *** D: James Algar. Narrated by Winston Hibler.   Disney's second True-Life feature shows wonderful footage of animal life in the plains including the birth of a buffalo calf. Parents, preview.   **V**

Volcano (1997) *** D: Mick Jackson. Tommy Lee Jones, Anne Heche, Gaby Hoffman, Don Cheadle, Jacqueline Kim, Keith David, John Corbett, Michael Rispoli, John Carroll Lynch.   Jones is the [supposed to be on vacation] head of Office of Emergency Management for L.A. when a volcanic eruption takes place. He and scientist Heche work together to second guess what it will do and save L.A. Definitely shows the potential power of and disaster from a volcanic eruption. You'll have to decide if it's for you, so preview. **[PG-13]** **V, DVD**

WarGames (1983) **1/2 (See 1900s)

NOTES

April Love (1957) **1/2 D: Henry Levin. Pat Boone, Shirley Jones, Dolores Michaels, Arthur O'Connell, Matt Crowley.   Musical remake of *Home in Indiana* with Boone visiting relatives farm in Kentucky due to some trouble with the wrong crowd back home. Uncle (O'Connell) has a skiddish horse that was a champion trotter. Boone and horse have an incident which causes the horse to trust him and reawakens his uncle's interest in life. He's coached on trotters by the neighbor, (Jones) for whom he falls. Clean family movie, lovely title song sung by Boone for whom it became a trademark.

Black Beauty (1971-British) **1/2 (See Literature)

Gallant Bess (1946) ** D: Andrew Marton. Marshall Thompson, George Tobias, Jim Davis, Clem Bevans, Donald Curtis, Chill Wills.   Story of a young boy who is trying to carry on the family dream of raising horses after the death of his parents. He's inducted into the Navy and sent overseas as a Seabee where he finds a horse to replace the one at home, who died. This "Bess" saves the lives of the men in his company. My family thinks this is a sweet and wonderful family film.

Glory (1956) ** D: David Butler. Margaret O'Brien, Walter Brennan, Charlotte Greenwood, John Lupton.   ·   O'Brien and Greenwood are impoverished owners of a champion racehorse who are trying to improve their lot while loving, caring for and racing their horse. **V**

Great Dan Patch, The (1949) **1/2 D: Joe (Joseph M.) Newman. Dennis O'Keefe, Gail Russell, Ruth Warwick, Charlotte Greenwood, Henry Hull, John Hoyt, Arthur Hunnicutt, Clarence Muse.   About legendary pacing horse Dan Patch and his amazing racing career with O'Keefe as his owner. **V**

Home in Indiana (1944) *** D: Henry Hathaway. Walter Brennan, Jeanne Crain, June Haver, Charlotte Greenwood, Lon McAllister, Ward Bond, Willie Best, George Cleveland.   Horse-racing story of trotters, a skittish horse, and a cantankerous old man which all works out in the end. Fun, clean family movie, remade as *April Love.*

Horse in the Gray Flannel Suit (1968) *** D: Norman Tokar. Dean Jones, Diane Baker, Lloyd Bochner, Fred Clark, Ellen Janov, Kurt Russell.   Disney comedy about an ad man (Jones) who figures out a way to use a horse for advertising in order to pay for his daughter's desire for a horse. Clean, fun film. [G] **V**

Horsemasters, The (1961) ** D: William Fairchild. Annette Funicello, Janet Munro, Tommy Kirk, Donald Pleasence, Tony Britton, Jean Marsh, John Fraser, Millicent Martin.   Originally shown in two parts on Disney's Sunday night TV show, this is the story of young people training at a British riding school and of Funicello overcoming her fear of jumping. Lovely scenery and clean family film. **V**

Horse Whisperer, The (1998) ***1/2 D: Robert Redford. Robert Redford, Kristin Scott Thomas, Sam Neill, Dianne Wiest, Scarlett Johansson, Chris Cooper, Cherry Jones, Ty Hillman, Jeanette Nolan, Don Edwards.   This film definitely needs to be previewed by the parents and edited for children to view. That said, there are still some wonderful things in this movie, which is based on the Nicholas Evan's novel of a young girl whose best friend is killed in the same accident in which she lost her leg and in which her horse was badly injured when a semi-truck struck them on an icy road. Her parents marriage is in trouble, her mother is a perfectionist executive who decides to do her job by phone and fax while she drives her daughter and the horse cross country to a famous horse "whisperer" (Redford) in Montana. Through her persistence, the horse whisperer works with the horse and her daughter to rehabilitate them and get them back "in the saddle" again. The part needing editing is the still married mother falling for Redford and vice versa, though she does end up choosing her marriage. Preview and see what you think. [PG-13] **V, DVD**

In Old Kentucky (1935) *** D: George Marshall. Will Rogers, Dorothy Wilson, Bill "Bojangles" Robinson, Russell Hardie, Louise Henry, Charles Sellon.   Cute family film of poor but good family vs rich family with less than admirable principles. A horse race is involved, Rogers appears in black face and Bill Robinson does some great dancing. A film I think every family will enjoy.

Kentucky (1938) *** D: David Butler. Loretta Young, Richard Greene, Walter Brennan, Douglass Dumbrille, Karen Morley, Moroni Olsen, Russell Hicks.   Oscar winner for Brennan in this tale of rival horse breeding families in the blue-grass country.   **V**

King of the Wild Stallions (1959) ** D: R. G. Springsteen. George Montgomery, Diane Brewster, Edgar Buchanan, Emile Meyer, Byron Foulger.   Horse is the star in this as he protects widow & son. Preview

Man From Snowy River, The (1982-Australian) ***1/2 (See Family Films)

Miracle of the White Stallions (1963) *1/2 (See WWII, Europe)

Misty (1961) *** D: James B. Clark. David Ladd, Pam Smith, Arthur O'Connell, Anne Seymour. Marguerite Henry's popular children's book comes to life with Ladd and Smith as the children who so want a wild pony from Chincoteague. Sweet family film.   **V**

Money From Home (1953) **1/2 (See Family Films)

My Friend Flicka (1943) *** D: Harlold Schuster. Roddy McDowall, Preston Foster, Rita Johnson, Jeff Corey, James Bell.   Story of a boy who loves a difficult to handle horse. Lovely color film.   **V**

National Velvet (1944) **** D: Clarence Brown. Mickey Rooney, Elizabeth Taylor, Donald Crisp, Anne Revere, Angela Lansbury, Reginald Owen, Norma Varden, Jackie "Butch" Jenkins, Terry Kilburn. Perhaps the best horse film of all time about a girl who is determined to follow in her mother's footsteps (mom swam the English channel) and do the unconventional: ride her horse in the famous Grand National Steeplechase. Young Taylor is grand as is Rooney at his tamed down best and the rest of the cast is simply superb. Just a bit of trivia: Taylor's mother, Anne Revere, was a direct descendent of the famous patriot Paul Revere. She won Best Supporting Actress Oscar. Don't miss this! Wonderful for entire family. **V, DVD**

Return to Snowy River (1988-Australian) **1/2 (See Family Films)

Scudda Hoo! Scudda Hay! (1948) ** D: F. Hugh Herbert. June Haver, Lon McCallister, Walter Brennan, Anne Revere, Natalie Wood.   Haver is a bright young girl and McCallister's life is devoted to his two mules.

Seabiscuit (2003) ** D: Gary Ross. Jeff Bridges, Chris Cooper, Toby Maguire, Elizabeth Banks, Gary Stevens, William H. Macy. Though more factual than the one below, this film is rather rough, so please preview before showing the children and edit where needed. **[PG-13] V, DVD**

Stallion Road (1947) ** D: James V. Kern. Ronald Reagan, Alexis Smith, Zachary Scott, Peggy Knudsen, Patti Brady, Harry Davenport.   Friends, vet Reagan and writer Scott vie for the heart of lovely neighbor and horsewoman Smith. Not the greatest film but does show the very real threat from an outbreak of anthrax, making it perhaps a valuable film to include in light of today's current events. Generally, a sweet old fashioned film.

Story of Seabiscuit (1949) **1/2 D: David Butler. Shirley Temple, Barry Fitzgerald, Lon McCallister, Rosemary DeCamp.   Fitzgerald plays incredible horse trainer O'Hara who is imported from Ireland to work for a racehorse owner. He sees a young colt with knobby knees and recommends the head-trainer keep him. They don't and O'Hara goes with the colt to the new owner. This colt becomes the famous, real-life Seabiscuit. Great family horse movie with Temple playing Fitzgerald's nurse niece.   **V**

Thoroughbreds Don't Cry (1937) **1/2 (See Music/Arts)

Thunderhead-Son of Flicka (1945) **1/2 D: Louis King. Roddy McDowall, Preston Foster, Rita Johnson, James Bell, Diana Hale, Carlton Young.   Sequel to *My Friend Flicka* has McDowall raising Flicka's offspring, Thunderhead, who's the first albino in three generations. There's a battle between Thunderhead and another stallion.

Medicine

All Mine to Give (1957) **1/2 Sweet family film including diphtheria. (See Family for more information.)

Dr. Ehrlich's Magic Bullet (1940) ***1/2 D: William Deterle. Edward G. Robinson, Ruth Gordon, Otto Kruger, Donald Crisp, Maria Ouspenskaya, Montagu Love, Sig Ruman, Donald Meek.   Wonderful film of 19th century German scientist who first developed chemotherapy for disease treatment. Robinson stands out as the dedicated and driven Dr. Ehrlich. **V**

Fantastic Voyage (1966) ***1/2 D: Richard Fleischer. Stephen Boyd, Raquel Welch, Edmond O'Brien, Donald Pleasence, Arthur O'Connell, William Redfield, Arthur Kennedy, James Brolin.   Part sci-fi, part medicine this is the story of a medical team that is miniaturized in order to be injected into an important patient to fix the medical problem and save his life. The discussion of how certain parts of the body and the immune system work is what makes me place this film in this category. A fun way to learn some interesting information. **V, DVD**

Florence Nightingale (1985) TVM D: Daryl Duke. Jaclyn Smith, Claire Bloom, Timothy Dalton, Jeremy Brett.   Color version of Miss Nightingale's story is well done, but not as accurate as older *White Angel*, below. Still a nice film showing most of her deed though some things have been changed from the way it really happened. Read some good biographies on her and compare!

Girl in White, The (1952) ** D: John Sturges. June Allyson, Arthur Kennedy, Gary Merrill, Mildred Natwick, James Arness.   True story about first woman ambulance surgeon, Emily Dunning Barringer, (1884-1961) who was also the first woman to be allowed to intern at a city hospital in the winter of 1902. Mostly factual, very interesting movie. For more information about her, read the book, *The First Woman Ambulance Surgeon* by Iris Noble, © 1962, published by Julian Messner, Inc.

Great Moment, The (1944) **1/2 D: Preston Sturges. Joel McCrea, Betty Field, Harry Carey, William Demarest, Franklin Pangborn, Grady Sutton, Louis Jean Heydt.   Based upon the discovery of anesthesia by dentist William Morton, I believe this film deserves a better rating than the original reviews gave it. The story may not be 100% factual, but it certainly conveys (without being gory) that facing surgery before anesthetia was something to be dreaded. The final 30 minutes with the trial surgery using ether for the first time is certainly "worth the price of admission." This would be an interesting film to use to whet the children's appetite for more information on this subject including the dispute over who was really the first to come up with anesthesia. I believe most commonly, the credit goes to Crawford W. Long of Jefferson, Georgia, thirty minutes from my home. Another great discussion point could be to point out the lack of antiseptics and the lack of knowledge about germs, which didn't come about for another 40 years from Louis Pasteur. (Thanks to my daughter, Rachel, for the medical information, which she studied independently in a "self-assignment" that came about because of her interest in medicine.) **V**

Madame Curie (1943) *** D: Mervyn LeRoy. Greer Garson, Walter Pidgeon, Henry Travers, Albert Basserman, Robert Walker, C. Aubrey Smith.   Biography of famous scientist who discovered radium and thus began the possibility of nuclear medicine, power, and arms. **V**

Sister Kenny (1946) ***1/2 D: Dudley Nichols. Rosalind Russell, Alexander Knox, Dean Jagger, Philip Merivale, Beulah Bondi, Dorothy Peterson.   Biography of the famous Australian nurse who initiated a successful therapeutic treatment for polio, and fought with the closed medical minds of the medical "elite" her entire life. Based upon the book, *And They Shall Walk*. Compare it with this excellent film. **V**

Story of Louis Pasteur, The (1936) ***1/2 D: William Dieterle. Paul Muni, Josephine Hutchinson, Anita Louise, Donald Woods, Fritz Leiber, Porter Hall, Akim Tamiroff. Oscar winning performance by Muni shows achievements of famous scientist including his friendship with Joseph Lister, though they have changed the timing of their face-to-face

meeting as well as altering/omitting some other facts. Why not read a biography of him and then watch the movie and compare? **V**

White Angel, The (1936) ** (See 1800s Europe)

Yellow Jack (1938) ** D: George B. Seitz. Robert Montgomery, Virginia Bruce, Lewis Stone, Stanley Ridges, Henry Hull, Charles Coburn, Buddy Ebsen, Andy Devine, Henry O'Neill, Sam Levene, Alan Curtis, William Henry.   Film shows how Dr. Walter Reed figured out the cause of Yellow Fever in Cuba and is mostly factual. Again, this is a good time to read about this important medical event and person and then compare to the movie.

NOTES

Literature

This section contains films based upon well-known works of literature (or writers) which you might read or study for their own literary value and then like to see transformed into film.

Please note: Just because Shakespeare or a work of literature is considered a "classic" by "authorities" does not mean that it is necessarily suitable for children or will even be acceptable to your family's values. Please be familiar with or read first before assigning works of "classic literature" to your children.

Adventures of Ichabod and Mr. Toad, The (1949) *** D: Jack Kinney, Clyde Geronimi, James Algar. Voices of Eric Blore, Pat O'Malley, John Ployardt, Colin Campbell, Claude Allister, The Rhythmaries. Cute adaptation of the classic Kenneth Grahme book, *The Wind in the Willows* which should be great fun to children. However, this version of Washington Irving's *The Legend of Sleepy Hollow* will leave most children afraid to go to sleep at night! So, if you see this one, watch the first part and skip the second, at least until they're older. The second story is narrated and sung by Bing Crosby. **V, DVD**

Adventures of Mark Twain, The (1944) *** (See 1800s-East)

Adventures of Sherlock Holmes, The (1939) ***1/2 D: Alfred Werker. Basil Rathbone, Nigel Bruce, Ida Lupino, Alan Marshal, Terry Kilburn, George Zucco, E. E. Clive, Mary Gordon.   Professor Moriarty plans to steal the Crown Jewels and Sherlock must stop him. It's been years since I've seen this film but cannot remember anything which might be objectionable. For safety's sake, view first but I think the Sherlock Holmes series with Rathbone and Bruce might be a fun way to introduce Sir Arthur Conan Doyle. **V**

Alice in Wonderland (1951) *** D: Clyde Geronimi, Hamilton Luske, Wilfred Jackson. Voices of Kathryn Beaumont, Ed Wynn, Richard Haydn, Sterling Holloway, Jerry Colonna, Verna Felton, Bill Thompson.   Animated Disney version of the classic Lewis Carroll story has some elements which may be frightening to younger children, especially Tweedle-Dum, Tweedle-Dee, and the Queen of Hearts, so parents should view this first to decide if they feel it's right for their children. There are some fun songs, "The Unbirthday Song," "I'm Late," and the vowel song sung by the caterpillar, one of my favorite characters. I must confess that I've always wondered if Carroll wrote this while on drugs. Other than the caterpillar, my children really didn't like this picture. **V**

All Creatures Great and Small (1974 U. S.-British) TVM D: Claude Whatham. Simon Ward, Anthony Hopkins, Lisa Harrow, Brian Stirner, Freddie Jones, T. P. McKenna.   Based upon the book of the same title by James Herriot. Ward plays the author as a young veterinarian who has come to work with an eccentric established vet named Siegfried (Hopkins). Not as good as the book, but a great way to introduce children to these wonderful books by Herriot, or use it to compare to the book after reading it. These are books NOT to be missed! Read them as family read-alouds if you must, but by all means, read it and the sequel. (*All Things Bright and Beautiful*) Above average.

Antony and Cleopatra (1973) *1/2 D: Charleton Heston. Charleton Heston, Hildegard Neil, Eric Porter, John Castle, Fernando Rey.   If you need a film version of Shakespeare's play, this is the only one around. View first if you must use it but I recommend waiting for a stage version in your area. **V**

Around the World in Eighty Days (1956) *** D: Michael Anderson. David Niven, Cantinflas, Shirley MacLaine, Robert Newton, Buster Keaton, Jose Greco, John Gielgud, Robert Morley, Marlene Dietrich, all-star cast.   A well done, Oscar winning (though a bit dated) version of Jules Vern's tale of the bet over whether or not a man could travel around the world in 80 days. The various locations and cultures open the door for many star cameo appearances as well as various studies. **V**

As You Like It (1936-British) *** D: Paul Czinner. Elisabeth Bergner, Laurence Olivier, Sophie Stewart, Henry Ainley, Leon Quartermaine, Felix Aylmer.   This is the only version of this famous Shakespearian comedy on film, to date. Bergner is hard to understand but generally this is a charming film. **V, DVD**

Babar The Movie (1989-Canadian-French) *** D: Alan Bunce. Voices of Gordon Pinsent, Gavin Magrath, Elizabeth Hanna, Sarah Polley, Chris Wiggins.   Feature length animated version of the classic children's book by Jean and Laurent de Brunhoff. This was a favorite of my youngest daughter's when she was little. Beware that the Rhino king could be frightening to children. My daughter felt that it showed good character as Babar cared about Celeste and worked to find her parents. [G]   **V**

Barretts of Wimpole Street, The (1934) *** D: Sidney Franklin. Norma Shearer, Fredric March, Charles Laughton, Maureen O'Sullivan, Katherine Alexander, Una O'Connor, Ian Wolfe.   **V**
(**1957** U.S.-British) **1/2 D: Sidney Franklin. Jennifer Jones, John Gielgud, Bill Travers, Virginia McKenna.   **V**
Story details the life of poet Elizabeth Barrett Browning and her romance with husband Robert Browning, also a poet. Amazing that she could write what she did with such a tyrannical father. View first to edit subject matter.

Beauty and the Beast (1991) ***1/2 D: Gary Trousdale, Kirk Wise. Voices of Paige O'Hara, Robby Benson, Jerry Orbach, Angela Lansbury, Richard White, David Ogden Stiers, Jesse Corti, Rex Everhart, Bradley Michael Pierce, Jo Anne Worley, Kimmy Robertson.   Well done animated classic tale by Disney. Bookish Belle sacrifices herself for her father and willingly remains as a hostage to the Beast. Wonderful animation of household objects along with a winning score make this story a treat. There is the story of an enchantment at the beginning, and a miraculous resurrection at the end which in many ways parallels rebirth through the love of Messiah. Parents may wish to view this first and see if it fits into your plan for your family. Overall, this is a story with many redeeming qualities and I feel the questionable items can be discussed of edited. Even my sophisticated graduate students like this. [G]   **V, DVD**

Belles on Their Toes (1952) *** D: Henry Levin. Myrna Loy, Jeanne Crain, Debra Paget, Jeffrey Hunter, Edward Arnold, Hoagy Carmichael.   Sequel to *Cheaper By the Dozen* (below) showing widowed Myrna Loy stepping into her husband's shoes to support her family as the first woman engineer of her field. It also shows the family working to stay together; the struggles, sacrifices, and camaraderie. A wonderful family film.

Big Red (1962) *** D: Norman Tokar. Walter Pidgeon, Gilles Payant, Emile Genest, Janette Bertrand, Doris Lussier.   From novel by Jim Kjelgaard, this is the story of a boy who must find work and ends up working for a wealthy dog owner and falls in love with an Irish setter. When the dog is injured and is going to be put down, the boy takes the dog, nurses him back to health and then returns him to his owner. A fine family film by Disney. **V, DVD**

Black Beauty (1971-British) **1/2 D: James Hill. Mark Lester, Walter Slezak.   Based on the book by Anna Sewell, this is the story of a horse who is passed from owner to owner in 19th C England and the treatment it receives from various owners. [G]   **V**

Born Free (1966-British) ***1/2 D: James Hill. Virginia McKenna, Bill Travers, Geoffrey Keen, Peter Lukoye.   Based upon the true story of Joy Adamson's about Elsa the lioness who was raised as a pet by two Kenya game wardens. A wonderful look at Africa, lions and their habits. Good family viewing. Sequel is *Living Free.* **V**

Caine Mutiny, The (1954) **** D: Edward Dmytryk. Humphery Bogart, Jose Ferrer, Van Johnson, Robert Francis, May Wynn, Fred MacMurray, E. G. Marshall, Lee Marvin, Tom Tully, Claude Akins. Naval officers mutiny against paranoid captain resulting in a court-martial. Court scene amazingly well acted. Based upon the Pulitzer Prize winning novel by Herman Wouk, which may or may not be good for children to read; I haven't read it so don't know. The film is very well done and interesting. View if concerned about content. **V, DVD**

Chariots of Fire (1981) ***1/2 (See Ancient Greece)

Charlotte's Web (1973) *** D: Charles A. Nichols, Iwao Takamoto. Voices of Debbie Reynolds, Henry Gibson, Paul Lynde, Agnes Moorehead, Charles Nelson-Reilly; narrated by Rex Allen.   Animated version of famous children's classic by E. B. White is charming and wonderful for all. Charlotte is a spider who comes to Wilbur [the pig's] farm one day. He's doomed for slaughter, so she weaves a message about him in her web: "Some Pig." This causes quite a stir and makes Wilbur a celebrity thus avoiding disaster. A tale full of warm fuzzies about an amazing friendship. For children of all ages. [G]   **V, DVD**

Cheaper by the Dozen (1950) *** D: Walter Lang. Clifton Webb, Myrna Loy, Jeanne Crain, Mildred Natwick, Edgar Buchanan.   Real-life turn of the century story of the Gilbreth family who had twelve children. Based upon the book by the same name, this is a wonderful look at Americana at its best. A great family film with a father who used home schooling techniques, even during the summer. Also included and interesting for discussion are his attitude toward Anne's dating and how that applies to us today. Lastly would be the appearance of Mildred Natwick as the representative for the (then) new "Planned Parenthood" and their reaction to this organization. A good discussion could be had about the difference in mindsets and thinking in less than 100 years on this issue. Read the book (edit it a bit) and compare.   **V**

Christmas Carol, A (See Holidays)

Cinderella (1950) ***1/2 D: Wilfred Jackson, Hamilton Luske, Clyde Geronimi. Voices of Ilene Woods, William Phipps, Eleanor Audley, Rhoda, Williams, Lucille Bliss, Verna Felton.   One of Disney's best animated films of classic fairy tale, with a few embellishments, namely the cute mice Gus and Jaq. Songs include, "A Dream is a Wish Your Heart Makes," "Bibbidi Bobbidi Boo," "Cinder-ell-e," "So This is Love."   **V**

Clarence the Cross-eyed Lion (1965) **1/2 (See Science/Nature)

Comedy of Errors (See Boys from Syracuse in Music/Arts)

David Copperfield (1935) **** D: George Cukor. Freddie Bartholomew, Frank Lawton, W. C. Fields, Lionel Barrymore, Madge Evans, Roland Young, Basil Rathbone, Edna May Oliver, Maureen O'Sullivan, Lewis Stone, Lennox Pawle, Elsa Lanchester, Una O'Connor, Arthur Treacher.   Excellent film adaptation of the Dickens's classic is well worth seeing for the entire family. David loses his precious father and then his mother, after she remarries a horrid man (Rathbone). He is sent from home and finds himself in a desperate situation. He is befriended by Micawber (Fields) and later taken in by his Aunt Betsey (Oliver). My children cheered when she sent Murdstone (Rathbone) packing! Don't miss this wonderful classic film of a great piece of literature. **V**

Emma (1996) *** D: Douglas McGrath. Gwyneth Paltrow, Jeremy Northam, Toni Collette, Greta Scacchi.   Charming, warm, wonderful adaptation of the Jane Austen comedy of manners about a headstrong young woman who decides to play matchmaker for others, yet is not in touch with her own feelings or of those around her. She learns of her feelings and becomes more aware of others as she matures in the film. One part of the film stands out as Emma loses patience with a woman who would try most of our patience as well, and the lesson she learns from her hasty words and uncharitable actions. A beautifully done film. [PG] **V**

Five Weeks in a Balloon (1962) **1/2 D: Irwin Allen. Red Buttons, Barbara Edenl, Fabian, Cedric Hardwicke, Peter Lorre, Richard Haydn, Barbara Luna.   Based on Jules Vern tale of a balloon expedition to Africa with some twists and turns reminiscent of *Around the World in Eighty Days*. Several cameos are included. **V**

From the Mixed-Up Files of Mrs. Basil E. Frankweiler (1995) TVM D: Marcus Cole. Lauren Bacall, Jean Marie Barnwell, Jesse Lee, Miriam Flynn, Mark L. Taylor, Emmett Walsh.   Based on the E. L. Konigsburg book, this is the story of two children who run

away from home and hide out in the NYC Metropolitan Museum and while there they try to solve a mystery about a statue. Read the book and then compare to the movie. My children enjoyed both.

Gentleman's Agreement (1947) *** D: Ella Kazan. Gregory Peck, Dorothy McGuire, John Garfield, Celeste Holm, Anne Revere, June Havoc, Albert Dekker, Jane Wyatt, Dean Stockwell, Same Jaffe. Oscar winning film version of Laura Z. Hobson novel. Writer (Peck) agrees to pretend to be Jewish and discovers rampant anti-Semitism. Should be viewed first by parents, but it is an interesting look at prejudice especially since this seems to be once again on the rise. Believers know that we (individually and as a nation) must bless the Jews or fall under the curse-part of the covenant God made with Abraham which was passed down to Issac (the child of Promise) and his lineage, "I will bless those who bless you, those who curse you I will curse." (Genesis 12:3) **V, DVD**

Grapes of Wrath, The (1940) **** D: John Ford. Henry Fonda, Jane Darwell, John Carradine, Charley Grapewin, Dorris Bowden, Russell Simpson, John Quqallen, O. Z. Whitehead, Eddie Quillan, Zeffie Tilbury, Daryl Hickman, Ward Bond, Charles Middleton, Tom Tyler, Mae Marsh. Jack Pennick.   Oscar winning film version of John Steinbeck's novel about life during the Great Depression and Dust Bowl. This is considered one of the great American films of all time, and off hand, I can't think of anything objectionable in it, but parents should probably view it first. It is the only film with which I am familiar covering the pure desolation of the land during this time and the hopelessness the depression brought. See what you think. **V**

Great Expectations (1946– British) **** D: David Lean. John Mills, Valerie Hobson, Bernard Miles, Francis L. Sullivan, Finlay Currie, Martita Hunt, Anthony Wager, Jean Simmons, Alec Guiness, Ivor Barnard, Freda Jackson, Torin Thatcher, Eileen Erskine, Hay Petrie.   Considered one of the greatest films ever made, this film adaptation is of Dickens' famous novel about a mysterious benefactor making a poor orphan a gentleman of means. Oscar winner could have some scary parts for younger ones, so parents view first. **V, DVD**

Guns of Navarone (1961) ***1/2 (See WWII, Europe)

Hamlet (1948-British) **** D: Laurence Olivier. Laurence Olivier, Eileen Herlie, Basil Sydney, Felix Aylmer, Jean Simmons, Stanley Holloway,, Peter Cushing.   Multiple Oscar winner and best film version of the classic play by Shakespeare. Parents need to know the play before showing to children to make sure they approve. It contains a ghost and other items to which some might object. **V, DVD** Remake in 1990 with Mel Gibson and Glenn Close is also well done. **[PG] V**

Harriet the Spy (1996) **1/2 D: Bronwen Hughes. Michelle Trachtenberg, Vanessa Lee Chester, Gregory Smith, Rosie O'Donnell, J. Smith-Cameron, Robert Joy, Eartha Kitt.   A young girl is encouraged by her nanny (O'Donnell) to keep a written record of everything she sees which eventually gets her in trouble with everyone and gives families some discussion material about relationships. Mostly for kids. Based upon the book by Louise Fitzhugh. **[PG] V**

Heidi (1968) TVM D: Dlebert Mann. Maximilian Schell, Jean Simmons, Michael Redgrave, Walter Slezak, Jennifer Edwards, Peter Van Eyck.   Well done film version of classic children's tale. Above average. **V, DVD**

Henry V (1945-British) **** D: Laurence Olivier. Laurence Olivier, Robert Newton, Leslie Banks, Renee Asherson, Esmond Knight, Leo Genn, Ralph Truman, Harcourt Williams, Ivy St. Helier, Ernest Thesiger, Max Adrian, George Cole, Felix Aylmer, Robert Helpmann, Freda Jackson, Jimmy Hanley, John Laurie.   If this play meets with your approval, then this film is worth viewing for more than just a fantastic rendition of Shakespeare's play. Olivier had the brilliant idea to film this as though it were being done in the Globe Theatre in the 1500s, for which he earned a special Oscar "for his outstanding achievement as actor, producer, and director in bringing *Henry V*

to the screen." If you plan to use this play, then don't miss this brilliant film version. If you are unfamiliar with the subject matter, view first. For the student, it might be better to read the play and then view, if it is your plan that the student read this play. **V, DVD**

Henry V (1989-British) ***1/2 D: Kenneth Branagh. Kenneth Branagh, Derek Jacobi, Brian Blessed, Alec McCowen, Ian Holm, Richard Briers, Robert Stephens, Robbie Coltrane, Christian Bale, Judi Dench, Paul Scofield, Michael Maloney, Emma Thompson, Geraldine McEwan.   Different, though powerful, version of famous Shakespearian play. You might want to view both this and the one above and compare and contrast the different "takes" on the same play. Also won an Oscar for Costume Design. The same cautions apply to this version as to the one above. **V, DVD**

Horatio Hornblower (1998) (See 1700s Europe)

Hound of the Baskervilles, The (1939) *** D: Sidney Lanfield. Basil Rathbone, Nigel Bruce, Richard Greene, Wendy Barrie, Lionel Atwill, John Carradine, Beryl Mercer, Mary Gordon, E. E. Clive.   First Sherlock Holmes movie in the series starring Rathbone as the title character, based on the books by Sir Arthur Conan Doyle. The story is a bit scary and so is the film version, even for 1939. Preview and decide if it fits your criteria. The story is of a creepy mansion at which a murder takes place and how Sherlock Holmes solves it. Be aware that in the story Holmes was a cocaine addict, thereby explaining the last line, "Quick Watson, the needle!" **V**

Huckleberry Finn (1939) *** D: Richard Thorpe. Mickey Rooney, Walter Connolly, William Frawley, Rex Ingram, Lynne Carver.   Thorpe managed to tone down Rooney, who plays a fine Huck in good adaptation of classic Mark Twain tale. **V**

Hunchback of Notre Dame, The (1939) ***1/2 D: William Dieterle. Charles Laughton, Sir Cedric Hardwicke, Thomas Mitchell, Maureen O'Hara, Edmond O'Brien, Alan Marshal, Walter Hampden, Harry Davenport, George Zucco, Curt Bois, George Tobias, Rod La Roque.   Laughton stars in this film version of the Victor Hugo classic tale as Quasimodo, the deformed bell ringer of Notre Dame. The atmosphere and location of medieval Paris is magnificently recreated. Parents need to decide if this is age appropriate before showing, but even if not, might be able to salvage some of the scenery. By far the best film version of this tale. **V, DVD**

Importance of Being Earnest, The (1952-British) *** D: Anthony Asquith. Michael Redgrave, Michael Denison, Richard Watts, Edith Evans, Margaret Rutherford, Joan Greenwood, Dorothy Tutin.   Oscar Wilde's wonderful comedy of manners set in Victorian England about a girl who says she can only marry a man named Ernest. Colorful costume film of a humorous play. Parents may wish to preview. **V, DVD**

Indian in the Cupboard, The (1995) *** D: Frank Oz. Hal Scardino, Lite-foot; Lindsay Crouse, Richard Jenkins, Rishi Bhat, Steve Coogan, David Keith, Sakina Jaffrey, Vincent Kartheiser, Nestor Serrano. Based on the children's book by Lynne Reid Banks, this is the story of a boy who receives an old cupboard for a birthday gift and finds that when he puts his plastic Indian inside, it comes to life. Read the book first and compare after previewing for appropriateness. **[PG] V, DVD**

Inheritance, The (1997) D: Bobby Roth. Meredith Baxter, Tom Conti, Cari Shayne, Thomas Gibson, Brigitta Dau, Paul Anthony Stewart, Brigid Brannagh, Michael Gallagher, Max Gail.   Wonderful film adaptation of Louisa May Alcott's story of a young woman, Edith (Shayne), who is raised as a companion to the daughter of a wealthy family. Edith has character and integrity in abundance as she shows time and again, especially when faced with the self-centered spitefulness of a distant cousin who comes to live with the family. This is the story of goodness, character and integrity over pettiness and spite. Don't miss it! Also known as *Alcott's Inheritance*. **[NR]**

I Remember Mama (1948) ***1/2 (See 1900s)

Ivanhoe (1952) ****1/2 (See Middle Ages)

Jane Eyre (1944) *** D: Robert Stevenson. Orson Welles, Joan Fontaine, Margaret

O'Brien, Henry Daniell, John Sutton, Agnes Moorehead, Elizabeth Taylor, Peggy Ann Garner, Sara Allgood, Aubrey Mather, Hillary Brooke.   Well done version of the classic Brontë story is somewhat slow moving in the beginning. First, decide if you want your child to read this story and if you do, then compare to this after reading the book. If you can find the one below, I prefer it.   **V**

Jane Eyre (1971-British) TVM D: Delbert Mann. George C. Scott, Susannah York, Ian Bannen, Jack Hawkins, Rachel Kempson, Jean Marsh, Nyree Dawn Porter.   Scott and York do fine jobs in this rendition of the classic Brontë story. After a parent reads the book, see if you decide that this is a story you want your child to read. My long time favorite, but may be harder to find.

Jane Eyre (1997) NR D: Robert Young. Samantha Morton, Ciaran Hinds, Gemma Jones, Richard Hawley, Peter Wright, Timia Berthonme.   An A&E production of the classic Brontë novel of the governess who falls in love with her employer, who also loves her. There's just one problem, his living wife who is totally insane. Of all the productions I have seen, this one is the best one, even rating better than my old favorite with Susannah York and George C. Scott. **V** (available from A&E)

Journey to the Center of the Earth (1959) *** D: Henry Levin. James Mason, Pat Boone, Arlene Dahl, Diane Baker, Thayer David, Alan Napier.   Colorful version of Jules Verne's story has old-fashioned flavor and is generally fun. There are a few parts that might be scary to the younger ones, but by and large, I believe most families will enjoy it.

Julius Caesar (1953) ***1/2 D: Joseph L. Mankiewicz. Marlon Brando, James Mason, John Gielgud, Louis Calhern, Edmond O'Brien, Greer Garson, Deborah Kerr, George Macready, Michael Pate, Alan Napier, Ian Wolfe, Douglas Dunbrille, Edmund Purdom.   Oscar winning production of Shakespeare's play of politics and power in Ancient Rome. Parents should preview this first.   **V**

Jungle Book (1942) *** D: Zoltan Korda. Sabu, Joseph Calleia, John Qualen, Frank Puglia, Rosemary DeCamp, Nobel Johnson.   Kipling story comes to life with Sabu as Mowgli. Remade by Disney as a cartoon. (See Family Films)   **V, DVD**

Keys of the Kingdom, The (1944) *** (See 1900s)

Kidnapped (1960) **1/2 D: Robert Stevenson. Peter Finch, James McArthur, Bernard Lee, Niall MacGinnis, John Laurie, Finlay Currie, Peter O'Toole.   Disney version of Robert Louis Stevenson's tale. Also made into a TV movie in 1995 and reportedly excellent though I've not seen the entire thing, so can't verify that. If you see it, proceed with caution until you know what's there. Both versions are available on **V.**

Kim (1950) ***1/2 D: Victor Saville. Errol Flynn, Dean Stockwell, Paul Lukas, Thomas Gomez, Cecil Kellaway.   Action film based on Kipling tale set in 1880s India about British troops quelling native uprising with the help of young Kim. This is the only film version. Parents, view first.   **V**

King Lear (1971-British) ***1/2 D: Peter Brook. Paul Scofield, Irene Worth, Jack MacGowran, Alan Webb, Cyril Cusack, Patrick Magee.   Photographed in Denmark, this is not the play to choose to introduce a child to Shakespeare. If you choose this one, have the child read the play first and then compare to the screen version. Preview first.   **V**

Lad: A Dog (1962) **1/2 D: Aram Avakam, Leslie H. Martinson. Peter Breck, Peggy McCay, Carroll O'Connor, Angela Cartwright, Maurice Dallimore.   Based on the book by Albert Payne Terhune about a dog who changes the life of a child. Breck and wife McCay raise collies. O'Connor moves into the neighborhood with crippled daughter Cartwright to do the same. Lad, Breck's dog, makes a huge impression on daughter Cartwright, who eventually gets one of his pups. Fine family film with good values.   **V**

Les Miserables (1947) *** D: Lewis Milestone. Michael Rennie, Debra Paget, Robert Newton, Sylvia Sidney, Edmund Gwenn, Cameron Mitchell, Elsa Lancaster.   Based on classic by Victor Hugo, this seems to be the best choice of many. Get the recording of the musical and listen. Preview

Little Lord Fauntleroy (1936) *** D: John Cromwell. Freddie Bartholomew, C. Aubrey Smith, Guy Kibbee, Dolores Costello Barrymore, Mickey Rooney, Jessie Ralph.   Based on the classic story by Frances Hodgson Burnett, young Bartholomew discovers that his deceased father was in line for an earldom which has now passed to him but he and his mother must move from N.Y. to England to live with his grandfather. He touches everyone with love and kindness. Lovely film, highly recommended. **V, DVD**

Little Women (1944) **** D: George Cukor. Katharine Hepburn, Joan Bennett, Paul Lukas, Frances Dee, Jean Parker, Edna May Oliver, Douglass Montgomery, Spring Byington.   Beautiful film adaptation of classic book by Louisa May Alcott has all the right elements. This one is the best. **V, DVD**
(1949) ** 1/2 D: Mervyn LeRoy. June Allyson, Peter Lawford, Margaret O'Brien, Elizabeth Taylor, Janet Leigh, Mary Astor.   This one also has its following, though not as well done, it is in color. **V**

Lost Horizon (1937) **** D: Frank Capra. Ronald Colman, Jane Wyatt, John Howard, Edward Everett Horton, Margo, Sam Jaffe, H. B. Warner, Isabel Jewell, Thomas Mitchell.   James Hilton's classic story of five people who survive incredible odds and stumble upon a strange Tibetan village where health and peace reign and it seems no one ever dies. Fascinating story and interesting discussion piece. **V, DVD**

Louis L'Amour's Crossfire Trail (2001) TVM D: Simon Wincer. Tom Selleck, Virginia Madsen, Wilford Brimley, Brad Johnson, Mark Harmon, David O'Hara, Christian Kane, Barry Corbin, Joanna Miles, Ken Pogue, Patrick Kilpatrick, Rex Linn, William Sanderson.   Based upon the book, three men escape a ship upon which they have been captured for a press gang. The man who inspired them dies before escaping, but Selleck makes a promise to him he aims to keep. To do so, he must return to the man's home and look after his ranch and his wife. Trouble ensues when the villain behind all the trouble sees Selleck standing between him and his goal. If you are a L'Amour fan, this is a well done film based upon his work, but it *must* be previewed by parents first for some needed editing. Also see *Shadow Riders*. **V**

Macbeth (1948) *** D: Orson Welles. Orson Welles, Jeanette Nolan, Dan O'Herlihy, Edgar Barrier, Roddy McDowall, Robert Coote, Erskine Sanford, Alan Napier, Peggy Webber, John Dierkes.   This is one you definitely have to see first to decide if you want to show it. I list it because the only other film of this Shakespearian play is rated R. Compare with the story Shakespeare wrote and I think you'll find it fairly accurate even with some of the more interesting camera angles and directorial decisions. **V**

Madeline (1998) *** D: Daisy von Scherler Mayer. Frances McDormand, Hatty Jones, Nigel Hawthorne, Ben Daniels, Stephane Audran.   Cute contemporary adaptation of Ludwig Bemelman's beloved children's book about an orphan girl always in trouble and the wise nun Miss Clavel (McDormand) who takes care of the orphans and orphanage. The children who like the book will like this. **[PG] V, DVD**

Man With a Million (1954-British) **1/2 D: Ronald Neame. Gregory Peck, Jane Griffiths, Ronald Squire, A. E. Matthews, Wilfrid Hyde-White, Reginald Beckwith.   Mark Twain's "The Million Pound Bank Note" is a cute and fun story of an American who is given the title sum of money in a bank note with the understanding that he cannot spend it, just show it and see what happens. All of this is done as a wager between two English gentlemen, and leads to a variety of problems. Good family film.

Master of Ballantree, The (1953) **1/2 D: William Keighley. Errol Flynn, Roger Livesey, Anthony Steel, Yvonne Furneaux.   Flynn stars in this adaptation of Robert Louis Stevenson's story of those who want to put Bonnie Prince Charles on the throne. Filmed on location in Scotland, Sicily and England. **V**

Midsummer Night's Dream, A (1935) *** D: Max Reinhardt. William Dieterle, James Cagney, Dick Powell, Joe E. Brown, Jean Muir, Hugh Herbert, Olivia de Haviland, Ian Hunter, Frank McHugh, Victor Jory, Ross Alexander, Verree Teasdale, Anita Louise, Mickey Rooney, Arthur Treacher, Billy Barty. Oscar winning film adaptation of Shakes pearian play has its good and bad points. Rooney goes a bit over the top as Puck and gets tiring after a while, but the play within the play at the end is wonderful! Mendelssohn's music by the same title is incorporated thereby giving you an introduction to it. Be sure to listen to it on its own, too. By far the best film version made and probably the best Shakespearian play on film for children.   **V**

Much Ado About Nothing (1992-British-U.S.) *** D: Kenneth Branagh. Kenneth Brannagh, Michael Keaton, Robert Sean Leonard, Keanu Reeves, Emma Thompson, Denzel Washington, Richard Briers, Kate Beckinsale, Brian Blessed, Richard Clifford, Ben Elton, Gerard Horan, Phyllida Law, Imelda Staunton, Jimmy Yuill.   Well done version of Shakespeare's comedy of Benedict and sharp-tongued Beatrice was filmed around and in a villa in Tuscany, but does need editing for some of the bawdy parts Shakespeare was known to include which are a bit too graphic. View first and edit before showing. [**PG-13**] **V, DVD**

Mutiny on the Bounty (1935) **** D: Frank Lloyd. Charles Laughton, Clarke Gable, Franchot Tone, Herbert Mundin, Eddie Quillan, Dudley Digges, Donald Crisp, Movita, Henry Stephenson, Spring Byington, Ian Wolfe, Mamo.   Based on the Nordhoff-Hall book about a mutiny led by Mr. Christian (Gable) against a tyrannical Captain Bligh (Laughton) while on a south sea voyage. Oscar winner for Best Picture. Don't bother with the remakes, just see this one. [The Mel Gibson remake is not suitable for children.]   **V**

Nancy Drew Carolyn Keene's series of mysteries for young girls has been famous with many readers since its debut in 1930. The older versions are the best ones and are now being republished. They are somewhat different from the newer versions. I remember reading both versions of *The Hidden Staircase Mystery* and finding that the ending of the older version was totally different and better! Hollywood decided to produce a series of films based on the character, with only two (*Nancy Drew, Detective,* [based on *The Password to Larkspur* Lane] and Nancy *Drew and the Hidden Staircase)* actually adapted from the books. These are fun for kids.

Nancy Drew, Detective (1938) **1/2   **Nancy Drew—Troubleshooter** (1939) **
Nancy Drew—Reporter (1939) **1/2   **Nancy Drew and the Hidden Staircase** (1939) **1/2

New Adventures of Pippi Longstocking, The (1988) ** D: Ken Annakin. Tami Erin, Eileen Brennan, Dennis Duan, Dianne Hull, George DiCenzo, John Schuck, Dick Van Patten.   Based on Astrid Lindgren's books about an amazing child who lives on her own while her father is at sea and how she makes friends with the neighbor children, gets in trouble with the authorities and must go to school, and thwarts criminals with no sweat. Fun for kids. [**G**]   **V, DVD**

O'Henry's Full House (1952) **1/2 D: Henry Hathaway, Howard Hawks, Henry King, Henry Koster, Jean Negulesco. Fred Allen, Anne Baxter, Charles Laughton, Marilyn Monroe, Gregory Ratoff, Jeanne Crain, Oscar Levant, Jean Peters, Richard Widmark, Farley Granger.   Five O'Henry stories come to life with the introduction by John Steinbeck. The stories are: "The Clarion Call," "Last Leaf," "Ransom of the Red Chief," "Gift of the Magi," and "Cop and the Anthem."

Old Yeller (1957) *** (See 1800s, West)

Oliver Twist (1948-British) **** D: David Lean. Alec Guiness, Robert Newton, John Howard Davies, Kay Walsh, Francis L. Sullivan, Anthony Newley, Henry Stephenson.   Best version of Dickens' story of a young boy who becomes involved with the nefarious Fagin and his gang of young thieves, headed by the Artful Dodger. Later made into the musical, *Oliver!* Preview and see what you think. (See Music/Arts)

Othello (1965-British) **** D: Stuart Burge. Lawrence Olivier, Frank Finlay, Maggie Smith, Joyce Redman, Derek Jacobi, Edward Hardwicke, Milk Gambon, John McEnery.   Excellently done film version of Shakespeare's play of Othello and the dreaded Iago. Investigate the subject matter before you show it and preview first. **V**

Persuasion (1995-British-U.S.-French) *** D: Roger Mitchell. Amanda Root, Ciaran Hinds, Susan Fleetwood, Corin Redgrave, Fiona Shaw, John Woodvine, Phoebe Nicholls, Samuel Est, Sophie Thompson, Judy Cornwell, Felicity Dean.   Jane Austen's story of a young woman who has never gotten over her love for an impoverished British officer, whose marriage proposal she was advised to refuse. Now, years later, fortunes have changed as she is the one in a lesser financial situation and comes into the officer's circle once again. A story of a girl with great character who meets adversity bravely and receives her hearts desire in the end. The details in this film are beautifully crafted, giving us an visual feast of 19th century English life. [PG]   V, DVD

Pollyanna (1960) ***1/2 D: David Swift. Hayley Mills, Jane Wyman, Richard Egan, Karl Malden, Nancy Olsen, Adolphe Menjou, Donald Crisp, Agnes Moorehead.   Delightful Disney film is a must-see for the whole family. The Eleanor Porter story comes to life as orphaned Pollyanna (Mills) comes to New England to live with her wealthy namesake, her Aunt Polly and touches and changes the lives of all around her with her sunshine and good cheer. Wonderful family film.   V, DVD

Pride and the Prejudice, The (1940) **** D: Robert Z. Leonard. Greer Garson, Sir Laurence Olivier, Edna May Oliver, Edmund Gwenn, Mary Boland, Maureen O'Sulivan, Karen Morley, Melville Cooper, E. E. Clive, Ann Rutherford, Jane Wyman.   Outstanding adaptation (and still my favorite of all the many remakes) of Jane Austen's novel of five sisters, all of marriageable age and their scheming mother. (my relative, Mary Boland) A young woman, Elizabeth, overhears a remark which tarnishes her view of the proud Mr. Darcy. They must each learn to see beyond the surface. The inimitable Edna May Oliver plays the formidable Lady Catherine DeBurg.   V

Pride and Prejudice (1996) **** D: Simon Langton. Colin Firth, Jennifer Ehle, Crispin Bonham Carter. A&E production of Austen's classic novel is incredibly well done, longer than the above version so includes more details of the story and in color, so is quite lovely to watch. Parents might wish to preview, but I think most will think it a lovely film. For me, a close second to the 1940 film.   V

Prince and the Pauper, The (1937) ***1/2 D: William Keighley. Errol Flynn, Billy and Bobby Mauch, Claude Rains, Alan Hale, Montagu Love, Henry Stephenson, Barton MacLane.   Exciting version of Mark Twain story of two look-a-like boys who meet and change places; one is the Prince of Wales and the other is a common pauper. Against all odds, Flynn helps the rightful king return to the throne. Wonderful score by Erich Wolfgang Korngold, who also wrote music for the *Adventures of Robin Hood* as well as other films, composed opera, and was a student of classical composer Gustav Mahler.   V

Princess Bride, The (1987) **1/2 D: Rob Reiner. Cary Elwes, Mandy Patinkin, Chris Sarandon, Christopher Guest, Wallace Shawn, Andre the Giant, Fred Savage, Robin Wright, Peter Falk, Peter Cook, Carol Kane, Billy Crystal, Mel Smith.   From the William Goldman novel of a young girl and her "one true love" who disappears. Her heart is frozen while awaiting his return, which happens in the nick of time to save her from a series of disasters. Parents may wish to view this first and see if it fits your criteria as it is a bit wacky and off-beat. [PG]   V, DVD

Rascal (1969) **1/2 D: Norman Tokar. Steve Forrest, Bill Mumy, Pamela Toll, Bettye Ackerman, Elsa Lanchester, Henry Jones.   Disney adaptation of Sterling North's autobiography about his childhood friendship with a raccoon is clean and fun for the entire family. Caution children about making pets of racoons as today, most are carriers of rabies.   [G]   V, DVD

Richard III (1955-British) ***1/2 D: Laurence Olivier. Laurence Olivier, John Gielgud, Ralph Richardson, Claire Bloom, Alec Clunes, Cedric Hardwicke, Stanley Baker, Pamela Brown, Michael Glough.   Shakespeare's play of insane 15th century British king and court. Please read all Shakespeare before allowing your children to read it or showing a film of it. Just because it's Shakespeare doesn't mean that it is appropriate for all ages, nor does every Shakespearian work match the values of every family.   V

Rodgers and Hammerstein's Cinderella (1964) TMV (See Music/Arts)

Romeo and Juliet (1968-British-Italian) ***1/2 D: Franco Zeffirelli. Leonard Whiting, Olivia Hussey, Milo O'Shea, Michael York, John McEnery, Pat Heywood, Robert Stephens. Narrated by Laurence Olivier.   An excellent production of the Shakespearian play, this film is most accurate in the actual ages (17 and 15, respectively) Shakespeare intended for the main characters in the tragic story of two young lovers kept apart by a dispute between their families. Parents, view first to see if this is okay with you. However, it IS the play, so then you must decide if the play is alright for your children. [PG] **V, DVD**

Secret Garden, The (1949) *** D: Fred M. Wilcox. Margaret O'Brien, Herbert Marshall, Dean Stockwell, Gladys Cooper, Elsa Lanchester. **V**
(1987) TVM D: Alan Grint. Gennie James, Barret Oliver, Jadrien Steele, Michael Hordern, Billie Whitelaw, Derek Jacobi, Lucy Getteridge. (Our favorite version) **V**
(1993) *** D: Agnieszka Holland. Kate Maberly, Heydon Prowse, Andrew Knott, Maggie Smith, Laura Crossley, John Lynch, Walter Sparrow, Irene Jacob. [G] **V, DVD**
Warm and wonderful story from the book by Frances Hodgson Burnett of an orphan girl who comes to stay with her guardian at his lonely estate. Late at night, she hears strange noises and goes to investigate. She finds her guardian's son, (or uncle's son, depending upon the version) a child recluse whom she is able to challenge and to bring out of his shell. With a friend named Dickon who has a way with animals, they discover and refurbish a walled garden to its former splendor.

Secret Life of Walter Mitty, The (1947) **1/2 D: Norman Z. McLeod. Danny Kaye, Virginia Mayo, Boris Karloff, Fay Bainter, Ann Rutherford, Florence Bates.   Kaye is a milquetoast who dreams of doing great deeds, and ends up in the right place at the wrong time thereby getting involved in international intrigue. Fun if you like Kaye's humor of which my children are fans.   **V, DVD**

Sense and Sensibility (1995) **** D: Ang Lee. Emma Thompson, Alan Rickman, Kate Winslet, Hugh Grant, James Fleet.   Wonderful production based upon the novel by Jane Austen, it is the tale of three sisters who find themselves impoverished and displaced upon their father's death. Of the oldest two, one is impulsive and flirtatious, the other is forced to be sensible and to suppress her feelings to help her mother and sisters carry on. An interesting character study of how different people handle life's challenges and of the social mores of the time. Won an Oscar for Best Screenplay Adaptation. Best suited for older children. There is some subject matter which parents may wish to view first, however, it can easily be edited and salvaged. Generally, a fabulously done film. [PG]   **V**

Shadow Riders, The (1982) TVM D: Andrew V. McLaglen. Tom Selleck, Sam Elliot, Ben Johnson, Katharine Ross, Geoffrey Lewis, Jeffrey Osterhage, Gene Evans, Harry Carey, Jr. Another Louis L'Amour tale about two brothers returning home from the Civil War, only to find that a renegade southerner has taken their siblings and other young people hostage. They go after them to get them back. Parents need to preview first for a few items, but this is a generally humorous film and much less violent than *Crossfire Trail*. Above average. **V, DVD**

So Dear to My Heart (1949) ***1/2 (See Family Films)

Sounder (1972) **1/2 D: Martin Ritt. Cicely Tyson, Paul Winfield, Kevin Hooks, Carmen Matthews, Taj Mahal, James Best, Janet MacLachlan.   Story of black sharecropping family in the 1930s, the hard times they face as well as the educational opportunities that come to the eldest son. Generally sweet, but does need editing for language. Discussions may be necessary about stealing, as well. Filmed in Louisiana. [G] **V**

Stuart Little (1999) *** D: Rob Minkoff. Geena Davis, Hugh Laurie, Jonathan Lipnicki, Jeffrey Jones, Julia Sweeney, Allyce Beasley, Brian Doyle-Murray, Dabney Coleman, Estelle Getty; voices of Michael J. Fox, Nathan Lane, Chazz Palminteri, Jennifer Tilly, Bruno Kirby, David Alan Grier, Steve Zahn.   Loosely based on the E. B. White book, this is the story of a mouse who is adopted by a human family but who is not loved by the family cat. The book is much better. [PG]   **V, DVD**

Swiss Family Robinson (1960) ***1/2 D: Ken Annakin. John Mills, Dorothy McGuire, James MacArthur, Janet Munro, Sessue Hayakawa, Tommy Kirk, Kevin Corcoran.   Fabulous Disney film of famous book about a shipwrecked family who must find a way to survive on a desert island. They not only survive, they thrive, even when rescuing damsels in disguise or being attacked by pirates. A must see, charming family film.   **V, DVD**

Tale of Two Cities, A (1935) **** (See 1700s)

Taming of the Shrew, The (1967-US- Italian) ***1/2 (See Renaissance)

Tarzan These films based on Edgar Rice Burroughs' classic tale were made from 1918 to 1998 and have included various Tarzans, the most famous of whom was Olympic swimmer Johnny Weissmuller, who also created the famous Tarzan call by yodeling, which was then played backwards! Some of these films include a heavy occultic theme, so you'll have to view them first to see which ones are safe for your family. There are forty films in all, too many to list here; just plan to preview any film you may rent or tape.

Three Musketeers, The (1948) **1/2 D: George Sidney. Lana Turner, Gene Kelly, June Allyson, Van Heflin, Angela Lansbury, Robert Coote, Frank Morgan, Vincent Price, Keenan Wynn, Gig Young.   A beautiful costume film of the Alexander Dumas tale with Kelly as D'Artangnan. Though the 1974/1975 version of the Three and Four Musketeers (respectively) are excellent productions, I do not think they are appropriate for children as they embellish and revel in the bawdy and immorality of the tale. Also, avoid the 1993 rendition. The 1948 version glosses over the involvement of the French Queen with the English Earl of Buckingham as well as some other parts included in the later versions. This allows the children some knowledge of this famous piece of literature without introducing them to the immorality of it.   **V**

Toby Tyler, or Ten Weeks with a Circus (1960) **1/2 D: Charles Barton. Kevin Corcoran, Henry Calvin, Gene Sheldon, Bob Sweeney, Richard Eastham, James Drury.   Disney film of children's book about a boy who runs away to join the circus at the turn of the last century. Preview.   **V**

To Kill a Mockingbird (1962) ***1/2 D: Robert Mulligan. Gregory Peck, Mary Badham, Philip Alford, John Megna, Brock Peters, Robert Duvall, Frank Overton, Rosemary Murphy, Paul Fix, Collin Wilcox, Alice Ghostley, William Windom; narrated by Kim Stanley.   Based on the novel by Harper Lee, Peck won an Oscar portraying (his favorite role as) a southern lawyer defending a black man against the rape of a white girl. This is a powerful film of prejudice as it is clearly proven that the physiological limitations of the accused make it impossible for him to be guilty. Peck must try to explain to his children what it's all about. His children are involved in trying to get a look at their neighbor, a recluse named Boo Radley, who later saves their lives. Preview and decide if this meets with your approval. Most schools have this book as required reading. See what you think.   **V, DVD**

Treasure Island (1950) ***1/2 D: Byron Haskin. Bobby Driscoll, Robert Newton, Basil Sydney, Walter Fitzgerald, Denis O'Dea, Ralph Truman, Finlay Currie.   Disney version of Robert Louis Stephenson's tale was filmed in England. It is a well done version, but should be viewed first for your family as parts can be pretty scary. You'll have to decide what's right for your family.   **V**

Twelfth Night (1996-British) **1/2 D: Trevor Nunn. Imogen Stubbs, Helena Bonham Carter, Toby Stephens, Nigel Hawthorne, Ben Kingsley, Richard E. Grant, Mel Smith, Imelda Staunton, Nicholas Farrell, Stephen Mackintosh.   Mostly accurate to the play, though certainly not to Shakespeare's time. Set in the 1890s this is a somewhat "campy" version and generally lots of fun. View first and see what you think. [PG]   **V**

20,000 Leagues Under the Sea (1954) **** D: Richard Fleischer. Kirk Douglas, James Mason, Paul Lukas, Peter Lorre, Robert J. Wilke, Carleton Young.   Excellent Disney adaptation of the Jules Verne classic tale of scientist Lukas and sailor Douglas meeting the

mysterious Captain Nemo (Mason). An Oscar winner for Art Direction and Special Effects, it includes an encounter with a giant squid.   **V, DVD**

Walk to Remember, A (2002) **1/2 (See Family)

War and Peace (1956-U.S-Italian) **1/2 D: King Vidor. Audrey Hepburn, Henry Fonda, Mel Ferrer, Vittorio Gassman, John Mills, Herbert Lom, Oscar Homolka, Anita Ekberg, Helmut Dantine.   Not the novel, by any stretch of the imagination, but perhaps a way for children to see it. Includes some well done battle scenes and a star studded cast.   **V**

Wuthering Heights (1939) **** D: William Wyler. Merle Oberon, Laurence Olivier, David Niven, Flora Robson, Donald Crisp, Geraldine Fitzgerald, Leo G. Carroll, Cecil Kellaway, Miles Mander, Hugh Williams.   Emily Brontë's novel isn't completed, but is an exceptionally well done film of the story of Heathcliff's doomed love. You will have to decide if this is appropriate subject matter for your children. **V, DVD**

Yearling, The (1946) ***1/2 D: Clarence Brown. Gregory Peck, Jane Wyman, Claude Jarman, Jr., Chill Wills, Margaret Wycherly, Henry Travers, Jeff York, Forrest Tucker, June Lockhart.   Marjorie Kinnan Rawling's story of a young boy's attachment to a fawn, who can only bring havoc as a pet to a family scratching its existence off the land. Beautifully filmed on location in Florida this is a lovely family film and one that will bring out the hankies!   **V**

Babes in Toyland (1961) **1/2 (See Music/Arts)

Ben Hur (1959) ***1/2 (See Ancient Rome)

Bishop's Wife, The (1947) *** D: Henry Koster. Cary Grant, Loretta Young, David Niven, Monty Woolley, James Gleason, Gladys Cooper, Elsa Lancaster.   Niven is a bishop who is so involved in building a bigger cathedral that he neglects his wife (Young) and loses his "joi de vivre." Grant is an angel who comes to help him rediscover what is *really* important in life. Remade as *The Preacher's Wife,* this one is my pick. A film about the importance of family and the choices we make. **V, DVD**

Christmas Box, The (1995) TVM D: Marcus Cole. Richard Thomas, Maureen O'Hara, Annette O'Toole, Kelsey Mulrooney, Robert Curtis-Brown, Michael Ensign.   After a twenty-three year absence, Maureen O'Hara returns to the screen in a film that makes you remember just how wonderful movies can be. Thomas and O'Toole are young parents desperately in need of larger quarters. O'Hara advertises for a housekeeper/caretaker as she is elderly and shouldn't stay alone. Thomas is career minded and driven, O'Toole is pretty well grounded and realizes that there is much she can learn from O'Hara. The real transformation comes in Thomas' character, but I can't tell you more or I'll give it away. Just don't miss this one and have the tissues ready. Above average. A film about the importance of family. **V**

Christmas Carol, A (1938) *** D: Edwin L, Marin. Reginald Owen, Gene Lockhart, Kathleen Lockhart, Terry Kilburn.   **V**
(1951-British) **** D: Brian Desmond-Hurst. Alastair Sim, Jack Warner, Kathleen Harrison. **V, DVD**
(1984) TVM D: Clive Donner. George C. Scott, Nigel Davenport, Frank Finlay. **V, DVD**
All tell the classic Dickens tale fairly faithfully. PLEASE preview before showing any version to children as Marley's ghost and the ghosts of the various Christmases can be quite frightening. You'll have to make the call on this one.

Christmas in Connecticut (1945) **1/2 D: Peter Godfrey. Barbara Stanwyck, Dennis Morgan, Sydney Greenstreet, Reginald Gardiner, S. Z. Sakall, Robert Shayne, Una O'Connor.   Stanwyck's a magazine writer who writes about the farm and marriage she *doesn't* have! Fat hits the fire when magazine publisher (Greenstreet) wants to come to her farm for Christmas *and* bring a sailor with him! Comedy of errors generally funny. My girls especially enjoyed the flapjack episode. Parents might wish to view first as Stanwyck is supposed to be married to Gardiner, but falls for Morgan. I think most will find it okay.   **V**

Christmas in My Hometown (1996) TVM D: Jerry London. Melissa Gilbert, Tim Matheson, Chris Makepeace, Travis Tritt.   An executive must cut jobs at the tractor factory that keeps his childhood hometown alive. There, he must deal with his past and the father he's not seen since childhood.

Christmas List , The (1997) TVM D: Charles Jarrott. Mimi Rogers, Rob Stewart, Stella Stevens, Bill Switzer.   My youngest daughter likes this movie, for the "good character" shown. A family reconnects and gets a new mom to boot. It mentions Santa, but my favorite part is the song at the end!

Come to the Stable (1949) *** D: Henry Koster. Loretta Young, Celeste Holm, Hugh Marlowe, Elsa Lancaster, Regis Toomey, Mike Mazurki.   French nuns in New England ask for help from the locals to build a facility for children. Another film I haven't seen for years, but remember warmly. Preview. **V**

Easter Parade (1948) ***1/2 (See Music/Arts)

Exodus (1960) *** (See 1900s)

Fiddler on the Roof (1971) *** (See Music/Arts)

Gentleman's Agreement (1947) *** (See Literature)

George Balanchine's The Nutcracker (1993) **1/2 (See Music/Arts)

Godspell (1973) **1/2 (See Music/Arts)

Going My Way (1944) **** (See Family Films)

Greatest Story Ever Told (1965) **1/2 (See Bible)

Heidi (1968) TVM (See Literature)

Holiday Affair (1949) *** D: Don Hartman. Robert Mitchum, Janet Leigh, Wendell Corey, Gordon Gebert, Henry (Harry) Morgan.   Delightful Christmas season story of widow Leigh, a comparison shopper who is inadvertently responsible for the loss of Mitchum's job and the zany things that happen from that point on. Corey [and now Mitchum] want to marry her and take care of her and her cute son. Remade in 1997 with David James Elliot (of JAG fame) playing Mitchum's part, but the original is the best. **V**

Holiday Inn (1942) ***1/2 (See Music/Arts)

It's a Wonderful Life (1946) **** D: Frank Capra. James Stewart, Donna Reed, Lionel Barrymore, Thomas Mitchell, Henry Travers, Beulah Bondi, Frank Faylen, Ward Bond, Gloria Grahame.   Small town boy Stewart falls in love with Reed. On their wedding day, the market crashes and he has to go to the family business to try and save it. They struggle against the town "boss" (Barrymore) until finally Stewart decides it would have been better to never have been born. So, his angel grants his wish and gives him a glimpse of what life would have been like in his town without him. Powerful film showing the importance of even the "smallest" life. **V, DVD**

Little Drummer Boy, The (1968) TVM D: Jules Bass. Arthur Rankin Jr. José Ferrer, Paul Frees, June Foray, Ted Eccles, Greer Garson, narrator.   Based upon the song, this is a sweet animated classic from my childhood. **V**

Man For All Seasons (1966-British) **** (See Reformation)

Meet John Doe (1941) *** (See Family Films)

Meet Me In St. Louis (1944) **** (See Music/Arts)

Miracle on 34th Street (1947) *** D: George Seaton. Maureen O'Hara, John Payne, Edmund Gwenn, Gene Lockhart, Natalie Wood, Porter Hall, William Frawley, Jerome Cowan.   Oscar winning, classic Valentine Davies story of Kris Kingle (Gwenn) who steps in to take the place of the drunken Santa for the Macy's parade. He gets the job for the rest of the season and meets the child of the woman who hired him (O'Hara) who doesn't believe in Santa and has passed her belief on to her child. He takes them on as a kind of challenge which ultimately results in a court trial to prove his identity. Charming story that you'll have to decide is right for your family or not, depending on how you feel about Santa stories. **V, DVD**

Nutcracker, The (See George Balanchine's The Nutcracker in Music/Arts, 1993) **

O'Henry's Full House (1952) **1/2 (See Literature)

Robe, The (1953) **1/2 (See Ancient Rome)

Rudolph the Red-Nosed Reindeer (1964) TVM D: Kizo Naga Shima, Larry Roemer. Narrator: Burl Ives. Voices of: Larry D. Mann, Billie May, Richard Raul Soles.   Like the Little Drummer Boy, a classic from my childhood based upon the famous song. Cute characterizations with darling puppets. **V**

Santa Clause, The (1994) *** D: John Pasquin. Tim Allen, Judge Reinhold, Wendy Crewson, Eric Lloyd, David Krumholtz, Peter Boyle, Larry Brandenburg, Mary Gross, Paige Tamada.   Harum-scarum divorced dad accidentally scares Santa off the roof and obeys the card he finds on him, puts on his suit and begins to become Santa, outside (which results in some funny scenes) and in. You'll have to decide if this is right for your family's values and how you feel about Santa movies. [PG] **V, DVD**

Ten Commandments, The (1956) **** (See Ancient Egypt)

White Christmas (1954) ** (See Music/Arts)

Yankee Doodle Dandy (1942) **** (See Music/Arts)

Miscellaneous

Schoolhouse Rock (1973) This series of videos was produced years ago for television, but are as fun today as they were then. They are still available from many places including www.school-house-rock.com

Grammar Rock Fun songs and cartoons teach the parts of speech and how they work. Includes: Unpack Your Adjectives; Interjections!; A Noun is a Person, Place or Thing; Lolly, Lolly, Lolly, Get Your Adverbs Here; Rufus Xavier Sarsaparilla (Pronouns); Busy Prepositions; Conjunction Junction; Verb! That's What's Happening; The Tale of Mr. Morton (Subject/Predicate)

American Rock More fun songs about American History. Includes: No More Kings (Pilgrims); The Preamble (Constitution); Mother Necessity (Inventions); Three Ring Government (President, Congress, Judiciary); Fireworks (July 4, 1776); Elbow Room (Louisiana Purchase); Sufferin' Till Suffrage (Suffragettes); The Shot Heard Round the World; Great American Melting Pot; I'm Just a Bill (How a Bill Becomes Law)

Multiplication Rock Songs to help children learn their multiplication tables and some of their rules and quirks. Includes: My Hero, Zero; Elementary, My Dear (2); Three is a Magic Number; The Four Legged Zoo; Ready or Not, Here I Come (5); I Got Six; Lucky Seven Sampson; Figure Eight; Naughty Number Nine; The Good Eleven; Little Twelvetoes

Science Rock Songs covering some basics of science in a fun and memorable way. Includes: The Body Machine (Digestion); Do the Circulation; Electricity, Electricity (Where it Comes From); Energy Blues (Different Sources of Energy); Interplanet Janet (Solar System); Them Not-So-Dry Bones (Skeletal System); A Victim of Gravity (What is Gravity)

Appendix

Finding the Movies You Want to See

There are various ways to go about finding the movies you wish to use.

1. The very best way is to begin taping movies from this book that you'd like to see as they come on television and begin to build your own family library of films. This is inexpensive as far as the investment in tapes go and the movies are free on television. As I understand it, the law allows you one personal copy for private use, just don't charge admission! On a T-120 tape (less than $1.00 each at Sam's) you can usually get THREE movies when taping on SLP (slow long play) or EP (extended play). Just keep an eye out for whatever movies in the book interest you and when they come on, tape them. Then, when you need them, you'll have them. If you haven't seen a copy of a film you want to see or tape, email AMC or TCM or whatever network you watch and request that they air that film. Most of them are very happy to hear from their viewers.

2. Most public libraries have a fairly good selection of videos, including many educational ones. Check out your local library and if they don't have a good selection, show them this book and give them some suggestions of where they could put some funds to good use. My library asks the home schoolers to let them know what we'd like them to add to the library and has purchased many items just for us. It never hurts to ask, so see what they say.

3. Try your local church library. You might be surprised at what some of them make available. My family's church has a fabulous library with many excellent videos. If your church doesn't have this option, perhaps it's time to suggest that they begin one. This is a real service to the members who can borrow books from the library instead of having to purchase them from a bookstore. As all homeschoolers know, coming up with funds for books you'd like to read can be a real challenge, so, when a library is offered, it is like a breath of fresh air to those who have access to it.

4. The next place to check would be local video rental stores. Blockbuster is the national leader and has a Classical, Family, Drama, Comedy, and Musical section in their stores. If you have more than one in your town, they are usually very helpful in calling another store if they don't have the video for which you are looking. Also, some of the smaller more independent stores may surprise you. Check with them if you can't find what you want elsewhere. Just be sure you go in and don't send your children by themselves. Some of them appear a bit "seamy."

5. The internet. I have not found an internet company as yet that has a large selection of films from this book for rental, but that doesn't mean someone won't come up with the idea some time soon. The place I found was www.cleanfilms.com, which has a few films, but not a large selection at this time. The other option which I have used is to check www.amazon.com and www.half.ebay.com and see if someone is selling the video for which you are looking. I have found videos there which are hard to find in the $5.00 or less range, which I found very surprising, so don't overlook this possibility or dismiss it thinking it will be too expensive. Sometimes, just the opposite is true. Also the History Channel (www.historychannel.com) and A & E (http://store.aetv.com/html) have some wonderful programs they have produced that are available on video tape. Be sure to check www.mentura.com as they carry quite a few of these and specialize in more of the documentary type of films for DVD rental as well as having some major releases.

6. Garage and yard sales. If you go to these you might be surprised at what you can find. One man's trash is another man's treasure, and you can find some amazing things at these sales for pennies. If you have friends and/or relatives who go to these regularly, give them a list of the titles for which you are searching.

INDEX

C

G

M

Q

R

S

T

U

V

W

Y

Z

NOTES

Bread For Life Books and Tapes

www.breadforlife.net
www.learningwiththemovies.co,
Email: breadforlife@mindspring.com
(706) 546-7214

Bread For Life Cookbook (vol. 1): contains over 160 recipes with the following categories: Yeast Breads; Quick Breads; Cereals; Desserts; Main Dishes; Milk Products; Miscellaneous; Dehydration. In the years since its release, it has gotten rave reviews. 52 pages. **$8.95**

Bread For Life Cookbook (vol. 2): contains over 250 recipes with research information on butter, honey, olive oil and recipes to make flavored butters, honeys and olive oils. Includes terms for olive oils so you don't get stuck purchasing an old one or one extracted with chemical solvents; grain nutritional facts, a combination chart to make complete proteins; A timetable for cooking grains and another one for beans; a sprouting chart and how to make bread with sprouted grains; an herb and a spice chart, a substitution chart, types of sweeteners and types of wheat, and that's just the glossary section! The recipe sections are as follows: Hor D'oeurves and More, Cereals and Breakfast Foods, Soups and Salads, Main Dishes, Desserts, Yeast Breads, (including information on what the various ingredients do and how to make bread with the **DLX, Dimension 2000, Bosch and by hand**), Quick Breads, Sourdough, Vegetables and Side Dishes, and Miscellaneous. Spiral bound for easy use in the kitchen. 184 pages. **$16.95**

Tea Time with Bread For Life: The heart of *Tea Time* is about spending time with those you love, bonding with each other, slowing life down for a short period of time, and making memories to treasure. This book is 104 pages, and includes the following information and recipes: Having a Family Tea Time, Making a Pot of Tea, How To Decaffeinate Any Tea, Tea History, Tea Accessories, Types of Afternoon Teas (Special Tea Cup Tea, Mother's Day Tea, Hat Tea, Cake/Cookie Tea, Chocolate Tea....! 29 in all!!), A Tea Tray Ministry, Varieties of Tea, Recipe sections include: Scones, Cookies and Bars, Quick Breads, Savories, Cakes and Trifles, Tea Biscuits, Toppings, "Cool" Tea Beverages, Links for Tea on the Internet, Tea Quotations for Copy work, Appendix: The Testimony of Others, Catalogue. **$6.50**

Some Common Nutritional Fallacies covers some of the nutritional errors on grain, honey and milk which dispute the word of God; these past "facts" are now being found by medical science to be untrue as in their research, medical doctors are now confirming what God wrote in His word, long ago. **$4.50**

The Coming Famine is a word from God Beth received in 1998 and wrote down concerning coming times. It is a call to pray and seek God's face, to find out what He is saying to YOU! **$4.50**

Bread For Life Audio Tape: a 90 minute excerpt from Beth's 5 1/2 hour class centering on some of the nutritional facts about freshly milled grains and why they provide superior nutrition and help to combat disease. **$5.00**

Bread For Life Class Video: a two tape video set of Beth's 5 1/2 hour class including the lecture which covers why refined, processed, man-made foods bring disease and how God's whole foods can repair, reverse and prevent the common diseases with which America is plagued. You will also see live demonstrations of making sandwich bread, filled breads, tortillas, muffins and pizza from dehydrated tomato powder! Also included are the audience's response to the food, the class, and the audience's questions. If you cannot attend a class, then this is the next best thing to being there. Many people who attend purchase videos so they can put stop and start the tape for better retention of all the information. Two videos, **$35.00**

Basic Breadmaking Video: a 45 minute video which covers how to begin using your mill (this shows the Magic mill, which required cleaning. With the Whisper mill, there is NO cleaning. The principles of use, however, are the same.); **how the mill works** (same as the Whisper mill); milling grains; **how to use the DLX**; making bread in the DLX; proofing yeast; bran, endosperm, pastry dough; lecithin; rising and triple rise; cleaning the DLX; **shaping and forming**: loaf bread, dinner rolls, hamburger buns; types of baking pans; **how to use the DLX blender**: flax seed; **roller/flaker mill**: oats to oatmeal, apple cinnamon oatmeal; proportion of water to grains; cleaning roller/flaker mill; **grain and spice mill**: grits; cleaning grain and spice mill; **baking bread**; risen bread, ready to bake; dinner rolls, risen, ready to bake; baked dinner rolls; sliced sandwich bread; types of bread knives; **warranty on DLX, lifetime warranty on Whisper mill**. For those who have had trouble making bread successfully, this tape has been 100% effective. **$15.00**

Advanced Breadmaking Video: 1 hour and 50 minutes. Live video demonstrations of making the following: Apple Cinnamon Coconut Bread; Apricot Walnut Bread; Croutons/Herb Bread; Cinnamon Rolls; Tortillas; Overnight Coffee Cake; Reuben Sandwich/French Bread; Garlic Breadsticks; Pizza; How to Convert Conventional Recipes to Freshly Milled Grains; use of Sucanat; Double Chocolate Bread; Shortnin'Bread; Biscuits;Types of Baking Powder; Scones; Clotted Cream; Cream Cheese Icing; Muffins: Orange, Streusel-